Over 400 Pivc in 16 Shakespeare Plays Analyzed

Hamlet, King Lear, Macbeth

Plus

Plantagenet Plays: Richard 11; Henry 1V, Parts 1 and 2; Henry V; Henry V1, Parts I, 2, 3; Richard 111

Plus

Julius Caesar; Antony and Cleopatra; Cymbeline; Titus Andronicus, Pericles

Richard J. Noyes

ISBN-13: 9781073875597
ISBN-10: 1073875598

The over-400 essential speeches in the 16 plays critiqued in this indispensable e-Book and paperback contains over 800 pages. This new and original volume is available on the Amazon Kindle App which can be downloaded free to most devices. It is a grand bargain, as a Kindle book or as an Amazon paperback, loaded with information, enlightenment and understanding.

Over 400 Pivotal Speeches in 16 Shakespeare Plays Critiqued

Table of Contents

DEDICATION

Over 400 Pivotal Speeches in 16 Shakespeare Plays Analyzed is dedicated to Boston University Professors of English Literature Robert Sproat and Harold White.

Professor Sproat was expert in sixteenth–and-seventeenth-century poetry. He read beautifully and made the writing come alive with feeling, meaning and matchless comparative analysis.

Professor White skillfully specialized in the works of Geoffrey Chaucer and William Shakespeare and brought to those subjects impressive knowledge of the history of both writers' eras.

Learning from Dr. Sproat and Dr. White motivated me to engage in the long-term study and enjoyment of English literature, and I will be ever grateful to have experienced university education at its finest.

INTRODUCTION

I've been reading, studying and enjoying William Shakespeare's plays, sonnets and poems for decades, and have regularly collected my favorite speeches and lines.

I recently reread this lengthy compendium. The review of accumulated speeches triggered a fresh reading of Will's* complete works with the express purpose of finding more language gems that I may have missed during previous readings.

In the better-late-than-never department, I quickly realized that in order to gain a full appreciation of the writing, the speeches needed explanation. Extended efforts on deciphering the meaning of the speeches, and the lines making up each speech, soon evolved into this book.

The format for *Over 400 Pivotal Speeches in 16 Shakespeare Plays Analyzed* took on the present form when I saw that each important speech needed a preamble and a summary. To my knowledge, this technique has not been used before, at least extensively. As you will see, it works well and improves understanding.

*'Will' Shakespeare

*In the interest of brevity, and absent disrespect, I call William Shakespeare 'Will' throughout this book. I called him 'Will' in my novel *Discovering Will's Lost Years*, an original work of fiction. Shakespeare's friends called him Will and he called himself Will, even using it in Sonnets 135 and 136 written to the 'Dark Lady.' The closing couplet of 136 includes his name.

'Make but my name, thy love, and love that still,
And then thou lovest me, for my name is 'Will.'

The use of 'Will' in the context of the previous Sonnet, 135, is often a little earthy, but the point about using Shakespeare's nickname in this book is sharpened.

I have the impression that too many people approach Will's writings while genuflecting on bended knee, or as George Bernard Shaw put it, engaging in excessive 'Bardolatry.'

From all the years of reading his work, I believe that Will was comfortable in his own skin, good company and easy in his relationships. In his time, he was referred to as 'good Will' and 'gentle Will.'

.

Part One

Three Great Tragedies:

Hamlet, King Lear, Macbeth

HAMLET

Pivotal Speeches Critiqued

Hamlet is based on an ancient Danish story. A previous version, often called the Ur, or original, *Hamlet* was probably written by Thomas Kyd, author of *The Spanish Tragedy*. It was performed in London around 1587. The manuscript was subsequently lost.

William Shakespeare's timeless version of *Hamlet*, published in 1603, is one of the great theatrical tragedies. The lead character, the eponymous Hamlet, plays the Prince of Denmark who mourns his late father, the King, who is also named Hamlet.

Upon the sudden death of King Hamlet, his brother Claudius becomes King and quickly marries Gertrude, the widowed Queen.

Young Hamlet is perplexed by his mother's sudden marriage to his uncle, a man he judges unworthy.

Next, we have an event that launches the play headlong toward its violent conclusion.

(MARCELLUS, Bernardo and Francisco, three military men attached to the King's army, guard the castle ramparts. A ghost appears two nights in a row. The soldiers tell Hamlet's friend Horatio about the incident, but he thinks they are credulous.

On the third night, Francisco and Bernardo talk at their posts and are soon joined by Horatio and Marcellus.

Marcellus. What, has this thing appeared again tonight?
Bernardo. I have seen nothing.
Marcellus. Horatio says 'tis but our fantasy,
And will not let belief take hold of him
Touching this dreaded sight twice seen of us.
Therefore, I have entreated him along
With us to watch the minutes of this night,
That if again this apparition come,
He may approve our eyes and speak to it. (28)

(Horatio enters and Marcellus wants him to confirm what he and the other soldiers saw the past two nights: 'He may approve our eyes and speak to it.' (28)

Next, the ghost enters, and the soldiers react. Bernardo says, 'In the same figure, like the King that's dead.' (41)

Marcellus asks, 'Thou art a scholar. Speak to it, Horatio.' (42)

In Elizabethan times, it was believed that ghosts, and other hobgoblins of the mind, could only be appealed to in Latin, hence the need for the educated Horatio. It's good that modern ghosts are multilingual. Otherwise, with our limited-in-Latin-language population, we'd be in big trouble.)

Horatio. What art thou that usurp'st this time of night, Together with that <u>fair and warlike form</u> (47) In which the majesty of <u>buried Denmark</u> (48) Did sometimes march? By Heaven I charge thee, speak.
Hamlet, 1.1, 21-49

(WITH the phrase beginning with 'fair and warlike form,' (47) Horatio describes the dead King Hamlet. Monarchs of the time were often referred to by the name of their country, hence Horatio's use of 'buried Denmark.' (48)

(THE ghost exits.* A soldier cries, 'See it stalks away!' (50) That line is a stage direction.

*The first folio doesn't tell how the ghost enters and exits. The custom is a trapdoor: given the use of the verb 'stalks' in line (50), this ghost enters and exits from offstage.

Horatio goes on to give the soldiers an example of old King Hamlet's exploits: 'Fortinbras of Norway' (82) met him in battle, and the former King 'Did slay this Fortinbras.' (86) By doing that, King Hamlet acquired all of Fortinbras' lands. Now, his son, young Fortinbras, is in Denmark with an army to recover the lands 'his father lost.' (104)

In the next passage, Horatio compares the death of old King Hamlet, and the possible trouble that might ensue in Denmark, to what happened in Rome when Julius Caesar was assassinated.)

Horatio. In the most high and palmy sate of Rome,
A little ere the mightiest Julius fell,
The graves stood tenantless, and the sheeted dead (115)
Did squeak and gibber in the Roman streets. (116)
As stars with trains of fire and dews of blood, (117)
Disasters in the sun, and the moist star (118)
Upon whose influence, Neptune's empire stands
Was sick almost to doomsday with eclipse.
Hamlet, 1.1, 50-120

(The speech above, delivered by Horatio, is where Will hits his stride with elevated poetry, and it continues throughout the play.

'The graves stood tenantless, and the sheeted dead' paints with words. (115)

We don't know how the dead 'Did squeak and gibber in the Roman streets.' (116) But I love the verbs. Is there a line omitted between this one and the next?

'As stars with trains of fire and dews of blood,' (117) is valuable imagery written for audiences who don't have the benefit of elaborate, electricity-generated special effects. 'Trains of fire' conjures stars shooting from horizon to horizon. 'Dews' drip with blood-red sparks.

'Disasters in the sun, and the moist star' (118) speaks of troubling omens and the moon's pull on the tides. Confirmed by 'Upon whose influence Neptune's empire stands was sick almost to doomsday with eclipse.' (119)

The first part of the last sentence is accurate. The tides are impacted by the moon's gravitational pull. The second part is also scientifically correct. Tides are higher when the moon is in eclipse. Will knew his science.)

(THE ghost appears again. They beseech it to speak, and when it won't they mean to strike it, dawn rises, the ghost exits. It was believed at the time that spirits, especially evil ones, only appeared at night and retreated to their hideaways at daybreak.

Bernardo says, 'It was about to speak when the cock crew.' (147)

Horatio. <u>And then it started like a guilty thing</u>
<u>Upon a fearful summons.</u> . . . . (148)
Marcellus. It faded on the crowing of the cock.
Some say that ever 'gainst that season comes
<u>Wherein Our Saviour's birth is celebrated,</u> (159)
<u>The bird of dawning singeth all night long.</u> (160)
And then, they say, no spirit dare stir abroad,
The nights are wholesome, then no planets strike,
No fairy takes nor witch hath power to charm,
So hallowed and gracious is the time.
Horatio. So have I heard and do in part believe it.
<u>But look, the morn, in russet mantle clad,</u>
<u>Walks o'er the dew of yon eastward hill.</u> (167)
Break we are watch up, and by my advice
Let us impart what we have seen tonight
Upon young Hamlet, for upon my life,
<u>This spirit, dumb to us, will speak to him.</u> (171)
Hamlet, 1.1, 147-171

(HORATIO is prompted by Bernardo's mention of the cock crowing. 'And then it started like a guilty thing upon a fearful summons.' (148) These lines are prized by actors who often pause between the well-placed verb 'started' and 'like.' They place emphasis on 'thing.' This timing sets up the second line finishing the dramatic thought smartly.

'Wherein Our Saviour's birth is celebrated,' (158) is an important line in Marcellus' response to the cock crowing: His moving speech on how the actions of planets and witches are interrupted by Christmas magic is a nice touch, and here Will is surely recalling beliefs learned during his boyhood in Stratford. Especially beautiful is the line, 'The bird of dawning singeth all night long.' (160)

In the second part of his speech, Horatio agrees in part with Marcellus. Then he speaks two poetic lines on the beauty of sunrise, 'But look, the morn, in russet mantle clad, walks o'er the dew of yon eastward hill.' (167)

Horatio realizes that the ghost won't speak to him, because he wants to talk to Hamlet. The final line cues the audience to what's coming: 'This spirit, dumb to us, will speak to him.' (171)

* * *

(IN the opening of scene two, Claudius, the recently-invested King, enters with Gertrude his new wife and Queen. Young Hamlet, son by her previous marriage to Old King Hamlet, is with them. Polonius, the Lord Chamberlain, and his son Laertes are in the assemblage.

Claudius speaks of how Old King Hamlet's death remains fresh in their minds and the need 'To bear our hearts in grief.' (3) This is hypocrisy on steroids.

He then instructs two courtiers, Voltimand and Cornelius, to go to Norway. The purpose of the mission is to convince young Fortinbras' uncle to rein in his warlike nephew and stop him from trying to regain the lands his father lost to old King Hamlet.

Next, Claudius learns that Laertes, who came back to Denmark to attend Claudius' coronation, wants to return to France. After making sure that Laertes' father Polonius agrees, Claudius gives permission.

Finally, Claudius addresses young prince Hamlet, 'But now, my cousin Hamlet, and my son—' (63) Nobles regularly called each other 'cousin,' which also meant kinsman.

In an aside, Hamlet answers with a much-quoted line that shows what he thinks of Claudius, 'A little more than kin and less than kind.' (64) By 'kind,' Hamlet means warmth, and a lack thereof.

In his entrance to the play, the audience sees that Hamlet is witty and caustic. The King asks, 'How is it that the clouds still hang on you.' (66)

Hamlet answers with a pun: 'Not so, my lord. I am too much i' the sun.' (67)

In 'Henry 1V, Part One,' 1.2, Hal says, 'I imitate the sun.'

Gertrude asks her son, who is dressed in black throughout the play, 'Good Hamlet, cast thy nighted color off.' (68) She goes on to wonder why his downcast looks seem to 'Seek for thy noble father in the dust.' (71) And then tells Hamlet that 'all that lives must die, passing through nature to eternity.' (72) He's mourning, and she's rationalizing.

Hamlet agrees that 'it is common.' (73) Gertrude asks, 'If it be, why seems it so particular with thee?' (74)

Hamlet. <u>Seems, Madam! Nay, it is. I know not "seems."</u> (76)
'Tis not <u>alone my inky cloak,</u> (77) good Mother,
Nor customary suits of solemn black.
Nor windy suspiration of forced breath—
No, nor <u>the fruitful river in the eye,</u> (80)
Nor the dejected havior of the visage,
Together with all forms, moods, shapes of grief—
That can denote me truly. These indeed <u>seem,</u> (83)

For they are actions that a man might play.
But I have that within which passeth show,
These but the trappings and the suits of woe. (86)
Hamlet, 1.2, 3-86

(HAMLET replies to his mother, 'Seems, Madam! Nay, it is. I know not "seems." ' (76) I see straightening of posture and a raised eyebrow. He agrees with his mother's generalization that people die, but bristles when she asks, in effect, why his father's death is unique to him.

Gertrude's attempt to put her husband's death in perspective for Hamlet strikes him as a little casual. We can't know Will's thought processes as he writes Gertrude's dialogue.

It does appear shat she's telling Hamlet, 'Look, bad stuff happens, let's move on.' However, that doesn't jibe with their later confrontations when she seems oblivious to his ridicule of the hasty marriage to her late husband's brother. This is a good example of why a labyrinthine play like *Hamlet* is subject to multiple interpretations. There's a lot going on in the thinking and motivations of all the characters.

Hamlet tells his mother that casting off 'alone my inky cloak,' (77) or black clothes, or stopping the weeping, 'the fruitful river in the eye,' (80) will not halt his mourning.

He returns to 'seem' (83) first used by his mother, and then inquiringly by him in line one, to follow with, 'For they are actions that a man might play.' (84) Remember, the words are being 'played' by an actor. Hamlet, the character, is an actor and a joy to play, if you are good enough to master the complexities of the role.

Hamlet concludes by saying that he holds his grief within. He's not wearing his heart on his sleeve, and the outer signs are 'but the trappings and the suits of woe.' (86) I love 'suits of woe.'

The dialogue between the Queen and her son is revealing of character and glossed with subtlety and layers of meaning. And the passage contains needed exposition in preparation for later mother-son confrontations.

The play is a convoluted puzzle, and each piece, this being one of them, fits into place like a bolt into its proper tap.)

* * *

(PICKING UP on Queen Gertrude's advice, King Claudius attempts through some quasi-religious guilt-dealing to put Hamlet's grief over his father's death in perspective. It is 'most incorrect to Heaven' (95) not to let go and let the dead rest.

Claudius also wants Hamlet to think of us 'As of a father.' (107 That's the last thing that Hamlet wants to do.

Both his mother and the King want Hamlet to forego his return to school at Wittenberg. Gertrude makes a motherly plea, 'I pray thee, stay with us, go not to Wittenberg.' (119)

We don't as yet know why, and it's likely the Hamlet doesn't know himself, but he relents, 'I shall in all my best obey you, madam.' (120)

Although we don't yet understand his underlying motives, the King acts pleased and proposes that 'the great cannon to the clouds shall tell,' (126) or let's drink to Hamlet's decision. Toasts and cannons going off was a royal tradition in several European countries of the time.)

* * *

(*Hamlet* is the longest and most seamless of all Will's plays. Is it his most accomplished play? That depends on your point of view. Based on the variety of disparate characters, such as Falstaff, plus superb storytelling, some people vouch for *I Henry IV*. Others favor *A Midsummer Night's Dream*.

I've spent countless hours critiquing all the plays and in particular *Macbeth* and *King Lear*. And *Hamlet*, by any measure, is easily the most complex and interpretation-resistant of all Will's plays.

Greatness is difficult to quantify. For now, let's focus on the emerging and shining structure of the play at hand: Horatio and others introduce the ghost of Hamlet's dead father; Hamlet agrees to stay on at Elsinore Castle with his mother and new stepfather; next, he lets us in on his colliding feelings; and we're just getting started. Lean in and read on.

The King, the Queen and their retinue exit. In a famed soliloquy, the conflicted Hamlet contemplates suicide while also revealing his opinion of Claudius and his mother's precipitate marriage to him.)

Hamlet. Oh, that this too too solid flesh would <u>melt</u>, (129)
<u>Thaw, and resolve itself into a dew!</u> (130)
Or that the Everlasting had not fixed
<u>His canon against self-slaughter!</u> (132) Oh, God! God!
<u>How weary, stale, flat, and unprofitable</u> (133)
<u>Seem to me all the uses of this world!</u>
Fie on 't, ah, fie! 'Tis an <u>unweeded garden</u>, (135)
That grows to seed, things rank and gross in nature
Possess it merely. That it should come to this!
But two months dead! Nay, not so much, not two.
So excellent a King, that was, to this,
<u>Hyperion to a satyr</u>. (140) So loving to my mother

That he might not beteem the winds of heaven
Visit her face too roughly. Heaven and earth!
Must I remember? Why, she would hang on him (143)
As if increase of appetite had grown
By what it fed on. And yet within a month— (145)
Let me not think on 't—Frailty, thy name is woman!
(146)
A little month, or ere those shoes were old
With which she followed my poor father's body,
Like Niobe, all tears. (149) —Why she, even she—
O God! A beast that wants discourse of reason
Would have mourned longer—married with my
uncle,
My father's brother, but no more like my father
Than I to Hercules. Within a month,
Ere the salt of most unrighteous tears (154)
Had left the flushing in her gallèd eyes,
She married. Oh, most wicked speed, to post
With such dexterity to incestuous sheets! (157)
It is not, nor it cannot, come to good. (158)
But break, my heart, for I must hold my tongue!
Hamlet, 1.2, 129-158

(IN the first two lines, Hamlet wishes that his body
could just 'melt' or 'thaw' (129) and go away. Then we
have the brilliantly poetic 'resolve itself into a dew!
(130)

14

Knowing that the wished-for resolution to his torment is impossible, Hamlet regrets that God made 'His canon against self-slaughter! (132) 'How weary, stale, flat, and unprofitable (133) seem to me all the uses of this world!' He wants to end his life, but is torn between wishes and fears. The religious beliefs of the time made suicide heretical.

He likens life to an 'unweeded garden' (135) This apt, but defeatist, metaphor sets up the core of Hamlet's speech, his disgust with his mother's quick marriage to Claudius.

With 'Hyperion to a satyr,' (140) Hamlet calls his dead father a Titan god and Claudius a debaucher who seduced his brother's wife into marriage too soon after the funeral.

Hamlet tells of how his mother 'would hang on him,'* (143) meaning that she was demonstratively in love with her former husband.

*Will used similar phrasing in other plays, for example, *Henry IV*, Part 2, 2.3. In a poetic epitaph to her husband, Lady Percy speaks of 'I, hanging on Hotspur's neck,' in remembrance of their affectionate life together. She also called him 'the mark and glass, copy and book, that fashioned others.' Look for similar wording in Ophelia's description of Hamlet. The charismatic Hotspur is one of Will's most fluent poets.

Back to the soliloquy: Hamlet broods on his mother's deep attraction to his father. Her rash decision to transfer endearment 'within a month' (145) to Claudius causes Hamlet to cry out the much-quoted, 'Frailty, thy name is woman!' (146)

'Like Niobe, all tears.' (149) This line refers to a woman in Greek mythology whose children were all slain.

'Ere the salt of most unrighteous tears (154) had left the flushing in her gallèd eyes, ties back to Niobe's tears. But Gertrude's grief was short-lived. To Hamlet's chagrin, and paraphrasing Will's words, she married within a month.

Hamlet laments further his mother's post, or hurry, 'to incestuous sheets.' (157) With accurate foreboding, he says, 'It is not, nor it cannot, come to good.' (158)

* * *

(SCENE TWO continues with a change of pace. Horatio and the soldiers join Hamlet onstage. Hamlet asks Horatio why he isn't back at Wittenberg. Horatio replies, 'My lord, I came to see your father's funeral.' (176) It's strange that Hamlet didn't see him there, or know he was at Elsinore, a possible structural slip.

Hamlet counters wittily: 'I pray thee do not mock me, fellow student. I think it was to see my mother's wedding.' (177)

Horatio: 'Indeed, my lord, it followed hard upon.' (178)

Hamlet. <u>Thrift, thrift, Horatio! The funeral baked meats</u>
<u>Did coldly furnish forth the marriage tables</u>. . . . (181)
<u>Methinks I see my father</u>. . . . (183)
<u>In my mind's eye, Horatio</u>. (185)
Horatio. I saw him once. He was a goodly King.
Hamlet. He was a man, take him for all in all.
<u>I shall not look upon his like again</u>. (188)
Hamlet, 1.2, 176-229

(Hamlet answers Horatio's political comment on the short duration between his father's death and his mother's remarriage with the sharp and oft-quoted, 'Thrift, thrift, Horatio! The baked funeral meats did coldly furnish forth the marriage tables.' (181)

We observe Will's build of Hamlet's persona as an actor. For an actor he is, and a skilled one who, as we now see, is mercurial and always fascinating.

The dialogue 'Methinks I see my father.' (183) 'In my mind's eye, Horatio,' (185) anticipates three things: Horatio calling Old Hamlet a goodly King;

Hamlet's much-copied compliment that, 'I shall not look upon his like again;' (188) and the certainty that he'll soon see his father's ghost.

Will constructed this intricate play so flawlessly that a high percentage of the lines cue something to come. Analyzing the key lines of the foremost speeches helps us to better recognize and appreciate the play's exemplary composition.

Horatio goes on to tell Hamlet that he and the other soldiers saw his father's ghost. Hamlet probes, 'saw you not his face?' (228)

'Oh yes, my lord, he wore his beaver up.' (229) This means that the old King's apparition wore armor.)

* * *

(Horatio and the others exit. Hamlet soliloquizes for the second time.)

Hamlet. My father's spirit in arms! All is not well.
<u>I doubt some foul play</u>. (256) Would the night were come!
Then sit still, my soul. Foul deeds will rise,
Though all the earth o'erwhelm them, to <u>men's eyes</u>. (258)
Hamlet, 1.2, 255-258

(In Elizabethan and Jacobean days, 'doubt' in line two didn't have its modern meaning. Hamlet believes there is 'foul play.' (256)

He is impatient for night to come so that he can see the ghost for himself. Although he thinks that what he finds will be too fanciful for most 'men's eyes' (258) to accept.

Hamlet also knows that the Devil sometimes comes disguised as a ghost. He is understandably wary that the ghost actually is his father's spirit.)

* * *

(SCENE THREE of act one opens in the home of Polonius, Lord Chamberlain in the court of King Claudius.

Polonius' son, Laertes, is about to leave for France. He gives advice to his younger sister, Ophelia. In essence, the counsel is: be circumspect when dealing with Hamlet.

Following this, Polonius enters to offer platitudinous advice to the departing Laertes and then to the smitten Ophelia.

Observe how Will uses these encounters for the purposes, among others, of character definition and storyline advancement. Also record that nearly everything in the play connects to Hamlet.

Laertes. For Hamlet, and a trifling of his favor,
Hold it a fashion and <u>a toy in blood</u>, (5)
<u>A violet in the youth of primy nature</u>, (6)
Forward, not permanent, sweet, not lasting,
The perfume and suppliance of a minute—
No more.
Ophelia. <u>No more but so?</u> (9)
Laertes. Think it no more.
<u>For Nature crescent does not grow alone</u>
<u>In thews and bulk, but as this temple waxes</u> (12)
The inward service of the mind and soul
Grows wide withal. Perhaps he loves you now.
And now no soil nor cautel doth besmirch
The virtue of '<u>his will.</u>' (16) But you must fear,
<u>His greatness weighed</u>, (17) his will is not his own,
For he himself is subject to his birth. . .
Then weigh what loss your honor may sustain
If with too credent ear you list his songs,
Or <u>lose your heart, or your chaste treasure open</u> (31)
To his umastered importunity.
Fear it, Ophelia, fear it, my dear sister,
And keep you in the rear of your affection,
Out of the shot and danger of desire.
The chariest maid is prodigal enough
If she <u>unmask her beauty to the moon</u>. (37)
Virtue itself 'scapes not calumnious strokes.

The canker galls the infants of the spring (39)
Too oft before their buttons be disclosed,
And in the morn and liquid dew of youth
Contagious blastments are most imminent.
Be wary, then, best safety lies in fear.
Youth to itself rebels, though none else near.
Ophelia. I shall the effect of this good lesson keep
As watchman to my heart. But, good my brother,
Do not, as some ungracious pastors do,
Show me the steep and thorny way to Heaven
Whilst, like a puffed and reckless libertine,
Himself the primrose path of dalliance (50) treads
And recks not his own rede.
Polonius. (Enters to give Laertes advice.) And these
few precepts in thy memory
Look thou character. . . .
Costly thy habit as thy purse can buy,
But not expressed in fancy—rich, not gaudy.
For the apparel oft proclaims the man, . . . (72)
Neither a borrower or a lender be, . . . (75)
To thine own self be true, (78)
And it must follow, as the night the day,
Thou canst not then be false to any man.
Hamlet, 1.3, 4-127

(LAERTES tells Ophelia that her infatuation, 'a toy
in blood,' (5) is an unimportant urge that will pass.

'A violet in the youth of primy nature' (6) indicates that Ophelia and Hamlet are young. We, of course, surmised that given Hamlet's recently studies at Wittenberg University in Germany.*

*Christopher Marlowe's *Doctor Faustus* was also educated at Wittenberg. Since the *Doctor Faustus* play predated *Hamlet*, did Will's idea to use Wittenberg spring from that?

Marlowe's revolutionary use of unrhymed blank verse in *Tamburlaine* influenced Will and other Elizabethan playwrights. Will admired Marlowe, and they became friends. Kit Marlowe gave Will help with some of his early plays.* During the year before Marlowe's murder, he and Will co-wrote a great play that was subsequently lost. At least that's how I wrote it in my novel 'Discovering Will's Lost Years and the Shakespeare-Marlowe Lost Play.'

*The OED recently gave Marlowe a co-writing credit for HenryV1, 1,2,3.

Back to *Hamlet* and the work at hand: Ophelia's response to her brother's advice—'No more but so?'—(9) tells us that she is not taking it seriously.

'For Nature crescent does not grow alone in thews and bulk, but as this temple waxes' (12) is Laertes saying that even as the body grows so does the mind and not always in good ways. 'His will' (16) or sexual cravings will also grow. Like his father, Polonius, Laertes' style is pompous and garrulous.

'His greatness weighed' (17) initiates lines in which Laertes warns Ophelia that Hamlet may well be King someday and perhaps his intentions toward you will change.

Therefore, if you are taken in by his wooing you may 'lose your heart, or your chaste treasure open' (31) to him.

Laertes continues to lay it on with a trowel warning Ophelia that if she is extravagant with her chastity and 'unmask her beauty to the moon,' (37) —a captivating phrase—is to risk disaster.

Polonius plays the heavy father. Clearly, with his forced advice to his sister, Laertes is his father's son. Not certain that he's convinced Ophelia not to sleep with Hamlet, Laertes likens him to a canker, one of Will's favorite metaphors: 'The canker galls the infants of the spring,' (39) and can ruin a fresh bud like you.

Ophelia answers her brother with respect, and then quickly gives him the needle. Don't give me all this counsel to be a good girl, if you're heading off to France to ignore your own advice and take 'the primrose path of dalliance.' (50) Nice dig, Ophelia.

Polonius picks up where Laertes left off with what have become cliché-ridden bits of advice to his

France-bound son. We include a few that have fallen into the language. Some people consider these lines profound, and that's fine. But over time, Polonius' advice has generally come to represent the preachings of an old fuddy-duddy.

Examples: 'For the apparel oft proclaims the man;' (72) 'Neither a borrower or a lender be;' (75) and 'To thine own self be true.' (78) It's probable that in his youth Will heard variations on these bromides.

After Laertes exits the stage, Polonius gives Ophelia more warnings about her affection for Hamlet. A good one: 'These blazes, daughter, give more light than heat.' (117) I'm not sure that Will originated this phrase. It is now typically phrased as giving more heat than light.

The best is, 'Do not believe his vows, for they are brokers.' (127) In the modern sense, daddy's saying that the guy you're gaga over is a huckster.

Ophelia is a sympathetic character, bright, beautiful, sensitive and possessing a good sense of humor. She is surrounded by overbearing men. Her father and brother are overprotective, stuffy and given to ornamental language. Hamlet, the man she loves, is increasingly entangled with his own problems. Watch with me as Ophelia, the prototypical victim, goes from being a seemingly happy young woman to one consumed by personal tragedy. Think about this: what destroys Ophelia?

* * *

(HORATIO, Marcellus and other soldiers saw the ghost of Hamlet's father in scene one. Now it's Hamlet's turn, and he's out on the ramparts with them.

They hear the blare of musical instruments and the noise of arms being shot off. Horatio asks Hamlet what it means.)

Hamlet. The King doth wake tonight and <u>takes his rouse</u>, (8)
Keeps wassail, and the swaggering uprising reels.
And as he drains his draughts of <u>Rhenish</u> (10) down,
The kettledrum and trumpet thus bray out
The triumph of his pledge.
Horatio. Is it a custom?
Hamlet. Aye, marry, is 't.
But to my mind, though I am native here
<u>And to the manner born,</u> (15) it is a custom
<u>More honored in the breach than the observance</u>. (16)
<u>This heavy-headed revel east and west</u>
<u>Makes us traduced and taxed of other nations</u>. (18)
They clepe us drunkards, and with swinish phrase

Soil our addition, and indeed it takes
From our achievements, though performed at height,
The pith and marrow of our attribute.
So oft it chances in particular men,
That for some vicious mole of nature in them, (24)
As in their birth—wherein they are not guilty,
Since nature cannot choose his origin—
(Ghost enters. This stage direction is not in the First
Folio. Hamlet speaks to the Ghost.)
Angels and minister of grace defend us!
Be thou a spirit of health or goblin damned,
Bring with thee airs from Heaven or blasts from Hell,
(42)
Be thy intents wicked or charitable,
Thou comest in such a questionable shape
That I will speak to thee. I'll call thee Hamlet,
King, Father, royal Dane. Oh, answer me.
Let me not burst in ignorance, but tell
Why thy canonized bones, hearsèd in death,
Have burst their cerements, why the sepulcher
Wherein we saw thee quietly inurned
Hath oped his ponderous and marble jaws (50)
To cast thee up again. What may this mean,
That thou, dear corse, again, in complete steel, (52)
Revisit'st thus the glimpses of the moon,
Making night hideous, and we fools of nature
So horribly to shake our disposition

With thoughts beyond the reaches of our souls?
Say, why is this? Wherefore? What should we do?
(Ghost beckons Hamlet. This stage direction is in the
First Folio.)
Marcellus. Look with what courteous action
It waves you to a more removèd ground.
But do not go with it.
Hamlet. It will not speak. Then I will follow it. . .
I do not set my life at a pin's fee, (65)
And for my soul, what can it do to that,
Being a thing as immortal as itself?
It waves me forth again. I'll follow it. . . . .
My fate cries out,
And makes each petty artery in this body
As hardy as the Nemean lion's nerve. (83)
Still I am called. Unhand me gentleman.
By Heaven, I'll make a ghost of him that lets me! (85)
I say, away! Go on. I'll follow thee.
Horatio. He waxes desperate with imagination. (86)
Marcellus. Something is rotten in the state of Denmark.
(89)
Hamlet, 1.4, 8-89

(IN Hamlet's first speech, he describes Claudius'
partying habits. With 'takes his rouse' (8) we learn that
the King likes a bottoms-up style.

27

And he favors 'Rhenish,'* (10) a German white wine from a region near the Rhine River.

*I'm always wondering where Will's particular creative thoughts come from. The 'Rhenish' may have come to mind from his reaction to Robert Greene, a contemporary, a university wit and a clever writer. Greene resented the relatively uneducated, but polymathic, Shakespeare's early successes, calling him an 'upstart crow' and 'Shake-scene.'

Greene was a larger-than-life man who might have been one of the inspirations for Falstaff. I wrote a passage in my novel *Discovering Will's Lost Years* in which Will learns from Richard Burbage's brother that Greene is infirm and destitute. Will visits Greene in his airless room above a shoemaker's shop. Greene is touched, apologizes to Will, and they reconcile. He tells Will that he is a tosspot and trencherman who was finally done in by 'a surfeit of Rhenish wine and pickled herring.'

Back to *Hamlet*: Horatio asks Hamlet if the new King's drinking and carousing is customary. Hamlet answers that he is familiar with court life and 'And to the manner born,' (15) a phrase that has lodged in the language. He goes on to say that the custom of extravagant carousing is 'More honored in the breach than the observance.' (16) Hamlet means that the practice is more honored by not doing it than doing it, a subtly intelligent point.

Hamlet goes on to tell his comrades that 'This heavy-headed revel east and west makes us traduced and taxed of other nations.' (18) Hamlet's saying that the inebriate conduct at Claudius' court demeans Scotland in the eyes of other country's leaders.

He adds that some men, meaning Claudius, are bit by 'some vicious mole of nature in them,' (24) they're born with and Nature cannot cure. This is more evidence of how Hamlet feels about his new stepfather, especially with 'vicious' and 'mole' imbedded in the cutting phrase.

I didn't include the final 11 lines (27-38) from Hamlet's speech ending with the word 'scandal.' For additional reference, this portion of the speech comes before the Ghost enters. Since these lines are among the most disputed as to meaning in all of Shakespeare, you may choose to read them on your own.

The gist is that immoral actions by a leader like Claudius infect the entire enterprise, in this case Scotland. My limitations* prevent me from offering more.

*A germane use of this word is spoken by Captain Fisby in *The Teahouse of the August Moon*: 'I've made peace with myself somewhere between my ambitions and my limitations.'

Back to Hamlet and the Ghost: As said earlier, ghosts of the period in which this play was written sometimes appear as the devil in disguise. Therefore, we have Hamlet's question: 'Be thou a spirit of health or goblin damned, bring with thee airs from Heaven or blasts from Hell.' (42) Hamlet remains unsure as to whether the Ghost is his father's spirit or the Devil incognito.

In his poetic questions to the Ghost, Hamlet wonders how the burial crypt's 'ponderous and marble jaws,' (50) an image-provoking phrase, have opened. Usually, if Will can't show a physical object onstage, his language materializes it.

'That thou, dear corse, again, in complete steel' (52) tells us that Will remembers that Horatio and the soldiers told him that in their earlier sighting the Ghost wore armor. He also mentioned it earlier in his brief soliloquy: 'My father's spirit in arms! All is not well.' 1.2, (255) Old Hamlet's spirit is dressed for battle. This signals Hamlet that he'd better, like his father's specter, gear up for a fight as well.

When Hamlet says, 'I do not set my life at a pin's fee,' (65) he's telling his companions that given the chance to talk with his dead father he's not about to measure his life's worth.

By seeing his fate in play, Hamlet feels 'As hardy as the Nemean lion's nerve.' (83) This massive and ferocious beast is impervious to weaponry. The lion is strangled by Heracles, son of Zeus, tough guys these mythological Greek heroes.

Horatio and Marcellus try to stop Hamlet from following the Ghost. He tells them to keep their hands off him, or 'I'll make a ghost of him that lets me!'* (85) Here, 'lets' means stops.

*The threat by Hamlet recalls similar dialogue from *Richard III*, 1.2. When Richard, called Gloucester before he becomes King, encounters a funeral cortege he orders that the coffin of a man he recently killed be set down, or 'I'll make a corse of him that disobeys.' In a preposterous exchange, that only a Will Shakespeare can make believable, Gloucester proceeds to seduce, on the spot, the dead man's widow.

Richard, along with Falstaff, Hamlet, Cleopatra, Othello, Imogen and Lear are among Will's choicest roles for actors playing Shakespeare.

Back to Hamlet exiting offstage with the Ghost: Horatio's 'He waxes desperate with imagination' (86) neatly cues Marcellus' enduring 'Something is rotten in the state of Denmark.' (89)

* * *

(HAMLET and the Ghost enter on another area of the stage. Hamlet tells the Ghost to speak because he intends to 'go no further.' (1) Does Hamlet mean distance or degree? If Will meant distance, it should read 'farther.')

Ghost. <u>My hour is almost come</u> (2)
When I to <u>sulphurous and tormenting flames</u> (3)
Must render up myself. . . .
I am thy father's spirit,
<u>Doomed for a certain term to walk the night</u> (10)
<u>And for the day confined to fast in fires</u> (11)
<u>Till the foul crimes done in my days of nature</u> (12)
Are burnt and purged away. But that I am forbid
To <u>tell the secrets of my prison house,</u> (14)
I could a tale unfold whose lightest word
Would <u>harrow up thy soul, freeze thy young blood,</u> (16)
Make thy two eyes, like stars, start from their spheres.
. . .
If thou didst ever thy dear father love—
Revenge his foul and most unnatural murder. . . .
<u>Murder most foul,</u> (27) as in the best it is,
But this most foul, strange, and unnatural.
Hamlet. Hast me to know 't, that I, with wings as swift
As meditation or thoughts of love,
<u>May sweep to my revenge.</u> (31)

Ghost. Now, Hamlet, hear.

'Tis given out that, sleeping in my orchard,

<u>A serpent stung me—so the whole ear of Denmark</u>

<u>Is by a forgèd process of my death</u> (36)

Rankly abused. But know, thou noble youth,

<u>The serpent that did sting thy father's life</u> (38)

Now wears his crown.

Hamlet. <u>Oh, my prophetic soul! My uncle!</u> (40)

Ghost. Aye, that incestuous, that adulterate beast.

With witchcraft of his wit, with traitorous gifts—

Of wicked wit and gifts, that have the power

So to seduce!—won to his shameful lust

The will of my most seeming-virtuous Queen.

O Hamlet, what a falling-off was there! . . .

<u>Though lewdness court it in a shape of Heaven.</u> (54)

So lust, though to a radiant angel linked,

Will sate itself in a celestial bed

And prey on garbage. . . .

Sleeping within my orchard,

My custom always of the afternoon,

Upon my secure hour thy uncle stole

With juice of cursed hebenon in a vial

And in the porches of my ears did pour

The <u>leprous distilment,</u> (64) whose effect

Holds such an enmity with blood of man

That swift as quicksilver it courses through

<u>The natural gates and alleys of the body,</u> . . . (67)

Thus was I, sleeping by a brother's hand

Of life, of crown, of Queen, at once dispatched—

Cut off even in the blossoms of my sin, (76)

Unhouseled, disappointed, unaneled, (77)

No reckoning made, but sent to my account

With all my imperfections on my head. . . .

But, howsever thou pursuest this act,

Taint not thy mind, nor let thy soul contrive

Against thy mother aught. Leave her to Heaven—

(86)

(Ghost exits.)

(THE Ghost answers Hamlet's demand that they 'go no further' with 'My hour is almost come,' (2) and I'll soon return to 'sulphurous and tormenting flames.' (3)

The first impression is that the Ghost is the Devil in disguise and comes from Hell. But the Ghost quickly says he is the spirit of Hamlet's father who is 'Doomed for a certain term to walk the night.' (10) 'And for the day confined to fast in fires.' (11) Like us, Hamlet wonders why this hellish punishment has been imposed on the Ghost.

He tells us, 'Till the foul crimes done in my days of nature,' (12) or life, are resolved. You, reader, like me, know this. But consider that this book is aimed at understanding the speeches, and that includes structure.

Remember, that most of Will's period audiences have not seen the play before. Of necessity, he assumes that they're new to it. In light of that, he patiently sets up the emerging story. Will's also thinking like Hamlet and carefully doles out the revelations about his character to the audience.

Will loves Hamlet. Will is Hamlet. The one character in all the plays most like Will: intelligent, sensitive, rational, nuanced, articulate. And, as we learn later, not without faults. To borrow the title of Tom Wolfe's novel, Hamlet is *A Man in Full*. The Prince of Denmark is the actor up on the stage facing this quandary, and he wants the audience to like him and feel sympathy for him.

Back to scene five: the audience is teased a bit when the Ghost tells Hamlet that he can't 'tell the secrets of my prison house,' (14) and wouldn't we like to know those. However, the intent here is to give Hamlet more reasons why he should free, what he's been told is his father's spirit, from a penal form of purgatory.

Will diverts to what the Ghost can reveal, and that's a tale that will 'harrow up thy soul, freeze thy young blood,' (16) and this grabs Hamlet's and the audience's attention. And here's an example of why the play is so popular. You're led on; wanting to know more, getting it, and then like Gertrude, Hamlet's mother, in her love for King Hamlet, would 'hang on him as if increase of appetite had grown by what it fed on.' We haven't even completed act one, and we're already hungry for more.

The Ghost employs a little guilt by telling Hamlet that if he loved his father, he will revenge his 'Murder most foul.' (27)

For now, Hamlet is sold and 'May sweep to my revenge.' (31) This line runs counter to the opinion of late 18th and early 19th-Century British author Samuel Taylor Coleridge's claim that Hamlet is a man who could not make up his mind.

USC Professor Frank Baxter didn't subscribe to this theory. His rejoinder, 'Hamlet has too much mind to make up.'

Hamlet's alleged dithering is largely explained by analyzing his actions in light of generally held Elizabethan religious beliefs. As we progress through the play, we'll look at some examples.

Another note on the subject of Hamlet's determinations: Sir Laurence Olivier directed and played Hamlet in his 1948 film of the same name. It is a wonderfully entertaining movie and very bad Shakespeare. The following was included in the opening titles: 'This is a story of a man who could not make up his mind.'

On another topic related to Olivier, too many actors play Shakespeare with an exaggerated, conversational tone, like chatting over the back fence. The poetry does not fit this method. Olivier, in his *Hamlet* and *Richard III* films, had the style exactly right with his clipped, fully accessible, and slightly presentational, declaiming delivery of Will's language.

Lest we forget, Hamlet promises to revenge his father's murder, but the Ghost is not about to settle for that and continues to make his case. To make certain that Hamlet is not carried away and will follow through on his promise, the Ghost provides damning evidence: 'A serpent stung me—so the whole ear of Denmark is by a forgèd process of my death rankly abused.' (37) The Danish people listen with their ears to a false tale from this serpent. Note the use of 'ear' in this sense and several lines later in another.

Reprising the serpent's swindle, 'The serpent that did sting thy father's life' now wears his crown.' (39)

Then the audience hears Hamlet's impulsive reaction, 'Oh, my prophetic soul! My uncle!' (40) Use of the word 'prophetic' suggests that Hamlet suspects all along that Claudius is guilty of some subterfuge. In commenting on his mother's sexual attraction to Claudius, Hamlet said in 1.2, 'It is not, nor it cannot, come to good.'

The Ghost speaks of Claudius' gift of wit, witchcraft and seduction 'Though lewdness court it in a shape of Heaven.' (54) This means that Claudius was clever enough to appear spiritual to Gertrude and fool her into bed.

Hamlet learns that his father's murder was accomplished by pouring poison into his ears. In strong poetry, the Ghost describes how the 'leprous distillment' (64) ran like quicksilver through 'The natural gates and alleys of the body.' (67) And he was 'Cut off even in the blossoms of my sin,' (76) or absent the chance to rectify his transgressions and not face perdition.

According to religious customs, Claudius' murder of Hamlet's father grows ever more egregious, as he left him 'Unhouseled, disappointed, unaneled,' (77) or without receiving the last rites of the church.

The Ghost's impassioned speech closes with him urging Hamlet not to blame his mother, 'Leave her to Heaven.' (86) This lovely, forgiving phrase became, as so many of Will's originals do, the title of a novel and a Hollywood film in which Gene Tierney's lead character was less than admirable. But since she left the stuffy Vincent Price for the heartthrob Cornel Wilde, many female viewers forgave her.

After the Ghost exits, Hamlet continues in soliloquy.)

Hamlet. O all you host of Heaven! O earth! What else?
And shall I couple hell? Oh. fie! Hold, hold my heart,
And you, my sinews, grow not instant old
But bear me stiffly up. <u>Remember thee!'</u> (95)
Aye, thou poor ghost, <u>while memory holds a seat</u> (96)
<u>In this distracted globe. Remember thee!</u> . . . (97)
<u>That one may smile, and smile, and be a villain.</u> (108)
At least I'm sure it may be so in Denmark.
<u>So, Uncle, there you are.</u> (110) Now to my word.
<u>It is 'Adieu, adieu! Remember me. I have sworn 't.</u>
(111)
(Marcellus and Horatio enter. Hamlet continues.)
Give me one poor request. . . .
Never make known what you have seen tonight. . . .
Nay, but swear 't. . . .
Upon my sword. . . .
(From under the stage, the Ghost cries out 'Swear.'
This stage direction is in the First Folio. Hamlet
continues.)
Never to speak of this that you have seen,
Swear by my sword. . . .
Ghost. (From under stage.) Swear.
Hic et ubique? <u>Then we'll shift our ground.</u> (156)
Horatio. O, day and night, but this is <u>wondrous
strange!</u> (163)
Hamlet. And therefore as a stranger give it welcome.

There are more things in Heaven and earth, Horatio,
Than are dreamt of in your philosophy. (167)
But come,
Here, as before, never, so help you mercy,
How strange or odd so'er I bear myself,
As I perchance hereafter shall think meet
To put an antic disposition on, (172)
That you, at such times seeing me, never shall,
With arms encumbered thus, or this headshake
Or by pronouncing some doubtful phrase—
The time is out of joint. (189) O cursèd spite
That ever I was born to set it right! (190)
Hamlet, 1.5, 1-190

('REMEMBER thee!' (95 and 97) is used twice in this soliloquy, as Hamlet promises to remember his father. And 'Remember me' in (111)

He's determined not to forget the advice from his father's spirit, 'while memory holds a seat' (96) in 'In this distracted globe. Remember thee!' (97) After all the insights he's just learned from the Ghost, Hamlet fears getting sidetracked and having things slip out of his 'globe' or head.

Like the actor he is, Hamlet is reminded of his 'word,' or prompt from the spirit: 'It is 'Adieu, adieu! Remember me. I have sworn 't.' (111)

After Horatio and Marcellus enter, Hamlet asks them not to speak about the Ghost with anyone. He keeps forcing the issue, and they continue to agree. Hamlet wants more confirmation, several times asking them to swear upon his sword. The Ghost chimes in from beneath the stage also asking the group to swear.

For some reason, Hamlet didn't want the oaths to be administered over the Ghost. He says, '*Hic et ubique*? Then we'll shift our ground.' (156) The Latin means here and everywhere.

Even after moving, the Ghost is below them, again ordering them to swear. The actor playing Hamlet looks to the stage floor and good naturedly, and to the audience's delight, says to the Ghost:

Hamlet. Well said, old mole! Canst work i' the ground so fast?
A <u>worthy pioneer!</u> (162) Once more remove, good friends.

(NOW we know why Will wrote it this way: the moving around is better stagecraft, and its humor relieves the heavy dialogue and dire warnings. By calling him 'worthy pioneer' (162) Hamlet likens the Ghost to a miner working fast underground.

I don't know why I like the following lines so much, but I do.)

Hamlet. There are more things in Heaven and earth, Horatio, (166)
Than are dreamt of in your philosophy.

(PRIOR to the two lines above, Horatio calls the ongoing events 'wondrous strange.'* (163) Hamlet simply tells him that there are more things happening around them than the philosophy taught at Wittenberg.

*Will favored the words 'strange' and 'wondrous.' They were used beautifully by Othello in 1.3 when he quotes his wife's comments on his earlier adventures:

Othello. She swore, in faith, 'twas strange, 'twas passing strange,
'Twas pitiful, 'twas wondrous pitiful.

(And the brilliant sentence spoken by Theseus in *A Midsummer Night's Dream*, 5.1: 'That is, hot ice and wondrous strange snow.')

Hamlet tells his comrades that when they see him 'put an antic disposition on,' (172) or act crazy, pretend not to notice. Reread the lines that follow.

Hamlet demonstrates how he'll use his arms and head to simulate the body language of a mentally disturbed person.

Hamlet closes act one with a neat couplet, 'The time is out of joint.' (189) And he curses, 'That ever I was born to set it right!' (190) We see his point. He's been dealt an unholy mess, and then told by his father's spirit that he's expected to clean it up.

Although not being a life-or-death situation like Hamlet's, the narrative reminds me of a letter sent home to Italy by a 19th-Century Italian immigrant to America: 'Not only are the streets not paved in gold, they are not paved at all, and we are expected to pave them.')

* * *

(AS act two opens, we're reminded that Laertes asked permission to go back to France. His father and the King granted his wish. Unless it's something about music, we don't know why Laertes was in France, nor do we know why he wishes to go back. Now, after the fact, Polonius asks himself the same question.

Before leaving, Laertes gave his sister, Ophelia, a long, junior-Polonius lecture on why she should not sleep with Hamlet. She listens with respect, but did tell her brother that when he got back to France he shouldn't walk the 'primrose path of dalliance,' a teasing counter.

Polonius now suspects that Laertes may wander onto the path and sends his servant, Reynaldo, off to France to spy on Laertes. As I'm sure you've already picked up, Polonius never uses one word to make a point when three or more are available. He is prolix to a fault.

Find out, Polonius long-windedly tells Reynaldo, if Laertes is involved in drinking, fencing, swearing, (24) gaming, whoring and tennis. Tennis? Yes, Will loves kidding the French over their addiction to tennis. You may recall in *Henry V*, 1.2 that the Dauphin sends King Henry a gift. He asks what is in the package, 'Tennis balls, my liege.'

Polonius interrupts his lengthy instructions to Reynaldo with: 'What was I about to say? By the mass, I was about to say something. Where did I leave?' (51) The American actor, Frank Morgan, who played the Wizard in *The Wizard of Oz* movie, would make a fine amusingly-confused Polonius.

Polonius' tedious wordiness is temporarily relieved when Ophelia enters to report to him on Hamlet's previously-predicted bizarre behavior, 'Oh, my lord, my lord, I have been so affrighted!' (74) She goes on.)

Ophelia. My lord, as I was sewing in my closet,

Lord Hamlet, with his doublet all unbraced,
No hat upon his head, his stockings fouled,
<u>Ungartered and down-gyved to his ankle</u>, (80)
Pale as his shirt, his knees knocking each other,
And with a look so piteous in purport
As if he had been loosèd out of Hell
To speak of horrors he comes before me.
Polonius. <u>Mad for thy love?</u> (84)
Ophelia. My lord, I do not know,
But truly I do fear it. . . .
<u>He took me by the wrist</u> (87) and held me hard.
Then he goes to the length of all his arm,
And with his other <u>hand thus o'er his brow</u> (89)
He falls to such perusal of my face
As he would draw it. Long he stayed so.
Polonius. <u>Come, go with me. I will go seek the King</u>.
(101)
This is the very ecstasy of love . . .
That hath made him mad.
Hamlet, 2.1, 24-101

(OPHELIA describes Hamlet's disordered clothes with his stockings bunched, or 'Ungartered and down-gyved to his ankle.' (80)

As Hamlet told Horatio in 1.5, (172) he would 'put an antic disposition on,' or fake madness.

Polonius asks, 'Mad for thy love?' (84) In Will's times, Elizabethans believed that people could be insane with love.

Ophelia replies that she doesn't know the answer. Then, from 'He took me by the wrist' (87) to 'hand thus o'er his brow' (89) is a rich stage-business-while-speaking opportunity for the actor playing Ophelia. Recall that Hamlet practiced the moves she's demonstrating in 1.5, 173-4

'Come, go with me. I will go seek the King.' (101) This is quintessential Polonius, a panicky old fusspot, overreacting and making mountains out of molehills. Don't first talk with Hamlet, rush to the King with some juicy gossip.

But Polonius has a deeper motivation. He thinks that the news of Hamlet's peculiar actions toward Ophelia might also prompt the King to prevent Hamlet from marrying below his station, and thereby save his daughter from him. Polonius is a meddler, but he's also a wily old party. Beyond his bumbling, he does have, as Lord Chamberlain, sufficient court-intrigue acumen.)

* * *

(SCENE TWO opens with the King and Queen, plus two new characters, Rosencrantz and Guildenstern.*

46

They're not clowns, but almost. Also, they resemble two halves of a whole, and can't be told apart. As we will learn, R & G were Hamlet's classmates at Wittenberg, and they are not at Elsinore by happenstance.

*The writer Tom Stoppard wrote a play, later made into a movie, called *Rosencrantz and Guildenstern are Dead*, a cockeyed view of *Hamlet*, with much of the action taking place behind the scenes. R & G are as confused in that version, as they are in this one.

King Claudius tells R & G of 'Hamlet's transformation,' (5) and that explains why they were summoned. The King and Queen want them to use their prior acquaintance with Hamlet to draw him out and learn why he is acting crazy. Keep in mind that Hamlet has 'put an antic disposition on.' Except for Horatio and Marcellus, nobody knows that.

Rosencrantz and Guildenstern go off agreeably to meet with Hamlet.

Scene two continues as Polonius enters with two representatives from Norway who seek permission for their army to cross Scotland on the way to fight Poland.

Remember that Young Fortinbras, the Norwegian military leader, wants to take back the land captured by old King Hamlet from Old Fortinbras. But, it appears that Young Fortinbras' uncle has, at least temporarily, diverted him from that goal. Claudius says that he will 'think upon this business,' (82) of letting them cross Scotland on the way to Poland.*

*Unless the borders were drastically different at that time, and I don't think they were, it makes no geographic sense to traverse Scotland en route to Poland. Do the Norwegian envoys have ulterior motives? We'll learn more in the play's resolution.)

* * *

(AFTER the delegates exit, Polonius, in increasingly ornate language, speaks to the King and Queen on Hamlet's behavior.

Polonius. My liege and madam, to expostulate
What majesty should be, what duty is
Why day is day, night night, and time is time, (88)
Were nothing but to waste night, day, and time.
Therefore, since brevity is the soul of wit (90)
And tediousness the limbs and outward flourishes,
I will be brief. Your noble son is mad.
Queen. More matter, with less art. (95)
Polonius. Madam, I swear I use no art at all.
That he is mad, 'tis true. 'Tis true 'tis pity,
And pity 'tis 'tis true—a foolish figure. (98)

More matter, with less art But farewell it, for I will use no art.

(POLONIUS' maundering , 'Why day is day, night night, and time is time,' (88) and his ludicrous, in the context of his talkiness, 'brevity is the soul of wit' (90) exasperates the Queen who instructs him, 'More matter, with less art.' (95) She wants some facts without decorative language.

And then Polonius is right back at it with, 'And pity 'tis 'tis true—a foolish figure.' (98) By 'figure' he means a mindless form of expression. Polonius can't help himself. He's trapped in a recitation of silly patter written by Will to give his audiences a few chuckles. When acted convincingly, bits like these are funny delivered by someone who's deadly serious while spouting nonsense.

Polonius goes on to tell Claudius and Gertrude that Hamlet gave Ophelia a letter in which he mentions, among other things, 'her excellent white bosom.' (113)

After more back and forth, Polonius goes on to tell his listeners that 'When I saw this hot love on the wing,' (132) a felicitous phrase, he took action telling Ophelia that Hamlet is, 'a Prince, out of thy star,' (141) or out of your league.'

'She took the fruits of my advice' (145) Polonius says and avoids contact with Hamlet. Being repulsed, Hamlet, according to Polonius' droll recitation

Fell into a sadness, then into a fast,
Thence to a watch, thence into a weakness
Thence to a lightness, and by this declension
Into the madness wherein he now raves
And all we mourn for.
Hamlet, 2.2, 86-151

(AMIDST his tyranny of verbosity, Polonius has it all wrong, but he delivers a nicely-paced description of Hamlet's lovesick descent into what he thinks is genuine looniness. These passages delight audiences who know what's going on while those onstage don't. Did Hitchcock learn a form of the MacGuffin from Will?)

* * *

(THE King, Queen and Polonius continue their banter on how to find out more about Hamlet's unhinged deportment. They know he walks in the castle lobby for hours at a time. Queen Gertrude and Polonius plan to hide behind an arras, or hanging curtain, and send Ophelia out to meet Hamlet and observe his behavior towards her.

The King and Queen exit. *Enter Hamlet reading on a book* is a notable stage direction from the First Folio.

Polonius asks Hamlet if he knows him: 'You are a fishmonger.' (174)

Later, Polonius asks 'What do you read, my lord?' (192)

Hamlet answers, 'Words, words, words.' (194)

Further on in the farcical exchange Hamlet describes the infirmities of old men. Among these he lists 'a plentiful lack of wit.' (201) Polonius misses the dig and in an aside, delivers to the audience what became a lasting cliché: 'Though this be madness, yet there is method in 't.' (207) He gives Hamlet some credit for making occasional sense.

Polonius says, 'I will most humbly take my leave of you.' (218)

In an inauspicious comment, Hamlet answers that Polonius can take nothing from him 'except my life,' (221) which he repeats twice more.

Hamlet, who's feigning madness while also teasing Polonius, remarks exasperatedly on 'These tedious old fools.' (223)
Hamlet, 2.2, 152-223

* * *

(ON his way offstage, Polonius spots Rosencrantz and Guildenstern entering. Unable to resist sticking his nose in, he says, 'You go to seek the Lord Hamlet. There he is.' (224)

Hamlet and R & G exchange in some risqué banter about the 'privates' (236) of Lady Fortune. Then it turns to why Lady Fortune 'sends you to prison hither.' (247)

R & G act surprised, 'Prison, my lord!' (248)

Hamlet tells them 'Denmark's a prison.' (249) R & G say they do not think so.

This play abounds in famous lines, and Hamlet speaks another: 'Why, then 'tis none to you, for there is nothing either good or bad but thinking makes it so. (255) To me it is a prison.'

R & G respond with, 'Why, then your ambition makes it one. 'Tis too narrow for your mind.' (258) They think that Hamlet's ambitions range beyond Denmark, and that's why he sees it as a prison.

Hamlet replies, 'Oh, God, I could be bounded in a nutshell and count myself a king of infinite space were it not that I have bad dreams.' (260) Hamlet's saying that Denmark's limited geography is not the problem. He could live in an acorn and still feel large. However what's he's dreaming about makes Denmark prison-like to him. This line refers back to (255) 'thinking makes it so.' R & G see the dreams as another indication that Hamlet is over-ambitious, and his dreams encourage his ambition, and are 'merely the shadow of a dream.' (264)

Hamlet answers, 'A dream itself is but a shadow.' (266)

Tired of the wordplay, Hamlet suggests, 'Shall we to the court? For, by my faith, I cannot reason.' (271)

Earlier, we mentioned British author Samuel Taylor Coleridge. He offered an interesting commentary on Hamlet's mind as 'Giving substance to shadows.' Hamlet knows exactly how to deal with the real world. An example follows, as Hamlet manipulates Rosencrantz and Guildenstern.

But first a reminder: except for Horatio, Marcellus and a few soldiers who are sworn to secrecy, every character in the play misreads Hamlet's intentions.

Hamlet asks R &G: 'In the beaten way of friendship, what make you at Elsinore?' (276) They claim it is simply a visit to see him. Hamlet sees through them, asks a few questions, and finally presses them: 'Come, deal justly with me . . . (284) You were sent for, and there is a kind of confession in your looks which your modesties have not craft enough to color.' (287)

We're including just the best lines of this act two, scene two passage and now continue: Through more verbal maneuvering, Hamlet draws R & G out, and they finally admit, 'My lord, we were sent for.' (303) Hamlet doesn't let on that he's faking insanity, but he does say that since they now know where each of them stands, there is no need to reveal the mutual understanding to the King.

He knows why his mood is down, but tells Rosencrantz and Guildenstern in marvelous prose poetry:

Hamlet. 'I have of late—but wherefore I know not—lost all my mirth, foregone all custom of exercises, and indeed it goes so heavily with my disposition that this goodly frame <u>the earth seems to me a sterile promontory.</u> (310) This <u>most excellent canopy, the air, look you, this brave, o'erhanging firmament, this majestical roof fretted with golden fire</u> (311)—why, it appears no other thing to me than <u>a foul and pestilent congregation of vapors.</u> (313) <u>What a piece of work is man!</u> (315) How noble in reason! How infinite in faculty! In form and moving how express and admirable! In action how like an angel! In apprehension how like a god! The beauty of the world! The paragon of animals! And yet, to me, <u>what is this quintessence of dust?</u> (319) <u>Man delights not me</u> (320)—no, nor woman either, though by your smiling you seem to say so.'

Hamlet, 2.2, 224-320

(MANY of the lines in *Hamlet* speak for themselves, such as, 'for there is nothing either good or bad but thinking makes it so.' (255) This is not only the rare favorable generalization, it also perfectly fits the dialogue surrounding it. You think of Denmark one way, gentlemen, I think of it differently.

'Why, then your ambition makes it one. 'Tis too narrow for your mind.' (258) Not knowing the actual reason for Hamlet's prejudice against Denmark, R & G guess that it's ambition. Since it sets up Hamlet's poetic 'bounded in a nutshell' (3) and 'king of infinite space' (260) lines, the exchange is useful. Then they get into dreams and shadows, and Hamlet says, in effect, let's drop this, I can't argue anymore.

After Hamlet induces Rosencrantz and Guildenstern to confess that they've come to Elsinore to spy on him, he tells them that he's become lackluster. Following ordinary complaints, Hamlet tells R & G that 'the earth seems to me a sterile promontory,' (310) or a headland he's trapped on with nowhere to go. In his second contemplation of suicide in the play, he's thinking of jumping off the cliff.

The buildups toward exalted language are always fun to follow. In this case, Hamlet's speech shifts from the audience visualizing him on a high bluff above the ocean to the roof of the Globe Theatre: 'this most excellent canopy,' 'this brave, o'erhanging firmament,' 'this majestical roof fretted with golden fire.' (311) The last one is especially image-rich, driven by the ideal verb 'fretted.'

Did you notice the 'look you' after 'canopy?' The actor playing Hamlet points to the Globe Theatre roof, now substituting for the sky, and tells the audience to look up at the canopy decorated with painted images of the heavens.

After lifting the audience with elevated poetry, with effects aloft to boot, Hamlet drops them by calling all that beauty 'a foul and pestilent congregation of vapors.' (313)

Then, back up again with the enduring 'What a piece of work is man!' (315) This is yet another creation that's become a cliché, as in 'he's a piece of work.'

Other praises of man follow, only to be demeaned again with, 'what is this quintessence of dust?' (319) Man delights not me'—(320) 'Quintessence,' or apotheosis, of dust is breathtakingly imaginative in re-highlighting Hamlet's despondency. It also ties to 'dust to dust' in the Book of Common Prayer.*

*This Protestant book was written, at least in part, by Edward VI, son of Henry VIII and Jane Seymour. He is the half-brother of Queen Elizabeth I, successor to Edward upon his death at 16, and daughter of Henry VIII and Anne Boleyn. Keep in mind that Hamlet is played at court before Elizabeth's death in 1603. She is the last Tudor ruler, and the intellectually-gifted Queen does not miss the allusion. She knew, admired and supported Will.

Even after her death, Will made respectful references to Queen Elizabeth I. In *A Midsummer Night's Dream*, 2.1, first shown in 1605, we have 'a fair vestal throned by the West.')

Hamlet's mood is not symptomatic of melancholy; he has persuasive reasons to be in the dumps. His beloved father dies suddenly, and his spirit presents to tell Hamlet that his brother, Hamlet's uncle, murdered him. Furthermore, the uncle, who is now King, seduced and married Hamlet's mother within a month. Who wouldn't be confused, bitter and bent on revenge?

Here's the thing: within the beliefs of the times, the spirit could be the Devil in disguise. How does Hamlet prove the spirit is telling the truth? Suddenly he finds potential help in solving his dilemma.)

* * *

(AT the close of the previous passage, Hamlet presses Rosencrantz and Guildenstern on why they smile

when he mentions 'Man delights not me'. (320) R &
G answer that if man does not delight Hamlet, how
will his welcome to the visiting players they met on
the way to Elsinore be received.

The arrival of traveling players at Elsinore is a
turning point in the play. Did you note that Will uses
R & G to introduce them. R & G are useful devices.
They set up
Hamlet's speeches, they reveal that the King is spying,
and now Hamlet can comment on the players to
them.)

Hamlet. <u>He that plays the King shall be welcome</u>, (332)
<u>His Majesty should have tribute of me.</u> (333) The
adventurous knight shall use his foil and target, the
lover shall not sigh gratis, the humorous man shall
end his part in peace, the clown shall make those
laugh whose lungs are tickle o' the sere, and the lady
shall say her mind freely or the <u>blank verse</u> (339) shall
halt for 't. <u>What players are they?</u>' (340)
Hamlet, 2.2, 320-420

(HAMLET immediately sees a use for the player king.
'He that plays the King shall be welcome, (332) his
Majesty should have tribute of me.' (333) Or I see a
use for him, and if he works out I'll pay him for it.

I didn't highlight them, but go back and read lines 333-339. Hamlet is an actor who, through Will, knows all the stock parts: the knight using his sword; the lover who shouldn't sigh too much; the bit player who is expected to perform adequately; and the clown who should make the audience laugh spontaneously, or on a hair-trigger.

Hamlet thinks of 'blank verse' (339) and what he might write for the player in the lady-part to deliver without stumbling.

He asks R & G, 'What players are they?' (340) He needs to know their fitness for the parody he has in mind. The speech is Will the writer and actor constructing a scene through Hamlet's character.

R and G tell Hamlet that these particular adult players work both in the city and on the road. Hamlet responds that they can make money either way.

Read this passage in full to gain insight into the ongoing battles between adult players of the Elizabethan and Jacobean periods and the increasingly popular boys' companies. Hamlet comments that the boys shouldn't harm the adult acting companies, since it is a profession that they will soon join: 'their writers do them wrong to make them exclaim against their own succession.' (368)

Following the repartee about the players, Hamlet shakes hands with R & G officially welcoming them to Elsinore with a bit of sarcasm. 'You are welcome. But my uncle-father and aunt-mother are deceived.' (393) A few lines later, 'I am but mad north-northwest. When the wind is southerly, I know a hawk from a handsaw.' (396) Hamlet's saying that he's crazy only part of the time, but the King and Queen don't know that.

Polonius enters to tell Hamlet what he already knows: players have arrived in the castle. Polonius reads the license to play the players gave him: 'The best actors in the world, either for tragedy, comedy, history, pastoral, pastoral-comical, historical-pastoral, tragical-historic, tragical-comical-historical-pastoral, scene individable or poem unlimited. Seneca cannot be too heavy, nor Plautus too light. (419) <u>For the law of writ and the liberty, these are the only men.</u>' (420

Theater-savvy audience members know these Roman writers, and will chuckle at the references. By including the mention of Seneca and Plautus, Will also kids himself. He lifts material from both these Roman writers. *Comedy of Errors*, for example, was based on two Plautus' plays. Sources of the Falstaff character are many and debatable. One of his elements could have come from Plautus.)

An able actor playing Polonius can make this classic speech amusing through inflection and business. Perhaps catching his breath, or clearing his throat, or dabbing his forehead at intervals.

'For the law of writ and the liberty, these are the only men.' (420) This means that the players can perform the Roman and Greek classics and also plays of the time.

* * *

(HAMLET greets the players, at least two of whom he knows. He remarks that one of the adult players is now 'valanced,' (442) or bearded.

Another is a young man who plays female roles. He has grown taller. Hamlet hopes that his voice has not 'cracked within the ring.' (447) Or like a coin that has fractured at the rim and has no worth.

Hamlet and the players recall and speak lines from plays they all know. This section is charming and worth reading in its entirety. They're getting reacquainted. Hamlet is seen by the players as a hospitable and erudite man they enjoy. The rapport is later useful when Hamlet instructs them on a play he wants performed before King Claudius.

Hamlet likes these players from his past theater experiences; just as Will understands and appreciates the members of his own London-based company. He writes for them and knows their capabilities in various roles. Will, the playwright, loves the upcoming inner play. This is what he does. He is, through Hamlet, in his element.

Meantime, Hamlet speaks to Polonius: 'Good my lord, will you see the players well bestowed? Do you hear, let them be well used, for they are the abstract and brief chronicles of the time.' (549) This beautiful sentence is the writer and actor Will speaking through Hamlet and expressing his love for theater people.

There's another point here regarding plays of the time and their commentary on society and its workings. Sometimes criticisms went too far, especially toward nobles, and punishment ensued. The Queen's Master of the Revels could prevent plays from opening, and closed down plays that were considered offensive, especially to the Crown. For example, language in Will's *Richard II* had to be amended before the play was allowed to open.

Richard II was shown during the time of the Essex plot against Queen Elizabeth. Participants in the conspiracy attended a performance. No doubt they approved of the play's theme that centered on the overthrow of a reigning monarch.

Back to the ongoing conversation: After Hamlet asks Polonius to see that the players are 'well bestowed.' (546) Polonius answers, 'My lord, I will use them according to their desert,' (552) or level.

'God's bodykins, man, much better. Use every man after his desert and who shall 'scape whipping? Use them after your own honour and dignity. The less they deserve, the more merit there is in your bounty.' (553)

Both of Hamlet's comments starting with the amusing 'God's bodykins' more or less say: don't treat people according to your evaluation of their rank, and even if you think they don't warrant your approval, it reflects well on you to treat them with respect. Also, don't be a snob, particularly after I've called them 'chronicles of the time.'

Hamlet knows the first adult player, and he remains onstage, as all other players exit with Polonius. Hamlet asks, 'Dost thou hear me, old friend? Can you play *The Murder of Gonzago*?' (562)

The player answers, 'Aye, my lord.'

'We'll ha 't tomorrow night. You could, for a need, study a speech of some dozen or sixteen lines which I would set down and insert in 't, could you not?' (565) The player agrees, and Hamlet continues, 'Very well. Follow that lord, and look you mock him not.' (570) Despite his previous derisive comments, Hamlet has a soft spot for Polonius, and doesn't want the players to make fun of him.)

Hamlet, 2.2, 442-570

* * *

(NEXT, Hamlet gives one of the great speeches in the play, great because the poetry is sublime and the range and content of his thoughts astonishing. I'll jump a step higher, it is one of the classic speeches in English literature, and an iridescent gift to actors who are up to the Hamlet role.)

Hamlet. <u>Now I am alone</u>. (575)
<u>Oh, what a rogue and peasant slave am I!</u> (576)
<u>Is it not monstrous to this player here</u>, (577)
But <u>in a fiction, a dream of passion</u>, (578)
Could force his soul so to his own conceit
That from her working all his visage waned,
Tears in his eyes, distraction in 's aspect,
A broken voice, and his whole function suiting
With forms to his conceit? And all for nothing!
For Hecuba!
<u>What's Hecuba to him or he to Hecuba</u>,
<u>That he should weep for her?</u> (585) What would he do
Had he <u>the motive and the cue for passion</u> (587)
That I have? He would <u>drown the stage with tears</u> (588)
And cleave the general ear with horrid speech,
Make mad the guilty and appal the free,
Confound the ignorant, and amaze indeed

The very faculties of eyes and ears.
Yet I,
A dull and muddy-mettled rascal, peak,
Like John-a-dreams, unpregnant of my cause, (595)
And can say nothing—no, not for a King
Upon whose property and most dear life
A damned defeat was made. Am I a coward?
Who calls me villain? Breaks my pate across?
Plucks off my beard and blows it in my face? (600)
Tweaks me by the nose? Gives me the lie i' the throat
As deep as the lungs? Who does me this?
Ha!
'Swounds, I should take it. For it cannot be
But I am pigeon-livered and lack gall
To make oppression bitter, or ere this
With this slave's offal. Bloody, bawdy villain!
Remorseless, treacherous, lecherous, kindless villain!
(609)
Oh, vengeance!
Why, what an ass am I! This is most brave,
That I, the son of a dear father murdered,
Prompted to my revenge by Heaven and Hell,
Must, like a whore, unpack my heart with words (614)
And fall a-cursing like a very drab,
A scullion!
Fie upon 't! Foh! About, my brain! Hum, I have heard
That guilty creatures sitting at a play (618)

Have by the very cunning of the scene
Been struck so to the soul that presently
They have proclaimed their malefactions; (621)
For murder, though it have no tongue, will speak
With most miraculous organ. I'll have these players
Play something like the murder of my father
Before mine uncle. I'll observe his looks,
I'll tent him to the quick. If he but blench,
I know my course. The spirit that I have seen
May be the Devil, and the Devil hath power
To assume a pleasing shape, (629) Yea, and perhaps
Out of my weakness and my melancholy,
As he is very potent with such spirits,
Abuses me to damn me. (632) I'll have grounds
More relative than this. (633) The play's the thing
Wherein I'll catch the conscience of the King.
Hamlet, 2.2, 575-634

(HAMLET's emotions are torn. Knowing what he faces after meeting his father's ghost, whose nerves wouldn't be shaky? Then, in rapid order, Hamlet pretends he's insane, repeatedly deals with the busybody Polonius who believes Hamlet is really crazy, copes with Rosencrantz and Guildenstern who are at Elsinore to spy on him, and uses visiting players to stage a play that may confirm that his uncle murdered his father.

The soilioquy, 'Now I am alone.' (575) contains a litany of confused thoughts emanating from a brilliant mind. Thanks to Will's uncanny writing skill, the monologue ranges from self-doubt to resolve.

Hamlet opens angry at himself: 'Oh, what a rogue and peasant slave am I!' (576) He's saying, I'm a bad person who is being mastered by outside sources that I can't control.

Then he says, 'Is it not monstrous to this player here,' (577) suddenly being the onstage actor the audience focuses on. As usual, Will's thinking of the acting while doing the writing.

Hamlet wonders whether he is 'in a fiction, a dream of passion.' (578) Or, is he like Hecuba, the Greek mythological Queen who wants to avenge her murdered son and is involved in all kinds of other brutal disorders. Thinking of himself playing a role in his own ongoing drama, Hamlet says, 'What's Hecuba to him or he to Hecuba, that he should weep for her?' (585)

Hamlet has 'the motive and the cue for passion' (587) and should 'drown the stage with tears. (588) Note the use of 'stage.' Will always writes for performance. Only a playwright and an actor could write lines like these.

But rather than take action he sits in a confused dream not even understanding what's going on around him and without a strategy, 'Like John-a-dreams, unpregnant of my cause.' (595)

Hamlet wonders why no one calls him a villain, or 'Plucks off my beard* and blows it in my face?' (600) In his temporary self-hatred, Hamlet believes that his lack of guts deserves insult.

*In *King Lear*, Regan plucks Gloucester's beard. In the Elizabethan period, this is considered a gross insult. It isn't the worst thing Gloucester suffers. Later, Regan's husband Cornwall gouges out his eyes.

Quickly, Hamlet switches from self-loathing to his hatred of Claudius, 'Remorseless, treacherous, lecherous, kindless villain!' (609) That's called covering your bases with a nice string of adjectives. I especially liked the poetic pairing of 'treacherous' and 'lecherous.' And 'kindless' is inventive in its place. Since Claudius, at least so far, seems to be having a good time, 'remorseless' also fits.

Just when we think Hamlet's spine stiffens, he's back to calling himself an ass who should be revenging his father's murder. Instead, he 'Must, like a whore, unpack my heart with words,' (614) or talk rather than act decisively.

Finally, Hamlet, in his intellectual, nonlinear way has it all worked out. He says 'Fie,' or forget it, and concentrates on furthering the scheme he has already hatched He muses that he's heard 'That guilty creatures sitting at a play' (618) have sometimes 'proclaimed their malefactions,' (621) or given away their guilt. These lines also serve as exposition. The audience has already listened in on Hamlet talking to the lead traveling player. Now the plan to ensnare the King expands into a stratagem.

As we've discussed before in this book, it was believed in Elizabethan days that the Devil could 'assume a pleasing shape,' (629) and pretend he was something he was not. And since he is weak and melancholy*, it's possible the Devil 'Abuses me to damn me.' (632)

Many people criticize Hamlet for appearing soft and indecisive. However, intelligent individuals act within the mores of their time. Operating within Elizabeth-era beliefs, Hamlet is understandably cautious about taking the Ghost's word and then killing Claudius. If he acts precipitously and is wrong, Claudius goes to Heaven and Hamlet lands in hell.

*Hamlet calls himself 'melancholy' with good reason. His sadness and suicidal tendencies in 1.2: 'How weary, stale, flat . . .' is plausible given the pickle he's in. Hamlet hasn't decided to become bowed down. His once-vital family and his life lie in ruins. Of course he's conflicted. It's impressive that he can handle so much discord with style.

And to fix things, or at least make them better, he must prove the sitting King a murderer, with something 'More relative than this,' (633) like the Ghost's word.

Hamlet ran the range of emotions and came out the other side a determined man. Given all the laying bare down to the soul in the soliloquy, think of the theatrical fever when Hamlet stands tall, and with flawlessly prepared exuberance utters the most famous couplet in all of Shakespeare:

The play's the thing
Wherein I'll catch the conscience of the King.
Hamlet, 2.2, 575-634

* * *

(THE opening of act three is largely exposition. King Claudius, Queen Gertrude, Rosencrantz, Guildenstern, Polonius and Ophelia meet.

R & G report that Hamlet was civil to them, but didn't reveal much. They mention that he knows of visiting players who are now in the castle and will play tonight. Claudius says that he'd like to see them play.

Gertrude exits, and the King tells Ophelia that while she talks to Hamlet, he and her father will listen in to determine whether Hamlet's madness is caused by love. The King says they have 'lawful espials,' (32) meaning that they have just cause to spy.

Polonius advises Ophelia to read a book as she walks about. Hamlet enters reading as well, and is so absorbed that he fails to notice Ophelia. Since Ophelia remains onstage, Hamlet's magnificent speech is not in soliloquy, but he thinks it is, and it is therefore revealing. As we learn next, Hamlet's recent resolution wavers.

Hamlet. <u>To be, or not to be—that is the question.</u> (56)
Whether 'tis nobler in the mind to suffer
<u>The slings and arrows of outrageous fortune,</u> (58)
Or <u>take arms against a sea of troubles</u> (59)
And by opposing end them. To die, to sleep—
No more, and by a sleep to say we end
<u>The heartache and the thousand natural shocks</u> (62)
That <u>flesh is heir to.</u> (63) 'Tis a confirmation
Devoutly to be wished. <u>To die, to sleep,</u> (64)
To sleep—perchance to dream. Aye, there's the rub,
For in that sleep of death what dreams may come
When we have <u>shuffled off this mortal coil</u> (67)
Must give us cause. There's the respect
That makes calamity of so long life.
<u>For who would bear the whips and scorns of time,</u>
(70)
The oppressor's wrong, the proud man's contumely

The pangs of déspised love, the law's delay,
The insolence of office and the spurns
That patient merit of the unworthy takes, (74)
When he himself might his quietus make
With a bare bodkin? (76) Who would fardels bear,
To grunt and sweat under a weary life,
But that the dread of something after death,
The undiscovered country from whose bourn (79)
No traveler returns, puzzles the will, (80)
And makes us rather bear those ills we have (81)
Than fly to others that we know not of? (82)
Thus conscience does make cowards of us all, (83)
And thus the native hue of resolution
Is sicklied o'er with the pale cast of thought,
And enterprises of great pitch and moment
With this regard their currents turn awry
And lost the name of action.—Soft you now!
The fair Ophelia! Nymph, in thy orisons
By all my sins remembered.
Hamlet, 3.1, 56-89

(THE first line 'To be, or not to be—that is the question,' (56) is Hamlet weighing whether to kill himself or not. We've been there before with the Prince, but he's back at it again.

With to suffer 'The slings and arrows of outrageous fortune,' (58) Hamlet asks if it's cowardly or brave to commit suicide, or put up a fight and 'take arms against a sea of troubles,' (59) As we know, he takes the latter course, but his contemplative mind cannot resist evaluating options.

Hamlet wouldn't make a good salesman. He thinks too much, and wouldn't get around to closing the sale. He is, however, the prototypical MIT student, as described in this amusing tale: Three students visiting France are falsely accused of a heinous crime and sentenced to die on the guillotine. The authorities ask whether they would like to lie on the block facing up or down. All three declare their bravery and choose to face the descending blade. Miraculously, the blade stops short of the necks of the Harvard and Yale students, and they are given their freedom on the grounds of divine intervention. The MIT student lays the back of his head on the block, looks up, and says, 'I think I see your problem.'

We return to a more serious issue and the most fascinating theatrical character invented to date. 'The heartache and the thousand natural shocks' (62) is my favorite line in the speech, especially the imaginative combination of the last three words. And 'flesh is heir to' (63) is an elegant way of saying that I'm sick of having life beat me up.

'To die, to sleep' (64) is also used back in line (60), both emphasizing a wish to die, sleep and end the 'natural shocks.' But wait—what if I dream after having 'shuffled off this mortal coil,' (67) a specific phrase picturing a molting snake. Will accomplishes two goals with the phrase, the visual one and the idea that death ends all of life's trials and tribulations. Two lines earlier, Hamlet mentions the chance of dreaming after death and how that's a 'rub,' (65) or obstacle. Will could also be citing a technical term for a surface fault, or rub, in the grass used in the game of lawn bowling.

Dreaming after death is an interesting perception coming from a conflicted mind. Hamlet then says, probably justifying his suicidal thoughts, that living a long life is a calamity.

'For who would bear the whips and scorns of time' (70) incisively reprises 'The slings and arrows of outrageous fortune' back in line three.

'That patient merit of the unworthy takes,' (74) means that meritorious men have to exercise forbearance when suffering abuse from lesser individuals.

'When he himself might his quietus make with a bare bodkin?' (76) Hamlet wonders whether he should kill himself with an unsheathed dagger.

Hamlet continues his thoughts on suicide, and, in a telling phrase, briefly considers the prospect of entering 'The undiscovered country from whose bourn,' (79) or border, or boundary, 'No traveler returns,' (80) and how that prospect 'puzzles the will,' (80) and leaves him confused about whether 'To be, or not to be,' back in (56).

Maybe it's better, Hamlet thinks, to 'bear those ills we have' (81) 'Than fly to others that we know not of.' (82) It took a lot of graceful and well-worth-rereading poetry for Hamlet to reach the point where he comes down on the side of not risking a visit to 'the undiscovered country' and sticking around 'to be.'

But he's still weighing his options: 'Thus conscience does make cowards of us all.' (83) Stewing over religious principles may delay action until it's too late.

The agonized thoughts about the pros and cons of action continue along the same lines, and then Hamlet notices Ophelia onstage. His thoughtful musings turn mean. I kind of wish Ophelia would say to him, 'Oh, Hamlet, get over yourself, there's more to life than pissing and moaning about everything.' Sorry for the irreverence, but as much as I admire his mindful inventions, and sympathize with his plight, Hamlet is a guy who takes himself very seriously.

The more I study Hamlet, the man, the more unfathomable he becomes. He reminds me of Churchill's comment on Russia: 'A riddle wrapped in a mystery inside an enigma.' Hamlet is a theatrical character puzzle that only Will could create.

Cleopatra is Will's most interesting woman. How about Hamlet and Cleopatra paired up? Call the cops!)

* * *

(IN the passage that follows, Hamlet knows that Polonius and Claudius listen in. He continues to feign madness in the hope that they will talk and reveal themselves. Also, he incorrectly believes that Ophelia is in league with her father and the King against him.

Ophelia reminds Hamlet of gifts he gave her. He denies the giving. She tells him that not only did he give gifts, he gave them with 'words of so sweet breath composed as made the things more rich.' (98) And then she tells Hamlet in a catchy phrase that 'Rich gifts wax poor when users prove unkind.' (101)

Insultingly, he asks Ophelia if she is 'honest,' (102) or chaste, on the discrediting basis that someone as beautiful as you seldom is. Her clever answer: 'Could beauty, my lord, have better commerce than with honesty?' (109) Or isn't it admirable to be both attractive and virtuous?

Hamlet tells her 'I did love you once.' (116) Ophelia says 'you made me believe so.' (117) He cruelly answers 'You should not have believed me.' (117)

Followed by, 'I loved you not.' (120) When she tells him 'I was the more deceived,' (121) he tells her: 'Get thee to a nunnery.' (122)

In Elizabethan days, 'nunnery' could mean either a cloister or a bordello. Given the denigration of Ophelia by Hamlet in the next paragraph, Will may have meant brothel.

The insults continue, as Hamlet tells Ophelia 'Be thou as chaste as ice, as pure as snow—thou shalt not escape calumny,' (140) or slander. He continues to bait her with typical Elizabethan satire on women, falsely accusing her that like most women she paints her face, dances lewdly and lisps.

To conclusively dash Ophelia's dreams, Hamlet says, 'I say we will have no more marriages. Those that are married already, all but one shall live; the rest shall keep as they are. To a nunnery, go.' (154) (Hamlet exits.) In the next-to-last sentence above, the 'all but one shall live,' refers to Claudius.

Hamlet may be feigning madness in order to get Claudius and Polonius behind the curtain to say something. It appears, however, that there is more to it. Given his cruelty toward Ophelia and his total rejection of her, I surmise that their previous relationship had more to it than courting and love talk. The emotions discussed above suggest a strong physical relationship.

Why is Hamlet victimizing and using Ophelia? He's clever enough to reveal the spying Polonius and Claudius without putting Ophelia through this torture. We know that he's beset with terrible problems, but does solving them have to include destroying Ophelia? And later Hamlet is just about as tough on his mother.

Possibly, due to his troublesome affair with the 'Dark Lady' of the Sonnets, Will is going through his own traumas and working them out through Hamlet. Now I'm getting too hung up with psychological undertones. Let's get back to enjoying the play.)
Hamlet, 3.1, 90-157

* * *

(THE gobsmacked Ophelia believes that Hamlet has gone mad. She still loves him, but his brutal spurning triggers her downward spiral into mental instability.)

Ophelia. Oh, what a noble mind is here o'erthrown!
The courtier's, soldier's, scholar's, eye, tongue, sword—
The expectancy and rose of the fair state, (160)
The glass of fashion and the mold of form, (161)
The observed of all observers—quite, quite down!
And I, of ladies most deject and wretched,

That sucked the honey of his music vows, (164)
Now see that noble and most sovereign reason.
Like sweet bells jangled, out of tune and harsh, (166)
That unmatched form and feature of blown youth
(167)
Blasted with ecstasy. Oh, woe is me, (168)
To have seen what I have seen, see what I see!
Hamlet. 3.1, 158-169

(IN Ophelia's speech on Hamlet's attributes, she calls him, 'The expectancy and rose of the fair state,' (160) meaning that he is destined to be king of Denmark. 'Rose,' denoting flawless attractiveness, is also a great compliment.

'The glass of fashion and the mold of form,' (161) tells us that Hamlet's a laudable specimen of manhood. In *Henry IV*, *Part Two*, 2.3, similar wording was used by Lady Percy in describing her late husband Hotspur: 'He was the mark and glass, copy and book, that fashioned others.'

Ophelia is miserable because she 'sucked the honey of his music vows,' (164) a theatrical line highlighted by the unlikely pairing of 'music' and 'vows.' 'Music' is also a marvelous adjective suggesting that Hamlet sweet-talked her.

Now his reason is 'Like sweet bells jangled, out of tune and harsh,' (166) and in a phrase that echoes (160 and 161) above, 'That unmatched form and feature of blown youth,' (167) now 'Blasted with ecstasy,' (168) or insanity, with 'Blasted,' the unlikely but ideal verb.

Didn't you love 'sweet bells jangled' in (166) above, Ophelia's metaphor for what she perceives as Hamlet's mixed-up mind?

And then the heartrending, 'Oh, woe is me,' (168) reshaped by Will from the King James Bible, Corinthians, 9:16—'Woe is unto me.' If he didn't remember reading the passage, Will likely recalled hearing it in church on a Stratford Sunday.)

* * *

(KING CLAUDIUS and Polonius enter. Claudius, corrupt as he is, but a wily politician to his toenails, picks up that Hamlet's talk doesn't sound crazy, or 'Was not like madness.' (172) Claudius sees a plot in the works. He thinks that Hamlet 'sits on brood,' (173) like a chicken ready to lay eggs. Will's metaphor comes out of his Stratford farming experiences.

Claudius decides to send Hamlet 'with speed to England' (177) where he hopes that a different scene will expel whatever is bothering him. In a superlative closing line, Claudius utters the unfading, 'Madness in great ones must not unwatched go.' (196)
Hamlet, 3.1, 170-196

(SCENE TWO of act three opens with Hamlet instructing the players on how to deliver their lines in the play-within-a-play crafted to snare King Claudius.

These dictates are Will, speaking through Hamlet, on the art of acting, particularly his own company's methods, as opposed to the competitors more flamboyant styles. Since Hamlet is also an actor, the directions flow authoritatively.

The future of the kingdom rides on the force and outcome of the upcoming scene. It is Hamlet's best, and likely last, opportunity to reveal Claudius' turpitude.)

Hamlet. Speak the speech, I pray you, as I pronounced it to you, <u>trippingly on the tongue.</u> (2) But if you mouth it, as many of your players do, I had as lief the town crier <u>spoke my lines.</u> (3) <u>Nor do not saw the air too much with your hand, thus, but use all gently.</u> (5) For in the very torrent, tempest, and, as I may say, whirlwind of passion, you must acquire and beget a temperance that may give it smoothness. Oh, it offends me to the soul to hear a robustious periwig-pated fellow to tear a passion to tatters, to very rags, to <u>split the ears of the groundlings,</u> (11) who <u>for the</u>

most part are capable of nothing but inexplicable dumb shows and noise. (12) I would have such a fellow whipped for o'erdoing Termagant—it out-Herods Herod. (15) Pray you, avoid it. . . .

Be not too tame neither, but let your own discretion be your tutor. Suit the action to the word, the word to the action, with this special observance, that you o'erstep not the modesty of nature. For anything so overdone is from the purpose of playing, whose end, both at the first and now, was and is to hold as 'twere the mirror up to Nature (24)—to show Virtue her own feature, (25) scorn her own image, and the very age and body of the time his form and pressure. Now this overdone or come tardy off, though it make the unskillful laugh, cannot but make the judicious grieve, the censure of the which one (29) must in your allowance o'erweigh a whole theater of others.

Hamlet, 3.2, 1-31

(I WROTE earlier, in another context, that Olivier is the ablest speaker of Will's dialogue. He delivers his lines, 'trippingly on the tongue.' (2) You may not know the meaning of every phrase, but you do understand each word.

Hamlet wrote the lines in question, and if they are not delivered according to his direction, he'd as soon the town crier 'spoke my lines' (3) It's not clear about how much direction was given to Elizabethan-era actors. Surely, the job description of modern-day directors wasn't in place. In any event, Hamlet's instruction to the players visiting Elsinore is theatrical direction at its acme.

'Nor do not saw the air too much with your hand, thus, but use all gently.' (5) Here, Hamlet demonstrates. This line is an example of how difficult it is to play this role. Although the lines mostly contain advice on speaking, the actor delivering them must use body language that fits the direction he's giving.

Will obviously dislikes the over-the-top acting practiced by many of his contemporaries. Hamlet warns the players not to 'split the ears of the groundlings.' (11) There are no groundlings at Elsinore, but the actual play is given in front of them. Then, they get insulted when Hamlet says that they 'for the most part are capable of nothing but inexplicable dumb shows and noise.' (12) London actors delivering that line in those unruly days, would give the groundlings a wink or grin, as if to say, 'just kidding.'

In case any of the players miss the point, Hamlet would have scene-chewers 'whipped for o'erdoing Termagant—it out-Herods Herod.' (15) Hamlet's warns the players not to copy the absurdly excessive acting and roaring speechmaking used in those old roles. With Termagant played as a screaming shrew and Herod as a loudmouth.

In describing the purpose of playing, it is, Hamlet says, 'to hold as 'twere the mirror up to Nature' (24) Note that Nature is capitalized. Elizabethans took Nature seriously.

In *King Lear: Pivotal Speeches Critiqued in Depth*, next up after *Hamlet*, I discuss in 1.2 how bad Edmund enlists Nature as chaos. In Elizabethan terms, this is heretical and nature red in tooth and claw. Will didn't like this. He believed in order and good government, and Hamlet's use of 'Nature' is in the best sense of the term.

And 'to show Virtue her own feature' (25) is along the same lines. Here, 'Virtue' refers to the Seven Heavenly Virtues countering the seven deadly sins. Will knew the religious side of life. As a boy, he studied the Catechism. With the advent of the Church of England and the threat of being named a recusant and face punishment, Will read *The Book of Common Prayer*. It's like the old saw, 'if you can't beat 'em, join 'em.'

Making 'the judicious grieve' and 'the censure of the which one' (29) is Hamlet saying to the players, don't offend intelligent theatergoers by trying for a cheap laugh from the less-sophisticated audience members.)

* * *

(AFTER the players go off to rehearse, Horatio enters. Before asking for his help, Hamlet says that he has no need to flatter his friend because there's no expected reward for it. 'No, let the candied tongue lick absurd pomp and crook the pregnant hinges of the knee.' (65) Hamlet's saying that he and Horatio don't need hypocrisy in the form of false talk and bowing and scraping.

Hamlet continues that 'Since my dear soul was the mistress of her choice,' (68) I picked you for my best friend. And he considers himself lucky that 'their blood and judgment are so well commingled.' (74) Hamlet is grateful to have Horatio for a friend. He likes and trusts him, and the feeling is mutual.

Although Hamlet previously said that he does not need to flatter Horatio, he does seem to butter him up with some fine poetry.)

Hamlet. 'Give me that man
That is not <u>passion's slave,</u> (77) and I will wear him
In my heart's core—aye, in my <u>heart of heart</u> (78)
As I do thee.'

Hamlet, 3.2, 76-79

(THE term 'passion's slave,' (77) refers to emotion.

The enduringly warm phrase 'heart of heart' (78) was invented by Will for this speech. The modern equivalent is heart of hearts. Either way, it means the compassionate and caring center of the heart

All this leads up to Hamlet telling Horatio of the special scene inserted into the play, and would he do the following.)

Hamlet. Observe my uncle. If his occulted guilt (85)
Do not itself unkennel in one speech
It is a damnèd ghost (87) that we have seen
And my imaginations are as foul
As Vulcan's stithy. (89) Give him heedful note,
For I mine eyes will rivet to his face
And after we will both our judgments join (91)
In censure of his seeming.
Hamlet, 3.2, 65-92

('IF his occulted guilt,' meaning his hidden guilt, (85) isn't revealed after hearing the speech, we have seen a 'damnèd ghost' (87) and it's a misreading as filthy 'As Vulcan's stithy,' (89) the forge used by the mythological Roman God of Fire working as a blacksmith. Although wreathed in smoke, we can see it through Will's words.

Saying, 'we will both our judgments join' (91) harkens back to earlier in the passage that preceded the speech, with Hamlet telling Horatio that their 'blood and judgment are so well commingled.' (74)

* * *

(THE main characters of the play gather for the performance by the traveling players. Hamlet continues to affect insanity. He says to Ophelia, 'Lady, shall I lie upon your lap?' (119) This refers to intercourse. Ophelia says no, and Hamlet replies, 'I mean, my head upon your lap.' (121)

Ophelia answers, 'Aye,' and Hamlet asks 'Do you think I mean country matters?' (123) His carnal innuendo then gets even more explicit.

The inner play goes on, as the characters simulate the Ghost's description of Claudius pouring poison into King Hamlet's ears and then plying the widowed Queen Gertrude with gifts.

The complex scene switches back and forth between Hamlet's interjections and the players' performances. The Queen in the inner play has professed her love to the new king, but she does have confused thoughts such as this odd, but meaningful in its context, couplet, 'A second time I kill my husband dead' (194) and 'When second husband kisses me in bed.' (195) And later, 'If, once a widow, ever I be wife!' (233)

Hamlet asks his mother, 'Madam, how like you this play?' (239)

She famously answers, 'The lady doth protest too much, methinks.' (240)

King Claudius asks Hamlet, 'What do you call the play?' (246)

'*The Mousetrap.*' (247) This is a perfect name for a play designed to prod the perpetrator of a crime to expose his sins and be caught. Hamlet goes on to tell Claudius that the play concerns Gonzago, a Duke of Vienna, and 'Tis a knavish piece of work,' (250) and 'we that have free souls, it touches us not,' (251) or it can't hurt us.

Note the 'piece of work' used in line (250) is reminiscent of, but different in meaning from, 'What a piece of work is man' in Hamlet's 2.2 monologue.

During the performance by the players, Ophelia affectionately prompts Hamlet's comments: 'You are as good as a chorus, my lord.' (255) Her behavior in this scene suggests that she is still hopeful that Hamlet will recover his wits and his love for her.

Hamlet sets up the next scene in the inset play with 'the croaking raven doth bellow for revenge.' (264)

Ravens and crows were seen as symbols of wickedness in Elizabethan times. A similar line was used in *Macbeth*, 3.2, 50 when Macbeth, pale from fear, sees crows as representations of his own evildoing: 'Light thickens, and the crow makes wing to the rooky wood.' Rooky, in this usage, could mean dreary or a place where more black birds gather, or both.

A player enters and pours poison into the sleeping Gonzago's ear. Hamlet announces that 'the murderer gets the love of Gonzago's wife.' (275)

Claudius rises stricken and calls for light. Hamlet says, 'What, frighted with false fire!' (277) Or, can't he handle a little play? Claudius exits with his retinue.

A pleased Hamlet says to Horatio, 'Why, let the stricken deer go weep . . .' (282) and 'get me a fellowship in a cry of players, sir.' (288) Looking for a share in a company of London players is exactly what Will was working on at the time.

The actor playing Horatio, who is a fellow player in Will's company, kids back that Hamlet's acting is only worth 'Half a share.' (290) Many in the audience get the inside joke.

Hamlet rejoices, 'I'll take the Ghost's word for a thousand pound. Didst perceive?' (297) He's saying that Claudius' reaction proves that the spirit of my father is legitimate.

Horatio replies, 'I did very well note him.' (301) In his joy, Hamlet calls for some music.
Hamlet, 3.2, 118-301

(I'VE given you highlights, with some reflective lines, from a long and superb passage. I hope that what I've included will inspire you to carefully read the full copy.

Have you seen it acted? If so, view it again. If a stage play is not available, look for a *Hamlet* film and, as you pause the recording, read along with the action. As known, and as crafted by Will, *Hamlet*, the play, is written to be performed for an audience's pleasure, and should be visualized as such while the speeches on the page are studied.)

* * *

(Rosencrantz and Guildenstern enter to report that the King left the play 'marvelous distempered' (312) and 'with choler.' (315)

They go on to tell Hamlet, in their insipid way, that his mother thought that 'Your behavior hath struck her into amazement and admiration.' (338) Hamlet replies, 'Oh, wonderful son that can so astonish a mother!' (340) R & G finally get to the point: 'She desires to speak with you in her closet ere you go to bed.' (343)

Hamlet calls for music at the end of the previous passage. Now players enter with recorders. As we know, Hamlet got R & G to admit that the King called them to Elsinore to spy on him. He's still not happy with them, and as a device to chastise them more he borrows a recorder. Reminder: Hamlet's frustrated, angry, needs to vent, and R & G are handy stooges. When he's finished with them, he baits Polonius.

Hamlet quizzes R & G on their ability to 'play upon this pipe.' (366) Continually prodded, they say, 'I know no touch of it, my lord.' (372)

Hamlet. <u>It is as easy as lying.</u> (373) Govern these ventages with your fingers and thumb, give it breath with your mouth, and it will discourse most eloquent music. . . .
Why, look you now, how unworthy a thing of you make of me! You would play upon me, <u>you would seem to know my stops, you would pluck out the heart of my mystery,</u> (381) you would sound me from my lowest note at the top of my compass—and there is much music, excellent voice, in this little organ— yet you cannot make it speak. 'Sblood, do you think I am easier to be played on than a pipe? Call me what

instrument you will, <u>though you can fret me, you cannot play upon me.</u> (387)

Polonius. (Enters.) My lord, the Queen would speak with you, and presently.

Hamlet. <u>Do you see yonder cloud that's almost in shape of a camel?</u> (392)

Polonius. By the mass, and 'tis like a camel indeed.

Hamlet. Methinks it is like a weasel.

Polonius. It is backed like a weasel.

Hamlet. Or like a whale?

Polonius. Very like a whale.

Hamlet. Then I will come to my mother by and by. <u>They fool me to the top of my bent.</u> (401) (All but Hamlet leave the stage.)

Hamlet. <u>'Tis now the very witching time of night,</u> (406) <u>When churchyards yawn</u> (407) and Hell itself breathes out

Contagion to this world. <u>Now could I drink hot blood,</u> (408)

And do such bitter business as the day

Would quake to look on. Soft! Now to my mother.

O heart, lose not thy nature, let not ever

<u>The soul of Nero enters this firm bosom.</u> (412)

Let me be cruel, not unnatural.

I will speak <u>daggers</u> (414) to her, but use none.

My tongue and soul in this be hypocrites,

How in my words soever she be shent,

To give them seals, never, my soul, consent!
Hamlet, 3.2, 338-417

(HAMLET tells Rosencrantz and Guildenstern 'It is as easy as lying' (373) to play the recorder, a pointed remark setting up the additional abuse.

With 'you would seem to know my stops, you would pluck out the heart of my mystery,' (381) Hamlet ties R & G's subterfuge to the pipe metaphor, and then it gets very personal. He accuses them of trying to steal his heart and its secrets.

Be assured, he tells them, 'though you can fret me, you cannot play upon me.' (387) In other words, you can tune the instrument, but don't use it to play me for a fool. Or, it could also mean that he doesn't welcome their trying to wear him down.

After he enters, Hamlet teases Polonius the politician into agreeing to most anything he thinks will please someone: 'Do you see yonder cloud that's almost in shape of a camel?' (392) Polonius accepts the suggestion and several more inane comparisons. Of course, he also thinks Hamlet's crazy and attempts to humor him.

'They fool me to the top of my bent.' (401) Dealing with three men he considers buffoons tests Hamlet's endurance.

After they exit the stage, Hamlet says, "Tis now the very witching time of night.' (406) In his mood, he expects the witches to come out and do their foul business, because he intends to do his.

Now, the surprising and delicious verb in a mood-altering phrase, 'When churchyards yawn'— (407) followed by 'Hell itself breathes out contagion to this world.' which certainly refers to the prevalence of the plague in London.

'Now could I drink hot blood' (408) naturally builds on the previous paragraph and anticipates the next frightful thought.

What with the invocation of witches and churchyards, and now citing Nero's dastardly act, Hamlet pleads with himself not to kill his mother. Don't let, 'The soul of Nero enter this firm bosom.' (412)

Hamlet's going to be tough on his mother and use words like 'daggers.' (414) And no matter how she reproaches him, it will not inhibit his later action.)

* * *

(SCENE THREE of act three opens with the vexed Claudius telling the weaseling Rosencrantz and Guildenstern about Hamlet, 'I like him not, nor stands it safe with us to let his madness range,' (1) or go unchecked.

Claudius goes on at length about how a King, meaning his brother, dying leaves a gulf, and how it soon widens and threatens the kingdom unless constrained. He orders R & G to get Hamlet to England: 'Arm you, I pray you, to this speedy voyage, for we will put fetters upon this fear, which now goes too free-footed.' (24) I can see the three of them, like characters out of Monty Python in a speeded-up film, sprinting, or free-footing, over hill and dale to merry England. Will's writing sure makes you see things.

The canny Claudius knows that his reaction to the meta-theatrical *Murder of Gonzago* revealed his guilt. He now views Hamlet as an existential threat.

R & G exit, and the equally unctuous Polonius enters to tell Claudius that Hamlet's headed to see his mother and that he'll hide behind the arras, or hanging curtain, to listen in. Polonius adds that he'll report anything he learns back to the King.

Polonius exits, and for the first time in the play Claudius is alone and speaking to the audience in soliloquy the truth as he knows it.)

Claudius. Oh, my offense is rank, it smells to Heaven.
<u>It hath the primal eldest curse upon 't</u>, (37)
A brother's murder. Pray can I not,

Though inclination be as sharp as will.
My stronger guilt defeats my strong intent, (40)
And like a man to double business bound, (41)
I stand in pause where I shall first begin,
And both neglect. What if this cursèd hand
Were thicker than itself with brother's blood,
Is there not rain enough in the sweet heavens (45)
To wash it white as snow? (46) . . . I am still possessed
Of those effects for which I did the murder—
My crown, mine own ambition, and my Queen. . . .
Help, angels! Make assay!
Bow, stubborn knees, and heart with strings of steel,
Be soft as sinews of the newborn babe!
All may be well. (72) (Claudius goes to one side of the stage and kneels in prayer. (Hamlet enters on the opposite side. This is his first time alone with Claudius.)
Hamlet. Now might I do it pat, now he is praying,
And now I'll do 't. And so he goes to Heaven, (74)
And so I am revenged. That would be scanned:
A villain kills my father, and for that
I, his sole son, do this same villain send
To Heaven.
Oh, this is hire and salary, not revenge. (79)
He took my father grossly, (80) full of bread,
With all his crimes broad blown, as flush as May,

And how his audit stands who knows save Heaven?
(82)
But in our circumstance and course of thought,
'Tis heavy with him. And am I then revenged,
To take him in the purging of his soul,
When he is fit and seasoned for his passage?
No!
Up, sword, and known thou a more horrid hent.
When he is drunk asleep, or in his rage
Or in the incestuous pleasure of his bed—
At gaming, swearing, or about some act
That has not relish of salvation in 't— (92)
Then trip him, that his heels may kick at Heaven
And that his soul may be as damned and black
As Hell, whereto it goes. My mother stays. (95)
This physic but prolongs thy sickly days. (96)
Claudius. (Now standing and facing the audience.)
My words fly up, my thoughts remain below. (97)
Words without thoughts never to Heaven go.
Hamlet, 3.3, 36-99

(WITH 'It hath the primal eldest curse upon 't,' (37)
Claudius compares murdering his brother to the
Biblical Cain who slew his brother Abel.

   'My stronger guilt defeats my strong intent' (40)
says that although Claudius desires to do something
to atone for his sins, his guilt is stronger, and he is

97

stuck in neutral 'And like a man to double business bound,' (41) he is not sure which of the two tasks to undertake and ends up doing neither.

Claudius' guilt-ridden mind imagines that his hand carries his brother's blood and wonders 'Is there not rain enough in the sweet heavens' (45) 'To wash it white as snow?' (46) These lines recall Macbeth 2.2 after he kills Duncan, 'Will all great Neptune's ocean wash this blood,' from his hands.

In his closing lines, Claudius reassures himself that he still has what he murdered for: crown, Queen, and ambition. He's talked it out and now feels that 'All may be well.' (72) To have the nerve to pull off murder and incest labels Claudius an optimist, cockeyed maybe, but surely audacious in the extreme.

Hamlet enters, sees Claudius praying, and says 'I'll do 't. And so he goes to Heaven.' (74) He has three reasons for not killing Claudius: It would end the play; Claudius is presently in a state of grace; and it would make Hamlet as bad as Claudius, since he killed Hamlet's father before he received absolution.

'Oh, this is hire and salary, not revenge,' (79) means that Hamlet doesn't want monetary compensation for killing Claudius, he wants legitimate revenge. And he won't get that if he kills Claudius while he's praying and sends him to Heaven.

Hamlet, being Hamlet, thinks everything through, and under the dire circumstances who can blame him for inaction?

With 'He took my father grossly' (80) Hamlet again refers to his father's dying in full sin without an opportunity to rectify his behavior in the eyes of God.

Moreover, Hamlet continues, only God knows Old Hamlet's catalog of wrongdoings, or 'how his audit stands who knows save Heaven?' (82) Hamlet thinks: not only did this villain Claudius kill my father, he also left him in a purgatorial state, and the only way I can relieve him of his suffering, and help him resolve his audit or account with God, is to avenge his death.

Hamlet decides that when Claudius in involved in some illicit behavior like drunkenness, gaming or incest 'That has not relish of salvation in 't.' (92) Yes, he'll kill Claudio. Oops! I've slipped into *Much Ado About Nothing*. Hamlet will kill him when Claudius has no chance of redemption.

'My mother stays' (95) signifies that Hamlet's not forgotten the admonition given in 1.5 by his father's spirit: 'do not to contrive against your mother, and 'Leave her to Heaven.'

Hamlet's acerbic exit line sums up his contempt of Claudius at hypocritical prayer: 'This physic but prolongs thy sickly days.' (96) This line confirms the point that in Elizabethan religious thinking it's believed that if you're killed in a state of grace you're sent straight to Heaven, not purgatory. If not in a state of grace, the victim goes to purgatory where sins can be expunged before entering Heaven, or possibly Hell.

Hamlet exits, Claudius stands and speaks the bitter truth as he understands it: (97)

'My words fly up, my thoughts remain below.
Words without thoughts never to Heaven go.'

It appears that Claudius knows he's going to purgatory and probably Hell afterward.)

* * *

(Polonius and Queen Gertrude talk in her closet or sitting room. Polonius tells Hamlet's mother that he'll hide behind the arras, or tapestry, and asks her to be firm with her son. She agrees, Polonius withdraws, Hamlet enters.
The Queen says, 'Hamlet, thou hast thy father much offended.' (8)

He answers, 'Mother, you have my father much offended.' (9)

She accuses him of answering with 'an idle tongue.' (11)

Hamlet says, 'you question with a wicked tongue.' (12) The Queen stands to leave and Hamlet tells her 'You shall not go till I set you up a glass,' (19) or mirror, so she can see 'the inmost part of you.' (20)

Gertrude asks, 'Thou wilt not murder me?' (21) And she cries for help.

Polonius hears her and shouts for help from behind the arras. Hamlet draws his sword and stabs through the tapestry.)

Hamlet. How now! A rat? Dead for a ducat, dead! (23)
Polonius. Oh, I am slain.
Queen. Oh me, <u>what has thou done?</u> (25)
Hamlet. <u>Nay, I know not. Is it the King?</u> (26)
Queen. Oh, what a rash and bloody deed is this!
Hamlet. A bloody deed! Almost as bad, good Mother,
<u>As kill a king and marry with his brother.</u> (28)
Queen. <u>As kill a king!</u> (29)
Hamlet. Aye, lady, 'twas my word. (He looks behind the tapestry.)
<u>Thou wretched, rash, intruding fool, farewell!</u> (31)
<u>I took thee for thy better.</u> (32) Take thy fortune. . . .
(To Gertrude.) Leave wringing of your hands. Peace! Sit you down,
<u>And let me wring your heart.</u> (35) For so I shall,
If it be made of penetrable stuff,
If damnèd custom have not brassed it so

That it be proof and bulwark against sense.

Queen. What have I done that thou darest wag thy tongue

In noise <u>so rude against me?</u> (39)

Hamlet. Such an act

That <u>blurs the grace and blush of modesty</u> (41)

Calls virtue hypocrite, takes off the rose

From the fair forehead of an innocent love,

<u>And sets a blister there</u> 44)—makes marriage vows

As false as dicers' oaths. Oh, such a deed

As from the body of contraction plucks

The very soul, and sweet religion makes

<u>A rhapsody of words.</u> (48) Heaven's face doth glow,

Yea this solidity and compound mass,

With tristful visage, as against the doom,

Is thought-sick at the act. . . .

Look here upon this picture, and on this,

<u>The counterfeit presentment of two brothers.</u> (54)

See what grace was seated on this brow—

Hyperion's curls, the front of Jove himself,

An eye like Mars, to threaten and command,

A station like the herald Mercury

<u>New-lighted on a heaven-kissing hill,</u> (59)

A combination and a form indeed

<u>Where every god did seem to set his seal</u> (61)

To give the world assurance of a man.

This was your husband. Look you now what follows.

Here is your husband, like a mildewed ear, (64)
Blasting his wholesome brother. Have you eyes? (65)
Could you on this fair mountain leave to feed
And batten on this moor? Ha! Have you eyes? (67)
You cannot call it love, for at your age
The heyday in the blood is tame, (69) it's humble,
And waits upon the judgment. And what judgment
Would step from this to this? . . .
Oh, shame! Where is thy blush? Rebellious Hell,
If thou canst mutine in a matron's bones,
To flaming youth let virtue be as wax
And melt in her own fire. Proclaim no shame
When the compulsive ardor (86) gives the charge
Since frost itself as actively doth burn,
And reason panders will.
Queen. O Hamlet, speak no more.
Thou turn'st mine eyes into my very soul, (89)
And there I see such black and grainèd spots (90)
As will not leave their tinct.
Hamlet. Nay, but to live
In the rank sweat of an unseamèd bed, (92)
Stewed in corruption, honeying and making love
Over the nasty sty— (94)
Queen. Oh, speak to me no more,
These words like daggers (95) enter in my ears.
No more, sweet Hamlet! (96)
Hamlet, 3.4, 7-96

(HAMLET hears a voice calling for help from behind the arras. He pulls his sword and thrusts through the curtain killing Polonius. His mother asks, 'What hast thou done?'

Hamlet answers, 'Nay, I know not. Is it the King?' (23) There's no state of grace in eavesdropping behind the curtain and no hesitation at all by Hamlet. He thinks it's Claudius and believes he's achieved his long-sought-for revenge.

Gertrude calls it a 'rash and bloody deed.' (26) Hamlet comes back at her with, 'As kill a king and marry with his brother.' (28)

Gertrude's 'As kill a king!' (29) reply tells us that she has no idea that her former husband, Hamlet's father, was murdered.

After Hamlet lifts or pulls aside the curtain and sees the dead Polonius, he says, 'Thou wretched, rash, intruding fool, farewell!' (31) 'I took thee for thy better,' (32) meaning Claudius.

How would you act or direct this business? If the curtain is split, pulling it aside is more sweeping and dramatic and lends more weight to calling Polonius a 'wretched, rash, intruding fool.'

It's a stark contrast when Hamlet tells his mother to stop wringing her hands and sit down, 'And let me wring your heart.' (35)

We must suspend disbelief that Gertrude is blind to her actions. She asks why Hamlet is talking 'so rude against me.' (39) He answers that her act of marrying so soon after his father's death 'blurs the grace and blush of modesty.' (41)

Hamlet pours it on telling his mother that she went from an innocent love with a rose on her forehead, 'And sets a blister there,' 44) or brands herself as a whore. Is see the actor playing Hamlet touching his forehead followed by the actor playing the Queen touching hers then jerking her hand away.

Hamlet tells his mother that her behavior makes the marriage vows gibberish or 'A rhapsody of words.' (48)

He then asks her to look at 'The counterfeit presentment of two brothers.' (54) 'Counterfeit' in this sense simply means that Will plans to have side-by-side portraits of Old Hamlet and Claudius hung on the stage. This is, of course, impractical and small-scale pictures, are usually used. Audiences must, through Hamlet's description, visualize the faces of the brothers. They've seen Claudius and the ghost of Old Hamlet onstage. Given the description that follows the latter character needs to be Hollywood handsome.

Hamlet describes his father as a combination of mythological legends like Hyperion, Jove, Mars and

Mercury. And that this perfect man, blessed by the qualities of these exalted gods, and 'New-lighted on a heaven-kissing hill,' (59) was fine enough to be deposited on a high hill.

'Where every god did seem to set his seal' (61) means that the perfection of every god mentioned above is testimony, he tells his mother, to how exemplary your dead husband and my father was.

And 'Here is your husband, like a mildewed ear,' (64) a marvelous turn of phrase, followed by the perfect verb 'Blasting his wholesome brother. Have you eyes?' (65) Then two lines later, while again showing his mother the portraits of both men, 'Have you eyes?' (67) How, Hamlet asks her, can you go from loving my father to lusting after this base individual.

Hamlet presses on, now a shade unfairly, telling his mother that at her age when 'The heyday in the blood is tame,' (69) or desire should be tempered, she should show better judgment. This may be so from his point of view, but obviously not from hers. Aside from marrying a lesser creature, it's presumptuous of him to question or dictate her sexual needs.

At this point in his writing career, Will sometimes shows an aversion to sexual activity, often viewing it as a destructive act. This may have been caused by the guilt he felt after indulging in a troubling affair with the Dark Lady of the Sonnets.

Hamlet mercilessly continues with accusations around the theme of where is her shame and how could 'compulsive ardor,' (86) or sexual desire consume her. There's a bit of the son not wanting to think of his mother having sex. It's also youth thinking that supercharged sex is the province of the young and not for old folks.

We're guessing at what Will's thinking as he writes this passage. In any event, the poetry gleams on. Hamlet can't let up and impels his mother to say that he's forced her to look 'into my very soul' (89) where she sees such 'such black and grainèd spots as will not leave their tinct.' (90) Despite his brutal approach Hamlet's gotten through, and Gertrude is so abashed that her vision is bereft of color.

Hamlet dismisses his mother's admission with a 'Nay' and directs more perturbation at her, saying that she lives 'In the rank sweat of an unseamèd bed.' (92) Making love isn't enough, he tells her, you have to do it in a messy bed. Another fitting verb describes her sexual adventures as being 'Stewed in corruption.' (93) The slimy bed is then called a 'nasty sty,' (94) a place, he imputes, where his mother and uncle are no more than rutting pigs.

We can imagine in this charged scene when Gertrude speaks of Hamlet's 'words like daggers' (95) that she is in tears, on her knees, hands clasped, voice pleading, 'No more, sweet Hamlet!' (96) The adjective 'sweet' fits the pleading, and is meant to touch him favorably. It's Will coming up with the perfectly-suited theatrical tone.)

* * *

(IS Hamlet done berating his mother? No, the lacerating scene goes on. It appears that Hamlet's pent-up fury is boundless. Will's scene management excels, and his poetry soars. But Hamlet's vitriol directed at his mother now seems excessive, with more to come. Does Will have other female-related issues beyond the trouble with sex mentioned above? Calling Dr. Freud!

Amateur speculation aside, I'm sure you've noticed that Will is Hamlet: intellectual, sensitive, multidimensional, possibly confused in his personal life. Will is infatuated with the highly-personalized character of Hamlet and can't get enough of him.

That is why this scene and the entire play are so long. I've always said that Will is the sole writer in history who doesn't need an editor. But analyzing this play leads me to believe he could have used one for this magnificent, but overly long creation. Where would I cut? I only edit when getting paid for it, just kidding. I think that even suggesting editing Will would prompt the Shakespeare cognoscenti to lynch me. In fact, they may do me in for having the impertinence to even write this book. Who is this pretend expert? Who does he think he is? What are his credentials? I plead *nolo contendere.*

King Lear and Macbeth: Pivotal Speeches Critiqued and much more follow. Analyzing the speeches of those masterpieces challenged me, but nothing like the stretch required of *Hamlet.* This is not complaining. I loved every minute.

Hamlet is structurally seamless, endlessly intriguing, layered, full of multiple meanings, endlessly complex, and the best play ever written.

Hamlet now returns to his attack on King Claudius. Although well-constructed, the content of the speech has been said before. However, it is theatrically effective and sets up a reappearance of the ghost.)

Hamlet. A murderer and a villain,
A slave that is not twentieth part the tithe (97)
Of your precedent lord, (98) a vice of kings,
A cutpurse of the empire (99) and the rule,
That from a shelf the precious diadem stole (100)
And put it in his pocket!— (101)

A king of shreds and patches (102)—
(Ghost enters. Hamlet talks to him.)
Save me and hover o'er me with your wings,
You heavenly guards! What would your gracious figure?
Queen. Alas, he's mad.
Hamlet. Do not come your tardy son to chide
That, lapsed in time and passion, lets go by
The important acting of your dread command? (108)
Oh, say!
Ghost. Do not forget. This visitation
Is but to whet thy almost blunted purpose. (111)
But look, amazement on thy mother sits.
Oh, step between her and her fighting soul.
Conceit in weakest bodies strongest works.
Speak to her, Hamlet.
Hamlet. How is it with you, lady?
Queen. Alas, how is 't with you
That you do bend your eye on vacancy (117)
And with the incorporal do hold discourse? (118)
Forth at your eyes your spirits wildly peep,
And as the sleeping soldiers in the alarm, (120)
Your bedded hairs, like life in excrements,
Start up and stand an end. (122) O gentle son,
Upon the heat and flame of thy distemper
Sprinkle cool patience. Whereon do you look?
Hamlet. On him, on him! Look you how pale he glares!

His form and cause conjoined, <u>preaching to stones,</u> (126)
Would make them capable. Do not look upon me,
Lest with this piteous action you convert
<u>My stern effects.</u> (129) Then what I have to do
Will want true color—tears perchance for blood. . . .
<u>Mother, for love of grace,</u> (144)
Lay not that flattering unction to your soul,
That not your trespass but my madness speaks.
It will but film and skin the ulcerous place,
While rank corruption, mining all within,
Infects unseen. Confess yourself to Heaven,
<u>Repent what's past, avoid what is to come,</u> (150)
<u>And do not spread the compost on the weeds</u> (151)
To make them ranker. Forgive me this my virtue,
<u>For in the fatness of these pursy times</u> (153)
<u>Virtue itself of vice must pardon beg</u>— (154)
Yea, curb and woo for leave to do him good.
Queen. <u>O Hamlet, thou hast cleft my heart in twain.</u> (156)
Hamlet. <u>Oh, throw away the worser part of it,</u> (157)
<u>And live the purer with the other half.</u>
Good night. But go not to my uncle's bed.
<u>Assume a virtue if you have it not.</u> . . . (160)
Refrain tonight,
And that shall lend a kind of easiness
To the next abstinence, the next more easy.

For use can almost change the stamp of nature, (168)
And either the Devil, or throw him out
With wondrous potency. Once more, good night.
And when you are desirous to be blest,
I'll blessing beg of you. (172) For this same lord,
(Gesturing towards Polonius.)
I do repent; (173) but Heaven hath pleased it so,
To punish me with this, and this with me,
That I must be their scourge and minister.
I will bestow him, and will answer well
The death I gave him. (176) So again good night.
I must be cruel only to be kind. (177)
Thus bad begins, and worse remains behind.
One word more, good lady.
Queen. What shall I do?
Hamlet. Not this, by no means, that I bid you do.
Let the bloat king tempt you again to bed,
Pinch wanton on your cheek, call you his mouse,
And let him, for a pair of reechy kisses
Or paddling in your neck with his damned fingers,
Make you to ravel all this matter out, (186)
That I essentially am not in madness, (187)
But mad in craft. . . .
Queen. Be thou assured if words be made of breath
And breath of life, I have no life to breathe (197)
What thou hast said to me.
Hamlet, 3.4, 97-217

(AFTER Hamlet calls Claudius a murderer he says that he's 'not twentieth part the tithe.' (97) This means that he's not even one twentieth of ten percent of his father, or the worth of 'your precedent lord.' (98

Hamlet calls Claudius a thief, or 'cutpurse of the empire' (99) who 'from a shelf the precious diadem stole,' (100) meaning that he plucked the crown and, in a lively phrase, 'put it in his pocket.' (101)

Then Hamlet calls Claudius 'A king of shreds and patches,' (102) or a fool or clown.

The ghost of Hamlet's father enters, Hamlet speaks to him, and the Queen, because she cannot see the ghost, thinks Hamlet's insane.

Hamlet asks the apparition that he not be chided for being tardy in fulfilling the 'The important acting of your dread command,' (108) or not having already killed Claudius.

The ghost tells Hamlet that the visit 'Is but to whet thy almost blunted purpose.' (111) He's there to remind Hamlet of his promise to avenge his murder. The spirit doesn't realize that Hamlet might doubt his authenticity.

The ghost sees that Gertrude is dumbfounded and asks Hamlet to speak to her. He does, and asks how she's doing. After what he's put her through, his dour conduct, and her not seeing the ghost, the question is laughable. When well-delivered, it gets a rise from audiences.

Trying to get her bearings, Gertrude asks her son how come 'you do bend your eye on vacancy' (117) 'And with the incorporal do hold discourse?' (118) What are you looking at and who are you talking to?

In a neat metaphor, she notes that Hamlet acts like 'sleeping soldiers in the alarm,' (120) and his usually well-kept hair 'Start up and stand an end.' (122) 'An' substitutes for 'on' in Elizabethan vocabulary.

Gertrude doesn't know what Hamlet's looking at, and he fails to comprehend that she can't see the specter. He keeps asking her to look, and he tells her that her former husband's mind and form working together would if 'preaching to stones' (126) make them understand.

This is a testing role for actors playing Gertrude. Rather than looking at the ghost that Hamlet sees and she doesn't, he tells her not to look at him since it may change his 'stern effects,' (129) or determination to deal not in tears but in blood.

Gertrude asks who he's speaking to, and he asks whether she can see or hear the ghost. Keeping in mind that the audience is in on the action, the actor could smile and use her hands in a throwaway motion. Even though Gertrude's been a bad girl of sorts, I'm now sympathizing with her. I can see 1930's

Hollywood-star Jean Harlow, in her sex-without-regret screen persona, playing Gertrude, though maybe in a black wig.

Although she loved Hamlet's father, the Gertrude after his death is philosophical and hard-edged about moving on. In 1.2, she tells Hamlet to stop wearing his black clothes and get over it, 'all that lives must die.' In this character development exchange, Will establishes the Gertrude character as light hearted, guilt-free and ready for whatever fate might deal, which, to Hamlet's dismay, is his hateful uncle.

'Mother, for love of grace,' (144) is Hamlet's plea that his mother not believe that what he is saying to her is spoken in madness. If she does, it will undermine her understanding of how serious the situation is.

Although not directly applicable in the usage above, in Elizabethan days the term 'grace' comes from subjects who hoped for a merciful king, not a strict one.

Hamlet asks his mother to 'Repent what's past, avoid what is to come,' (150) 'And do not spread the compost on the weeds,' (151) or don't make bad conditions worse by continuing to canoodle with Claudius.

'For in the fatness of these pursy times' (153) means that they are living in puffy excess. This line is completed by 'Virtue itself of vice must pardon beg'— (154) Although the meanings differ somewhat, I wonder if this line prompted La Rochefoucauld's aphorism 'Hypocrisy is the homage vice pays to virtue.'

And we come to one of Will's best dramatic lines, 'O Hamlet, thou hast cleft my heart in twain.' (156) To which Hamlet lays down the skillful response, 'Oh, throw away the worser part of it, and live the purer with the other half.' (157)

Like a proficient prosecutor pounding out the points in the summary to a jury, Hamlet not only tells his mother not to go to her husband's bed, he adds 'Assume a virtue if you have it not.' (160) Even if you don't feel virtuous, act like you are, a classic example of the child becoming the parent.

'For use can almost change the stamp of nature,' (168) or, if you stay out of my uncle's bed tonight, abstinence through practice can become habitual.

Gesturing toward Polonius' body, Hamlet says that he repents, and knows he 'will answer well the death I gave him.' (176) This comment introduces the second revenge theme of the play: Polonius' son Laertes returns from France and seeks revenge for his father's murder.

Revenge plays were popular in Elizabethan days. In the final acts, most every main character ends up dead.

Vengeance was not considered complete unless murderers burn forever in Hell and their souls don't go to Heaven.

'I must be cruel only to be kind.' (177) This famed apology line rings in the theater.

After all of Hamlet's instructions and admonitions, Gertrude still asks what she should do. Hamlet shifts into sex education to tell her to stay out of Claudius' bed. If you go there, he warns, he will seduce you again with words and caresses. He will 'Make you to ravel all this matter out,' (186) or disclose Hamlet's plan designed to help her resist ardor.

And if she divulges 'That I essentially am not in madness, but mad in craft,' (187) she risks, like the proverbial ape, falling out of a high birdcage and breaking her neck.

Gertrude's overwhelmed by Hamlet's words. Along with her illusions, they have taken her breath away. She says, 'I have no life to breathe.' (197)

Commencing now, and continuing into acts four and five, Hamlet is under guard, or close observation, from the King and henchmen like Rosencrantz and Guildenstern. Gertrude and Hamlet discuss his upcoming travel to England accompanied by, 'my two school-fellows, whom I will trust as I will adders fanged.' (203) That's R & G following the King's orders to escort Hamlet.

He has other ideas about their attempt to 'marshal me to knavery,' (205) or roguish behavior. It's good sport, Hamlet says, to have the engineer, or plotter 'Hoist with his own petar.' (207) He will mine underneath them and 'blow them at the moon.' (209)

I see the actor delivering these lines grinning and flinging his arms upward at the thought of blowing up R & G with their own bomb. Like innumerable Shakespeare lines, 'Hoist with his own petard' is widely used, and often wrongly as though a petard was a spear rather than an incendiary device.

As we've seen, Hamlet switches between mild respect for Polonius and belittlement. As he says good night to his mother, he moves toward the dead body and announces, 'I'll lug the guts into the neighbor room.' (212)

* * *

(IN scene one of act four, Claudius asks Gertrude 'How does Hamlet?' (6) She answers, 'Mad as the sea and wind when both contend,' (7) meaning that she's not confiding in Claudius.

She goes on to tell him that Hamlet killed Polonius. This news fills the King with dread, and he tells

Gertrude that Hamlet's 'liberty is full of threats to all,' (14) and 'we will ship him hence,' (30) or get him out of the country.

Claudius also notes that they need to keep the murder quiet and find some way to excuse Hamlet. For his own protection from someone he knows might try to kill him, Claudius' first priority is to get Hamlet away from him.

Rosencrantz and Guildenstern enter. The King tells them, 'Hamlet in madness hath Polonius slain,' (34) and orders them to fetch the body and bring it to the chapel.)

Hamlet, 4.1, 6-34

* * *

(R & G find Hamlet in the brief scene two. He speaks in feigned madness telling them that they are the King's sponges currying favor. They don't get what he's talking about, and he tells them that 'A knavish speech sits in a foolish ear,' (25) or fools misconstrue hostile words.)

* * *

(SCENE three of act four opens with the King telling aides that it's dangerous for Hamlet to be on the loose, but 'must not we put the strong law on him,' (3) because 'He's loved of the distracted multitude,' (4) a relative phrase labeling people who are taken in by appearances and not by actions. We know from Ophelia's 3.1 description of Hamlet that he is 'the mould of form.' I wonder whether these references to Hamlet's appeal to the common people reflects Queen Elizabeth's contemporary dilemma when she decides to rid herself of Essex who is plotting to seize the crown..

Hamlet enters. He talks in faux-mad riddles about the whereabouts of Polonius' body. When asked by Claudius where Polonius is, Hamlet tells that he's at supper, but not himself eating, rather 'A certain convocation of politic worms are e'en at him.' (22) Although Hamlet is practicing feigned insanity, the retort is bitterly satirical. He's, of course, including the King among those political worms around the court who are eating Polonius' body.

The King asks again where Polonius is. Hamlet answers that if the King can't find him in Heaven 'seek him i' the other place yourself,' (36) an excellent jab. Hamlet adds that if you don't find the body 'within this month, you shall nose him as you go up the stairs into the lobby.' (37) Faking madness or not, Hamlet's sardonic phrase stays with you.

The King and Hamlet banter more about his upcoming boat-trip to England. After Hamlet exits the King gives final orders to R & G on the urgency of getting Hamlet onto the boat. After they exit, Claudius soliloquizes on his real intent.)

King. Follow him at foot, tempt him with speed aboard.
Delay it not, I'll have him hence tonight.
Away! <u>For everything is sealed and done</u> (58)
<u>That else leans on the affair.</u> Pray you make haste.
(R & G exit. The King continues in soliloquy.)
And, England, if my love thou hold'st at aught—
As my great power thereof may give thee sense,
<u>Since yet thy cicatrice looks raw and red</u> (62)
After the Danish sword, and thy free awe
Pays homage to us—thou mayst not coldly set
Our sovereign process, which imports at full,
By letters congruing to that effect,
<u>The present death of Hamlet. Do it, England,</u> (67)
For like the hectic in my blood he rages,
And thou must cure me. till I know 'tis done,
Howe'er my haps, my joys were ne'er begun.
Hamlet, 4.3, 36-70

(KING CLAUDIUS uses 'speed' and 'haste' in urging R & G to deliver Hamlet to England, 'For everything is sealed and done that else leans on the affair.' (58) He's made a deal with England, and he wants it quickly consummated.

'Since yet thy cicatrice looks raw and red' (62) is Claudius warning England that Danish power* can rip off the scab and make them bleed again if they don't obey his orders sent by letter to pursue 'The present death of Hamlet.' (67)

*Claudius refers to the continuing Norse raids on England, the largest one occurring in 1013.

In saying 'Do it, England,' (67) Claudius is speaking of the King of England.

Since Hamlet is his wife's son, Claudius doesn't have him killed in Denmark. He shifts the task to England's King under threat of punishment if he fails to carry it out. Claudius may be a rat, but he's a nervy, political rat who knows how to pull the levers of power. Keep this scene in mind as prelude to a delicious hoodwink.

* * *

(REMINDER: Before his death, Old King Hamlet won a battle against Norway's Old Fortinbras and captured land. In scene four of act four, Young Fortinbras is itching to get it back and requests permission to cross Denmark in order to invade

Poland. The last we heard of this, Claudius told Norway's envoys that he would think about it. He also appealed to Fortinbras' uncle, aka Old Norway, to get the young upstart to stand down.

Unlike Hamlet, Fortinbras, like Hotspur in *Henry IV*, is a soldier and a man of action who's inclined to march and consider the consequences later. As an American admiral once said, it's much easier to apologize than ask permission. And now Fortinbras is in Denmark without his uncle's consent.

We open scene four of act four with Fortinbras ordering his captain to call on the Danish King and tell him that they're marching across Denmark on the way to Poland. If the King resists, Fortinbras will go to see him and 'express our duty in his eye,' (6) or face-to-face.

Hamlet enters with Rosencrantz and Guildenstern to ask the captain what's going on. The mission is explained, and Hamlet asks if it's against mainland Poland or some outpost.

Captain. Truly to speak, and with no addition,
We go to gain a little patch of ground (18)
That hath in it no profit but the name.

(THIS is another of Will's sharp-pointed truisms, a language gift on the futility of war, followed by

Hamlet reflecting on the words. He bemoans the waste of lives in a battle over a triviality.

Hamlet rues the obstacles, like being exiled to England, that impede revenge for his father's murder. He wonders if he's being cowardly, or having 'craven scruples of thinking too precisely on the event.' (40)

On the other hand, he compares his own hesitation with the ambition-driven, 'tender prince' (48) Fortinbras. Who's not worrying about sacrificing the lives of his men, even though, according to Hamlet, the upcoming battle is 'an eggshell,' (53) or trifle, and a 'quarrel in a straw.' (55) Although he does admire Fortinbras' mettle to fight over a bagatelle 'When honor's at the stake.' (56)

Hamlet comes back to 'How stand I then that have a father killed, a mother stained,' (57) 'And let all sleep,' (59) or do nothing about it, while 'twenty thousand men' (60) die in battle over 'a fantasy and trick of fame,' (61) or delusion, and 'Go to their graves like beds,' (62) a touching simile.

Hamlet concludes his trial by thought: 'Oh, from this time forth, my thoughts be bloody or be nothing worth!' (65) As said, he's not like Fortinbras and Hotspur, who, at the slightest provocation, leap into the saddle, draw swords and yell 'charge.'

Hamlet would not be a successful military leader. The battle would be over before he got there. The hesitations, in his current dilemma, don't come from a man who can't make up his mind. He just needs to think personal, life-and-death issues through a little longer in order to make appropriate decisions.*

Read this subtle scene in its entirety. Retain Fortinbras' Denmark entry as a placeholder for future reference.

*American WW11 general, George S. Patton, said something like: eighty-percent of a good plan today is better today than one-hundred percent of a perfect plan tomorrow. Said differently, it's best to stay one step ahead of your enemies. Waiting too long to attack and missing the moment was Union General George B. McClellan's fatal flaw during the Civil War.) *Hamlet*, 4.4, 6-65

* * *

(IN the next scene, 4.5, Queen Gertrude, Horatio and a Gentleman talk about Ophelia's madness. Unlike Hamlet's imitation insanity, this is real and sad. At first, the Queen refuses to see her, but the Gentleman says that Ophelia needs pity.

Ophelia talks of her father, Polonius, fears the world's trickery, makes strange sounds and 'Spurns enviously at straws,' (6) or battles with negligible things.

The Gentleman also says that people suffering Ophelia's kind of madness don't know what they 'aim at,' (9) or truly know what is causing their anguish. He goes on to say that people in this state 'botch the words up to fit their own thoughts,' (10) meaning their mixed-up minds cause them to mix up words.

In an aside, the Queen says, 'Each toy seems prologue to some great amiss.' (18) She is saying that small incidents now turn into bigger issues that engender guilt and suspicion: 'So full of artless jealousy is guilt, it spills itself in fearing to be spilt.' (20) Trying to hide guilt often leaks it.

The Gentleman, who is excited to find Ophelia, enters with her. The First Folio says that Ophelia enters 'distracted' or acting crazy. She sings, and after the King enters, the tunes become explicitly bawdy. In some versions of *Hamlet* in performance, Ophelia also plays the lute. This scene needs careful reading. It is loaded with mixed messages.

In one of her ribald ditties, she sings 'before you tumbled me, you promised me to wed.' (63) If true, this line implicitly reveals a sexual relationship with Hamlet before he rebuffed her. If so, the love affair was more emotionally involving than previous dialogue suggests. And therefore it is more likely that Hamlet's cruel rejection of Ophelia instigated her descent into madness.

Before she exits, Ophelia says of her dead father, 'I cannot choose but weep to think they should lay him i' the cold ground.' (69) And then ominously, 'My brother shall know of it.' (70)

She adds touchingly: 'Come my coach! Good night, ladies, good night, sweet ladies, good night, good night.' (72) The rhythm and wording of the first line of verse is familiar. I'll propose that the author of the American folk song 'Good Night, Ladies!' was inspired by Ophelia's exits lines.

Horatio also exits when the King tells him to follow Ophelia. 'Follow her close, give her good watch, I pray you.' (74)

Hamlet, 4.5, 6-74

* * *

(CLAUDIUS talks with Gertrude, as scene five continues: following that, Laertes enters in a sweat, and the play cascades towards resolution.)

King. Oh, this is the poison of deep grief. It springs
All from her father's death. (76) O Gertrude, Gertrude,
When sorrows come, they come not single spies,
But in battalions! (78) First, her father slain.
Next, your son gone, and he most silent author

Of his own just remove. The people muddied.
Thick and unwholesome in their thoughts and whispers,
For good Polonius' death. <u>And we have done but greenly</u> (83)
<u>In huggermugger to inter him.</u> Poor Ophelia
Divided from herself and her fair judgment,
Without the which we are pictures, or mere beasts.
Hamlet, 4.5, 76-88

('It springs all from her father's death.' (76) This line indicates that Claudius does not know of Hamlet's rejection of Ophelia.

'When sorrows come, they come not single spies, but in battalions!' (78) This is a finely-drawn and much-quoted metaphor that nicely fits the scene. Speaking of fitting in, we see that the myriad elements of the play slot into place like pieces in a puzzle.

'And we have done but greenly in huggermugger to inter him.' (83) After blaming Hamlet a few lines above, Claudius admits that they've acted like greenhorns in botching the aftermath of Polonius' murder.

And if all that isn't bad enough, Claudius tells Gertrude that Ophelia's 'brother is in secret come from France.' (88)

* * *

(THE royal couple hear noises outside, and the King calls for his 'Switzers,' (96) or Swiss guard.

Another gentleman comes onstage to announce that 'young Laertes in a riotous head, o'erbears your officers. The rabble call him lord,' (102) and cry, 'Laertes shall be King!' (106)

Gertrude calls them 'false Danish dogs!' (110)

Laertes breaks in with his armed gang of Danes, and thinking Claudius killed his father says, 'O thou vile King, give me my father!' (116)

The Queen tells Laertes to calm down. Claudius tells her not to fear 'There's such divinity doth hedge a king,' (123) meaning that the gods encircle a King with a protective boundary, so let Laertes speak his piece. You've got to credit Claudius. He is one cool dude.

Claudius' divinity doth hedge a king' reminds us of Richard 11, 3.2, 'not all the water in the rough rude sea can wash the balm off from an anointed king.' With Bolingbroke ready to usurp him, Richard believes the gods will protect him.

Laertes demands 'Where is my father?' (126) The King says 'Dead.' The Queen chimes in with 'But not by him.' (128) Gertrude may love Hamlet, but she loves Claudius more.

Laertes wants to know how Polonius died, and 'Let come what comes, only I'll be revenged most thoroughly for my father.' (135) The parallel revenge plots are reaffirmed.

At this point, Claudius is not giving Hamlet away and tries to put the death of Polonius in perspective by telling Laertes that he may 'draw both friend and foe' (142) in pursuit of his revenge. To get Laertes off his trail, Claudius tells him, 'I am guiltless in your father's death.' (149) With Hamlet out to kill him, Claudius doesn't want another assassin on his trail.

Ophelia enters and Laertes sees that she is mad: 'Oh heavens! Is 't possible a young maid's wits should be as mortal as an old man's life?' (160) As I'm sure you've noted, Laertes is a bit full of himself, and his lofty speech advertises it.

Ophelia doesn't acknowledge her brother, sings more ditties and speaks a penetrating line: 'Oh, you must wear your rue with a difference,' (183) or your cause of sorrows is different from mine.

Before singing another song on her father's death, Ophelia says, 'They say a' made a good end.' (186) This phrase recalls Pistol's wife, the tavern Hostess, describing Falstaff's dying moments in *Henry V*, 2.3: '. . . a' made a finer end.'

Following Ophelia's exit, Laertes speaks bitterly about his late father: 'His means of death, his obscure funeral,' (213) and 'No noble rite or formal ostentation,' (215) or ritual pomp.

The King answers, 'And where the offense is let the great ax fall.' (219) Hoping that Hamlet will soon be dead at the hands of the English King, Claudius stalls Laertes.)

Hamlet, 4.5, 88-219

* * *

(IN the brief scene six of act four, a servant in Elsinore castle tells Horatio that 'Seafaring men' (2) wish to speak to him. They are shown in, and a sailor gives Horatio a letter from Hamlet. The gist is that the ship carrying Hamlet, along with Rosencrantz and Guildenstern, to England was waylaid by pirates. The crew of the two ships grappled, Hamlet ended up a prisoner of the pirates, and R & G sailed on to England.

Hamlet's letter also asks Horatio to give the sailors access to the King, for they have letters for him as well.

Hamlet concludes his letter to Horatio by asking him to come to him 'with as much speed as thou wouldest fly death. I have words to speak in thine ear will make thee dumb—' (25) The letter goes on to say that the sailors will bring Horatio to Hamlet.

And so we have a twist that entwines the two revenge plots. Hamlet will be back at Elsinore bent on revenge against the King for killing his father. As we know, Laertes is already in the castle seeking revenge for his father's murder. Read on as the cascade of events becomes a cataract.)

* * *

(BACK in Elizabethan days, there were no act separations, or breaks for food and drink, and scene changes were made on the fly. Audiences sat or stood during 'the two hours' traffic of our stage,' *Romeo and Juliet*, 1.1, although it was much longer than two hours for *Hamlet*.

Scene seven closes act four. In this scene, the King and Laertes extensively talk and plot. We highlight some of the best lines from the speeches to give you framework and insight into the events that constitute the plot before you go back and read the entire passage.

Claudius tells Laertes that he's surely heard 'That he which hath your noble father slain pursued my life.' (4) He's saying we need to get this really bad guy.

Laertes asks, 'Why you proceeded not against these feats, so crimeful and so capital in nature,' (7) meaning that since the crimes are so obviously heinous why didn't you have Hamlet killed.

Claudius says there are 'two special reasons.' (10) 'The Queen his mother lives almost by looks,' (12) and 'the great love the general gender bear him.' (18) We've read this before; Hamlet resembles a Greek god, or a Roman hero like Marc Antony. The King knows that since his wife and the general public love Hamlet he needs to be discreet in the means of murdering him. Do 'discreet' and 'murder' belong in the same sentence?

Laertes recounts the death of his father and 'a sister driven into desperate terms,' (26) 'But my revenge will come.' (29)

Claudius advises, 'Break not your sleeps for that,' (30) or don't lose sleep over it. I'm not dull and think 'it pastime. You shortly shall hear more.' (33) The king is saying: don't get over-eager, Laertes. He's also thinking that he will shortly have good news from England. Let's avoid any messes around the castle that will upset the Queen or the local folk loyal to Hamlet. Let the news come from England that Hamlet fell off his horse or died of a fever.

Just when Claudius thinks that he's calmed Laertes and is about to rid himself of Hamlet through a clean, far-off solution, a messenger come onto the stage with 'Letters, my lord, from Hamlet. This to your majesty, this to the Queen.' (38) The actor playing Claudius should give the audience a who-needs-this take.

The King reads the letter aloud to Laertes. In short it says that Hamlet is 'set naked on your kingdom. Tomorrow shall I beg leave to see your kingly eyes' (45) where he will 'recount the occasion of my sudden and more strange return,' (47) Claudius fears a deception.

Laertes says 'let him come,' (55) and 'I shall live and tell him to his teeth "Thus didest thou," ' (57) or you killed my father.

King Claudius has a plan, or 'exploit now ripe in my device,' (65) under which Hamlet will die, and even his mother will 'call it accident.' (68) Claudius tells Laertes that a gentleman from Normandy told him of Laertes' skill in fencing. And here we have the germ of the contrivance.

Claudius induces Laertes to confirm his love of his father and 'To show yourself your father's son in deed more than in words.' (127)

Laertes is so eager for payback that he offers 'To cut his throat i' the church.' (128)

The King warns, 'No place indeed should murder sanctuarize.' (129) The two previous lines tie back to Hamlet's earlier reluctance to kill Claudius at prayer on the grounds that it would send Claudius to Heaven and Hamlet to Hell: 'I'll do 't. And so he goes to Heaven.' 3.3

To further keep Laertes at bay, Claudius tells him that 'Revenge shall have no bounds.' (130) This contradicts his warning that cutting Hamlet's throat in church wouldn't be a smart idea. In any event, the King tells Laertes to stay out of sight once Hamlet's back in the castle.)

Hamlet, 4.7, 4-130

(THE scene-seven conniving between Claudius and Laertes continues. Claudius praises Laertes' swordsmanship to Hamlet and put a wager on the outcome of a friendly fencing match.

As you read and reread the dialogue, note how Will arranges the pieces in this chess-game-like play. Did Will ever sit back, take a breath and ask himself, 'Which maneuver comes next?' Or, 'what is the projected outcome of this particular character's next move?'

I suspect that given his enormous output over brief periods, that Will's agile thinking and faultless logic just pours onto the page. He instinctively knows where he's been in the plot, where he now is, and where he's going.

Sport nonpareils have similar instincts, Pele in soccer, for example, and Wayne Gretsky in hockey.

Gretsky famously said, 'I skate to where the puck is going to be, not where it has been.'

The greats in any endeavor see the field, and as Emerson wrote, 'It is difficult to see the field within the field.'

Let's now get back to Claudius and Laertes in act four, scene seven, colluding on how to kill Hamlet.)

King. He, being remiss,
Most generous and free from all contriving, (136)
Will not peruse the foils, so that with ease,
Or with a little shuffling, you may choose
A sword unbated, (139) and in a pass of practice
Requite him for your father.
Laertes. I will do 't,
And for that purpose I'll anoint my sword.
I bought an unction of a mountebank
So mortal that but dip a knife in it, (144)
Where it draws blood no cataplasm so rare,
Collected from all simples that have virtue (146)
Under the moon, (147) can save the thing from death
That is but scratched withal. I'll touch my point
With this contagion, that if I gall him slightly,
It may be death.
King. Therefore this project
Should have a back or second, that might hold
If this did blast in proof. (155) Soft, let me see—

We'll make a solemn wager on your cunnings. (156)
I ha 't,
When in your motion you are hot and dry— (159)
As make your bouts more violent to that end—
And that he calls for drink, I'll have prepared him
A chalice for the nonce, (161) whereon but sipping,
If he by chance escape your venomed stuck,
Our purpose may hold there.
Hamlet, 4.7, 135-163

(THE King tells Laertes, that Hamlet is a bit careless and 'Most generous and free from all contriving.' (136) Said differently, Hamlet, despite his faults, is noble and not of a suspicious nature. Therefore, he won't notice that one of the sharp tips is uncovered, or 'A sword unbated,' (138) and Laertes can choose that one and make a fatal thrust.

Laertes likes the idea, but to provide a little more insurance he bought poison from a charlatan so 'So mortal that but dip a knife in it,' (144) and nick someone that it will likely kill.

Poison herbs, or 'simples' (146) gathered 'Under the moon,' (147) or under the moon's rays, were thought to be, at that time, particularly lethal.

We see Claudius nodding, licking his lips and scheming further. He posits that if for some reason, the two ideas 'blast in proof' (155) or blow up like misfired artillery they need a third device to kill Hamlet.

While the King thinks on the endgame, he says, 'We'll make a solemn wager on your cunnings.' (156) He'll further delude Hamlet and make him think the fencing match is all a harmless game by getting him to lay a friendly bet on the outcome.

Claudius has the final piece of the murderous plan. In the event that neither of our plans work, Hamlet will be 'hot and dry' (159) and need drink. In that case, 'I'll have prepared him a chalice for the nonce,' (161) or a goblet laced with poison.

In their shared goal to murder Hamlet the plotters have three tricks up their doublets: unbated sword, envenomed tip, poisoned drink. The preceding poetic passage is masterful in its expository structure. We're now well-prepared for the play's resolution.)

* * *

(BUT first, Queen Gertrude enters with woeful news.)

Queen. One woe doth tread upon another's heel,
So fast they follow. Your sister's drowned, Laertes.
Laertes. Drowned! Oh, where?
Queen. There is a willow grows aslant a brook (167)

That shows his hoar leaves in the glassy stream.
There with fantastic garlands did she come
Of crowflowers, nettles, daisies, and long purples
(170)
That liberal shepherds give a grosser name,
But our cold maids do dead-men's-fingers call them.
(172)
There on the pendent boughs her coronet weeds
Clambering to hang, an envious sliver broke, (174)
When down her weedy trophies and herself
Fell in the weeping brook. Her clothes spread wide,
(176)
And mermaidlike awhile they bore her up— (177)
Which time she chanted snatches of old tunes, (178)
As one incapable of her own distress,
Or like a creature native and indued (180)
Unto that element. But long it could not be
Till that her garments, heavy with their drink,
Pulled the poor wretch from her melodious lay (183)
To muddy death.
Hamlet, 4.7, 164-183

(Ophelia's drowning is difficult, if near impossible, to depict onstage. It can be shown effectively on film. That said, do we really need a visual representation when the passage paints in poetry? How many times have we seen a tree bent over a stream with its leaves reflecting in the water? 'There is a willow grows aslant a brook.' (167)

The Queen tells of how Ophelia came garlanded 'Of crowflowers, nettles, daisies, and long purples.' (170) The myths about 'crowflowers,' or buttercups is extensive. They symbolize many things, including childlike behavior, poison, ingratitude, chastity and more.

Will used flowers to characterize insanity. In *King Lear*, 4.4., Cordelia talks of her father on the Dover heath being

As mad as the vexed sea, singing aloud,
Crowned with rank fumiter and furrow weeds,
With burdocks, hemlock, nettles, cuckoo flowers,
Darnel. And all the wild weeds that grow
In our sustaining corn.

Note that like Ophelia, Lear is 'singing aloud.' I venture that 'cuckoo' as a synonym for insanity originated in line three's 'cuckoo flowers.'

Back to Queen Gertrude's description of Ophelia's drowning, 'But our cold maids do dead-men's-fingers call them' (172) refers to the 'long purples,' or orchises, in the line describing the array of flowers garlanding Ophelia. It is also a vulgarity used by uncouth herdsmen.

'Clambering to hang, an envious sliver broke' (174) means that when Ophelia reached to hang her crown of weeds on a branch, it gave way and she fell into the brook.

'Fell in the weeping brook' (176) calls us back to 'willow' in the first line of the Queen's second speech.

'Her clothes spread wide, and mermaidlike awhile they bore her up' (177) is fine descriptive poetry. We see Ophelia buoyed along the flowing stream.

The sad 'Which time she chanted snatches of old tunes,' (180) increases the pity for the doomed Ophelia.

'Or like a creature native and indued' (180) suggests that Ophelia looks at home in the water. The line also ties back meaningfully to 'mermaidlike.'

Similarly, 'Pulled the poor wretch from her melodious lay,' (183) links nicely to the Queen's earlier mention of how 'she chanted snatches of old tunes.' The 'old tunes' reference makes us feel the sadness of Ophelia's death all the more. My favorite line from the *Hello Dolly* score is: 'One of your old favorite songs from way back when.'

Hearing the story of his sister's death heightens the fury of the rushing-offstage Laertes. The King and Queen dash off to intercept him before he prematurely 'requites' his revenge on Hamlet.)

(JUST when the unending tensions or horrors are about to make a play collapse under its own tragic weight, Will sends in the clowns.

In *Macbeth*, 2.3, we are distracted from the terror inside the castle by the risible Porter at the gate, as he postulates 'Lechery, sir, it provokes and unprovokes. It provokes the desire, but it takes away the performance. Therefore, much drink may be said to be an equivocator with lechery.'

When King Lear's two costly mistakes rocket the play toward its grim conclusion, the unnamed Fool is right there to remind him in audacious terms of the errors. In line five of his comical critique of Lear actions in 1.4, the Fool tells him, 'Set less than thou throwest,' or don't wager more than you can risk losing, a poke in the ribs to Lear who has incautiously given up his kingdom and banished his favorite daughter.

As we see in *Hamlet*, the two revenge issues collide, and we have King Claudius and Laertes conniving against Hamlet. It's heavy going as audiences prepare for what promises to be a bloody conclusion. Suddenly, to open act five, Will inserts two clownish grave diggers with shovels at work on Ophelia's plot.

For full effect you need to read the scene in its mirthful entirety. The two clowns assume that Ophelia committed suicide, and is therefore, according to current rites, not due a Christian burial.)

Clown One. Is she to be buried in Christian burial that willfully seeks her own salvation? . . . How can that be unless she drowned herself in her own defense?

Clown Two. Will you ha' the truth on 't? If this had not been a gentlewoman, she should have been buried out o' Christian burial. (28)

Clown One. Why, there thou say'st. And the more pity that great folks should have countenance (30) in this world to drown or hang themselves more than their even Christian. Come, my spade.

(The Second Clown exits, Clown One digs and sings nonsensical ditties. Hamlet and Horatio enter.)

Hamlet. Has this fellow no feeling of his business, that he sings at grave-making?

Horatio. Custom hath made it in him a property of easiness. (76)

(The singing grave digger throws a skull up out of the grave.)

Hamlet. That skull had a tongue in it, and could sing once. (83) How the knave jowls it to the ground, as if it were Cain's jawbone, that did the first murder. (84) It might be the pate of a politician which this ass now o'erreaches—one that would circumvent God, might it not? . . . (85)

Or of a courtier, which could say "Good morrow, sweet lord! How dost thou, good lord?" This might be my lord Such-a-one that praised my lord Such-a-one's horse when he meant to beg it, might it not? . . . (94)

Why, e'en so. And now my Lady Worm's chapless and knocked about the mazzard with a sexton's spade. . . . (96)

(The still-singing grave digger tosses up another skull at Hamlet's feet. Imagine the groundlings elbowing ribs and making merry, as they delight in Hamlet's skull examinations and sarcastic wordplay. He continues.)

Hamlet. There's another. Why may not that be the skull of a lawyer? Where be his quiddities now, his quillets, his cases, his tenures, and his tricks? (108) Why does he suffer this rude knave now to knock him about the sconce with a dirty shovel, and will not tell him of his action of battery? Hum! This fellow might be in 's time a great buyer of land, with his statutes, his recognizances, his fines, his double vouchers, his recoveries, to have his fine pate full of fine dirt? (111) Will his vouchers vouch him no more of his purchases, and double ones too, than the length and breadth of a pair of indentures? . . . (116)

144

(The grave digger's head pops up. Hamlet asks him whose grave he is digging, and nine lines later 'How long hast thou been a grave-maker?'' 153)

Clown. One that was a woman, sir, but, rest her soul, she's dead. . . . (146)

Of all the days i' the year, I came to 't that day our last King Hamlet o'ercame Fortinbras. (155)

Hamlet. How long is that since?

Clown. Cannot you tell that? Every fool can tell that. It was the very day that young Hamlet was born, he that is mad, and sent into England. . . . (164)

I have been sexton here, man and boy, thirty years. . . . (177)

Here's a skull now. This skull has lain in the earth three and twenty years. . . . (191)

A pestilence on him for a mad rogue! A' poured a flagon of Rhenish on my head once. This same skull, sir, was Yorick's skull, the king's jester.

Hamlet. Let me see. (Holds skull while closely inspecting it.) Alas, poor Yorick! (202) I knew him Horatio—a fellow of infinite jest, of most excellent fancy. He hath borne me on his back a thousand times, (204) and now how abhorred in my imagination it is! My gorge rises at it. Here hung those lips that I have kissed I know not how oft. Where be your gibes now? Your gambols? Your songs? Your flashes of merriment that were wont to set the table on a roar?

Not one now, to mock your own grinning. <u>Quite chopfallen?</u> (211) <u>Now get you to my lady's chamber and tell her, let her paint an inch thick,</u> (212) to this favor she must come—make her laugh at that. . . .
To what base uses we may return, Horatio! <u>Why may not imagination trace the noble dust of Alexander till he find it stopping a bunghole?</u> . . . (224)
As thus: Alexander died, Alexander was buried, Alexander returneth into dust; the dust is earth; of earth we make loam; and <u>why of that loam, whereto he was converted, might they not stop a beer barrel.</u> (233)
'Imperious Caesar, dead and turned to clay, might stop a hole to keep the wind away.' (237)
Hamlet, 5.1, 1-237

('IF this had not been a gentlewoman, she should have been buried out o' Christian burial.' (28) The grave diggers don't like digging a plot for a suicide that doesn't belong in their sacred graveyard, but some unsanctified elsewhere, like at a crossroads. Since they're assuming Ophelia committed suicide, rather than death by accidental drowning, the two clowns are being unfairly and amusingly sanctimonious.

'And the more pity that great folks should have countenance.' (30) Of course, they say, she gets a pass because she's somebody, and we sure wouldn't have that privilege. Will knew the thinking and language of Elizabethan-age menials.

'Custom hath made it in him a property of easiness.' (76) Horatio's saying that the digger has been at his otherwise depressing job for so long that he's comfortable with it and can be happy in his thoughts and singing snatches of silly tunes.

A skull tossed up by the grave digger lands at Hamlet's feet. Prompted by the singing from below, he comments, 'That skull had a tongue in it, and could sing once.' (83) At the risk of correcting Will, the line could have read 'and did sing once too.' Forgive my irreverent editing.

'How the knave jowls it to the ground, as if it were Cain's jawbone, that did the first murder.' (84) It would be fine, Hamlet's saying, for the grave digger to fling the jawbone of the man who, like Cain, killed his brother. But now he's thoughtlessly hurling the skull of what could be an admirable person.

'It might be the pate of a politician which this ass now o'erreaches—one that would circumvent God, might it not?' (85) Hamlet tells Horatio, for all that fool digging down there knows, this might be the skull of a politician who could outtalk God.

Like most of the selected copy, the 'Or of a courtier' section (94) is written to tickle the audience.

This worth rereading passage is clever at parodying boot-licking courtiers.

'And now my Lady Worm's chapless and knocked about the mazzard with a sexton's spade.' (96) Imaging a worm-eaten, jawless skull being batted around like a bowling pin by the grave diggers shovel is visually amusing wordplay.

As I wrote in the introduction to this book, Will, as a young man, clerked for two Stratford lawyers. If you doubt that, read the following about the possible owner of a skull, 'Where be his quiddities now, his quillets, his cases, his tenures, and his tricks?' (108)

Will also helped his father, John Shakespeare, in his buying and selling of land. 'This fellow might be in 's time a great buyer of land, with his statutes, his recognizances, his fines, his double vouchers, his recoveries, to have his fine pate full of fine dirt?' (111) More: 'Will his vouchers vouch him no more of his purchases, and double ones too, than the length and breadth of a pair of indentures?' (116)

The easy access to the lingo of the law and land deals is not something you research or just casually know. Even a talent of Will's stature wouldn't think to use these inside terms unless they were part of his participating experiences.

The grave diggers' head pops up out of the trapdoor in the stage. Hamlet asks him whose grave he's digging, 'One that was a woman, sir, but, rest her soul, she's dead.' (146) He's speaking of Ophelia, but Hamlet, who's been away, doesn't know she's dead. The line also alerts the audience to the episode that follows this analysis.

At this late point in the play, where Will is building toward the resolution, he re-introduces the Fortinbras name, albeit Old Fortinbras, by asking the grave digger how long he's been at his business: 'Of all the days i' the year, I came to 't that day our last King Hamlet o'ercame Fortinbras. (155)

Hamlet asks him how long ago was that. Like most all of Will's plotting, one line sets up the next, 'Cannot you tell that? Every fool can tell that. It was the very day that young Hamlet was born, he that is mad, and sent into England.' (164)

And then the clincher, 'I have been sexton here, man and boy, thirty years.' (177) It appears from the dialogue that Hamlet's thirty years old. Considering his Wittenberg student status, the apparent young love with Ophelia and the general tone of his place in the noble hierarchy, I thought him to be a much younger man.

The clownish grave digger bends down into the trapdoor, retrieves another skull and shows it to Hamlet, 'Here's a skull now. This skull has lain in the earth three and twenty years.' (191) This line tends to confirm Hamlet's current age at about thirty.

The grave digger tells Hamlet that it's the skull of Yorick, the King's, or Old Hamlet's, jester. Hamlet asks to see it, meaning to hold it. And, in a great theatrical moment, Hamlet gazes at the skull and utters a famous line, 'Alas, poor Yorick!' (202)

Following some touching and worth rereading remembrance lines about Yorick, Hamlet tells Horatio that 'He hath borne me on his back a thousand times.' (204) This suggests that Hamlet is around seven years of age when Yorick dies 'three and twenty years' ago, and jibes with previous dialogue hints that Hamlet is now about thirty. Maybe he's a postdoc at Wittenberg University.

Quite chopfallen?' (211) Hamlet, being Hamlet, can't resist an audience-pleasing quip at his beloved Yorick's expense—Yorick's skull lacking jaws recalls 'Lady Worms chapless' (96) above.

'Now get you to my lady's chamber and tell her, let her paint an inch thick, (212) reminds us of Hamlet's harsh likening of Ophelia to a harlot in the 3.1 'Get thee to a nunnery' speech. 'I have heard of your paintings too, well enough. God hath given you one face and you make yourselves another.'

Hamlet muses about what uses our dust could be used for, 'Why may not imagination trace the noble dust of Alexander till he find it stopping a bunghole? (224) And a few lines later, 'why of that loam, whereto he was converted, might they not stop a beer barrel.' (233) And now our rascally minds know what 'bunghole' really means.

Even Julius Caesar, about whom Will wrote a play at about the same time as *Hamlet*, is satirized by the eponymous Hamlet, 'Imperious Caesar, dead and turned to clay, might stop a hole to keep the wind away.' (237)

We don't know why Will, through Hamlet, chose to make sport of esteemed leaders of the past. Possibly, it reflects current political thinking toward the end of Elizabeth's long reign and the subconscious need to reject the old and start anew. It may also be an allusion to the fall of Essex, who was a national hero of the English people.)

* * *

(HAMLET and Horatio stand out of sight, as Ophelia's funeral procession, including the King, Queen, Laertes, others, arrives in the graveyard. The priest announces that since 'Her death was doubtful,' (250) meaning that it could have been suicide, 'She should in ground unsanctified have lodged.' (252)

'Shards, flints and pebbles should be thrown on her. Yet here she is allowed her virgin crants, her maiden strewments and the bringing home of bell and burial.' (257) The priest allows that even though Ophelia may be a suicide and died without receiving the last rites of the church, she will receive some kind of dignified burial even though, in the eyes of the church, she doesn't deserve it. Hard objects being thrown is what she deserves, not flowers strewn on a maiden's grave.

The priest also mentions 'bell and burial.' 'Bell' is part of 'bell, book and candle' the Catholic rite of excommunication. The 'bell' tolls for excommunicants.)

Laertes. Lay her i' the earth.
And from her fair and unpolluted flesh
May violets spring! I tell thee, churlish priest, (262)
A ministering angel shall my sister be
When thou liest howling.
Hamlet. (Unobserved by the mourners and off to one side of the stage.)
What, the fair Ophelia! (265)
Queen. (Spreading flowers.) Sweets to the sweet. (266)
Farewell.
I hoped thou shouldst have been my Hamlet's wife,
I thought thy bride bed to have decked, sweet maid,

And not have strewed thy grave.

Laertes. Oh, treble woe

<u>Fall ten times on that cursèd head</u> (270)

Whose wicked deed thy most ingenious sense

Deprived thee of! Hold off the earth a while

Till I have caught her once more in mine arms.

(Laertes jumps into the grave.)

<u>Now pile your dust upon the quick and dead</u> (274)

Till of this flat a mountain you have made

To o'ertop old <u>Pelion</u> or the skyish head (276)

Of blue <u>Olympus.</u> (277)

Hamlet. (Moving across the stage.) What is he whose grief

Bears such an emphasis? <u>Whose phrase of sorrow</u> (279)

Conjures the wandering stars and makes them stand

Like wonder-wounded hearers? <u>This is I,</u>

<u>Hamlet the Dane.</u> (280) (He jumps into the grave.)

Laertes. The Devil take thy soul! (They scuffle.)

Hamlet. Thou pray'st not well.

I, prithee, take thy fingers from my throat,

For though I am not splenitive and rash,

Yet have I in me something dangerous,

Which let thy wisdom fear. Hold off thy hand. . . .

I loved Ophelia. <u>Forty thousand brothers</u> (292)

Could not, with all their quantity of love,

Make up my sum. What wilt thou do for her? . . .

Hear you, sir.
What is the reason that you use me thus?
I loved you ever. But it is no matter,
Let Hercules himself do what he may,
The cat will mew and dog will have his day. (315)
King. (Speaking to Laertes.)
Strengthen your patience in our last night's speech.
(317)
We'll put the matter to our present push.
Good Gertrude, set some watch over your son.
This grave shall have a living monument. (320)
An hour of quiet shortly shall we see,
Till then, in patience our proceeding be.
Hamlet, 5.1, 241-320

('I tell thee, churlish priest, (262) is Laertes telling off the rude cleric for speaking ill of his sister. Laertes heaps it on by saying that unlike the impertinent priest, Ophelia in death will be a 'ministering angel' while he howls in Hell.

'Sweets to the sweet.' (266) This is the farewell of Queen Gertrude to the woman she hoped would be Hamlet's wife. The opening phrase of her speech has fallen into common use.

'Fall ten times on that cursèd head' (270) is Laertes blaming Hamlet for his sister's death.

'Now pile your dust upon the quick and dead.' (274) Will popularized the phrase 'quick and dead,' meaning both alive and dead. However, the phrase is used in the *King James Bible*, and in other works predating Elizabethan days.

As we said earlier, Laertes tends to get carried away with his rhetoric. In lines (276) and (277) he asks that he and Ophelia's body be covered with dust higher than Pelion and Olympus two mountains in Greece.

Hearing what he believes is a brother's over-grieving magniloquence, Hamlet strides across the stage to Laertes in the faux-grave trapdoor saying: 'Whose phrase of sorrow pretends to make the stars stop moving.' (279) Who does this guy think he is?

'This is I, Hamlet the Dane.' (280) I'm the Prince of Denmark, and you're not. Hamlet tells Laertes to stop choking him, as they tussle in Ophelia's grave. The humorist Garrison Keillor said something like, 'Tragedy is misunderstood comedy.' First, we have Horatio and Hamlet discussing Yorick's skull tossed up out of his grave. Now, we have the lover and the brother scrapping in the dead Ophelia's grave.

'Forty thousand brothers' (292) is Hamlet telling Laertes that a brother's love is no match for what he felt for Ophelia. At the risk of committing heresy, Hamlet's 'get thee to a nunnery' treatment of Ophelia in 3.1 makes his current declaration of all-consuming love a shade suspect, even hypocritical. I know he was feigning madness at that point in the play, but in no other scene was desperate love demonstrated. After Hamlet killed her father, why didn't he immediately seek Ophelia out and comfort her?

'The cat will mew and dog will have his day.' (315) Hamlet tells Laertes that he can rant all he wants, but I will have my say. You're correct, the common phrase 'every dog has his day' derives from this line.

'Strengthen your patience in our last night's speech.' (317) Knowing Laertes' hasty conduct, King Claudius reminds him to hold off on killing Hamlet. We'll get him soon with a sword thrust or poisoned wine.

After Claudius asks Gertrude to keep an eye on her son, he adds 'This grave shall have a living monument.' (320) He means that Hamlet will also soon have a grave.)

* * *

(SCENE TWO, the final scene of the play, opens with Hamlet and Horatio talking in Elsinore Castle. Hamlet tells his friend what happened on board the ship carrying him to England. Hamlet couldn't sleep and heard a ruckus. He said he'd learned some lessons like, 'When our deep plots do pall.' (8) Failure is something we can learn from he tells Horatio and continues with a distinguishable line 'There's a divinity that shapes our ends, roughhew them how we will.' (10) This can be read as fatalistic. Or Hamlet could be saying that if we start things badly God will bail us out.

Since many of Will's lead characters, especially in the tragedies, are both bad and fatalists, I prefer the optimistic interpretation of the 'divinity' line. Hamlet is surely not a bad person in the thoroughgoing sense that Claudius is. But his treatment of Ophelia and his excessive bullying of his victimized-by-Claudius mother doesn't make him the embodiment of benevolence.

Getting back to the scene, Hamlet goes on to tell Horatio that the noises on the ship prompted him to investigate.)

Hamlet. Up from my cabin,
My sea gown scarfed about me, in the dark
<u>Groped I to find out them, had my desire,</u>
<u>Fingered their packet,</u> (14) and in fine withdrew
To mine own room again, making so bold,
My fears forgetting manners, <u>to unseal</u>
<u>Their grand commission</u> (18) where I found,
Horatio—
Oh royal knavery—an exact command,

157

Importing Denmark's health and England's too,
With ho! Such bugs and goblins in my life
That, on the supervise, no leisure bated.
<u>No, not to stay the grinding of the ax,</u>
<u>My head should be stuck off.</u> . . . (24)
<u>Ere I could make a prologue to my brains</u>
<u>They had begun the play</u>— (31) I sat me down,
Devised a new commission, wrote it fair. . . .
<u>It did me yeoman's service.</u> (36) Wilt thou know
The effect of what I wrote? . . .
An earnest conjuration from the King,
As England was his faithful tributary,
As love between them like the palm might flourish
As peace should still her wheaten garland wear
And stand a comma 'tween their amities . . .
Horatio. How was this sealed?
Hamlet. Why, even in that was Heaven ordinant.
<u>I had my father's signet in my purse,</u>
<u>Which was the model of that Danish seal</u>— (50)
Folded the writ up in the form of the other.
Subscribed it, gave 't the impression, placed it safely,
The changeling never known. Now the next day
Was our sea fight, and what to this was sequent
Thou know'st already.
Horatio. So Guildenstern and Rosencrantz go to 't.
Hamlet. <u>Why, man, they did make love to this</u>
<u>employment.</u> (57)

They are not near my conscience, their defeat
Does by their own insinuation grow. . . .
Horatio. Why, what a King is this! (62)
Hamlet. He that hath killed my King and whored my
mother, (64)
Popped in between the election and my hopes . . . (65)
To let this canker of our nature (69) come
In further evil.
Hamlet, 5.2, 12-70

(After hearing the fighting, Hamlet went to find R &
G. They were not in their cabin. 'Groped I to find out
them, had my desire, fingered their packet,' (14) and
found the orders from King Claudius R & G were
carrying to the King of England.

Hamlet went back to his cabin 'to unseal their
grand commission' (18) and learn that without delay,
'No, not to stay the grinding of the ax, my head should
be struck off.' (24) England was not even going to
take time to sharpen the ax before lopping Hamlet's
head off. The cliché 'have no ax to grind' may have
predated the play, but it's likely that the line in the play
increased its use.

'Ere I could make a prologue to my brains, they had
begun the play' (31) is Hamlet, through Will, seeing
the letter from Denmark to England as a prologue in
this play within a play. So he wrote a new commission

for R & G to carry to the King of England, and 'It did me yeoman's service.'* (36)

*Yeomen were hardworking farmers reputed to be good soldiers. A variation, 'He did yeoman's work' is another Will-generated Cliché.

Unlike Claudius, who threatened England with invasion unless they killed him, Hamlet, in his rewritten letter, offers peace to England if they kill R & G.

Horatio asks how Hamlet made it official. 'I had my father's signet in my purse, which was the model of that Danish seal' (50) meaning that Hamlet had his dead father's ring and used that as the official stamp.

Horatio comments that R & G really went at their traitorous behavior towards Hamlet who responds, 'Why, man, they did make love to this employment.' (57) And having insinuated themselves into a situation below their stations they deserve what they got, which is 'put to sudden death.' (46)

'Why, what a King is this!' (62) Horatio's saying that Claudius is a rat. Also, this exclamation from Horatio is a good example of a setup line for Hamlet's next speech.

Hamlet answers, 'He that hath killed my King and whored my mother, (64) Popped in between the election and my hopes,' (65) or bypassed the electoral process in Denmark and Hamlet's chance to succeed his father. You may recall that Claudius fears Hamlet's popularity among the people. He knows that if an election was held Hamlet would win. So he jumped in and grabbed the crown while Hamlet was away at university.

Did you notice 'canker of our nature' (69) with 'canker' popping up again to describe Claudius as some kind of larva growing on the natural order of things.

Finally, on the passage above, Hamlet's actions against R & G aboard the ship carrying him to execution took guts. He showed that he could act fast and handily reshuffle the deck.)

* * *

(IN this play, Osric is a courtier in the supercilious mold of the toadying Oswald in *King Lear*. Given to overelaborate language, Osric enters to tell Hamlet that King Claudius has arranged a fencing match between him and Laertes.

Hamlet mocks Osric and outdoes his embroidered wordplay. But first, Osric welcomes Hamlet back to Denmark. Hamlet thanks him and asks Horatio, 'Dost know this water fly?' (83) A bug skidding about the surface of a pond is a useful metaphor for the foppish Osric.

There's also some good business going on. Osric has deferentially doffed his hat, and Hamlet teases him about putting it back on. 'Put your bonnet to his right use, 'tis for the head.' (96) Osric tells Hamlet that it's hot, and Hamlet says that it's cold. Then they discuss how sultry it is. This foolishness is fun for the audience, most of whom enjoy seeing a lickspittle like Osric made fun of. It's also a useful expositional device in preparation for the upcoming finale.

But we're not there yet, and Osric speaks of Laertes qualities, 'an absolute gentleman, full of most excellent differences, of very soft society and great showing.' (113) In short, Laertes is handsome and well-bred.

In just one well-written line, Hamlet satirizes Osric's oleaginous drivel about Laertes with, 'I know to divide him inventorially would dizzy the arithmetic of memory.' (118) Or, Laertes is so wonderful that we'd run out of numbers trying to remember and quantify his attributes.

After Osric's overly long, but worth-reading recital on the terms of the King's bet, e.g., 'The King hath wagered with him six Barbary horses, against the which he has imponed, as I take it six French rapiers . . .' (154) Osric goes on to tell Hamlet 'The King, sir, hath laid, sir, that in a dozen passes between yourself and him, he shall not exceed you three hits.' (172)

Although amusing in pricking Osric's pretensions, much of the badinage serves as exposition. Osric asks Hamlet if he agrees with the terms and can he report that back to the King. Hamlet tells him, 'To this effect, sir, after what flourish your nature will.' (187) He's saying, yes you can tell the King I'm ready, and I know it will take many more words than are necessary.

After Osric exits, Hamlet says to Horatio, 'He did comply with his dug before he sucked it.' (196) Put in modern terminology, Osric was punctilious from infancy and couldn't even nurse without first making a ceremony out of it.

A lord enters to tell Hamlet that the King is ready for him. He adds that 'The Queen desires you to use some gentle entertainment to Laertes before you fall to play.' (213) Said differently, try to make up with Laertes. Hamlet responds, 'She well instructs me,' (214) and the lord exits.

Horatio says, 'You will lose this wager, my lord.' (219)

Hamlet answers, 'I do not think so. Since he went into France I have been in continual practice. I shall win at the odds. But thou wouldst not think how ill all's here about my heart—but it is no matter.' (223) Is this a premonition?

Horatio tells his friend that if he's not fit, he will get the King to delay the match.)

Hamlet. Not a whit, <u>we defy augury.</u> (230) There's special providence in the <u>fall of a sparrow.</u> (231) If it be now, 'tis not to come; if it be not to come, it will be now; if it not be now, yet it will come. <u>The readiness is all.</u> (234)
Hamlet, 5.2, 83-234

(THE 'we defy augury' (230) reference means that Hamlet isn't interested in signs that may portend good or bad outcomes. Even though Hamlet has foreboding, he rejects it on the grounds that the end result is in God's hands.

Will probably derived the 'fall of a sparrow' phrase from Matthew 10:29: 'One of them shall not fall on the ground without your father.' Hamlet's a believer, and whether he falls or not is preordained.

The brilliant 'not be now' lines from this classic speech are Hamlet saying that his fate is already determined. And if not now, it will be later. One of the best lines in the play sums this up: 'The readiness is all.' (234)

Edgar in *King Lear,* 5.2 uses a similar line with 'Ripeness is all.')

* * *

(The King, the Queen and their retinue, including Osric, enter. Prompted by the King, Hamlet and Laertes shake hands. Hamlet apologizes to Laertes, saying 'His madness is poor Hamlet's enemy' (250) and ending the speech with the imaginative,
'I have shot mine arrow o'er the house, and hurt my brother.' (254)

Laertes tentatively accepts the apology, with a caveat: 'in terms of honor I stand aloof . . . (257) 'To keep my name ungored.' (261) He wants a higher authority to declare that his reputation is undamaged. It's interesting that he seems to value his good name more than his father's murder by Hamlet.

Also, Laertes apparently doesn't know about Hamlet's mistreatment of Ophelia, his dead sister. But we're reading too much into Laertes' words. Complicit with the King, Laertes is there to kill Hamlet. And it would make Hamlet suspicious should Laertes give absolute forgiveness.

Laertes and Hamlet choose foils for their fencing match. Laertes doesn't like the feel of the first one he selects and says 'let me see another.' (275) This foil is the lethal one. Keep in mind that the poisoned wine is a backup in the event that Laertes doesn't kill Hamlet with a thrust of his unbated sword tip. Moreover, the uncovered sword point is envenomed with the poison Laertes bought from the charlatan.

The King describes the odds in the match and then gives a short, but informative speech.)

King. Set me the stoups of wine upon that table.
If Hamlet give the first or second hit,
<u>Or quit in answer of the third exchange</u>, (280)
Let all the battlements the ordnance fire.
<u>The king shall drink to Hamlet's better breath,</u>
<u>And in the cup a union shall he throw</u> (283)
Richer than that which four successive kings
In Denmark's crown have worn. Give me the cups,
And let the kettle to the trumpet speak,
The trumpet to the cannoneer without,
The cannon to the Heavens, the Heaven to earth,
"Now the King drinks to Hamlet." Come, begin,
And you, the judges, bear a wary eye.
Hamlet, 5.2, 250-297

(AS a diversion from his main intent, King Claudius announces that if Hamlet scores two hits on Laertes 'Or quit in answer of the third exchange,' (280) meaning that if he retaliates successfully, 'The king shall drink to Hamlet's better breath, and in the cup a union shall he throw.' (283) The 'union' is supposed to be a rare gem, but in reality it is the poison pill intended to kill Hamlet.

The bout begins. Hamlet claims a hit. Laertes contests it. Hamlet asks for a judgment. Osric delivers a noted line, 'A hit, a very palpable hit.' (292)

The King offers Hamlet a drink, Hamlet declines. They play again. Hamlet scores another hit that Laertes acknowledges. The King announces 'Our son shall win.' (297)

Queen. He's fat and scant of breath.
Here, Hamlet, take my napkin, rub thy brows.
<u>The Queen carouses to thy fortune, Hamlet.</u> (300)
King. Gertrude do not drink.
Queen. I will, my lord, I pray you pardon me. (302
King. (Aside.) It is the poisoned cup, it is too late. (303)
Hamlet, 5.2, 298-318

('The Queen carouses to thy fortune, Hamlet.' (300) 'Carouses' means she's taken a big chug of the poisoned wine.'

Laertes and Hamlet resume the match. Laertes says, 'Have at you now!' (313) Does Laertes stab Hamlet in the back? After Hamlet is wounded the two tussle. During the grappling, they swap rapiers, resume fencing and Hamlet cuts Laertes. The Queen collapses.

Osric asks the wounded Laertes how he's doing. Laertes: 'I am justly killed with mine own treachery.' (316)

Hamlet asks after the Queen. The King says 'she swounds to see them bleed.' (318)

Queen. No, no, the drink, the drink! —O my dear Hamlet—
The drink, the drink! I am poisoned. (Dies.)
Hamlet. Oh, villainy! Ho! Let the door be locked.
Treachery! Seek it out.
Laertes. (Crumples.) It is here, Hamlet. Hamlet, thou art slain.
No medicine in the world can do thee good,
In thee there is not half an hour of life.
The treacherous instrument is in thy hand,
Unbated and envenomed. The foul practice
Hath turned itself on me. Lo, here I lie
Never to rise again. Thy mother's poisoned.
I can no more. The King, the King's to blame.
Hamlet. The point envenomed too!
Then, venom, to thy work. (He stabs Claudius.)
All. Treason! Treason! (334)
King. Oh, yet defend me, friends, I am but hurt.
Hamlet. Here, thou incestuous, murderous, damnèd Dane,
Drink off this potion. (336) Is thy union here?

Follow my mother. (The King dies.)

Laertes. He is justly served.

It is a poison tempered by himself.

Exchange forgiveness with me, noble Hamlet. (340)

Mine and my father's death come not upon thee,

Nor thine on me! (Laertes dies.)

Hamlet. Heaven make thee free of it. (343) I follow
thee.

I am dead, Horatio. Wretched Queen, adieu! (344)

You that look pale and tremble at this chance,

That are but mutes or audience to this act,

Had I but time—as this fell sergeant, Death,

Is strict in his arrest (348) —oh, I could tell you—

But let it be. Horatio, I am dead,

Thou livest. Report me and my cause aright

To the unsatisfied. (351)

Horatio. Never believe it.

I am more an antique Roman than a Dane.

Here's yet some liquor left. (353)

Hamlet. As thou 'rt a man,

Give me the cup. Let go—by Heaven, I'll have 't.
(354)

O good Horatio, what a wounded name,

Things standing thus unknown, shall live behind me!
(356)

If thou didst ever hold me in thy heart,

Absent free from felicity a while,

And in this harsh world would draw thy breath in
pain
To tell my story.
What warlike noise is this?
Osric. <u>Young Fortinbras, with conquest comes from
Poland,</u> (361)
To the ambassadors of England gives
This warlike volley.
Hamlet. Oh, I die, Horatio,
The potent poison quite o' ercrows my spirit.
<u>But I do prophesy the election lights
On Fortinbras. He has my dying voice.</u> (367)
So tell him, with the occurrents, more or less,
Which have solicited. The rest is silence. (Hamlet
dies.)
Horatio. <u>Now cracks a noble heart. Good night,
sweet Prince,
And flights of angels sing thee to thy rest!</u> (371)
Hamlet, 5.2, 319-371

(WE wonder who yells, 'Treason! Treason!' (334) *All*
is in the script, but who is it. Whoever they are, they
don't take any action even when Hamlet, after
stabbing him, pours poisoned wine into Claudius'
mouth: 'Here, thou incestuous, murderous, damnèd
Dane, drink off this potion.' (336) In the same line
and the next, Hamlet adds mockingly, 'Is thy union

here? Follow my mother.' In other words, drink the poison you claimed was a precious pearl that killed my mother.

'Exchange forgiveness with me, noble Hamlet.' (340) Laertes says, the deaths are not on you and me.

It appears that Hamlet forgives the dead Laertes, but he does say that Heaven, or God, will: 'Heaven make thee free of it.' (343)

Then, he turns to Horatio: 'I am dead, Horatio. Wretched Queen, adieu!' (344) In Elizabethan speech, wretched meant many things. Here, it affectionately means sad and pitiable.

'Had I but time—as this fell sergeant, Death, is strict in his arrest' (348) means that the officer who represents death is going to act quickly, therefore, 'Report me and my cause aright to the unsatisfied.' (351) Please tell the truth about me to those who don't know what really happened at Elsinore.

Horatio tells Hamlet don't be so sure I'm going to be around to tell it, 'I am more an antique Roman than a Dane. Here's yet some liquor left.' (353) He grabs the goblet of poisoned wine and says, in effect, I'm one of those Roman soldiers, like Marc Antony, who, once the battle's lost, kill themselves.

The dying Hamlet has some spark left and wrests the cup away from Horatio, 'Give me the cup. Let go—by Heaven, I'll have 't.' (354) 'Things standing thus unknown, shall live behind me!' (356) No one knows the truth about what happened here, Horatio, and you need to live to tell it.

Osric interrupts the death scene with some necessary exposition, 'Young Fortinbras, with conquest comes from Poland,' (361)

Hamlet affirms his wishes for a successor as King of Denmark, 'I do prophesy the election lights on Fortinbras. He has my dying voice.' (367)

'Now cracks a noble heart. Good night, sweet Prince, and flights of angels sing thee to thy rest!' (371) Horatio speaks simple, pure poetry to his best friend. It is the finest eulogy in English literature.)

* * *

(Fortinbras, his military aides, and the English Ambassador enter.)

Fortinbras. This quarry cries on havoc. (375) O proud Death,
What feast is toward in thine eternal cell
That thou so many princes at a shot (376)
So bloodily hast struck?
Ambassador. The sight is dismal,
And our affairs from England come too late.
The ears are senseless that should give us hearing,

To tell him his commandment is fulfilled,
That Rosencrantz and Guildenstern are dead. (382)
Where should we have our thanks?
Horatio. Not from his mouth
Had it the ability of life to thank you.
He never gave commandment for their death. (385)
But since, so jump upon this bloody question,
You from the Polack wars, and you from England,
Are here arrives, give order that these bodies
High on a stage be placèd to the view,
And let me speak to the yet unknowing world
How these things came about. (391) So you shall
hear
Of carnal, bloody, and unnatural acts, (392)
Of accidental judgments, casual slaughters,
And deaths put on by cunning and forced cause,
(394)
And, in this upshot, purposes mistook
Fall'n on the inventors' heads. (396) All this can I
Truly deliver.
Fortinbras. Let us haste to hear it,
And call the noblest to the audience.
For me, with sorrow I embrace my fortune.
I have some rights of memory in this kingdom, (400)
Which now to claim my vantage doth invite me.
Horatio. Of that I shall also have cause to speak,

And from his mouth whose voice will draw on
more. (402)
But let this same be presently performed,
Even while man's minds are wild, let more
mischance
On plots and errors happen.
Fortinbras. Let four captains
Bear Hamlet, like a soldier, to the stage. (407)
For he was likely, had he be put on,
To have proved most royally. (409) And for his
passage
Speak loudly for him.
Take up the bodies. Such a sight as this
Becomes the field, (412) but here shows much amiss.
Go, bid the soldiers shoot.
Hamlet, 5.2, 375-413

(WHEN Fortinbras says, 'This quarry cries on havoc.'
(375) He means that that the number of dead bodies
suggests a massacre. He follows with 'so many princes
at a shot' (376) a curiously modern expression.

The visiting English ambassador announces 'That
Rosencrantz and Guildenstern are dead.' (382)
Hamlet's ruse worked. His rewritten letter to the King
of England doomed the former classmates who
turned against him. The utter banality of Rosencrantz
and Guildenstern made them more ominous.

174

The ambassador wonders who they can thank: Horatio tells him 'He never gave commandment for their death.' (385) He knows that Hamlet tricked Claudius and also the English, but he's not giving away his friend.

Horatio asks that the bodies be placed on a high stage, 'And let me speak to the yet unknowing world how these things came about.' (391)

Lines 392-396 sum up the play. The murder of old King Hamlet and the hasty marriage to his brother's widow: 'carnal, bloody, and unnatural acts,' (392) plus the accidental death of Ophelia; her father, Polonius, being in the wrong place at the wrong time; R & G's subterfuge backfiring on them; the final carnage at the fencing match. The lines, 'Of accidental judgments, casual slaughters, and deaths put on by cunning and forced cause,' (394) recap in stirring poetry the remaining elements of the tragedy.

Horatio ends with 'And, in this upshot, purposes mistook fall'n on the inventors' heads.' (396) In short, the creators of these misadventures have no one to blame but themselves.

Fortinbras, being the strongman he is, doesn't hesitate to fill Denmark's power vacuum. 'For me, with sorrow I embrace my fortune. I have some rights of memory in this kingdom,' (400) meaning that Old King Hamlet took land away from my father, and now

175

that young Hamlet's no longer alive I will reclaim it along with the Kingship of Denmark.

Horatio says that Hamlet agreed with Fortinbras' claim: 'And from his mouth whose voice will draw on more.' (402) But before I tell you about his affirmation of your succession, let's get the funeral ceremony underway before he have more mishaps.

'Let four captains bear Hamlet, like a soldier, to the stage.' (407) Fortinbras' memorable line deserves an echo. Especially with the big-hearted 'For he was likely, had he be put on, to have proved most royally.' (409) It takes a strong, confident person like Fortinbras, on the path to the takeover of a kingdom, to admit that if Hamlet had become King he would have made a good one.

'Such a sight as this becomes the field,' (412) is Fortinbras saying that the number of dead in the hall resembles a battlefield, echoing his observation in (375).

SUMMARY

Three dues ex machina arrive onstage on cue: The ghost of Hamlet's father; the traveling players; and Fortinbras. Each of these plot devices propels the play smartly toward its resolution.

William Shakespeare's universality, or his ability to write comfortably about all types of people operating in varied situations, leaves us shaking our heads in admiring wonder. And the protean character of Hamlet is his greatest dramatic creation.

Hamlet is arguably the best play ever written. It is seamless in structure, yet so full of double and hidden meanings that we read everything we want or need into it. It is the crowning achievement of Will's career.

Although, *I Henry IV* advocates present persuasive reasoning that their favorite, with its wide-ranging cast of characters, is the better play. That may be true, but Prince Hamlet alone is a cast of characters. Okay, you're right, Falstaff also fills the playbill.

Perhaps we can settle this by agreeing that Hamlet is Will's supreme tragic figure, and Falstaff his leading comedic formation.

And just as Falstaff needs his gang of miscreants and Prince Hal's misbehavior to position him in his milieu, Hamlet needs Horatio as a wise anchor and later the muscular Fortinbras to save the kingdom.

– – –

KING LEAR

Pivotal Speeches Critiqued

LEAR, King of prehistoric Britain, is about to abdicate and divide his kingdom. One-third each will go to the Dukes' Albany and Cornwall who are married to Lear's daughters, Goneril and Regan.

The final third goes to either the King of France or the Duke of Burgundy. Both vie for the hand of Cordelia, a younger daughter. Since women couldn't own property at the time, Lear's daughters are either married to, or will marry, the three prospective rulers. Sound complicated? This is only the beginning.

Other important characters include two Earls, Kent and Gloucester. The soon-to-be–banished Kent remains an ally of Lear and he turns up throughout the play.

Gloucester is a lecherous old man who has an older legitimate son, Edgar. Gloucester jiggled fortune's wheel by also begetting Edmund who has cause for bitterness, as he was illegitimate through no fault of his own. Since property goes to the older, legitimate son, Edmund has a grudge against Edgar.

The tragedies of Gloucester and Lear run parallel. Both are compelling. Lear's is made greater by his soaring language and the range of characters around him, in particular his three daughters.

King Lear is an epic story requiring careful study to better appreciate and understand the key speeches that are fundamental to the structure of the play. We'll work through it and gain rewarding insights along the way. Let's move right into the first critiqued passage.

(EDMUND listens in to his father's mean-spirited description of his illegitimacy. No wonder Edmund is bitter.)

Gloucester. Though this knave came saucily into the world before he was sent for, yet was his mother fair, there was good sport at his making, and the whorseon must be acknowledged. . . . (20)
He hath been out nine years, and away he shall again. (33) The king is coming.
King Lear, 1.1, 20-33

(THE first sentence (20) is a masterpiece of character definition. While Gloucester speaks of his bastard son, Edmund, he succeeds in defining himself as a different kind of bastard.

As he openly derides him in front of Kent, Gloucester shows no respect for Edmund. And since he is illegitimate and can't hold land, the only thing Edmund's fit for is being away, as he has been for nine years, 'and away he shall again.' (33) As we'll see, the clever and devious Edmund has different ideas.)

* * *

(AS said above, we have analog plots, so dexterously interwoven that they rise and fall together:

(1) Gloucester and his two sons, Edgar and Edmund.

(2) Lear and his three daughters: Goneril and Regan, the unprincipled ones are hard to tell apart, plus the impolitic but admirable Cordelia,

Lear has already decided to divide his kingdom.* Now, he formally announces it.

*Dividing Britain after her death was feared by the childless Elizabeth 1, the last of the Tudor rulers, who died in 1603. However, when James 1 of Scotland succeeded Elizabeth he united Scotland, England and Ireland. King Lear was performed about three years later. Shakespeare's *Macbeth*, the next play we analyze, was written as a tribute to King James, who was a 47th cousin of Banquo.

Back to Lear: In review, the dukes Cornwall and Albany, married to Lear's daughters Regan and Goneril, are each heirs' apparent to one-third of the kingdom.

The sovereign heads of France and Burgundy* are also in attendance at Lear's court. They vie for the hand of Cordelia, Lear's youngest daughter and her third of royal property.

*In the middle ages, Burgundy, now southern France, was about the same size as France to the north.

The three princesses listen to their father talk of their dowries. Reminder: since women could not own property at that time, the possessions go to their husbands.)

Lear. Give me the map there. Know that we have divided
In three our kingdom. And 'tis our fast intent
To shake all cares and business from our age,
Conferring on them younger strengths while we
Unburdened crawl toward death. (42) Our son of Cornwall,
And you, our no less loving son of Albany,
We have this hour a constant will to publish

Our daughters several dowers, that future strife
May be prevented now. The Princes, France and
Burgundy,
Great rivals in our youngest daughter's love,
Long in our court have made their amorous sojurn,
(48)
And here are to be answered. Tell me, my daughters,
Since now we will divest us both of rule,
Interest of territory, cares of state,
Which of you shall we say doth love us most? (52)
That we our largest bounty may extend
Where nature doth with merit challenge. Goneril,
Our eldest-born, speak first.
Goneril. Sir, I love you more than words can wield the
matter,
Dearer than eyesight, space, and liberty,
Beyond what can be valued, rich or rare,
No less than life, with grace, health, beauty, honor,
As much as child e'er loved or father found
A love that makes breath poor and speech unable (61)
Beyond all manner of so much I love you.
Cordelia. (Aside.) What shall Cordelia do? Love and be
silent. (62)
Lear. Of all these bounds, even from this line to this,
With shadowy forests and with champaigns riched.
With plenteous rivers and wide-skirted meads,
We make thee lady. To thine and Albany's issue

Be this perpetual. What says our second daughter,
Our dearest Regan, wife to Cornwall? Speak.
Regan. I am made of that self-metal as my sister,
And prize me at her worth. In my true heart
I find she names my very deed of love,
Only she comes too short. That I profess
Myself <u>an enemy to all other joys</u> (75)
Which the most precious square of sense professes,
And find I am alone felicitate
In your dear Highness' love.
Cordelia. (Aside.) Then poor Cordelia!
And yet not so, since I am sure my love's
<u>More ponderous than my tongue.</u> (79)
Lear. To thee and thine hereditary ever
Remain this ample third of our fair kingdom,
No less in space, validity and pleasure
Than that conferred on Goneril. Now, our joy,
Although the last, not least, to whose young love
The vines of France and milk of Burgundy
Strive to be interested, what can you say to draw
<u>A third more opulent that your sisters?</u> (87) Speak.
Cordelia. Nothing, my lord.
Lear. <u>Nothing will come of nothing.</u> . . . (92)
Mend your speech a little,
Lest it mar your fortunes. . . .
Let it be so. Thy truth then be thy dower.
For, by the sacred radiance of the sun,

The mysteries of Hecate, (112) and the night,
By all the operation of the orbs (113)
For whom we do exist and cease to be,
Here I disclaim all my paternal care,
Propinquity and property of blood, (116)
And as a stranger to my heart and me
Hold thee from this forever. The barbarous Scythian,
(118)
Or he that makes his generation messes
To gorge his appetite shall to my bosom
Be as well neighbored, pitied, and relieved
As thou my sometime daughter. (122)
King Lear, 1.1, 38-296

(IN line five of his first speech, Lear makes clear that he expects to die soon, wants to break up his kingdom, and in stark language, 'Unburdened crawl toward death.' (42)

I like the wording in Lear's mention of how the princes of France and Burgundy 'have made their amorous sojurn' (48) to compete for Cordelia's hand. We immediately pick up that it's likely that both princes are more interested in Cordelia's land than they are in her hand. Look for a twist on this conjecture.

Lear is typical of the quick-tempered, hard to stomach, autocratic renaissance father we also see in

Romeo and Juliet and *Cymbeline*. Well into his first speech of this passage, Lear describes the division of the kingdom among the daughters, but first he demands declarations of unconditional love as a kind of competition, 'Which of you shall we say doth love us most?' (52) Note the use of the royal 'us' and 'we.'

Lear's request is utter folly and silly, but it is crucial to the play and precipitates the breakdown of him and his kingdom.

Near the end of Goneril's hypocritical paean, she goes to the roof with, 'A love that makes breath poor and speech unable.' (61)

Cordelia, who is nothing if not straightforward, wants nothing to do with this claptrap, and says in an aside, 'Love and be silent.' (62)

Regan tries to outdo Goneril's bunk by saying that her love of her father is so great that she is 'an enemy to all other joys. (75)

Cordelia remains conflicted by all this absurdity, understands that love is complicated and 'More ponderous than my tongue.' (81) Lear teases her out, and as his favorite, he tempts her with a more choice piece of Britain than he plans for her sisters, 'A third more opulent that your sisters?' (87) When asked to speak, she has nothing to say to which Lear responds, 'Nothing will come of nothing,' (92) an ominous statement that turns up throughout the play. Here it means that if Cordelia can't kiss up to her father and tell him how wonderful he is, he's giving her nothing in return. Specifically, she's not getting one-third of the kingdom.

It's not shown in the dialogue above, but Cordelia, in her honesty, tells her father that 'when I shall wed' (103 she would need to share 'Half my love with him.' (104) This isn't welcome news for the egomaniacal Lear, especially following the sycophantic drivel from Goneril and Regan. It also suggests that Cordelia will never make a good politician.

In his rejection speech to Cordelia, Lear mentions, 'The mysteries of Hecate,' (112) and 'the operation of the orbs. (113) He believes that Cordelia's actions are unduly influenced by Hecate, a Greek goddess, who is chiefly known for her witchcraft, and the 'orbs' or stars that decide the fates.

Lear promptly disowns Cordelia, including 'Propinquity and property of blood,' (116) meaning she is no longer part of the family and gets no property to boot. He even compares 'thou my sometime daughter' (122) to a savage Russian, or 'Scythian.' (118)

Kent attempts to intercede, and is banished by Lear for his trouble: 'Come not between the dragon and his wrath.' (124) Lear's ostracizing of Kent is focal to the play.

Later in the passage, Cordelia tells her father 'If for I want that glib and oily art, to speak and purpose not,' (228) or she's sorry she can't say things she doesn't mean.

She adds, 'But even for want of that for which I am richer,' (233) or actions should come before words.

As it turns out, through lengthy back and forth, Burgundy is less admirable than France and only wants Cordelia's dowry. France takes her penniless, 'She is herself a dowry,' (243) and later invades Britain to restore her.

Goneril and Regan know they have made out well, but are still wary given the sudden banishments of Cordelia, 'He always loved our sister most,' (294) and then Kent's ejection. They've long known of their father's fierce temper, but the recent sudden outbursts, 'Tis the infirmity of his age,' (296) against long-time favorites has them thinking defensively.)

* * *

(AS scene two opens, Gloucester's bastard son and our emerging evildoer, cries out that life is unfair. In Elizabethan terms, he is a heretic who doesn't believe in the stars.

Edmund soliloquizes, speaking the truth as he understands it.)

187

Edmund. Thou, Nature, art my goddess, to thy law (1)
My services are bound. Wherefore should I
Stand in the plague of custom, and permit
The curiosity of nations to deprive me,
For that I am some twelve or fourteen moonshines
(5)
Lag of a brother? Why bastard? Wherefore base?
When my dimensions are as well compact,
My mind as generous and my shape as true,
As honest madam's issue? (9) Why brand they us
With base? With baseness? Bastardy? Base, base?
Who in the lusty stealth of nature take (11)
More composition and fierce quality
That doth, within a dull, stale, tired bed
Go to the creating a whole tribe of fops
Got 'tween asleep and wake? Well, then,
Legitimate Edgar, I must have your land. (16)
Our father's love is to the bastard Edmund
As to the legitimate—fine word, "legitimate!"
Well, my legitimate, if this letter speed
And my invention thrive, Edmund the base
Shall top the legitimate. (21) I grow, I prosper,
Now, gods, stand up for bastards. (22)
King Lear, 1.2, 1-22

In line one of scene two, 'Thou, Nature, art my goddess, to thy law,' (1) Edmund enlists 'Nature' as chaos, meaning that as a non-believer in the stars he has the right to do as he pleases. He also chooses 'law' at the end of the line. In Edmund's terms, law is actually lawlessness.

This is nature red in tooth and claw. Will didn't like this. He believed in order and good government.

Generally, Elizabethans accepted that

(1) God decides individual fates.

(2) Fortune executes fates.

(3) Stars carry out fates.

And, if an individual, like Edmund, doesn't believe these tenets, he is a heretic.

Most pleasing is, 'I am some twelve or fourteen moonshines' (5) younger than my brother. I liked the twelve or 'fourteen', rather than twelve or thirteen. This conveys that Edmund is not overburdened with particularity; he has bigger things in mind. It also argues that he should not be discriminated against just because his brother is a year older.

Edmund goes on to complain that even though he is a bastard and called base, his mind and his 'compact,' or well put together body are just as good 'As honest madam's issue.' (9) This, of course, refers to Gloucester's wife and Edgar, his older brother's mother.

189

'Who in the lusty stealth of nature take' (11) is Edmund comparing his father to an animal in heat.

Then Edmund comes to the point that it's all well and good that his brother Edgar is legitimate, and he's not. The problem is that Edgar gets his father's land, and he doesn't. To counter that dismal reality, Edmund creates his own: 'Legitimate Edgar, I must have your land.' (16) Watch out, Edgar, villains like your brother always make their perfidy known to the audience.

Moreover, 'base' Edmund has a scheme, and if it works he 'Shall top the legitimate.' (21)

Will gave actors playing Edmund an audience-pleasing closing line, 'Now, gods, stand up for bastards.'* (22)

*The Bastard Faulconbridge in Will's play *King John* is illegitimate with a different point of view. He is proud of his heritage. His mother confesses to sleeping with Richard the Lion-Hearted. Since he doesn't respect the man married to his mother, the man he thought was his father, Faulconbridge is delighted with the news. Will also made Faulconbridge a regular guy, a brave fighter and a gifted poet, with a penchant for amusing argot, like:

Zounds! I was never more bethumped with words
Since I first called my brother's father dad.

* * *

(GLOUCESTER, Edmund's father, enters scene two of act one confused by recent developments and complaining.

Edmund produces a letter ostensibly written by his older brother that tells of Edgar's plans to take over his father's estate. Gloucester falls for it.

The following passage includes prose and poetry. First the poetry.)

Gloucester. Kent banished thus! And France in choler parted!
And the king gone tonight! Subscribed! His power! (24)
Confined to exhibition! All this done
Upon the gad! Edmund, how now! What news? (26)

(Many lines later, Edmund lies about Edgar's intentions.)

Edmund. I have heard him oft maintain it to be fit that, sons of perfect age and fathers declining, the father should be as ward to the son, and the son manage his revenue. (78)

Gloucester. Oh, villain, villain! Unnatural, detested, brutish villain! Worse than brutish! Go, sirrah, seek him, aye, apprehend him! Abominable villain! Where is he? . . .

These late eclipses in the sun and moon portend no good to us. (112) Though the wisdom of nature can reason it thus and thus, (113) yet nature finds itself scourged by the sequent effects. Love cools, friendship falls off, brothers divide. In cities, mutinies; in countries, discord; in palaces, treason; and the bond cracked 'twixt son and father. This villain of mine comes under the prediction, there's son against father. The King falls from bias of nature, there's father against child. We have seen the best of our time. (121) Machinations, hollowness, treachery, and all ruinous disorders follow us disquietly to our graves. (122) Find out this villain, Edmund, it shall lose thee nothing. Do it carefully. And the noble and true-hearted Kent banished! His offense, honesty! 'Tis strange. (Exits.)

Edmund. (Soliloquy.) This the excellent foppery of the world, that when we are sick in fortune—often the surfeit of our own behavior—we make guilty of our disasters the sun, the moon, and the stars, as if we were villains by necessity, (132) fools by heavenly

192

compulsion' knaves, thieves, and treachers by spiritual predominance; drunkards, liars, <u>and adulterers by an enforced obedience of planetary influence</u>; (135) and all that we are evil in, by a divine thrusting on—an admirable evasion of whoremaster man to lay his goatish disposition to the charge of a star! My father compounded with my mother under the dragon's tail, and my nativity was under Ursa Major, so that it follows that I am rough and lecherous. Tut, I should have been that I am the maidenliest star in the firmament twinkled on my bastardizing. Edgar—<u>and pat he comes like the catastrophe of the old comedy.</u> (145) My cue is villainous melancholy, with a sigh like Tom o' Bedlam Oh, these eclipses do portend these divisions! Fa, sol, la, mi.

Edgar. <u>Some villain hath done me wrong.</u> (180)

Edmund. (Later aside.) I do serve you in this business. <u>A credulous father, and a brother noble,</u> (195)
Whose nature is so far from doing harms
That he suspects none, on whose foolish honesty
<u>My practices ride easy. I see the business.</u> (198)
Let, me, if not by birth, have lands by wit.
All with me's meet that I can fashion fit.

 King Lear, 1.2, 1-200

(Gloucester, Edmund's father, rants about Lear's recent actions: 'And the king gone tonight!

Subscribed! His power! (24) confined to exhibition!' This means that Lear has given away his power and is now dependent.

And all this done, 'Upon the gad! Edmund, how now! What news?' (26) I liked the 'Upon the gad!' This is Gloucester's continued complaining about Lear taking action and making changes off the top of his head that end up badly. Beyond that, he wants more news, and Edgar gives him a heavy dose.

And here we commence analyzing the prose portion of the exchange.

Taking advantage of his father being all heated up, Edmund tells him of Edgar's forged letter that describes how 'the father should be as ward to the son, and the son manage his revenue.' (78)

Gloucester, who is hot-tempered and credulous, calls Edgar a villain among other choice terms.

Later in the scene, he says, 'These late eclipses in the sun and moon portend no good to us.' (112) This line tells us that Gloucester, unlike the heretical Edmund, is orthodox and believes in the stars. Gloucester goes on to say, 'Though the wisdom of nature can reason it thus and thus,' (113) meaning that although there is a rational explanation he's not willing to accept that eclipses occur normally. There must be some supernatural underlying cause for all the calamities we face. Gloucester ties all this to Edgar by turning more against him and deciding that 'We have seen the best of our time.' (121)

Unlike the poetical Lear, Gloucester's language is typically more pedestrian. But here, he aggregates his enumeration of hopelessness in prose poetry: 'Machinations, hollowness, treachery, and all ruinous disorders follow us disquietly to our graves.' (122)

Gloucester exits, and in soliloquy the cynical and disbelieving Edmund says we are fools to blame the stars for our own follies, 'as if we were villains by necessity,' (132) 'and adulterers by an enforced obedience of planetary influence.' (135)

Edgar enters, and cynical Edmund speaks the line of the night, 'and pat he comes like the catastrophe of the old comedy.' (145) Even though in Jacobean days 'catastrophe' means last act, the phrase gets an eruption of laughter from modern audiences, because it can also allude to someone's rear end.

When the unworldly and unfortunate Edgar utters 'Some villain hath done me wrong' (180) to his sly brother, I immediately thought of innocent-acting Gloucester, Richard *III* to be, commiserating with his brother Clarence who wonders why he is being sent to the Bloody Tower. After Clarence departs to his doom, Gloucester says:

'Simple, plain Clarence! I do love thee so

That I will shortly send thy soul to heaven.'
Richard III, 1.1

Also, Edgar's 'hath done me wrong' almost simultaneously reminds me of the lyrics from *Frankie and Johnnie*, 'He was my man, but he done me wrong.'

In the scene-two closing soliloquy, Edmund, the consummate cynic, gives us two crafty lines: 'A credulous father, and a brother noble.' (195) The remainder of the play bears out Edmund's characterizations of his father and brother.

Read again the facile line, 'My practices ride easy. I see the business.' (198) Said differently and less stylishly, Edmund is saying I'll win because my father is gullible and my brother is too honest for his own good.)

* * *

(GONERIL, Lear's repellent daughter, complains about her father's behavior to her aide, Oswald.

The scene takes place in the palace of Goneril's husband, the Duke of Albany.)

Goneril. Did my father strike my gentleman for chiding of his fool? . . .
By day and night he wrongs me. Every hour

<u>He flashes into one gross crime or other</u> (3)
That sets us all at odds. I'll not endure it.
His knights grow riotous, and himself upbraids us
On every trifle. When he returns from hunting,
I will not speak with him. . . .
<u>Idle old man</u>, (16)
That <u>would still manage those authorities</u> (17)
That he hath given away! Now, by my life,
Old fools are babes again, and must be used
<u>With checks as flatteries</u> (19) when they are seen
abused.
King Lear, 1.3, 1-26

(THE verb 'flashes' is descriptive and well-placed in line three to describe Lear's erratic behavior: 'He flashes into one gross crime or other.' (3)

Goneril calls her father an 'Idle old man,' (16) who 'would still manage those authorities' (17) he gave up. Who does my father think he is, she says, he's no longer King, but thinks he has the same rights.

'With checks as flatteries' (19) at the close of her speech, the disloyal Goneril says that she isn't about to baby or flatter 'Old fools' who act like babies, and she will punish her father when he misbehaves.

Goneril is fed up with Lear and plans to boot him out, but first she writes to her equally-objectionable sister Regan for support 'To hold my very course.' (26)

* * *

(KENT, banished by Lear, is one of the more enduring characters in the play. He shows up disguised in Albany's palace having altered his speech and 'razed my likeness,' (4) meaning that he's shaved his beard off.

Lear asks Kent questions, is taken in by his disguise, and hires him as an aide.)

Kent. I do profess to be no less than I seem—to serve him truly that will put me in trust, to love him that is honest, to converse with him that is wise and says little, to <u>fear judgment</u>, (17) to fight when I cannot choose, and <u>to eat no fish</u>. . . . (18)
I can keep honest counsel, ride, run, <u>mar a curious tale in telling it</u>, (34) and <u>deliver a plain message bluntly.</u> (35) That which ordinary men are fit for, I am qualified in, and the best of me is diligence.
King Lear, 1.4, 14-37

(KENT is a good salesman and would be convincing in a modern job interview, saying what the prospective employer wants to hear. For example, he does 'fear judgment,' (17) or judgment day, and therefore believes in God.

He lets the Protestant boss know that he will 'eat no fish,' (18) and consequently is not Catholic.

He also professes to be a straight talker, and not one to 'mar a curious tale in telling it,' (34) by speaking fancifully like the hangers-on at court. Accordingly, he will 'deliver a plain message bluntly.' (35)

Undoubtedly, Lear asks Kent, when can you start?)

* * *

(A KNIGHT, one of many in the King's train, enters to tell Lear that he is not being treated with respect.)

Knight. My lord, I know not what the matter is, but, to my judgment, your Highness is not <u>entertained with that ceremonious affection as you were wont.</u> (62) <u>There's a great abatement of kindness</u> (65) as well in the general dependents as in <u>the Duke himself</u> (66) I beseech you pardon me, my lord, if I be mistaken, for my duty cannot be silent when I think your Highness wronged.

Lear. Thou but rememberest me of mine own conception. <u>I have perceived a faint neglect of late,</u> (73) which I have rather blamed as mine own jealous

curiosity than as a very pretense and purpose of unkindness.
King Lear, 1.4, 61-76

(WHEN the knight says that Lear is not being 'entertained with that ceremonious affection as you were wont,' (62) he's acknowledging that although Lear gave up the responsibilities of office, he wants and deserves the pomp and circumstance of royalty.

The knight also wants Lear to have the respect of his daughter, 'There's a great abatement of kindness.' (65)

The knight goes on to include 'the Duke himself.' (66) However, at this point in the play Albany doesn't know that his wife, Goneril, is planning to oust her father from the palace. As we'll learn, Albany is not a louse like Cornwall, Regan's husband.

Lear answers the knight with, 'I have perceived a faint neglect of late,' (73) Given Goneril's attitude toward him, that's putting it mildly.

Following that exchange, Oswald, Goneril's servant, arrives in the wrong place at the wrong time for his second rebuke. In lieu of berating Goneril, Lear cuffs Oswald and Kent trips him, 'you base* football player,' (95) This action seals the deal for Kent, as Lear gives him money, "There's earnest of thy service.' (105)

*An obvious anachronism. However, near the turn of the 17th-Century football players were held in low esteem.

The audience, especially the groundlings, delights in seeing the supercilious Oswald knocked about.)

* * *

(LEAR'S Fool is the savviest and gutsiest court jester created by Will. That said, Lear's clever, unnamed Fool has estimable competitors, like Touchstone in *As You Like It* and Feste in *Twelfth Night*.

King Lear's imaginative Fool knows how to insult without getting punished. Many jesters go too far and pay the price.*

*'This is a practice as full of labor as a wise man's art.' Viola, *Twelfth Night*, 3.1.

All the keen banter of the Fool and Lear isn't shown here, but it's worth reading in its entirety.)

Some samples follow: But first, the Fool sees Lear giving Kent money and offers Kent his fool's cap, or coxcomb, 'you were best take my coxcomb.' (109) Kent asks 'Why, fool?' (110) The Fool replies in daring language to both Kent and Lear.)

Fool. Why, <u>for taking one's part that's out of favor.</u> (111) Nay, an thou canst not smile as the wind sits, thou'lt catch cold shortly. There, take my coxcomb. Why, this fellow hath banished two on 's daughters, and done the third a blessing against his will. If thou follow him, thou must needs wear my coxcomb. (115) 'How now, Nuncle! Would I had two coxcombs and two daughters. . . .

If I gave them all my living, I'd keep my coxcombs myself. There's mine, beg another of thy daughters. (122)

Lear. Take heed, sirrah, the whip. (128)

Fool. Sirrah, I'll teach thee a speech. . . .

Mark it, Nuncle:

Have more than thou showest,

Speak less than thou knowest,

Lend less than thou owest,

Ride more than though goest,

Learn more than thou trowest,

Set less than thou throwest. (136)

Leave thy drink and thy whore

And keep in-a-door,

And thou shalt have more

Than two tens to a score. (140)

Kent. This is nothing, fool. (141)

Fool. Then 'tis like the breath of an unfee'd lawyer. (142) You gave me nothing for 't. Can you make no use of nothing, Nuncle?

Lear. Why, no, boy, <u>nothing can be made out of</u> <u>nothing</u>. (145)

Fool. Dost thou know the difference, <u>my boy,</u> (151) between a bitter fool and a sweet

fool? . . .

That lord that counseled thee

To give away thy land,

Come place him here by me,

Do thou for him stand.

<u>The sweet and bitter fool</u> (158)

Will presently appear—

The one in motley here,

The other found out there.

Lear. Dost thou call me fool, boy?

Fool. <u>All thy other titles thou hast given away. That</u> <u>thou wast born with.</u> . . . (163)

When thou clovest thy crown i' the middle and gavest away both parts, thou borest thine ass on thy back o'er the dirt. <u>Thou hadst little wit in thy bald crown when</u> <u>thou gavest the golden one away.</u> (176) If I speak like myself in this, let him be whipped that finds it so. . . . I have used it, Nuncle, ever since <u>thou madest thy</u> <u>daughters thy mother. For when thou gavest them the</u> <u>rod and puttest down thine own breeches.</u> . . . (187)

I marvel what kin thou and thy daughters are. They'll have me whipped for speaking true, thou'lt have me whipped for lying, and sometimes I am whipped for

holding my peace. I had rather be any kind o' thing than a fool. And yet <u>I would not be thee, Nuncle.</u> (203) <u>Thou hast pared thy wit o' both sides and left nothing i' the middle.</u> (204) Here comes one o' the pairings.
King Lear, 1.4, 105-206

(MOST Elizabethan characters only speak the truth in soliloquy. Fools speak it in company. The badinage is amusing. It also serves as exposition just in case the audience misses the enormity of Lear's mistakes.

Opening the passage, the Fool immediately recognizes Kent in disguise and brazenly calls him a fool in front of Lear 'for taking one's part that's out of favor,' (111) or getting ostracized for sticking up for Cordelia when she is banished by her father.

Then the Fool describes Lear's mistakes with his daughters and tells Kent, 'If thou follow him, thou must needs wear my coxcomb. (115) In other words, if you're stupid enough to follow Lear after what he's done to you should be wearing my jester's cap.

He even has the effrontery to mock Lear and offer the cap to him, 'There's mine, beg another of thy daughters.' (122) to which Lear warns the fool with, 'Take heed, sirrah, the whip.' (128)

In line five of his comical speech to Lear, the Fool tells him, 'Set less than thou throwest,' (136) or don't wager more than you can risk losing—a poke in the ribs to Lear who has given up his kingdom and exiled his favorite daughter.

Then the unabashed Fool ties gambling to drinking and whoring and tells Lear that if he follows the advice he'll make a profit, or more 'Than two tens to a score.' (140)

Kent doesn't like the Fool's insinuations against his new boss: 'This is nothing, fool.' (141)

The Fool's, 'Then 'tis like the breath of an unfee'd lawyer,' (6) sets up the next 'nothing' line. He's saying that the words of a lawyer who isn't getting paid aren't worth much.

In response to a prod from the Fool, Lear repeats a line he uses earlier with Cordelia: 'nothing can be made out of nothing.' (145)

And then, the Fool dares to refer to Lear as 'my boy.' (151) This insult after he's already called him 'Sirrah,' or boy, back in line (128).

Next, in another rhyme, the Fool calls Lear, 'The sweet and bitter fool,' (158) implying that Lear is more the 'bitter fool.'

The abuse piles on as Lear asks if he is being called a fool. The Fool comes right back with the cutting, 'thy other titles thou hast given away. (163) That thou wast born with.'

To make sure that Lear is spared nothing, The Fool tells him that breaking up his crown makes him like the proverbial idiot who carries his own donkey on his back. And as punctuation, 'Thou hadst little wit in thy bald crown when thou gavest the golden one away.' (176)

Perhaps the Fool's best dig is, 'thou madest thy daughters thy mother. For when thou gavest them the rod and puttest down thine own breeches. . . .' (187) The Fool tells Lear he's an old fool who is now the child to his own children and asks to be beaten.

As said above, these lines also serve as exposition within the Fool's dialogue. Will wants to make certain that the less-acute audience members know exactly how impetuous Lear has been. Further, they delight in having the Fool tell off the boss and not get punished for it.

Lear challenges him, and the Fool piles on by saying he'd rather be anything but a fool, except, 'I would not be thee, Nuncle.' (203)

In the final confirmation of his mistakes, and to bait him with the 'nothing' word Lear likes to use, the Fool tells Lear that he's given up his crown to the two bad daughters 'and left nothing i' the middle,' (204) for himself or the wrongly exiled Cordelia.

That Lear takes the vitriol stretches credulity. Despite his spoken resentment, Lear realizes that it's all true, and in order to move forward he needs to hear it. However, Lear's motivations and reactions are debatable.

The Fool's role as instigator takes a master actor able to say hard things and through costume, body language, grins and tone make his getting away with it without penalty believable.

We've highlighted and interpreted selected lines in the preceding passage. Beyond this framework and for full appreciation of Will's brilliant dialogue, go back and read it whole.)

* * *

(GONERIL enters frowning prompting Lear to comment on it: 'Methinks you are too much of late i' the frown.' (208)

The Fool jumps in to again remind Lear that he is now nothing.

Goneril repeats her earlier exaggerated accusations that Lear and his retinue of knights and other hangers-on are causing problems. They go back and forth leading to a legendary Lear line.)

Fool. Thou wast a pretty fellow when thou hadst no need to care for her frowning. <u>Now thou art an O</u>

without a figure. (213) I am better than thou art now.
I am a fool, thou art nothing.

Goneril. Not only, sir, this your all-licensed fool (220)
But other of your insolent retinue (221)
Do hourly carp and quarrel, breaking forth
In rank and not to be endurèd riots.

Fool. For, you know, Nuncle,
The hedge sparrow fed the cuckoo so long
That it had it head bit off by it young. (236)
So out went the candle, and we were left darkling.
(237)

Goneril. Here do you keep a hundred knights and
squires,
Men so disordered, so deboshed, and bold,
That this our court, infected with their manners,
Shows like a riotous inn. Epicurism and lust
Make it more like a tavern or brothel (266)
Than a graced palace.

Lear. Darkness and devils! (273)
Saddle my horses, call my train together.
Degenerate bastard! I'll not trouble thee.
Yet have I left a daughter. . . . (276)
How ugly didst thou in Cordelia show!
That, like an engine, wrenched my frame of nature
(290)
From the fixed place, drew from my heart all love
And added to the gall. O Lear, Lear, Lear!

Beat at this gate that let thy folly in (293)
And thy dear judgment out! . . . (294)
Hear, Nature, hear, dear goddess, hear! (297)
Suspend thy purpose (298) if thou didst intend
To make this creature fruitful.
Into her womb convey sterility.
Dry up in her the organs of increase, (301)
And from her derogate body never spring
A babe to honor her! If she must teem,
Create her child of spleen, that it may live
And be a thwart denatured torment to her.
Let it stamp wrinkles in her brow of youth.
With cadent tears fret channels in her cheeks,
Turn all her mother's pains and benefits
To laughter and contempt, that she may feel
How sharper than a serpent's tooth it is (310)
To have a thankless child! . . .
Yet have I left a daughter (327)
Who I am sure is kind and comfortable. (328)
When she shall hear this of thee, with her nails
She'll flay thy wolvish visage. (330) Thou shalt find
That I'll resume the shape which thou dost think
I have cast off forever. Thou shalt, I warrant thee.
King Lear, 1.4, 208-332

(THE fool tells Lear, 'Now thou art an O without a
figure,' (213) or that he is a zero.

209

In line one of her next speech, Goneril mentions 'your all-licensed fool,' (220) or a fool who can get away with anything. Just like 'other of your insolent retinue.' (221) She continues to lie about the actions of Lear's aides. If she is truth-telling, it would be said in soliloquy.

Nice comparison to Goneril, as the Fool speaks of the sparrow getting its 'head bit off by young,' (236) meaning that the sparrow's been feeding young cuckoos, and in return for the favor they bite the sparrow's head off. The Fool completes the putdown by reminding Lear that when his daughters figuratively bit his head off the candle went out, and we were 'left darkling,' (237) or in the dark.

To finally drive her father out, Goneril adds more lies saying that Lear's men are making her palace, 'more like a tavern or brothel.' (266) This is the final insult Lear will take from Goneril, and we hear his 'Darkness and devils!' (273) a fitting pagan oath.

Several lines later, and not shown above, we have 'That, like an engine, wrenched my frame of nature' (290) indicates that Lear feels that Goneril has put him on the rack. In Elizabethan times and later, many mechanical devices are called engines.

And then we have, 'Beat at this gate that let thy folly in.' (293) The actor playing Lear smacks himself on the head. Adding to that: 'And thy dear judgment out'!

(294) It's a sane thing for Lear to say. He is mad at himself for giving up his crown.

'Hear, Nature, hear, dear goddess, hear!' (297) Lear pleads with the goddess of affection to 'Suspend thy purpose' (298) in making Goneril able to bear children: 'Dry up in her the organs of increase.' (301) Talk about angry old men.

Following other select lines that call for rereading, we have the unfading:

'How sharper than a serpent's tooth it is
To have a thankless child!' (310)

'Yet have I left a daughter,' (327) meaning Regan who he is off to visit. Still hopeful, Lear adds that he is sure she is 'kind and comfortable.' (328) We'll see how that works out, especially in light of a letter Goneril sent to her sister. I doubt it was packed with love and affection for daddy.

Lear believes that when Reagan hears the news of Goneril's bad behavior 'She'll flay thy wolvish visage.' (330) Now there's a line sprouting with images.)

* * *

(IN the brief scene five, Kent departs with a letter   .
Lear has written to Regan. Next, the Fool continues
to berate Lear who cries for help.)

Fool. If thou wert my fool, Nuncle, I'd have thee
beaten for being old before thy time. (45)
Thou shouldst not have been <u>old till thou hadst been
wise</u>.* (46)

*A variation is 'Too soon old too late smart,' an old
Dutch proverb. I wonder if it predated Will. In my
novel *Discovering Will's Lost Years*, I wrote scenes with
Will in the Netherlands as a scribe with the English
Army.

Lear. Oh, let me not be mad, not mad, sweet Heaven!
<u>Keep me in temper</u>. (49) I would not be mad.
King Lear, 1.4, 45-49

(THE Fool nails Lear's mistakes again by telling him
that not only did he grow old before he was ready,
(45) he shouldn't have grown 'old till thou hadst been
wise.' (46) The Fool is telling Lear that he's a
blockhead who should be beaten for being old and
stupid. In modern vernacular, the Fool constantly
reminds Lear that he's screwed-up royally.
Recognizing his own errors compounded by the

mirror the Fool keeps shoving in his face is driving Lear over the edge.

In saying 'Keep me in temper,' (49) or don't let me go mad, Lear pleads that his four bodily humors–Sanguine, Phlegmatic, Melancholy, Choleric–be kept proportionate.)

* * *

(THE following night, in scene one of act three, Edmund is in his father's castle. Edgar enters, they fake a fight, Edgar leaves, Edmund wounds himself, his father Gloucester enters, and Edmund blames his brother for the wound. 'Look sir, I bleed.' (42)

Gloucester is again persuaded of Edgar's treachery, 'Strong and fastened villain!' (79) 'Would he deny his letter? (80) Edmund now has two pieces of fake evidence against Edgar: the letter and the wound.

Cornwall and Regan join the scene. Like Lear, Gloucester complains about the ingratitude of children, in his case Edgar: 'Oh, madam, my old heart is cracked, is cracked!' (91)

Edmund confirms to Regan that Edgar 'was of that consort,' (99) or a party to the riotous knights attending Lear.

Kent delivers Lear's letter to his daughter Regan. She is not touched. If her father's retinue of knights shows up, she will be out.

Regan. I have this present evening from my sister
Been well informed of them, and with such cautions
That if they come to sojurn at my house,
I'll not be there.
King Lear, 2.1, 42-106

POOR old Lear was planning to live with Goneril for a month and then Regan. Things are not looking up for him.)

* * *

(AS mentioned earlier, Kent, banished by Lear for supporting the disowned Cordelia, is a battler who keeps showing up.* Still in disguise, he meets outside Gloucester's castle with Oswald, Goneril's steward. You may recall that the two don't like each other. Earlier, Kent got money from Lear for tripping Oswald, who now asks Kent, 'What dost thou know me for?' (14)

*As Woody Allen famously said, '80 percent of success is showing up.'

214

Kent. A knave, a rascal, an <u>eater of broken meats</u>; (15) a base, proud, shallow, beggarly, three-suited, hundred-pound, filthy, worsted-stocking knave; a lily-livered, action-taking knave; a whoreson, glass-gazing, superserviceable, <u>finical rogue</u>; (19) one-trunk inheriting slave; one that wouldst be a bawd in way of good service, and art nothing but the composition of a knave, beggar, coward, pander, and the son and heir of a mongrel bitch—one whom <u>I will beat into clamorous whining if thou deniest the least syllable of thy addition</u>. . . . (26)
Such smiling rogues as these,
<u>Like rats, oft bite the holy cords a-twain</u> (80)
Which are too intrinse to unloose; smooth every passion
That in the natures of their lords rebel;
Bring oil to fire, snow to their colder moods;
Renege, affirm, and turn their halcyon beaks
With every gale and vary of their masters,
Knowing naught, like dogs, but following.
A plague upon your epilectic visage!
Smile you my speeches, as I were a fool?
Goose, if I had you upon Sarum plain,
<u>I'd drive ye cackling home to Camelot</u>. (90)
King Lear, 2.2, 14-157

(THE abuse Kent hurls at Oswald rivals Falstaff's and Hal's traded disparagements in the *Henry IV* plays. Clearly, Kent doesn't respect Oswald's type of snobbish servant, especially one who's working for Goneril who has just evicted her father, the disguised Kent's benefactor.

The entire harangue is amusing, and has the groundlings rolling about the pit. A favorite in line one: 'eater of broken meats.' (15) Kent says that Oswald eats leftovers discarded by his masters above.

Atypically, Will uses 'knave' four times in Kent's arsenal of insults directed at Oswald. I wonder why he did this rather than substituting such synonyms as rascal, villain and varlet.

I like the creativity behind the entire arsenal of insults: 'finical rogue' (19) is particularly good with its ridiculous image of a fussy scoundrel.

Kent even challenges Oswald to contradict one iota of the withering criticism and, 'I will beat into clamorous whining if thou deniest the least syllable of thy addition.' (26)

Oswald as the 'rogue' is attacked by Kent again, this time smiling as he breaks up marriages: 'Like rats, oft bite the holy cords a-twain.' (80) Marvelous.

The last line of Kent's invective, after he calls Oswald a goose, 'I'd drive ye cackling home to Camelot,' (90) is priceless, although I have no idea what it means. And I doubt that a toady like Oswald would be welcome at Camelot.

Cornwall attempts to halt Kent's polemic with, 'What is his fault?' (94) The straight line initiates Kent's farcical reply, 'His countenance likes me not,' (96) or, I don't like his looks.

After Cornwall asks Kent whether his face or others around him are not likable, the nothing if not straightforward Kent says, 'I have seen better faces in my time.' (99) It may be an impolitic answer, but you've got to admire Kent's guts.

Hearing Kent's insinuations, plus his loaded accusations against Oswald, Goneril's steward, Cornwall orders, 'Fetch forth the stocks!' (132)

Regan, always ready to make anybody in trouble more miserable, adds, 'Put in his legs.' (157)

* * *

(CORNWALL and Regan exit. Kent has a brief exchange with a commiserating Gloucester before he exits. Then Kent delivers a metaphor-rich soliloquy.)

Kent. Good king that must approve the common saw,
Thou out of Heaven's benediction comest
To the warm sun!
Approach, thou beacon to this underglobe, (170)

217

That by thy comfortable beams I may
Peruse this letter. Nothing almost sees miracles
But misery. I know 'tis from Cordelia,
Who hath most fortunately been informed
Of my obscurèd course, and shall find time
From this enormous state, seeking to give
Losses their remedies, <u>All weary and o'erwatched</u>,
(177)
Take vantage, heavy eyes, not to behold
<u>This shameful lodging</u>. (179)
Fortune, good night. Smile once more, <u>turn thy wheel!</u>
(180)
King Lear, 2.2, 167-180

(LINE three of Kent's soliloquy mentions the warm
sun, and next he urges, 'Approach thou beacon to this
underglobe.' (170) He wants the sun to rise faster so
he can read Cordelia's letter.

The first five lines are necessary rereading. They
signify Kent's appreciation of the miracle of sunrise.

Later, with 'All weary and o'erwatched, (177) Kent
says that he's stayed up too long.

Next, I see the actor first looking down at his legs
in the stocks, 'This shameful lodging,' (179) looking
at the audience with a smile or grin, and twirling an
arm like a roulette croupier cueing the final line below.

Kent's closing line restates the Elizabethan belief that everybody's fastened on Fortune's wheel, now up, now down. Kent says, I'm down now, so Fortune 'turn thy wheel! (180)

This comic, but arresting, interlude between Oswald and Kent stands up well by itself. Mostly, though, like the Fool's badgering of Lear, it's constructed by Will as audience-based relief between Lear's multiple misfortunes and the continuing cascade of tragic events.)

* * *

(Next, in the short scene three of act two, we return to the parallel plot of Gloucester, his sons Edmund and Edgar, and the adversities they encounter on the path to resolution.)

Edgar. I heard myself proclaimed,
And <u>by the happy hollow of a tree</u> (2)
Escaped the hunt. No port is free, no place,
That guard and most unusual vigilance
Does not attend my taking. Whiles I may 'scape
I will preserve myself, and am bethought
To take <u>the basest and poorest shape</u> (7)
That ever penury in contempt of man
Brought near to beast. <u>My face I'll grime with filth,</u> (9)

Blanket my loins, <u>elf all my hair in knots</u>, (10)
And with presented nakedness outface
The winds and persecutions of the sky.
The country gives me proof and precedent
Of <u>Bedlam beggars</u>, (13) who with roaring voices
Strike in their numbed and mortified bare arms
Pins, wooden pricks, nails, <u>sprigs of rosemary</u>, (16)
And with this horrible object, from low farms,
Poor pelting villages, sheepcotes and mills,
Sometime with lunatic bans, sometime with prayers,
Enforce their charity, Poor Turlygood! Poor Tom!
That's something yet. <u>Edgar I nothing am</u>. (21)
King Lear, 2.3, 2-21

(THANKS to Edmund's chicanery, Edgar, on the run from their father, Gloucester, hides in the forest, 'by the happy hollow of a tree escaped the hunt.' (2) Edgar feels lucky to have found a hiding place in a hollowed-out tree.

Like Kent, he adopts a disguise. In Edgar's case, it is of 'the basest and poorest shape . . .' (7)

How would you act this scene? Would you come out with a dirty face, 'My face I'll grime with filth,' (9) your hair tangled, 'elf all my hair in knots,' (10) and wearing a loincloth? Or would you perform the business while speaking the lines?

Will gives few stage directions. Subject to informal direction by modern standards, Elizabethan actors play their roles pretty much as they wish, although they do get specific hints through the dialogue.

Period audiences know about the threat of 'Bedlam beggars,' (13) people released from Bedlam Hospital for the insane in London roaming the countryside and begging.

Edgar talks of sticking pins and nails in his arms. Beggars did this to get 'sprigs of rosemary.' (16) Now there's a miming opportunity for actors.

With 'Edgar I nothing am,' (21) he's saying that he needs the disguise to save his life. Note again that the use of 'nothing' recurs throughout the play.

Not knowing every Elizabethan custom, we need to work through the language. Will's audiences instantly knew what Edgar was talking about and nudged each other.)

* * *

(LEAR and his Fool see Kent in stocks outside Gloucester's castle. The Fool loves this, 'Ha, ha! He wears cruel garters.' (7)

Later, Kent explains that when Oswald, Goneril's messenger, acted 'saucily against your Highness' (41) he pulled his sword to fight him, and, for his impertinence, they put him in stocks.

Lear is unwell, he hunted all day and had no supper. He rode all night and has had no breakfast.

Then he learns that Regan and Cornwall won't speak with him.

They finally come out, and Goneril joins them. Cornwall weakly protests to Regan of her father's plight, but he's under her thumb: the 'thankless' daughters want no part of their father and his train of knights. Lear is stricken.)

Lear. Oh, how <u>this mother</u> (56) swells up toward my heart!
<u>Hysterica passio</u>, (57) down, thou climbing sorrow,
Thy elements below! Where is this daughter? . . .
Bid them come forth and hear me,
Or at their chamber door I'll beat the drum
Till it cry sleep to death. . . .
<u>Oh, me, my heart, my rising heart!</u> (121) But down!
Regan. <u>Oh, sir, you are old,</u> (148)
Nature stands in you on the very verge
Of her confine. <u>You should be ruled and led</u> (150)
By some discretion that discerns your state
Better than you yourself. Therefore I pray you
That to our sister you do make return.
Say you have wronged her, sir.

Lear. Dear daughter, I confess that I am old,
Age is unnecessary. <u>On my knees I beg</u> (157)
That you'll vouchsafe me raiment, bed, and food.
Regan. <u>I pray you, Father, being weak, seem so.</u> (204)
Lear. <u>You Heavens, give me that patience, patience I
need!</u> (274)
You see me here, you gods, a poor old man,
As full of grief as age, wretched in both.
If it be you that stirs these daughters' hearts
Against their father, fool me not so much
To hear it tamely. Touch me with noble anger,
And let not women's weapons, water drops,
Stain my man's cheeks! No, you unnatural hags,
<u>I will have such revenges on you both</u> (282)
That all the world shall—I will do such things—
What they are, yet I know not, but they shall be
The terrors of the earth. You think I'll weep.
No, I'll not weep.
I have full cause of weeping, but this heart
Shall break into a hundred thousand flaws
Or ere I'll weep. <u>Oh fool, I shall go mad!</u> (289) (Exit.)
Gloucester. (Enters.) Alack, the night comes on, and <u>the
bleak winds
Do sorely ruffle.</u> (303) For many miles about
<u>There's scarce a bush.</u> (304)
Regan. Oh sir, to willful men
<u>The injuries that they themselves procure</u> (306)

Must be their schoolmasters. (307) Shut up your doors.
He is attended by a desperate train,
And what they may incense him to, being apt
To have his ear abused, wisdom bids fear.
King Lear, 2.4, 7-310

(IN lines one and two of Lear's first speech in this passage, he speaks of 'this mother' (56) and 'Hysterica passio.' (57) He is in torment. His heart wells up in pain, his breath is short, and he feels smothered. Lear is coming apart in mind and body.

At the close of the speech, Lear groans, 'Oh, me, my heart, my rising heart!' (121) His heart is in his throat. This is a scene in which an able actor generates audience sympathy through voice and body language.

Cornwall and Regan enter, and she offers her usual sympathy: 'Oh, sir, you are old.' (148) Regan adds that her father is on the borderline of being able to care for himself and 'You should be ruled and led.' (150)

Lear is reduced to pleading, 'On my knees I beg.' (157) Regan answers that plea with the cutting, 'I pray you, Father, being weak, seem so.' (204) The message being: you're nothing now so don't try to act like you're not.

Lear's final speech of the passage begins with, 'You Heavens, give me that patience, patience I need! (274)

Since Lear now faces reality, this is the most important portion of the passage.

So Lear finally accepts that his daughters have no use for him and want him out of their lives. He turns from self-pity to calling them hags and, 'I will have such revenges on you both.' (282)

In the closing sentence, Lear moves from fear of going mad to predicting it: 'Oh fool, I shall go mad!' (289)

After Lear exits, Gloucester, who had entered earlier, describes the raging storm Lear faces on the barren heath: 'the bleak winds do sorely ruffle.' (303) And to make sure that the audience knows how bleak it is, Gloucester tell us that, 'There's scarce a bush.' (304) If you were playing Gloucester's role, would you spread your arms wide and look house left and right?

Regan continues the cold-hearted words toward her father: 'The injuries that they themselves procure' (306) 'Must be their schoolmasters.' (307) In other words, it's time that stubborn men like Lear learned a lesson.

Will carefully built up our dislike of Regan and Goneril as selfish, heartless termagants. It's difficult to believe that they weren't always this way, and why didn't Lear see it earlier. Clearly, the dramatic thrust is that they acted subserviently toward their father while he was King and had all his power. Once it was transferred to them, they saw their father as nothing but a powerless pest. Character will out at any level when power and riches are there for the plucking. Cordelia has strong character, Goneril and Regan are mean, shallow, acquisitive opportunists.)

* * *

(WITH no time gap and with necessary exposition, we find that Lear has one success in the previous encounter: he got Kent released from the stocks.

Kent and a Gentleman meet on a stormy heath, and, in the opening scene of act three, we learn more of value. We can imagine the peripatetic Kent out on the blustery heath, but why is the Gentleman to Cordelia we met earlier there? Is he expecting Cordelia to arrive from France?

The Gentleman is asked by Kent, Where's the King?)

Gentleman. Contending with the fretful elements.
Bid the wind blow the earth into the sea,
Or swell the curlèd waters 'bove the main,
That things might change or cease; tears his white hair. (7)
Which the impetuous blasts, with eyeless rage,

Catch in their fury, and make nothing of;
Strives in his little world of man to outscorn
The to-and-fro conflicting wind and rain.
This night, wherein the cub-drawn bear would couch,
The lion and the belly-pinchèd wolf (13)
Keep their fur dry, unbonneted (14) he runs,
And bids what will take all.
Kent. Sir, I do know you,
And dare, upon the warrant of my note,
Commend a dear thing to you. There is division,
Although as yet the face of it be covered
With mutual cunning,' twixt Albany and Cornwall,
(21)
Who have—as who have not that their great stars
Throned and set high (23)—servants, who seem no
less,
Which are to France the spies and speculations (24)
Intelligent of our state—what hath been seen,
Either in snuffs and packings of the Dukes, (26)
Or the hard reign which both of them have borne
Against the old kind king, or something deeper,
Whereof by chance these are but furnishings
But true it is, from France there come a power (30)
Into this scattered kingdom, who already,
Wise in our negligence, have secret feet
In some of our best ports and are at point
To show their open banner. . . .

For confirmation that I am much more
Than my outwall, open this purse and take
What it contains. If you shall see Cordelia—
As fear not but you shall—show her this ring, (47)
And she will tell you who your fellow is
That yet you do not know. Fie on this storm!
I will go seek the King.
King Lear, 3.1, 3-49

(AS indicated in the introduction to this scene, we learn from Cordelia's Gentleman that Lear 'tears his white hair,' (7) in a storm so fierce that 'The lion and the belly-pinchèd wolf,' (13) starving as they may be, stay in their caves.

Lear, in his desperate anger, runs amok without a hat, or 'unbonneted.' (14)

In line five of Kent's speech, we discover, 'With mutual cunning, twixt Albany and Cornwall,' (21) that the inheritors of Lear's kingdoms, are scheming.

And even though, 'Throned and set high' (23) by destiny, they, like all kings, have disloyal servants, 'Which are to France the spies and speculations' of Britain. (24)

'Either in snuffs and packings of the Dukes, (26) means that Cornwall and Albany are rivals for power who don't like each other and seek to undermine. This is no surprise given that Regan and Goneril are whispering subterfuge in their husbands' ears.

So, 'from France there come a power' (30) tells us that the King of France, who promised to invade Britain and regain his wife Cordelia's lost property, has landed at Dover.

Kent sends the Gentleman off to find Cordelia at Dover and 'show her this ring,' (47) which will confirm to Cordelia that Kent knows what is happening.)

* * *

(THE Fool is with him, as Lear declaims in the storm on another heath. He utters two memorable lines in three emotive speeches.

I recall James Earl Jones in the 1970's, with his resonant voice and solid physicality, making these speeches to a fixated audience.)

Lear. <u>Blow, winds, and crack your cheeks!</u> (1) Rage! Blow!
You cataracts and hurricanoes, spout
<u>Till you have drenched our steeples, drowned the cocks!</u> (3)
You sulphurous and thought-executing fires,
Vaunt couriers to <u>oak-cleaving thunderbolts,</u> (5)

<u>Singe my white head!</u> (6) And thou, all-shaking thunder,
<u>Smite flat the rotundity o' the world!</u> (7)
<u>Crack nature's molds, all germens spill at once</u> (8)
<u>That make ungrateful man!</u>
King Lear, 3.2, 1-9

(BETWEEN the preceding speech and the one that follows, the Fool tells Lear that asking help from his daughters is better than enduring this storm: 'Here's a night pities neither wise man nor fool.' (13)

Lear. Rumble thy bellyful! Spit, fire! Spout, rain!
Nor rain, wind, thunder, fire, are my daughters.
<u>I tax not you, you elements, with unkindness.</u> (16)
<u>I never gave you kingdom, called you children,</u> (17)
You owe me no subscription. Then let fall
Your horrible pleasure. Here I stand, your slave,
<u>A poor, infirm, weak, and despised old man.</u> (20)
But yet I call you servile ministers
That have with <u>two pernicious daughters</u> (22) joined
Your high-engendered battles 'gainst a head
So <u>old and white as this.</u> (24) Oh, oh! 'Tis foul! . . .
I am a man
<u>More sinned against than sinning.</u> (59)
Kent. Alack, bareheaded!
Gracious my lord, hard by here is a hovel.

<u>Some friendship will it lend you 'gainst the tempest.</u>
(62)
King Lear, 3.2, 1-62

(THIS is poetic declaiming for an actor. Did you picture James Earl Jones, or another actor, out there on the stage? Who of us, under great stress, hasn't wanted to go to a cliff, and rather than jump off, let loose a shattering primal scream?

'Blow, winds, and crack your cheeks!' (1) is immortal. Do you see the old, white-haired man of the cartoon, with his billowed cheeks and whooshing breath, looking not unlike our image of Lear?

'Till you have drenched our steeples, drowned the cocks!' (3) Now that's a storm to match Lear's anger, with water sloshing above the weathercocks, or weathervanes, on church steeples. No wonder the Fool told Lear that dealing with your bad daughters is better than being out in this.

As an actor in the Lear role, would you point to your head, as you ask the lightning to 'Singe my white head!' (6) 'Singe' is an exemplary verb matched with 'oak-cleaving thunderbolts.' (5)

Some lines are unbelievably imaginative, like: 'Smite flat the rotundity o' the world!' (7) I see Atlas shrugging off the world, sounds like Ayn Rand, and stomping it flat. In acting that line would you smack

231

your fist against something then bang your foot on the stage floor?

'Crack nature's molds, all germens spill at once that make ungrateful man!' (8) In other words, break the molds used to shape man, and while doing so spill the seeds that create life. Lear is really angry. Flattening the world isn't enough. He wants to stamp out the possibility of humans continuing to exist. No question, Will knew how to make an emphatic point and while doing it produce great theater.

In part two of his tirade, Lear switches and doesn't choose to blame the elements for his misfortunes. Unlike the bitterness towards his daughters, he says, 'I tax not you, you elements, with unkindness.' (16) And the mordant, 'I never gave you kingdom, called you children,' (17) Therefore, you don't owe me anything like they do,

'A poor, infirm, weak, and despised old man' (20) is irresistible to an audience, most of whom are already on Lear's side.

But Lear does indict the elements for conspiring with 'two pernicious daughters' (22) against a head as 'old and white as this.' (24)

Later in the scene, in a triumph of regretful self-pity, that also happens to be accurate, Lear sums up in an impassioned speech-closing line that he is 'More sinned against than sinning.' (59)

Late in this scene, Kent finds Lear on the heath and brings him to a hovel for protection. 'Some friendship will it lend you 'gainst the tempest.' (62)

* * *

(IN scene three of act three, we're back with Gloucester and his nefarious bastard son Edmund. Not understanding Edmund's double-dealing ways, Gloucester confides that he's learned that 'There's a division betwixt the Dukes,' (8) Albany and Cornwall. This line echoes Kent's similar comment in 3.1, (21).

Gloucester also tells Edmund that he has a letter divulging that 'There is part of a power already footed,' or landed. (13) He urges that they must help Lear.

Edmund has no compunction about double-crossing his father, going to the Dukes with the invasion news and getting paid for it, ergo the self-serving and scornful, 'The younger rises when the old doth fall.' (26)

King Lear, 3.3, 8-26

* * *

(AS we learned at the conclusion of scene two, Lear, along with the Fool and Kent, take refuge from the storm in a cave on a heath. Now we are in scene four of act three, where Lear, in stirring poetry, laments the fate of the poor.)

Lear. Poor naked wretches, wheresoe'er you are,
That bide the pelting of this pitiless storm,
How shall your <u>houseless heads and unfed sides,</u> (30)
<u>Your looped and windowed raggedness,</u> (31) defend you
From seasons such as these? Oh, I have ta'en
Too little care of this! Take physic, pomp.
<u>Expose thyself to feel what wretches feel,</u> (34)
<u>That thou mayst shake the superflux to them</u>
<u>And show the Heavens more just.</u> (35)
 King Lear, 3.4, 28-35

(THE always eloquent Lear wonders how unfortunates with their 'houseless heads and unfed sides' (30) can live in this kind of weather.

'Your looped and windowed raggedness,' (31) tells us that not only are the poor homeless and hungry they are also dressed in rags fill of holes.

Now that he's exposed to harsh elements, Lear realizes that as king he hasn't understood the poor or helped them enough. He asks that 'pomp,' or the privileged, should 'Expose thyself to feel what wretches feel,' (34) and share the wealth, or 'shake the superflux to them and show the Heavens more just.' (35)

It's a loose analogy, but as someone once said: to better understand democracy get out of the library and into the subway. Or, in this case, get out of the castle and onto the heath on a tempest-tossed night. We never guessed that Lear becomes a sudden populist. I'm reminded of a current American politician with flying white hair.)

* * *

(EDGAR enters in his Poor Tom O' Bedlam lunatic disguise. After cavorting about wearing nothing but a blanket and speaking nonsense, Lear asks him, 'What hast thou been?' (86) To prove his insanity, Edmund goes into a crazed and seamy speech that surely pleased many in the audience.)

Edgar. A servingman, proud in heart and mind, that curled my hair, wore gloves in my cap, served the lust of my mistress's heart and did the act of darkness with her, swore as many oaths as I spake words and broke them in the sweet face of Heaven. One that slept in the contriving of lust and waked to do it. Wine loved

235

I deeply, dice dearly, and in woman outparamoured the Turk. <u>False of heart, light of ear, bloody of hand, hog in sloth, fox in stealth, wolf in greediness, dog in madness, lion in prey.</u> (95) Let not the creaking of shoes nor the rustling of silks betray thy poor heart to woman.

King Lear, 3.4

(LEAR is so impressed by Edgar's speech that he tears off his clothes and runs naked around the heath in the pelting rain. With his usual nifty language, the Fool cautions, 'Prithee, Nuncle, be contented, 'tis a naughty night to swim in.' (114)

Will gives his male audiences, through Edgar's zany speech, a risqué change of pace after all the heavy weather, pun intended.

Let's applaud the strung-out list Edgar uses to define his imitation self: 'False of heart, light of ear, bloody of hand, hog in sloth, fox in stealth, wolf in greediness, dog in madness, lion in prey.' (94) I expect Will could easily add another dozen or two dubs.

Gloucester enters, doesn't recognize his good son Edgar in madman disguise and asks Lear, 'What, hath your grace no better company?' (147) Edgar responds with, 'The Prince of Darkness is a gentleman,' (148) a sharp retort that also matches up nicely with the 'act of darkness' in line (89), and later with 'angler in the lake of darkness.' 3.6, (8)

Kent tells Gloucester that Lear's 'wits begin to unsettle.' (167) Gloucester replies, and who can blame him, 'His daughters seek his death.' (168)

To further verify his Tom o' Bedlam costume, Edgar closes the scene with an old English ballad:*

Child Rowland to the dark to the dark tower came.
His word was still 'Fie, foh, and fum,
I smell the blood of a British man.
King Lear, 3.4, 86-189

('Child' in this balladic sense means a young man who is probably a combatant.)

*This early ballad was later adapted by Robert Browning into a mid-19th-Century poem titled *Childe Roland to the Dark Tower Came*.

Browning claimed that the idea came to him in a dream. I take his point; I once dreamt that I wrote *Beowulf.*)

* * *

(NEXT, in scene five in Gloucester's castle, the iniquitous Edmund meets with Cornwall and divulges the letter his father, the Earl of Gloucester, confided to him: 'This is the letter he spoke of, which approves him an intelligent party,' (11) or spy for France.

Edmund gets his reward when Cornwall tells him, 'True or false, it hath made thee Earl of Gloucester,' (18) or you now have your father's title as a reward.

Ratting out your own father to get his job, now there's filial loyalty. Even the modern mafia, with their 'honor thy father' code, wouldn't tolerate that.

Will is the undisputed master at creating appalling people who are absent any redeeming qualities. Iago may top the list, but Edmund is in the conversation, along with Tamora and Aaron the Moor from *Titus Andronicus*, Richard III, Angelo in *Measure for Measure*, and several more. And we can't forget Regan and Goneril from the play in review. Who are your favorite villains?)

* * *

(IN scene six of act three, Lear, Edgar, Kent and the Fool take haven in a house near the castle. Lear has achieved madness, or at least advanced senility. Edgar continues to pretend he is unhinged.

In his dementia, Lear puts the absent Goneril and Regan on trial. What an acting moment this scene is.

Enjoy the snippets of aberrant banter among Edgar, the Fool and Lear, until Gloucester reenters to disclose a plot against Lear's life.)

Edgar. Frateretto calls me, (7) and tells me Nero is an angler in the lake of darkness. (8) Pray, innocent, and beware the foul fiend.
Fool. He's mad that trusts in the tameness of a wolf, a horse's health, a boy's love, or a whore's oath. (17)
Lear. I'll see their trial first. Bring in the evidence.
Thou robèd man of justice, (37) take thy place.
And thou, this yokefellow of equity, (38)
Bench by his side. You are the commission, (39)
Sit you too. . . .
Arraign her first. 'Tis Goneril. I here take my oath before this honorable assembly, she kicked the poor King her father. . . . (49)
Then let them anatomize Regan, (80) see what breeds about her heart. Is there any cause in nature that makes these hard hearts?
Gloucester. (Enters.) Good friend, I prithee take him in thy arms.
I have o'erheard a plot of death upon him. (96)
There is a litter ready, lay him in 't,
And drive toward Dover, friend, where thou shalt meet
Both welcome and protection. Take up thy master.

If thou shouldst dally half an hour, his life,
With thine and all that offer to defend him,
Stand in assurèd loss.
King Lear, 3.6, 7-102

(EDGAR, still playing Tom o' Bedlam, gives a peculiar speech in which he includes a demon, 'Frateretto calls me,' (7) and Nero the depraved Roman emperor, who Edgar ties to a superb phrase, 'an angler in the lake of darkness.' (8)

Will favors the word 'darkness,' also using it as a euphemism for sexual intercourse. It was mentioned earlier by Edgar in 3.4, (148) 'and did the act of darkness with her.'

The Fool has gone a little over the edge himself and spouts a bawdy ditty: 'He's mad that trusts in the tameness of a wolf, a horse's health, a boy's love, or a whore's oath. (17) As we read earlier in Edgar's 3.4 virtuoso list vilifying Oswald, Will can sure write a conglomeration of phrases for disturbed minds.

Moving erratically in and out of sanity, Lear, in this scene, retains a modicum of reason, as he continues the trial of Goneril and Regan in absentia. He uses the mock-mad Edgar as the judge, or 'robèd man of justice.' (37) The Fool as lawyer, 'this yokefellow of equity,' (38) and tells Kent, 'You are o' the commission,' (39) or jury, and orders him to sit on the bench.

Following the assignments, Lear's charge to Goneril is the farcical and verb-rich 'she kicked the poor King her father.' (49)

Then we have the surprising verb-noun combination of 'anatomize Regan.' (80) 'See what breeds about her heart.'

The scene is an actor's reverie. The possibilities for voice inflections, business, costume are endless.

Then, in a deft touch, Will changes the mood. Gloucester enters to inform Kent, 'I have o'erheard a plot of death upon him,' (96) and they trundle the endangered Lear off to Dover.)

* * *

(IN act three, scene seven, Regan, Goneril, Kent and servants talk in Gloucester's castle. Cornwall announces that 'The army of France is landed.' (1)

Thanks to his son Edmund's treachery they all blame Gloucester. Regan says, 'Hang him instantly.' (4) Goneril wants to 'Pluck out his eyes.' (5) Cornwall orders, 'Pinion him like a thief.' (23) He then discusses (24) whether they can or cannot punish him.

Gloucester is brought in, tied to a chair, and Regan plucks his beard, a gross humiliation.

Keeping in mind that he's a prisoner in his own house, Gloucester then lectures them on hospitality.

After they badger him about where Lear is, he tells them, 'I am tied to the stake, and I must stand the course.' (53) Regan asks why Gloucester sent her father to Dover.

Back to Cornwall, who, after telling his men to pinion Gloucester, speaks on what they can or cannot do to punish him.)

Cornwall. Though well we may not pass upon his life (24)
Without the form of justice, yet our power
Shall do a courtesy to our wrath, which men
May blame but not control. Who's there? The traitor?
Gloucester. (Brought in on the chair.) By the kind gods, 'tis most ignobly done
To pluck me by the beard. . . . (36)
Naughty lady,
These hairs that thou dost ravish from my chin
Will quicken and accuse thee. I am your host. (39)
With robbers' hands my hospitable favors (40)
You should not ruffle thus. What will you do?
Regan. Wherefore to Dover, sir?
Gloucester. Because I would not see thy cruel nails
Pluck out his poor old eyes, (57) nor thy fierce sister
In his anointed flesh (58) stick boarish fangs.

The sea, with such a storm as his bare head
In hell-black night endured, would have buoyed up,
And quenched the stellèd fires. (61)
Yet, poor old heart, he holp the heavens to rain.
If wolves had at thy gate howled that stern time,
Thou shouldst have said, "Good porter, turn the key."
(63)
All cruels else subscribed. But I shall see
The wingèd vengeance overtake such children. (66)
King Lear, 3.7, 1-66

(IN the line, 'Though well we may not pass upon his life,' (24) and in the three lines that follow, Cornwall says that they don't have the power to punish Gloucester, but they're angry enough to do it anyway.

After he suffers the degredation of a beard plucking, 'To pluck me by the beard,' (36) a deeply rude humiliation, Gloucester admonishes them with 'I am your host,' (39) and 'With robbers' hands my hospitable favors' (40) are ruffled.

The point here is that in pagan times the law of hospitality is sacred. The tradition of hosting is designed to encourage travel and communication. Gloucester accuses Cornwall, Regan and Goneril of twice violating that precept.

'Pluck out his poor old eyes,' (57) may not have been the best thing for Gloucester to mention in reference to protecting Lear's well-being. Earlier, in line five, Goneril threatened Gloucester with 'Pluck out his eyes.'

'In his anointed flesh (58) means that because Lear is King, he is divine and should not be desecrated by one of his daughters 'boarish fangs,' an impeccable adjective-noun pairing.

Gloucester tells the group holding him prisoner that Lear was bareheaded out in a storm so fierce and with seas so high they could have 'quenched the stellèd fires,' (61) or the stars.

They should have opened the gates, taken him in, 'Thou shouldst have said, "Good porter, turn the key." (63)

Given what soon happens to him, it is portentous in his closing line that Gloucester says that he will see, 'The wingèd vengeance overtake such children.' (66) And since Cornwall puts out both of his eyes, he will not see his premonition.)

Cornwall. 'Out, vile jelly! (81)
Where is thy luster now?'
King Lear, 3.7

(CORNWALL gouges out Gloucester's other eye, with his theatrically compelling but hideous phrase combining 'vile' and 'jelly.' (81)

244

A servant to Gloucester challenges Cornwall. They fight and Cornwall is wounded. Regan takes a sword and runs the servant through from behind, a fitting act for a backstabber.

Gloucester cries out for his son, Edmund, and the hateful Regan gleefully gives Edmund's unforgivable conduct toward his father away.)

Regan. Thou call'st on him that hates thee. It was he (88)
That made the overture of thy treasons to us,
Who is too good to pity thee.
King Lear, 3.7, 88-108

(HEARING Regan's spite in the three lines above, starting with (88) Gloucester realizes that he is wrong about his good son, Edgar: 'Kind gods, forgive me that, and prosper him!' (92)

Regan, in character, responds to the blind Gloucester by ordering her guards to, 'Go thrust him out at gates, and let him smell his way to Dover.' (93)

Cornwall, gravely wounded from the servant's stab, exits with Regan.

His loyal servants help the blinded Gloucester: "I'll fetch some flax and whites of eggs to apply to his bleeding face. Now, Heaven help him!' (108) Will neatly juxtaposes Cornwall's and Regan's barbarity with the servants' compassion.)

* * *

(EDGAR, still in his Tom o' Bedlam garb, is on the heath. His now blind father enters guided by an old man who Gloucester shoos away, 'Thy comforts can do me no good at all.' (17)
The old man responds 'you cannot see your way.' (19)

Gloucester. I have no way and therefore want no eyes.
I stumbled when I saw. (21) Full oft 'tis seen,
Our means secure us, and our mere defects
Prove our commodities. (23) Ah, dear Son, Edgar,
The food of thy absèd father's wrath (24)
Might I might live to see thee in my touch, (25)
I'd say I had eyes again! (26)
King Lear, 4.1, 17-26

('I stumbled when I saw,' (21) and defects 'Prove our commodities,' (23) means that Gloucester realizes that when he had eyes he didn't see the truth about Edgar, and now that he's blind he does. Elegant poetry conveys a human insight.

'The food of thy abusèd father's wrath' (24) Gloucester's saying that his own anger has victimized his son.

'Might I might live to see thee in my touch, (25) is heartrending, especially when followed by the imaginative, 'I'd say I had eyes again! (26)

(The old man accompanying Gloucester sees Edgar and calls him a 'Madman and beggar too.' (32) I like Gloucester's answer.)

Gloucester. He has some reason, else he could not beg. (33)
I' the last night's storm I such a fellow saw,
Which made me think a man a worm. My son
Came then into my mind, and yet my mind
Was then scarce friends with him. I have heard more since.
<u>As flies to wanton boys are we to the gods, (37)</u>
<u>They kill us for their sport.</u>
King Lear, 4.1, 32-38

(THE second speech in this passage closes with legendary lines, commencing with, "As flies to wanton boys . . .' (37) Gloucester is not praising the gods. Rather, he says that we are powerless, and they do what they want with us.

In addition to being cynical and pessimistic, the lines are fatalistic, never a good idea in a play of this period. Gloucester feels deep guilt over his mistreatment of son Edgar. Blindness at the hands of Cornwall leaves him bitter and depressed. He intends to do something about his fate and asks for Edgar's help.)

Gloucester. There is a cliff whose high and bending head
Looks fearfully in the confinèd deep.
Bring me but to the very brim of it,
And I'll repair the misery thou dost bear
With something rich about me. From that place
I shall <u>no leading need</u>. (81)
King Lear, 4.1, 76-81

(IN his third speech, Gloucester wants to go to Dover and leap off a cliff that over- hangs the channel, a place from which I shall 'no leading need.' (81) In pagan times, it was considered noble to kill yourself. If you think that *King Lear* has been good so far? Stay with me, it gets even better.)

* * *

(ON the next day, in the second scene of act four, we have an oily twist. Edmund and Goneril, now there's a matching set, meet in her husband Albany's palace.

Then Albany shows up and . . .)

Goneril. I must change arms at home and <u>give the distaff</u> (17)
Into my husband's hands. This trusty servant
Shall pass between us. Ere long you are like to hear,
If you dare venture in your own behalf,
A mistress's command. Wear this. Spare speech.
<u>Decline your head.</u> (22) This kiss, if it durst speak,
Would stretch thy spirits up into the air.
<u>Conceive,</u> (24) and fare thee well.
Edmund. <u>Yours in the ranks of death.</u> (25) (He exits.)
Goneril. Most dear Gloucester.
Oh, the difference of man and man!
To thee a woman's services are due,
<u>My fool usurps my body.</u> (28) (Albany enters.)
Albany. O Goneril!
You are not worth the dust which the rude wind
Blows in your face. I fear your disposition.
That nature which contemns its origin
Cannot be bordered certain in itself.
<u>She that herself will sliver and disbranch</u> (34)
<u>From her material sap,</u> (35) perforce must wither
And come to deadly use.

Goneril. No more, the text is foolish.

Albany. Wisdom and goodness to the vile seems vile.
<u>Filths savor but themselves</u>. (39) What have you done?

Tigers, not daughters, what have you performed?

A father, and a gracious agèd man

<u>Whose reverence even the head-lugged bear would lick</u>, (42)

<u>Most barbarous, most degenerate</u>, (43) have you madded!

Goneril. <u>Milk-livered man!</u> (50)

Thou bear'st a cheek for blows, a head for wrongs,

Why hast not in thy brows an eye discerning

Thine honor from thy suffering; that not know'st

Fools do those villains pity who are punished

Ere they have done their mischief. <u>Where's thy drum?</u> (54

France spreads his banners in our noiseless land,

With plumèd helm thy state begins to threat.

Whiles thou, a moral fool, sit'st still and criest

<u>'Alack, why does he so?</u> (58)

Albany. See thyself, devil!

Proper deformity seems not in the fiend

So horrid as in woman. . . .

Thou changèd and self-covered thing, for shame,

Bemonster not thy feature. Were 't my fitness

To <u>let these hands obey my blood</u>, (64)

They are apt enough to dislocate and tear
Thy flesh and bones. Howe'er thou art a fiend
A woman's shape doth shield thee.
Messenger. (Enters.) O my good lord, the Duke of
Cornwall's dead,
Slain by his servant, going to put out
The other eye of Gloucester.
Albany. This shows you are above,
You justicers, that these our <u>nether crimes</u> (79)
<u>So speedily can venge.</u> (80) But, oh, poor Gloucester!
Lost he his other eye?
Goneril. (Aside.) One way I like this well,
But being widow, and my Gloucester with her,
<u>May all the building in my fancy pluck</u> (86)
<u>Upon my hateful life.</u> (87) Another way,
The news is not so tart.
King Lear, 4.2, 17-88

(IN line one of Goneril's first speech to Edmund, she says, 'give the distaff,'* (17) meaning that she will hand Albany an implement used in weaving, since all he's good for is woman's work.

*In the modern sense, 'distaff' is occasionally used as a synonym for female, as in 'on the distaff side.' I doubt that a female journalist would use the patronizing term.

251

In the last line of the speech, after Goneril kisses Edmund, 'Decline your head' (22) she tells him to 'Conceive,' (24) or think about it. She wants to marry him and dump Albany. Knowing that he will acquire her land if he can displace Albany, shifty Edmund gets the message, and answers, 'Yours in the ranks of death.' (25)

After Edmund exits, and before Albany enters, Goneril says of the husband she wants to dispose of, 'My fool usurps my body.' (28)

Albany lets Goneril know what he thinks of her. Near the end of his vitriolic speech, he says, 'She that herself will sliver and disbranch,' (34) or if Goneril cuts herself off 'From her material sap,' (35) or family, she will die.

Of all the acrimony Albany hurls at Goneril for mistreating her father, my favorite is, 'Filths savor but themselves.' (39)

Albany piles on by telling Goneril that she's abused her father, a man 'Whose reverence even the head-lugged bear would lick.' (42) Not even a baited bear wounded in the head would treat him in a way that is 'Most barbarous, most degenerate.' (43)

Reread the lines from 'Milk-livered man!' (50) and 'Alack, why does he so?' (58)
Goneril tells Albany that he's a weakling who should stop preaching and wake up to the fact that he's a fool

who can't even comprehend the insults directed at him. Moreover, she says, France has landed on our shores and you aren't doing anything about it: 'Where's thy drum? (54

Later in the speech, after he's had his fill of her venom, Albany tells Goneril that if he were strong enough he would, 'let these hands obey my blood,' (64) or tear her apart.

In his second speech, after the messenger enters with the news of Cornwall's death, Albany mentions 'nether crimes,' (79) or crimes performed on earth.

In the following line he says, 'So speedily can venge,' (80) meaning that the stars can quickly avenge a wrongdoing by man.

In her concluding aside, the underhanded Goneril plots her next moves. She says, 'May all the building in my fancy pluck,' (86) or her dream palace can fall in ruins if she can change 'my hateful life' (87) and marry Edmund, or as Goneril calls him in the previous line, Gloucester. Reminder: Edmund got the title, Earl* of Gloucester when he betrayed his father to Cornwall.

*In the lexicon of the period, Earl and Duke were equal titles, although Earl was more widely used.)

* * *

(SCENE three of act four opens with Kent and Cordelia's Gentleman attendant talking in the French camp at Dover,

We first learn that Cordelia's husband, the King of France, left Dover and returned to France on important business.

Cordelia remains in Dover, and when the Gentleman attendant delivers letters from her father, 'an ample tear trilled down' (14) her delicate cheek. 'Trilled' is an unusually effective verb as opposed to trickle. Trilled conveys the visual impression of a quavering note, similar to a teardrop zigzagging down Cordelia's cheek.

The Gentleman goes on tell Kent that while reading the letters Cordelia 'once or twice heaved the name of 'Father.' (27) This phrase tells us that the big-hearted Cordelia holds no resentment towards her father and loves him unconditionally.

Next, Kent shows his faith in the belief that the stars control the fates.)

Kent. It is the stars,
The stars above us, govern our conditions,
Else one self mate and mate could not beget
<u>Such different issues</u>. (36)
King Lear, 4.3, 14-36

(KENT says that the stars' governance explains how 'Such different issues,' (36) or how Cordelia and her sisters can come from the same parents.)

* * *

(THE just-analyzed scene three of act four occurs one day after scene two. The next three scenes take place shortly after scene three and all on the same day. With most elements in place, the play sprints toward its recognitions, reconciliations and resolutions. Now, how's that for some fancy alliteration? See how Will inspires us.)

* * *

(IN scene four, the next in discussion, Cordelia remains in Dover now accompanied by French soldiers. She knows of her father's troubles and wants to find and help him.)

Cordelia. Alack, 'tis he. Why, he was met even now
As mad as the vexed sea, (2) singing aloud,
Crowned with rank fumiter and furrow weeds, (3)
With burdocks, hemlock, nettles, cuckoo flowers, (4)
Darnel. And all the wild weeds that grow
In our sustaining corn. A century send forth. (6)

Search every acre in the <u>high-grown field,</u> (7)
And bring him to our eye. What can man's wisdom
In the restoring his <u>bereavèd</u> sense?
He that helps him take <u>all my outward worth</u>. (10)
King Lear, 4.4, 1-10

(CORDELIA recognizes that Lear, her father, is 'As mad as the vexed sea.' (2)

This is confirmed when she says he is 'Crowned with rank fumiter and furrow weeds,' (3) and more, including 'burdocks, hemlock, nettles, cuckoo flowers, Darnel.' (4)

She summarizes his costume under the word 'Darnel,' a term encompassing many indigenous wildflowers, a colorful visualization of mad Lear careering about the bleak and windswept heath garlanded in growth.

As mentioned in the introduction to this scene, soldiers attend Cordelia, and she orders one-hundred troops, or 'A century send forth' (6) to find her father in the summer, or 'high-grown field.' (7)

Emphasizing Cordelia's need to find her 'bereavèd' father, she offers to those who help him 'all my outward worth,' (10) or means.

A messenger enters to tell Cordelia, 'The British powers are marching hitherward.' (21)

* * *

(IN scene five of act four, Regan and Oswald, Goneril's steward, meet in Gloucester's castle.)

Regan. My lord is dead, Edmund and I have talked,
<u>And more convenient is he for my hand</u> (31)
<u>Than for your lady's.</u> You may gather more.
<u>If you do find him, pray you give him this,</u> (33)
And when your mistress hears thus much from you,
I pray desire her call her wisdom to her.
So, fare you well.
If you do chance to hear of <u>that blind traitor</u>, (37)
Preferment falls on him that cuts him off.
King Lear, 4.5, 30-38

(REGAN tells Oswald that since . her husband Cornwall is dead, Edmund is more convenient 'for my hand than for your lady's,' (31) meaning Goneril. Now we have the sisters competing for Edmund.

Then Regan asks Oswald, 'If you do find him, pray you give him this.' (33) She gives Oswald something for Edmund, but we don't know what it is, and it's never explained or referred to again.

Planning ahead in the interest of having no obstacles to Edmund's retaining the Earl of Gloucester title, Regan tells Oswald that if he meets

Edmund's father 'that blind traitor,' (37) he will be rewarded for killing him.

Such drama: will Edmund stick with Goneril, or go over to Regan? I sense he'll hold out for the best deal. Read on for more of Will's delicious backbiting dialogue and intrigue.

But first, we revisit Edmund and Gloucester, as the old man pursues suicide.)

* * *

(EDGAR, in rustic garb, and Gloucester his blind father climb a hill towards a Dover cliff.

Gloucester says, 'Methinks you're better spoken,' (10) He still doesn't realize that the man accompanying him is his son.)

Edgar. Come on, sir, here's the place. Stand still.
How fearful
And dizzy 'tis to cast one's eyes so low!
The crows and choughs that wing the midway air
Show scarce so gross as beetles. (14) Halfway down
Hangs one that gathers samphire, (15) dreadful trade!
Methinks he seems no bigger than his head.
The fishermen walk upon the beach
Appear like mice, and yond tall anchoring bark
Diminished to her cock–her cock a buoy (19)

Almost too small for sight. The murmuring surge
That on the unnumbered idle pebbles chafes (21)
Cannot be heard so high. I'll look no more,
Lest my brain and the deficient sight
Tumble down headlong.
Gloucester. (On knees.) O you mighty gods!
This world I do renounce, (35) and in your sights
Shake patiently all my afflictions off.
If I could bear it longer and not fall
To quarrel with your great opposeless wills,
My snuff and loathèd part of nature (39) should
Burn itself out. If Edgar live, oh, bless him!
Now, fellow, fare thee well.
King Lear, 4.6, 10-75

(IN line six of the speech, Edgar describes the scene below the cliff's edge to his father. 'The crows and choughs that wing the midway air show scarce so gross as beetles.'
(141) The cliff is so high that the birds look like tiny insects. 'Choughs,' also called jackdaws, a kind of crow, live in many environments including cliffsides.

Edgar says that halfway down 'Hangs one that gathers samphire.' (15) He's talking about a hovering bird collecting a pungent, parsley-like plant that grows on chalky cliffs. Will Shakespeare visited the Dover cliffs while traveling with players, and the firsthand details show it. Wherever he went everything was seen, and nothing was missed or forgotten.

'Diminished to her cock—her cock a buoy' (19) means that a tall ship in the distance looks as tiny at the small boat pulled behind it.

Edgar then speaks of 'the unnumbered idle pebbles chafes.' (21) They are so high he tells his father that they cannot hear the waves shifting the pebbles. This reference reminds me of line one from Sonnet 60, 'Like as the waves make toward the pebbl'd shore.'

Gloucester then prays on his knees to gods 'This world I do renounce.' (35) Another notable line is, 'My snuff and loathèd part of nature.' (39) He wants his world snuffed out like a candle burned to the quick.

This, worth-rereading in its entirety, speech is an anachronistic Christian sermon against suicide. As said earlier, in pagan times there would be no objection to it.

Gloucester tumbles forward. Thanks to Edgar's careful positioning away from the edge, Gloucester doesn't fall, but being blind is fooled into thinking he has.

Edgar speaks to his father, as though they were on the beach looking up at the cliff. 'Look up a-height.' (58) Edgar pretends that he saw a devil 'It was some fiend' (72) parting from his father as he jumped. And some illustrious gods 'have preserved thee.' (74) Gloucester is talked into it, as he says, 'I do remember now.' (75) And that ends the poetic, moving lesson on suicide.)

* * *

(SCENE SIX continues, as Lear enters still fancifully adorned with wildflowers. Gloucester, not able to see him, recognizes Lear's' voice, 'Is 't not the king? (108) Lear responds, 'Aye, every inch a king.' (109) This proud answer is rational, but Lear continues to randomly lecture, while interspersing sane language.

Next, he expounds on adultery, justifying it as it pertains to Gloucester's fathering of Edmund his bastard son. Halfway through the speech below Lear swivels to his black-hearted daughters' sexual appetites.)

Lear. When I do stare, see how the subject quakes.
I pardon that man's life. What was thy cause?
Adultery?
Thou shalt not die. Die for adultery! No.
The wren goes to 't, and the small gilded fly
Does lecher in my sight.
Let copulation thrive, for Gloucester's bastard son
<u>Was kinder to his father than my daughters</u> (117)

261

Got 'tween the lawful sheets. (118)
To 't, luxury, pell-mell! (119) For I lack soldiers.
Behold yond simpering dame,
Whose face between her forks presages snow,
That minces virtue and does shake the head
To hear of pleasure's name.
The filchew, nor the soiled horse, goes to 't (124)
With a more riotous appetite.
Down from the waist they are Centaurs,
Though women all above.
But to the girdle do the gods inherit,
Beneath is all the fiend's.
There's Hell, there's darkness, there's the sulphurous
pit,
Burning, scalding, stench, consumption, fie, fie, fie!
Pah, pah! Give me an ounce of civet, good
apothecary, to sweeten my imagination. (132) There's
money for thee. (133)
Gloucester. Oh, let me kiss that hand! (135)
Lear. Let me wipe it first, it smells of mortality. (136)
Gloucester. O ruined piece of nature! This great world
(137)
Shall so wear out to naught.
King Lear, 4.6, 110-138

(IT is quite a reach for Lear to say that Edmund,
Gloucester's bastard son 'Was kinder to his father

than my daughters' (117) who were 'Got 'tween the lawful sheets.' (118) However, Lear may not know of Edmund's perfidy.

Lear is carried away, as he tells how his daughters go 'To 't, luxury, pell-mell! (119) For full effect, we need to substitute lust for 'luxury.'

'The filchew, nor the soiled horse, goes to 't. with a more riotous appetite.' (124) Lear claims that his daughters are more sexually insatiable than animals such as skunks and grazing horses.

In the next-to-last line of this astounding speech, Lear suddenly realizes that his mind is in the gutter. He asks: 'Give me an ounce of civet, good apothecary, to sweeten my imagination.' (132) Imagine the actor in the Lear role using dismissive body language, or a grin as the line is delivered.

Then quickly back to caring for sad Gloucester with, 'There's money for thee.' (133)

Gloucester becomes so emotional he says to Lear, 'Oh, let me kiss that hand!' (136) Lear knows he is dying, and comes back with the startling, 'Let me wipe it first. It smells of mortality.' (137)

Blind Gloucester senses Lear's condition and ties it to his world which has also come apart, 'O ruined piece of nature! This great world shall so wear out to naught.' (137)

Now there's a theatrical exchange. No puzzle why actors love playing Shakespeare.)

* * *

(WE'RE still in scene six of act four. Edgar remains onstage. He remarks on Lear's continuing speech on the vagaries of life—not shown here—but worth reading.

Within Lear's rambling discourse, one line stands out, 'Plate sin with gold and the strong lance of justice hurtless breaks.' (169) Prior to this line, Lear comments on how poor people on the wrong side of the law usually get a raw deal. However, the rich can cover up their wickedness with money thereby avoiding justice.

Edgar reacts with, 'Oh, matter and impertinency mixed! (178) Reason in madness!' (179) Edgar allows that although Lear is mad, he can still make sense within a barrage of gibberish.)

(Lear recognizes Gloucester and gives him advice, highlighted by a pair of undying lines.)

Lear. If thou wilt weep my fortunes, take my eyes.
I know thee well enough. Thy name is Gloucester.
(181)

Thou must be patient, we came crying hither.
Thou know'st the first time that we <u>smell the air,</u> (183)
We wawl and cry. I will preach to thee. Mark. . . .
<u>When we are born, we cry that we are come</u> (186)
<u>To this great stage of fools.</u> This 's a good block.
It were a delicate strategem to shoe
A <u>troop of horse with felt</u>. (189) I'll put 't in proof,
And <u>when I have stol'n upon these sons-in-law,</u> (190)
Then, kill, kill, kill, kill, kill, kill!
King Lear, 4.6, 169-191

(THE early lines in the speech are touching. Lear recognizes Gloucester, 'I know thee well enough. Thy name is Gloucester.' (181) Lear preaches patience, and using inventive language speaks of babies crying when they first 'smell the air.' (183)

Through careful dialogue, the advice in the preceding paragraph is linked to lines six and seven in Lear's speech, beginning with 'When we are born we cry that we come to this great stage of fools.' (186) It is celebrated poetry, and once again note the use of 'stage,' as representing the world. The stage was Will's life.

The final two lines are directed with clear intent at Albany and Cornwall, his daughters' husbands, and men he considers disloyal to a former king. Lear will shoe a 'troop of horse with felt,' (189) like felt from a blocked hat, and 'when I have stol'n upon these sons-in-law,' (190) he will kill them, six times over. (Lear exits.)

* * *

(SCENE SIX continues with Oswald, Goneril's steward, entering. Reminder: Regan told Oswald that if he killed Gloucester there would be a reward. He sees Gloucester: 'The sword is out that must destroy thee.' (233)

Edgar intercedes. Oswald calls him a 'bold peasant' and challenges him to a fight. 'Darest thou support a published traitor?' (236)

Edgar tells Oswald in Kentish vernacular, ''Good gentleman go your gait, and let poor volk pass.' (242) Put differently, move along and let us alone.

Oswald responds with, 'Out, dunghill! (248) They fight, Edmund kills him, and while dying Oswald asks Edgar to 'take my purse' (251) and 'bury my body.' (252) In pagan times, with the risk of ghosts flitting about, it was considered bad luck not to be buried.)
King Lear, 4.6, 233-252

* * *

(A DAY later, in scene seven, King Lear lies on a cot asleep in a tent at the French camp, Cordelia enters and speaks to him. Following her speech, Lear awakes.

This is an immensely affecting reconciliation scene requiring sensitive and subtle acting.)

Cordelia. O my dear father! Restoration (26)
Hang thy medicine on my lips, (27) and let this kiss
Repair those violent harms that my two sisters
Have in thy reverence made! . . .
Was this a face
To be opposed against the warring winds?
To stand against the deep dread-bolted thunder?
In the most terrible and nimble stroke
Of quick, cross-lightning? . . . He wakes. . . .
How does my royal lord? How fares your majesty?
Lear. You do me wrong to take me out o' the grave.
(44)
Thou art a soul in bliss, (45) but I am bound
Upon a wheel of fire (46) that mine own tears
Do scald like molten lead. . . . (47)
I am a very foolish fond old man,
Fourscore and upward, (61) not an hour more nor less,
And, to deal plainly,
I fear I am not in my perfect mind. . . . (63)
Do not laugh at me,
For, as I am a man, I think this lady (68)

To be my child Cordelia. . . .
Be your tears wet? Yes, faith. I pray weep not.
If you have poison for me, I will drink it. (71)
I know you do not love me, for your sisters
Have, as I do remember, done me wrong.
You have some cause, (74) they have not.
Cordelia. No cause, no cause. (75)
King Lear, 4.7, 26-75

(BEFORE kissing her father, Cordelia asks that 'Restoration' (26) will 'Hang thy medicine on my lips.' (27) 'Hang,' a fine verb in just the right position.

After Lear awakes, he tells Cordelia, 'You do me wrong to take me out o' the grave.' (44) At this point he prefers to die.

Lear tells Cordelia, 'Thou art a soul in bliss,' (45) or a personification from paradise: and, since he is bound 'Upon a wheel of fire,' (46) she cannot help him. Lear is exhausted, confused, senile, but still capable of great poetry.

'Wheel of fire' evoking Hell, contrasts beautifully with the celestial 'soul in bliss.'

And the stirring imagery contains a blinding finish with Lear saying that his tears 'scald like molten lead.' (47) It was written for performance, and when done movingly fills the throat and moistens the eyes.

We learn that Lear is 'Fourscore and upward,' (61) or over 80.

Lear's comment that, 'I fear I am not in my perfect mind,' (63) is a sign that he's coming back.

And then the melting, 'I think this lady to be my child Cordelia.' (68)

In a closing passage from act four, Will suddenly changes the mood by having Lear say, in recognition of his guilt for having wronged Cordelia, 'If you have poison for me, I will drink it.' (71)

Reconciliation comes with Lear saying, 'You have some cause,' (74) to hate me for unfairly banishing you, while your sisters do not. In her simple, direct style, Cordelia replies, 'No cause, no cause.' (75)

* * *

(TO open act five, Edmund, Regan and Goneril are with the British armies at Dover. Both women suspect Edmund's affiliation with the other. Regan tells Edmund that he has 'bosomed' (13) with Goneril and adds 'Be not familiar with her.' (16)

Although preparing for war, Goneril, in an aside, says she 'had rather lose the battle' (18) than have Regan 'loosen him and me.' (19) As we now learn, Edmund, the gamesman, has other priorities.)

Edmund. To both these sisters I have sworn my love,
Each jealous of the other, as the stung
Are of the adder. (57) Which of them shall I take?
Both? One? Or neither? Neither can be enjoyed
If both remain alive. (59) To take the widow
Exasperates, makes mad her sister Goneril,
And hardly shall I carry out my side,
Her husband being alive. (62) Now then we'll use
His countenance for the battle, which being done,
Let her who would be rid of him devise
His speedy taking off. (65) As for the mercy
Which he intends to Lear and Cordelia,
The battle done, and they within our power,
Shall never see his pardon, (68) for my state
Stands on me to defend, not to debate. (69)
King Lear, 5.1, 13-69

(SINCE he's sworn his love to both of them, Edmund knows that Goneril and Regan are jealous and suspicious of each other's intentions toward him: 'Each jealous of the other, as the stung are of the adder.' (57) Edmund's saying that a person bitten by a snake is suspicious of the snake. Given the sisters' actions and intentions, the metaphor fits.

Edmund debates which one to take, but understands that, 'Neither can be enjoyed (59) if both remain alive. Give him this: Edmund is a realist.

He's skeptical of hooking up with Goneril with 'Her husband being alive. (62) Now Albany's on Edmund's list of potential victims.

Five lines from the end of the speech, Edmund hopes that Goneril will devise 'His speedy taking off,' (65) or find a way to kill her husband Albany. Although he's up to it, this would relieve Edmund of the task.

A few lines later, Edmund schemes that Lear and Cordelia 'Shall never see his pardon,' (68) nor will he allow implementation of Albany's plan to show mercy to Lear, or the soon-to-be-defeated-in-battle French army loyal to Cordelia.

Edmund concludes by saying that he has too much at stake to 'debate' (69) anything, he must strike now.)

* * *

(IN scene two of act five, the French and English armies engage in battle. Following the clash, Edgar tells his father, Gloucester, that 'King Lear hath lost, he and his daughter taken.' (6)

Gloucester wants to stay put, but Edgar takes his hand saying. 'Ripeness is all.* Come on.' (11)
King Lear, 5.2, 6-11

*This line recalls 'the readiness is all' from *Hamlet*, 5.2.)

* * *

(SCENE three of act five concludes the play. In the next passage, early in the scene, Lear and Cordelia talk of their fate following capture. They are being taken away under guard on orders from Edmund. As we know, he wants them dead clearing an even wider path in his power grab.

Cordelia asks her father whether they will see 'these daughters and these sisters,' (7) meaning Regan and Goneril.

As said, this book is about analyzing the principal speeches in *King Lear*. The critiques are multipurpose, but the chief goal is full appreciation of the language.

The next speech is Lear's answer to Cordelia's question. Delivered by a consummate actor, the poetry would make the angels weep.)

Lear. No, no, no, no! <u>Come, let's away to prison.</u> (8)
<u>We two alone will sing like birds i' the cage.</u> (9)
When thou dost ask me blessing, I'll kneel down
And ask of thee forgiveness. So we'll live,
And <u>pray, and sing, and tell old tales, and laugh</u> (12)
<u>At gilded butterflies,</u> and hear poor rogues

Talk of court news. And we'll talk with them too,
Who loses and who wins, who's in, who's out, (15)
And take upon 's the mystery of things (16)
As if we were god's spies. And we'll wear out,
In a walled prison, pacts and sects of great ones (18)
That ebb and flow by the moon. (19)
King Lear, 5.3, 8-19

(LEAR'S mind remains patchy. In his dotage, he is happy to find Cordelia. So happy he says 'Come, let's away to prison.' (7) He wants to be with her and have her forgiveness.

In his newfound delight with her company, he says, 'We two alone will sing like birds i' the cage.'* (9) Three lines later, Lear tells Cordelia that they will 'pray, and sing, and tell old tales, and laugh at gilded* butterflies.' (12) I found it charming that that he wants them to 'laugh at gilded butterflies,' or poseurs at court.

*It's likely that the 1900 song, 'I'm only a bird in a gilded cage' is derivative of these lines.

Lear, living in the past, tells Cordelia that they'll gossip about court life: 'Who loses and who wins, who's in, who's out.' (15) This phrase fits the society of any era.

How poetic are the closing lines where Lear tells Cordelia that they'll be like 'god's spies,' as they try to understand 'the mystery of things,' (16) or dark secrets.

When Lear says they'll examine the 'pacts and sects of great ones,' (18) he's thinking of his own ups and downs, and the way king's fortunes 'ebb and flow by the moon.' (19)

* * *

(AS Lear and Cordelia are led away, bad Edmund tells the guard, in a fate-sealing order, 'To be tender-minded does not become a sword,' (31) or soldier. In other words, show no mercy to these two.

Edmund tells Albany that Cordelia and Lear are under guard and await trial. Albany reminds Edmund that he's no longer in charge of anything.

Regan and Goneril enter still bickering over who owns Edmund. Regan tells Goneril, 'Lady, I am not well.' (73) Her 'full-flowing stomach' (74) is full of bile. No wonder, loving sister Goneril has poisoned her.

Albany arrests Edmund 'On capital treason,' (83) calls his wife Goneril a 'gilded serpent' (84) and tells her that she's not getting Edmund, and that Regan has first rights on him. For Regan, that's called getting what you deserve, although upcoming events render the issue moot.

A herald enters to read from a scroll that calls Edmund a 'manifold traitor.' (113) Edmund, in armor, throws down his glove and is ready to fight. Edgar steps in to order his brother, 'Draw thy sword.' (127) They fight, and Edmund falls but is not yet dead.

Goneril tells Albany that he's been fooled. He says, 'Shut your mouth, dame.' (154) Her love letter to Edmund was found on Oswald's body. Albany tells her, 'read thine own evil.' (156) Goneril tells him, 'the laws are mine, not thine' (158) and leaves. Albany send guards after her.

Out of character, the dying Edmund admits 'What you have charged me with, that have I done.' (162)

With expressive opening lines, Edgar continues to be big-hearted, and in line one offers to make peace, 'Let's exchange charity.' (166)

Edgar. Let's exchange charity.
I am no less in blood than thou art, Edmund. (167)
If more, the more thou hast wronged me.
My name is Edgar, and thy father's son. (169)
The gods are just, (170) and of our pleasant vices
Make instruments to plague us.
The dark and vicious place where thee he got (172)
Cost him his eyes.
Edmund. Thou hast spoken right, 'Tis true.

<u>The wheel is come full circle. I am here</u>. (174)
King Lear, 5.3

('I am no less in blood than thou art, Edmund.' (167) Even though I was conceived out of wedlock, I'm just as titled as you are.

'My name is Edgar, and thy father's son,' (169) means we are who we are because the gods are right.

Then Edgar says 'The gods are just.' (170) Contrast that with his father's earlier, 'As flies to wanton boys are we to the gods, they kill us for their sport.' Edgar is a believer. His father, in the depths of despair, is a cynic.

Edgar speaks of 'The dark and vicious place where thee he got' (172) to tell Edmund that if he hadn't been born it would not have 'Cost him his eyes,' meaning their father.

Edmund admits that his brother is right, 'The wheel is come full circle.' He started out wrong and ended, 'I am here,' (174) the same way. It is a resolution of sorts.

Following the exchange above, Albany asks after Gloucester, the blinded father, Edgar answers that his heart 'Burst smilingly,' (198) meaning, in his buoyant and caring language, that his father died happily.)

(A gentleman enters holding a knife and crying for help. Edgar asks him, 'What means this bloody knife?' (222)

Gentleman.
<u>'Tis hot, it smokes</u>. (223)
It came even from the heart of—oh, she's dead! . . .
(To Albany.) Your lady, sir, your lady. And her sister
By her is poisoned. She hath confessed it.
Edmund. I was contracted to them both. <u>All three</u> (227)
<u>Now marry in an instant</u>. . . .
Yet Edmund was beloved.
The one the other poisoned for my sake,
And after slew herself. . . .
He hath commission for thy wife and me
<u>To hang Cordelia in the prison</u> (254) and
To lay the blame upon her own despair,
That she <u>fordid herself</u>. (255)
King Lear, 5.3, 222-255

(THE Gentleman's opening line ''Tis hot, it smokes' (223) is an actor's gift of language and business.

When Edmund hears the news that Goneril and Regan are dead, he says ironically that the three of them 'Now marry in an instant,' (227) meaning he knows that he'll die in an instant.

Given all the onstage deaths in Will's plays, I'm surprised he didn't give audiences the satisfaction of seeing Goneril stab herself.

Edmund says, 'I pant for life' and 'Some good I mean to do.' (243) Before dying, he asks attendants to run and rescind the order to kill Cordelia, but they arrive too late.

Three lines from the end of his speech, Edmund tells Albany that his wife, Goneril, gave the order 'To hang Cordelia in the prison.' (254) Then claim that she 'fordid herself,' (255) or committed suicide.)

* * *

(Lear enters carrying the dead Cordelia.)

Lear. Howl, howl, howl, howl! Oh, you are men of stones.
Had I your tongue's and eyes, I'd use them so
That Heaven's vault should crack. (259) She's gone forever.
I know when one is dead and when one lives.
She's dead as earth. Lend me a looking-glass.
If that her breath will mist or stain the stone,
Why, then she lives. . . .
This feather stirs, she lives. (265) If it be so,
It is a chance which does redeem all sorrows (266)

That ever I have felt. . . .
I plague upon you, murderers, traitors all!
I might have saved her. Now she's gone forever.
Cordelia, Cordelia! Stay a little. Ha!
What is 't thou say'st. <u>Her voice was ever soft,</u> (272)
<u>Gentle and low, an excellent thing in woman.</u>
<u>I killed the slave that was a-hanging thee.</u> . . . (273)
<u>And my poor fool is hanged!</u> (304) No, no, no life!
<u>Why should a dog, a horse, a rat, have life</u> (306)
And thou no breath at all? Thou'lt come no more,
Never, never, never, never, never!
<u>Pray you, undo this button.</u> (309) Thank you, sir.
Do you see this? Look on her, look, her lips,
Look there, look there!
King Lear, 5.3, 257-311

(LEAR'S third line, 'That Heaven's vault should crack,' (259) is an admirable expression of grief.

Sadly, as though willing his daughter to be alive, Lear asks for a mirror to see if she has breath. Then, 'This feather stirs, she lives.' (269) And if she does, 'It is a chance which does redeem all sorrows.' (266) Lear is desperate for a chance to relieve his guilt. This sequence is breathtaking theater.

Halfway through the speech, knowing Cordelia is dead, and now prizing her qualities, Lear says in admiration, 'Her voice was ever soft, gentle and low, an excellent thing in woman.' (272) This confirms the impression that Regan and Goneril's voices were harsh.

'I killed the slave that was a-hanging thee. . . .' (273) Lear had some revenge, even if it wasn't against Edmund who ordered Cordelia's death.

'And my poor fool is hanged!' (304) A clever switch in the use of 'hang.' In that period the word 'fool' is often used as a term of endearment, in this case towards Cordelia. This is sadly followed, on the same line by, 'No, no, no life!'

And then the lament, 'Why should a dog, a horse, a rat, have life.' and his beloved Cordelia dies. (306) Given the proper intonation, this line moistens eyes.

Three lines from the end, 'Pray you, undo this button.' (309) Lear asks this before in the play, and it signals that before he dies his heartbeat is uncontrollable.

Albany tells Edgar and Kent, who has entered the scene, 'You, to your rights,' (300) meaning that they are welcome to the advantages of staying. Edgar stays on. Kent is dying, 'My master calls me, I must not say no.' (322)

SUMMARY

This masterful play has acting parts personifying several people with tragic flaws: The miscalculation of dividing the kingdom, plus Lear's credulous whims, makes him a tragic figure who happens to be a fine poet.

The bitterness with which Edmund resents his bastardy to the point of deadly pursuits is another tragic flaw.

We need to include the malicious temperaments of Goneril and Regan.

Gloucester's vanity and gullibility allows him to believe Edmund's lies about his good son Edgar. Gloucester loses his title, his eyes and his life. He is, however, rewarded with moving reconciliation moments with Edgar.

\- \- \-

MACBETH

Pivotal Speeches Critiqued

MACBETH, written around 1606, is one of Will's shortest, most seamless and greatest plays. It was written as a compliment to the Scottish-born King James the First, Queen Elizabeth the First's successor. King James was also a 47th cousin of Banquo.

Who is responsible in this Scottish tragedy? Is it the fates represented by the Weird Sisters, or witches; Macbeth's character; Lady Macbeth's ambition; or all three?

Next, the witches talk of past, present, and future.

Witch 1. When shall we three meet again
In thunder, lightning, or rain?
Witch 2. <u>When the hurly-burly's done</u>, (3)
<u>When the battle's lost and won.</u>
Witch 3. That will be ere the set of sun.

Witch 1. Where's the place?
Witch 2. Upon the heath.
Witch 3. There to meet with Macbeth.
Witch 1. I come, Graymalkin. (8)
All. Paddock calls.—Anon (9)
Fair is foul, and foul is fair. (11)
Hover through the fog and filthy air.
Macbeth, 1.1, 1-12

(WITH spelling current for that time, the version above is in the 1623 First Folio.

Witch two says they will meet again, 'When the battle's lost and won.' (3) The recent battle with Norway was lost until Macbeth came, and then it was won.

Witch one calls for her demon in the form of a gray cat named 'Graymalkin.' (8)

All the witches say 'Paddock calls,' (9) meaning their frog. Anticipating a later scene, I fear for the frog.

Then they chant, 'Fair is foul, and foul is fair.' (11) They're saying that everything's topsy-turvy.

What an acting and makeup opportunity the Weird Sisters are; all long fingernails, crooked fingers, pointed chins, hairs growing out of warts, flying hair, craggy voices and flayed costumes.

In the introduction to his masterful screenplay for *A Streetcar Named Desire,* Tennessee Williams described a darkened cloud formation as resembling 'the torn garments of witches.')

* * *

(DUNCAN, King of Scotland, enters with his sons, Malcolm and Donalbain, along with Lennox, a Scottish nobleman. They meet a sergeant bleeding from wounds of battle. Malcolm asks him how it's going: 'Say to the King the knowledge of the broil.' (6)

Sergeant. Doubtful it stood,
As <u>two spent swimmers that do cling together</u> (8)
<u>And choke their art.</u> . . .
For brave Macbeth—<u>well he deserves that name</u>— (16)
Disdaining fortune with his brandished steel,
Which <u>smoked with bloody execution,</u> (18)
Like valor's minion carvèd out his passage
Till he faced the slave,
Which ne'er shook hands, nor bade farewell to him,
<u>Till he unseamed him from the nave to the chaps,</u> (22)
And fixed his head upon our battlements.
Macbeth, 1.2, 7-23

(THE 'two spent swimmers that do cling together' (8) line is an inspired metaphor for two armies fighting to a standstill.

The sergeant goes on to tell his listeners that Macbeth is brave and 'well he deserves that name,' (16) for his sword 'smoked with bloody execution.' (18) The verb 'smoked' rewards us with a picture. It also tells us that for all his later faults, Macbeth is courageous in battle.

The next-to-last line, 'Till he unseamed him from the nave to the chaps,' (22) confirms the earlier 'bloody execution.' The verb 'unseamed' is ideal in its place.

The sergeant continues by saying the 'Norweyan lord' (31) was supplied with more arms and men and 'Began a fresh assault' (33) on the Scottish army. At this time, Norway was the enemy of Scotland.

Duncan, the king, asks the sergeant whether Macbeth and Banquo were 'dismayed' by this. And here we learn that Banquo is an ally of Macbeth.)

Sergeant. Doubly redoubled strokes upon the foe.
Except they mean to bathe in reeking wounds,
Or memorize another Golgotha, (40)
I cannot tell—
But I am faint, my gashes cry for help. (42)
Macbeth, 1.2, 38-42

(THE line, 'Or memorize another Golgotha' (40) tells us that the carnage was such that it resembled a huge burial ground like Golgatha, the burial site of Jesus and myriad others.

'But I am faint, my <u>gashes cry</u> for help,' is touching, 'gashes cry' is brilliant. (42)

Did you notice that, like the sergeant, many of Will's messengers talk more ornately than the lead characters?

Ross, another nobleman, enters to announce 'The victory fell on us.' (57)

* * *

(With their dialogue exhibiting impressive character definition, the wicked witches are back talking mischief and preparing to prophecy Macbeth's fate.)

Witch 1. Where hast thou been Sister?
Witch 2. Killing swine.
Witch 3. Sister, where thou?
Witch 1. A sailor's wife had chestnuts in her lap,
And mounched, and mounched, and mounched.
'Give me,' quoth I.
'Aroint thee, witch!' the <u>rump-fed ronyon</u> cries. (6)

Her husband's to Aleppo gone, master o' the Tiger,
(7)
But in a sieve I'll thither sail
And, like a rat without a tail, (9)
I'll do, I'll do, I'll do. . . .
And the very ports they blow,
All the quarters that they know
I' the shipman's card.
I will drain him dry as hay.
Sleep shall neither night nor day
Hang upon his penthouse lid. (20)
He shall live a man forbid. (21)
Weary se'nnights nine times nine (22)
Shall he dwindle, peak, and pine.
Though his bark cannot be lost, (24)
Yet it shall be tempest-tost. (25)
Look what I have. . .
Here I have a pilot's thumb, (28)
Wrecked as homeward did he come.
Witch 3. A drum, a drum!
Macbeth doth come.
All. The weird sisters hand in hand, (32)
Posters of the sea and land
Thus do go about, about.
Thrice to thine, and thrice to mine,
And thrice again, to make up nine.
Peace! The charm's wound up.

(FOUR lines into Witch One's description of the sailor's wife 'mounching' chestnuts, she describes her as a 'rump-fed ronyon,' (6) which is a double meaning in that she is broad in the beam and likes to gorge on meat.

A line later, she mentions that the husband of the woman munching chestnuts is 'master o' the Tiger,' (7) a ship that's like a 'sieve.'

Witch One follows that by saying she is 'like a rat without a tail.' (9) When magic creatures, like Witch One, take the form of an animal something is missing. We now know it's the holes in the 'sieve'-like ship.

Witch One jinxes the sailor with, 'sleep will 'Hang upon his penthouse lid,' (20) or upper lid. Nice adjective, 'penthouse,' then and now.

She continues the malediction, 'He shall live a man forbid,' (21) or damned.

'Weary se'nnights nine times nine.' (22) The witches see spiritual value, especially the fulfillment of goals, in the number nine. Witch One curses the master of the Tiger to spend eighty-one 'se'nights,' or weeks awake in storms.

Two lines later, when the witch says, 'Though his bark cannot be lost,' (24) she admits that she doesn't have the power to sink it. The next line, 'Yet it shall be tempest-tost' (25) reveals that she can do some damage. This witch knows her limitations.

But she doesn't lack confidence in her abilities: 'Here I have a pilot's thumb.' (28) Meaning that she spends most of her time sinking ships, which is a contradiction of her earlier admission of being unable to sink the Tiger. Come on, Witch One, make up your mind.

When 'The weird sisters' call themselves 'weird' at the start of their chant at the end of this passage, they're announcing that they are the three fates who control the destiny of individuals, as Witch One did with the captain of the ship Tiger.

Specifically, 'weird' in the sense it's being used suggests fate-inducing powers, rather than the modern usage.

The remainder of the incantation, beginning with, 'The weird sisters . . .' (32) is a shade childish, surely interpolated or written by someone other than Will. The witch's words are not on the same level as the tragic effects they produce.)

* * *

(Macbeth and Banquo, both Scottish army generals, enter the onstage heath.)

Macbeth. <u>So foul and fair a day I have not seen.</u> (38)

Banquo. What are these?

So withered, and so wild in their attire,

That look not like the inhabitants o' the earth

And yet are on 't? Live you? Or are you aught

That man may question? You seem to understand me,

By each at once her choppy finger laying

Upon her skinny lips. You should be women,

<u>And yet your beards forbid me to interpret</u> (46)

That you are so.

Macbeth. Speak, if you can. What are you?

Witch 1. All hail, Macbeth! Hail to thee, Thane of Glamis!

Witch 2. All hail, Macbeth! Hail to thee, Thane of Cawdor!

Witch 3. All hail, Macbeth, <u>that shalt be King hereafter!</u> (49)

Banquo. <u>Good sir, why do you start, and seem to fear</u> (51)

Things that do sound so fair? i' the name of truth,

Are ye fantastical, or that indeed

Which outwardly ye show? My noble partner

You greet me with present grace and great prediction

Of noble having and of royal hope.

That he seems rapt withal. To me you speak not.

If you can look into the seeds of time

And say which grain will grow and which will not,

Speak then to me, who neither beg nor fear
Your favors nor your hate.
Witch 1. (All to Banquo.) Lesser than Macbeth and
greater.
Witch 2. Not so happy, yet much happier.
Witch 3. Thou shall get kings, though thou be none.
(67)
So all hail, Macbeth and Banquo.
Macbeth. Stay, you imperfect speakers, tell me more.
By Sinel's death (71) I know I am Thane of Glamis,
But how of Cawdor? The Thane of Cawdor lives,
A prosperous gentleman and to be King (73)
Stands not within the prospect of belief,
No more than to be Cawdor. Say from whence
You owe this strange intelligence? Or why
Upon this blasted heath you stop our way
With such prophetic greeting? Speak, I charge you.
Macbeth, 1.3, 38-77

(MACBETH'S opening line of this passage, 'So foul
and fair a day I have not seen,' (38) is a deliberate echo
of the witch's speech in 1.1(1) Macbeth is also alluding
to the weather and the fortunes of battle, as the
witches do in 1.1, (3)

In the next-to-last line of Banquo's first speech,
he thinks the witches are women, 'And yet your
beards forbid me to interpret' (46) that. In most, if not

all, literature witches are exclusively female, a strange tradition. However, in the 1692 Salem, Massachusetts trials two men were executed for allegedly practicing witchcraft. Thirteen women were hanged, not a fair tally. I blush to say that one of the tarnished judges, and the official minister of the trials, was the Reverend Nicholas Noyes. I am cursed by bell, book and candle and plead for your undeserved mercy.

Getting back to Banquo's reference to 'beards,' it was believed that women with facial hair were inherently wicked. You may recall from the film *The Wizard of Oz* that the Wicked Witch of the West, brilliantly played by the actress Margaret Hamilton, had some facial sprouts.

The three witches, representing in order past, present and future, hail Macbeth. The third hail, 'That shalt be King hereafter,' (49) causes a physical reaction in Macbeth. Banquo asks him, 'Good sir, why do you start, and seem to fear.' (51) He starts because what he has wished for years has been presented to him.

The witches address Banquo. Witch Three tells him, 'Thou shall get kings, though thou be none.' (57) As I'm sure you've deduced, this prophecy is why Macbeth plans to kill Banquo.

'By Sinel's death' (71) means that Macbeth knows that he became Thane of Glamis when his father died.

What he doesn't know is why the witches named him Thane of Cawdor, 'A prosperous gentleman and to be King,' (73) someone who lives. This is a mistake in the text. Macbeth knows that the Thane of Cawdor has been captured by the Norwegian army. Incidentally, a Scottish 'thane' is roughly equivalent to a British earl or duke.

The witches disappear. In dialogue that follows but not shown above, Banquo says, 'The earth hath bubbles as the water has,' (79) meaning that you can't change the fates. He understands that the three witches constitute the three fates.

Still trying to figure it all out, Banquo asks, 'Were such things here as we do speak about?' (83) He adds, 'Or have we eaten on the insane root? (84) He wonders, out loud to Macbeth whether they have taken henbane or hemlock.

In then saying to Banquo, 'Your children shall be kings,' (86) Macbeth, as we shall see, doesn't take the witch's prophesies lightly.)

* * *

(WE'VE already met Ross, a nobleman. He enters accompanied by Angus, another noble, with a very Scottish name.

They tell Macbeth that Duncan, the King, is rewarding him, for bravery in battle, the title Thane of Cawdor. Macbeth protests that the Thane of Cawdor lives. Angus reports that Cawdor consorted with the enemy and is under penalty of treason.

Macbeth says to himself in an aside that the best is yet to come. He wants to be king. He's had a taste, now he wants nothing less than the entire meal. Macbeth then says about Banquo, in a warning, expressed in a continuing aside, 'Do not hope that your children shall be kings.' (117)

Note: The word 'Aside' does not appear in the First Folio. Apparently, it was assumed that the actors could figure out the places for asides from the copy. Since Will is an actor, thinks like an actor, and writes for actors, this is understandable.)

* * *

(NEXT, Banquo speaks on what is happening, followed by Macbeth's revealing aside.)

Banquo. That, trusted home,
Might yet enkindle you unto the crown,
Besides the Thane of Cawdor. But 'tis strange.
And oftentimes to win us to our harm,
The instruments of darkness tell us truths, (124)

Win us with honest trifles, to betray's
In deepest consequence.
Cousins, a word, I pray you. (127)
Macbeth. (Aside.) Two truths are told (128)
As happy prologues to the swelling act (129)
Of the imperial theme. . . .
This supernatural soliciting
Cannot be ill, cannot be good, If ill,
Why hath it given me earnest of success, (132)
Commencing in a truth? I am Thane of Cawdor.
If good, why do I yield to that suggestion
Whose horrid image doth unfix my hair
And make my seated heart knock at my ribs,
Against the use of nature? Present fears
Are less than horrible imaginings.
My thought, whose murder yet is but fantastical, (139)
Shakes so my single state of man that function
Is smothered in surmise, and nothing is
But what is not. . . .
If chance will have me King, why, chance may crown
me. (143)
Without my stir.
Macbeth, 1.3, 120-144

(COMPARE Banquo's lines, three through the end of
his speech, with Hamlet's mistrust of the ghost who

tells him dread things. Both have good reasons to watch out for a devil in disguise.

The line, 'The instruments of darkness tell us truths' (124) says that the devil tells us truths at first to lead us on, and then we live by his lies.

'Cousins, a word, I pray you' (127) is Banquo's last line of his speech. All nobles called themselves 'cousins,' which also means 'kinsman.'

Macbeth's initial lines in his aside are so vivid they confirm that he thought of being king before he heard the Witch's prophecy. The first line is, 'Two truths are told.' (128) This is followed by the theatrical, 'As happy prologues to the swelling act of the imperial theme.' (129) Macbeth sees the action being played out that will lead him to become king.

Macbeth then asks himself, if the augury is ill founded, 'Why hath it given me earnest of success, commencing in a truth?' (132) Or, how can the witches come from hell, if they tell the truth?

Later in the aside, he thinks, 'My thought, whose murder yet is but fantastical.' (139) This gives away that Macbeth is already contemplating murder.

Two lines from the end of his speech, Macbeth says, 'If chance will have me King, why, chance may crown me.' (143) Macbeth thinks he doesn't have to do anything to become king. But the Weird Sisters know he is impatient.)

* * *

(DUNCAN, the Scottish King, and his sons Malcolm and Donalbain are in the castle at Forres, about 25 miles from Inverness. Malcolm reports to his father that the Thane of Cawdor, whose title Macbeth now holds, has been executed for treason.)

Malcolm. My liege,
They are not yet come back. But I have spoke
With one that saw him die, who did report
That very frankly he confessed his treasons,
Implored your Highness' pardons, and set forth
A deep repentance. <u>Nothing in his life</u> (7)
<u>Became him like the leaving it.</u> He died
As one that had been studied in his death
To throw away the dearest thing he owed
As 'twere a careless trifle.
Duncan. There's no art
<u>To find the mind's construction in the face.</u> (13)
He was a gentlemen on whom I built
An absolute trust.
(Macbeth, Banquo, others enter.)
Macbeth. And our duties
Are to your throne and state and children and servants,

Which do but what they should, by doing everything
Safe toward your love and honor. (27)
Duncan. We will establish our estate upon
Our eldest, Malcolm, whom we name hereafter
The Prince of Cumberland. (39) Which honor must
Not unaccompanied invest him only,
But signs of nobleness, like stars, shall shine
On all deservers. From hence to Inverness, (42)
And bind us further to you.
Macbeth. (Aside.) The Prince of Cumberland! That is a
step. (48)
On which I must fall down or o'erleap, (49)
For in my way it lies. Stars, hide your fires,
Let not light see my black and deep desires. (51)
The eye wink (52) at the hand, yet let that be
Which the eye fears, when it is done, to see.
Macbeth, 1.4, 3-53

(HALFWAY through his speech describing the Thane of Cawdor's death, Malcolm utters the famous line, 'Nothing in his life became him like the leaving it.' (7) An elegant, and subsequently much-repeated, way of saying he made a good end.

Duncan excuses himself for trusting Cawdor by saying there's no way 'To find the mind's construction in the face.' (13) That's a debatable point. Some people believe that until the age of fifty you're stuck with the face you were born with. After that, you are responsible.

Macbeth enters with murder on his mind and offers Duncan a gush of hypocrisy ending with the goal of making everything 'Safe toward your love and honor.' (27)

To Macbeth's dismay, Duncan then names his son heir apparent, 'The Prince of Cumberland.' (39)

Three lines later, Duncan adds 'From hence to Inverness.' (42) He plans a royal progress to Macbeth's castle.*

*Elizabeth 1 went on many royal visits that in several cases left the noble hosts destitute for the expense of it all. Given Macbeth's plans for mayhem, Duncan's royal progress is timely.

In Macbeth's next aside, he says to himself, 'The Prince of Cumberland! That is a step.' (48) He doesn't like news of that hindrance to his goals. And he goes on with, 'On which I must fall down or o'erleap,' (49) meaning he plans to kill the King.

'Let not light see my black and deep desires' (51) describes Macbeth's wish that the stars will go out so that his fellow nobles won't see through his immoral plans.

The 'eye wink' (52) at the hand, or be blind to what I plan to do.

We can bet that Macbeth whipped his horse back to his castle at Inverness ahead of Duncan and his train. Macbeth needs to talk to Lady Macbeth. After Will's skillful framework in the first four scenes, we're now really getting into it.)

* * *

(WE'RE at Inverness Castle with Lady Macbeth awaiting her husband. She reads a letter from him describing his meeting with the witches. The letter relates Macbeth's goals and the need for her help in achieving them. Are you rubbing your hands in anticipation? Or are you thinking ahead to where the Macbeth's will be kneading their bloody hands in fear?

The letter also tells of the King awarding Macbeth the title, Thane of Cawdor. After entering the scene, Macbeth informs Lady Macbeth that the weird sisters saluted him with 'All hail, Macbeth, that shalt be King hereafter!' (1.3, 49) We pick up the letter-reading from that point, followed by Lady Macbeth's explicit reactions in illimitable poetry.)

Lady Macbeth. (Reads her husbands' letter.) 'This have I thought good to deliver thee, <u>my dearest partner of greatness,</u> (10) that though mightst not lose the dues of rejoicing by being ignorant of what greatness is promised thee. Lay it to thy heart and farewell.'

Lady Macbeth. (Soliloquy.) Glamis thou art, and Cawdor, and shalt be

What thou art promised. <u>Yet do I fear thy nature</u>. (17)

<u>It is too full o' the milk of human kindness</u> (18)

<u>To catch the nearest way</u>, (19) Thou wouldst be great,

<u>Art not without ambition</u>, (20) but without

The illness should attend it. What thou wouldst highly,

That wouldst thou holily—wouldst not play false,

And yet wouldst strongly win. Thou'dst have, great Glamis,

That which cries 'Thus thou must do, if thou have it,

<u>And that which rather thou dost fear to do</u> (25)

Than wishest should be undone. Hie thee hither,

That I may pour my spirits in thine ear,

And chastise with the valor of my tongue

<u>All that impedes thee from the golden round</u> (29)

Which fate and metaphysical aid doth seem

To have thee crowned withal.

Messenger. (Enters.) The King comes here tonight. . . . Our Thane is coming.

Lady Macbeth. The raven himself is hoarse

<u>That croaks the fatal entrance of Duncan</u> (40)

<u>Under my battlements</u>. Come, you spirits

That tend on mortal thoughts, <u>unsex me here</u>, (42)

And fill me, from the crown to the toe, topfull
Of direct cruelty! Make thick my blood,
Stop up the access and passage to remorse, (45)
That no compunctious visitings of nature
Shake my fell purpose, nor keep peace between
The effect and it! Come to my woman's breasts, (48)
And take my milk for gall, you murdering ministers,
Wherever in your sightless substances
You wait on nature's mischief! Come, thick night, (51)
And pall thee in the dunnest smoke of Hell,
That my keen knife not see the wound it makes,
Nor Heaven peep through the blanket of the dark (53)
To cry 'Hold, hold!' (Macbeth enters.)
Great Glamis! Worthy Cawdor!
Greater than both, by the all-hail hereafter!
Thy letters have transported me beyond
This ignorant present, and I feel now
The future in the instant.
Macbeth, 1.5, 10-58

(MACBETH tells her that Duncan is coming tonight
and leaves 'Tomorrow, as he purposes.' (61) That line
can be read two ways: he will leave dead or alive.)

Lady Macbeth. Oh, never,
Shall sun that morrow see!
Your face, my Thane, is a book where men (63)

302

May read strange matters. To <u>beguile the time,</u>
<u>Look like the time, bear welcome in your eye,</u> (65)
Your hand, your tongue. Look like the innocent flower
<u>But be the serpent under 't.</u> (67) He that's coming
Must be provided for. And you shall put
<u>This night's great business into my dispatch,</u> (69)
Which shall to all our nights and days to come
Give solely sovereign sway and masterdom.
Macbeth, 1.5, 61-71

(IN line one and continuing into line two of Macbeth's letter, he calls Lady Macbeth, 'my dearest partner of greatness,' (10) and we learn that he depends on her.

After finishing reading the letter, and in the beginning of her soliloquy, Lady Macbeth gives us insight into her husband's character with, 'Yet do I fear thy nature.' (17) And she punctuates this with the lasting comment on his temperament, 'It is too full o' the milk of human kindness.' (18) Peppered with 'To catch the nearest way,' (19) or resort to assassination.

Then, with her devious mind catching on to what needs to be done to clear the way for her husband, she says, 'Art not without ambition,' (20) is needed. Substitute assassination for ambition, and we see that the wicked plan is hatched.

As her speech continues, five lines later Lady Macbeth says, 'And that which rather thou dost fear to do.' (25) This means that her husband wishes to kill Duncan and seize the crown, but he's afraid to do it himself. She knows he'd like to have it, and it cries out to him, but he'll hesitate.

By saying, 'All that impedes thee from the golden round,' (29) Lady M. is telling her husband that where he is lacking in spirit and valor in his search for the crown will be facilitated by her.

After finishing her first speech, a messenger enters to inform Lady Macbeth that Duncan is on his way to Inverness. She says that the raven, in her view a symbol of evil, 'croaks the fatal entrance of Duncan.' (40) Said differently, it is fate that Duncan is coming 'Under my battlements,' and as a consequence, it is fated that he should die.

Although unflinching until now, Lady Macbeth does say in the next line, 'unsex me here,' (42) or make me a man. This wish contrasts with her opinion that Macbeth doesn't have it in him to commit murder.

But she goes on with 'Stop up the access and passage to remorse.' (45) Or, don't let that part of me work, the part of the body in which remorse is found.

I've seen actors saying, 'Come to my woman's breasts, and take my milk for gall, you murdering ministers.' (48) Actors with the voice and business to relay the poetry make the moment riveting.

'Come, thick night, and pall thee in the dunnest smoke of Hell,' (51) is striking poetry. 'Hold, hold,' finishes Lady Mabeth's wish that no good spirits 'peep through the blanket of the dark.' (53) Love the cute verb 'peep' amid all the treachery, particularly with Heaven potentially saying 'Hold, hold.'

In her final speech of the passage, after Macbeth enters, Lady M. counsels her husband to put on a good face for the king. She knows that he is not the actor that she is, and he gives away his feelings. His face, she says, 'is a book where men may read strange matters,' (63) an excellent phrase.

'Beguile the time,' (65) she advises Macbeth, 'Look like the time, bear welcome in your eye.' 'But be the serpent under 't.' (67) Leave the murder to me and put 'This night's great business into my dispatch' (69) she concludes, and that will deliver the crown.

Going back a few lines, I thought using 'beguile' (65) as a verb was inventive.

Lady Macbeth's foreboding series of speeches in scene five of act one are prime among Will's speeches.)

* * *

(IN scene six of act one, Duncan and his entourage, including Banquo, arrive at Macbeth's Inverness castle. Lady Macbeth greets them and offers food. Duncan wonders where Macbeth is.)

* * *

(SCENE SEVEN opens with Macbeth in recognizable soliloquy. When that ends, Lady Macbeth enters to find, as she earlier predicted, that her husband's recent resolve on the murderous mission has gone wobbly.)

Macbeth. <u>If it were done when 'tis done then 'twere well</u> (1)
<u>It were done quickly.</u> If the assassination
Could trammel up the consequence, and catch,
With his surcease, success, that but this blow
Might be the <u>be-all and the end-all</u> here, (5)
But here, <u>upon this bank and shoal of time,</u> (6)
<u>We'd jump the life to come.</u> But in these cases
We still have judgment here, that we but teach
<u>Bloody instructions,</u> (9) which being taught return
To <u>plague the inventor,</u> (10) This even-handed justice
Commends the ingredients of our poisoned chalice
To our own lips.
He's here in double trust.

First, as I am his kinsman and his subject,
Strong both against the deed. Then, as his host,
Who should against his murderer shut the door,
Not bear the knife myself. Besides, this Duncan
Hath borne his faculties so meek, hath been
So clear in his great office, that his virtues
<u>Will plead like angels trumpet-tongued</u> against (19)
The <u>deep damnation of his taking-off.</u> (20)
And pity, like a naked newborn babe,
Striding the blast, or Heaven's cherubim horsed
Upon the sightless couriers of the air,
Shall blow the horrid deed in every eye,
That tears shall drown the wind. I have no spur
To <u>prick the sides of my intent,</u> (26) but only
<u>Vaulting ambition, which o'erleaps itself</u> (27)
And falls on the other.
Macbeth, 1.7, 1-28

(THE first two lines, 'If it were done . . . (1) are storied.

Line five includes 'be-all and the end-all,' (5) long since fallen into the language.

And here, 'upon this bank and shoal of time, we'd jump the life to come,' (6) a fluent and pertinent phrase meaning that if Duncan is killed right now Macbeth can't enjoy his newfound honors like the title Thane of Cawdor.

Four lines later, Macbeth wonders whether following 'Bloody instructions' (9) would lead someone to come back and murder him, or as Will put it, 'plague the inventor.' (10)

Over the next several lines, Macbeth acknowledges that Duncan has been a good King and anybody found guilty of murdering him will be subject to the 'deep damnation of his taking-off,' (20) or murder. Setting that up in the previous line, Macbeth says that Duncan's virtues 'Will plead like angels trumpet-tongued' (19) against killing him. My goodness, that's fine language.

In 'prick the sides of my intent,' (26) Macbeth imagines that his intent, is a nonliteral horse, and he has no spurs to make it go faster. It is a language-loaded section of the speech that you should carefully reread for full appreciation of how original word combinations flow off Will's quill like an opened faucet.

In the last two lines, Macbeth finds he only has 'Vaulting ambition, which o'erleaps itself' (27) and vaults over the figurative horse. Also, if he leaps too high he'll fail.)

* * *

(LADY M. enters to tell Macbeth that Duncan has supped. Macbeth inquires whether the King has asked for him, and she tells him, of course.

Next, Macbeth reveals to her his reconsidered feelings about the planned murder.)

Macbeth. We will proceed no further in this business.
He hath honored me of late, and I have bought
Golden opinions from all sorts of people,
Which would be worn now in their newest gloss, (33)
Not cast aside so soon.
Lady Macbeth. Was the hope drunk (35)
Wherein you dressed yourself? Hath it slept since?
And wakes it now, to look so green and pale
At what it did so freely? From this time (37)
Such I account thy love. Art thou afeard?
To be the same in thine own act and valor
As thou art in desire? Wouldst thou have that
Which thou esteem'st the ornament of life
And live a coward in thine own esteem, (42)
Letting 'I dare not' wait upon 'I would,'
Like the poor cat i' the adage. . . .
What beast was 't then
That made you break this enterprise to me? . . .
I have given suck, and know
How tender 'tis to love the babe that milks me.
I would, while it was smiling in my face,

Have plucked my nipple from his boneless gums
And dashed the brains out, (57) had I so sworn as you
Have done to this.
Macbeth. If we should fail?
Lady Macbeth. We fail!
But screw your courage to the sticking-place (60)
And we'll not fail. When Duncan is asleep—
Whereto the rather shall his day's hard journey
Soundly invite him, his two chamberlains
Will I with wine and wassail (64) so convince
That memory, the warder of the brain,
Shall be a fume, and the receipt of reason
A limbec only. (67) When in swinish sleep
Their drenchèd natures lie as in a death,
What cannot you and I perform upon
The ungarded Duncan? What not put upon
His spongy officers, who shall bear the guilt (71)
Of our great quell?
Macbeth, 1.7, 31-83

(WITH, 'Which would be worn now in their newest gloss,' (33) Macbeth says that he likes the idea of the new honors from Duncan, like the title Thane of Cawdor, and he'd like to wear them for awhile. It's an excuse for action, but the new title and recognition temporarily feed his ego.

Lady Macbeth rejects his plea out of hand and replies to her husband's default on his promise to kill Duncan. She asks him if he was drunk when he made it: 'Was the hope drunk wherein you dressed yourself?' (35)

Then, in lines four and five, she increases the pressure of her boot on his neck by asking, 'From this time such I account thy love,' (37) or you don't love me anymore.

Four lines later she asks whether he will 'live a coward in thine own esteem.' (42)

I thought, *this is guilt-dealing at its best*, but it quickly rises to a higher level.

Lady M. tells Macbeth that if she had failed him like he's failing her she would have 'dashed the brains out' (57) of her nursing baby, even 'while it was smiling in my face.' Now there's a vow that has to get Macbeth's attention. It sure gets mine even though I've read it many times.

Unwisely, Macbeth asks his wife what they would do if the plot to kill Duncan failed. She really turns up the heat with the unforgettable, 'screw your courage to the sticking-place.' (60)

She plans to get Duncan's aides drunk, 'with wine and wassail,' (64) and then close the deal by blaming them for his murder, 'His spongy officers, who shall bear the guilt.' (71) Incidentally, 'wassail' means carouse, which comes from the German *gar aus*, or bottoms up. Note the 'spongy' aptly standing in for the overworked 'drunk.'

Then the skillful, worth rereading two lines leading up to 'A limbec only.' (67) She's saying that with all the alcohol she will provide, the grooms' memories and brains will be distilled like wine.

Thanks to Lady M's surpassing sales job, Macbeth is sold, and ends act one with a good exit line, 'False face must hide what the false heart doth know.' (83) Macbeth is learning. The line echoes his wife's earlier admonition that his face 'is a book where men may read strange matters,' or he needs to be a better actor.)

* * *

(IN the opening scene of act two, Banquo and his son Fleance walk and talk in the courtyard of Macbeth's castle, then exit.

Banquo. <u>How goes the night, boy?</u> (1)
Fleance. <u>The moon is down,</u> (2) I have not heard the clock.
Banquo. Hold, take my sword. <u>There's husbandry in Heaven.</u> (4)
<u>Their candles are all out.</u> (5) Take thee that too.
A heavy summons lies like lead upon me,

And yet I would not sleep. Merciful powers,
<u>Restrain in me the cursèd thoughts that nature</u> (8)
<u>Gives way to in repose!</u>
Macbeth, 2.1, 1-9

(When the scene opens with, 'How goes the night, boy?'— (1) Banquo, in this case, says 'boy' affectionately to his son.

Fleance responds with, 'The moon is down.' (2) As we know, variations on the moon being down, or having some influence, often recur in Will's plays.

'There's husbandry in Heaven.' (4) 'Their candles are all out' (5) means that the heavens are thrifty and don't waste light.

Banquo's final two lines above beginning with, 'Restrain in me the cursèd thoughts—' (8) This means that he dreams bad things but doesn't think about them when awake.

Next, Macbeth enters, and Banquo speaks of the witches: 'I dreamed last night of the three weird sisters. To you they have showed some truth.' (20) Since his mind is on killing Duncan, Macbeth is not interested in hearing about the witches and thinking about their prophecy: 'I think not about them.' (22) Or, Macbeth may be diverting Banquo from the witch's prophecy to show him that being King is not on his mind.)

(BANQUO and Fleance exit. Macbeth speaks to his servant, who also exits. Macbeth delivers a memorable soliloquy from a tortured mind.)

Macbeth. Go bid thy mistress, <u>when my drink is ready</u>, (31)
She strike upon the bell. Get thee to bed. (Servant exits.)
<u>Is this a dagger which I see before me</u>, (33)
The handle toward my hand? <u>Come, let me clutch thee</u>. (34)
I have thee not, and yet I see thee still.
Art thou not, fatal vision, sensible
To feeling as to sight? Or art thou but
<u>A dagger of the mind</u>, (38) a false creation,
Proceeding from the heat-oppressèd brain?
I see thee yet, in form as palpable
As this which now I draw.
Thou marshal'st me the way that I was going,
And such an instrument I was to use.
Mine eyes are made the fools o' the other senses,
Or else worth all the rest. I see thee still,
<u>And on thy blade and dudgeon gouts of blood</u>, (46)
Which was not so before. There's no such thing.
It is the bloody business which informs
Thus to mine eyes. Now o'er the one-half world

Nature seems dead, and wicked dreams abuse
The curtained sleep. Witchcraft celebrates
Pale Hecate's offerings, and withered murder, (52)
Alarmed by his sentinel, the wolf,
Whose howl 's his watch, (54) thus with his stealthy
pace,
With Tarquin's ravishing strides, (55) toward his
design
Moves like a ghost. Thou sure and firm-set earth,
Hear not my steps, which way they walk, for fear
The very stones prate of my whereabouts,
And take the present horror from the time
Which now suits with it. Whiles I threat, he lives.
Words to the heat of deeds too cold breath gives. (61)
I go, and it is done. The bell invites me.
Hear it not, Duncan, for it is a knell
That summons thee to Heaven, or too Hell. (64)
Macbeth, 2.1, 31-64

(BEFORE his grand soliloquy, Macbeth orders his
servant to have Lady Macbeth ring a bell 'when my
drink is ready.' (31) It was traditional that the lady of
the house fix her husband's posset of wine, eggs and
spice to help him sleep.

Macbeth's soliloquy of the mind, an actor's and
audience's delight, commences with 'Is this a dagger
which I see before me.' (33) The handle is nearest to

315

him, as he says, 'Come, let me clutch thee.' (34) Even though he sees the knife, he can't grab it and realizes that it's 'A dagger of the mind.' (38)

Macbeth's hallucinating brain reveals that 'on thy blade and dudgeon gouts of blood.' (46) The blade and handle were clean when the imagined dagger first appeared.

About three-quarters of the way through, when Macbeth is excited almost to the point of incoherence, he rails about the witchcraft goddess, Hecate, and 'withered murder,' (52) or skeletons. He even likens his fevered words to the wolf, 'Whose howl's his watch,' (54) or tells the time by howling.

'With Tarquin's ravishing strides' (55) recalls the lustful Tarquin rushing toward his barbarous deed in Shakespeare's *The Rape of Lucrece*.

Two couplets end the scene. The first ending with 'cold breath gives.' (61) Then, a bell rings prompting the second couplet closing with Duncan being summoned 'to Heaven, or too Hell.' (64) Did Will write both, or was either of them added later by another writer? We'll never know, but if you think like me, the second one is better.)

* * *

(LADY MACBETH and her husband discuss the night's depravity, starting off with making Duncan's aides inebriated patsies.)

Lady Macbeth. <u>That which made them drunk hath made me bold,</u> (1)
What hath quenched them hath given me fire.
Hark! Peace!
<u>It was the owl that shrieked, the fatal bellman,</u> (3)
<u>Which gives the stern'st good night</u>. (4) He's about it.
The doors are open, and the surfeited grooms
Do mark their charge with snores. I have drugged their possets,
That death and nature do contend about them,
Whether they live or die. . . .
Alack, I am afraid they have awaked
And 'tis not done. <u>The attempt and not the deed</u> (11)
<u>Confounds us.</u> Hark! I laid their daggers ready,
He could not miss 'em. Had he not resembled
<u>My father as he slept,</u> (13) I had done 't.
Macbeth. Methought I heard a voice cry '<u>Sleep no more!</u> (34)
<u>Macbeth does murder sleep</u>' (36)—the innocent sleep,
<u>Sleep that knits up the raveled sleeve of care,</u> (37)
The death of each day's life, sore labor's bath,
Balm of hurt minds, great nature's second course,

Chief nourisher in life's feast. . . .
Still it cried 'Sleep no more' to all the house,
'Glamis hath murdered sleep, and therefore Cawdor
Shall sleep no more, Macbeth shall sleep no more.'
Lady Macbeth. Who was it that thus cried? Why, worthy Thane,
You do unbend your noble strength to think
So brainsickly of things. Go get some water
And wash this filthy witness from your hand. (47)
Why did you bring these daggers from the place?
They must lie there. Go carry them, and smear
The sleepy grooms with blood. . . . (49)
Infirm of purpose!
Give me the daggers. The sleeping and the dead (53)
Are but as pictures. 'Tis the eye of childhood
That fears a painted devil. (55) If he do bleed,
I'll gild (56) the faces of the grooms withal,
For it must seem their guilt. (Exits)
Macbeth. Whence is that knocking? (58)
How is 't with me when every noise appals me?
What hands are here? Ha! They pluck out mine eyes!
Will all great Neptune's ocean wash this blood (60)
Clean from my hand? No, this my hand will rather
The multitudinous seas incarnadine, (62)
Making the green one red.
Lady Macbeth. (Reenters.) My hands are of your color, (64) but I shame

To wear a heart so white. (65) I hear a knocking
At the south entry. Retire we to our chamber.
A little water clears us of this deed. (67)
How easy is it then! Your constancy
Hath left you unattended. Hark! More knocking.
Get on your nightgown, lest occasion call us
And show us to be watchers. Be not lost
So poorly in your thoughts.
Macbeth, 2.2, 1-74

(LADY MACBETH's announcement: 'That which made them drunk hath made me bold' (1) tells us that the wine she drank with Duncan's grooms didn't make her sleepy. It gives her, as drink will do, more false courage. Or does it give her a temporary sense of power?

'It was the owl that shrieked the fatal bellman.' (3) This line, plus the one that follows, 'Which gives the stern'st good night,' (4) can be read two ways. The bellman could be the one who went around the city ringing his bell and crying 'All's well,' or it could be the 'fatal bellman' who rings his bell before a hanging. It's more likely the latter.

When, six lines later, Lady Macbeth says, 'The attempt and not the deed confounds us,' (11) she means that if they are caught in Duncan's room with the daggers they will hang for it.

'My father as he slept' (13) is an eerie line. She would have murdered Duncan herself, but he 'resembled' her father. It's always heartening when killers show some compassion. Inserting this line shows again that Will had an innate sense of human nature. I've read surviving-witness accounts of mass murderers walking through a fear-filled crowd, looking at some people and passing them by only to shoot the next one

The speeches above and their noted excerpts included here are useful. But, for full appreciation, the scene requires reading in its entirety. For example, after Lady Macbeth's unusual comment about her father in the paragraph above, there is extensive back and forth between the murderous couple.

Before Macbeth's imaginary 'sleep no more' (34) and 'Macbeth does murder sleep,' (36) speech he tells his wife that Duncan's grooms said their prayers before sleeping. Macbeth wanted to add 'Amen' to their 'God Bless us' (28) but it 'Stuck in my throat.' (32) We learn through this insightful writing that fear of retribution, regret, and guilt began the moment he committed murder.

After Macbeth hears the cry 'Macbeth does murder sleep,' he speaks of 'innocent sleep' and speaks several fine poetic lines on the subject: the memorable one being, 'Sleep that knits up the raveled sleeve of care.' (37)

Will wrote some bloody plays, *Titus Andronicus*, *Richard III*, *Cymbeline*, for example, but nothing like the blood-soaked Macbeth. The creepy lines resonate. Following Duncan's murder, Lady M. tells her husband to 'wash this filthy witness from your hand.' (47) She asks him why he didn't leave the daggers in the room and go back and smear 'The sleepy grooms with blood.' (49) He's won't go back, so she does.

Jane Greer, playing the icy femme fatale opposite Robert Mitchum in the 1947 film noir *Out of the Past*, would have been a worthy Lady Macbeth.

Back to the play at hand: No need to stew, Lady Macbeth tells her husband, 'The sleeping and the dead are but as pictures.' (53) And only a child 'fears a painted devil.' (55) How gruesomely effective that is, especially punctuated in the next line with the almost-comical verb 'gild.' (56) Now, there's a verb for you.

Macbeth starts his next speech with 'Whence is that knocking? (58) Then, more knocking occurs. This signifies to the audience that Macbeth's castle isn't just a hellish place of unnatural death. There are people outside, and life goes on. Will realized that the audience was stretched too far, and needs to be brought back. The knocking has further meaning, and we'll get to that.

Macbeth can't wash the blood off his hands and wonders, 'Will all great Neptune's ocean wash this blood' (60) away. He doesn't think so, and believes that his hand will make 'The multitudinous seas incarnadine,' (62) or red. That's called emphasizing a point. You can see actors like Orson Welles and Kenneth Branagh holding audiences rapt. I would like to have seen Sarah Siddons, Ellen Terry and Judith Anderson, among others, playing Lady Macbeth.

Judith Anderson could effortlessly project evilness, a necessary skill in playing Lady Macbeth. She personified wickedness as the mad Mrs. Danvers in the 1940 Hitchcock film *Rebecca*. With her insinuating, coaxing voice, she almost induced Joan Fontaine to jump onto the rocks below from a high Manderley window: 'It would be so easy.'

Back to *Macbeth*: in her final speech of this spellbinding scene, Lady M. returns from her blood-smearing mission to further incriminate Duncan's grooms. She tells her husband, 'My hands are of your color,' (64) but she wouldn't want 'To wear a heart so white,' (65) or be cowardly like him. Ouch! The scene ends with more knocking, as Lady Macbeth suggests that they go to their chamber and wash off the blood: 'A little water clears us of this deed.' (67) More knocking is heard, and Macbeth makes a pathetic wish that it would 'Wake Duncan.' (73)

* * *

(WHEN the tension becomes too taut, the audience needs something they can legitimately laugh at. Otherwise, the play could fall flat.

The vulgar Porter at the gate fills that role nicely. He greets Lennox, who we've already met, and Macduff, another Scottish nobleman, who becomes a crucial character in the play. Note that once Macduff appears, the appearances of Lady Macbeth diminish.)

Porter. <u>Here's a knocking indeed!</u> (1) If a man were porter of Hell Gate, he should have old turning the key. Knock, knock, knock! Who's there, i' the name of Beelzebub? Here's a farmer who hanged himself on th' expectation of plenty. . .
Anon, anon! <u>I pray you remember the porter.</u> (23)
Macbeth, 2.3, 1-21

(NOTE the porter's first sentence, 'Here's a knocking indeed! (1) We're reminded of the earlier knocking heard by the Macbeth's but with a different slant. Thomas De Quincy, in his 1823 essay 'On the Knocking at the Gate in *Macbeth*,' believes that the knocking is introduced to remind audiences of the horror of the murders contrasted with the nighttime quiet in the castle. We can't know Will's original intent. Was the knocking a tension-breaker, or did he have in mind a more cerebral use as in De Quincey's interpretation? We do know that Will writes for the audience, and if the knocking has two purposes all the better.

Starting with the second sentence and continuing through, not included in the copy above, to the final sentence of the speech, 'I pray you remember the porter,' (23) he is dreaming. He only wakes up, after having kept Lennox and Macduff outside waiting, to ask for a tip.

Macduff asks the porter why he was so late in answering the knocks. He responds that he was carousing and drink 'is a great provoker of three things.' (27) Macduff plays along by asking him 'What three things does drink especially provoke?' (29)

Porter. Marry, sir, nose-painting, sleep, and urine. Lechery, sir, it provokes and unprovokes. <u>It provokes the desire, but it takes away the performance</u>. (33) Therefore, much drink may be said to be an equivocator with lechery.
Macbeth, 2.3, 31-33

(THE first few lines of the second Porter's speech contain all three things he thinks drink provokes, but we suggest that you read the remainder on your own. We do include the much-used-since 'desire' and 'performance' (33) quote, a relatively accurate truism.)

* * *

(SCENE THREE continues in the castle with Macbeth entering and keeping cool until Macduff discovers Duncan's dead body. His emotion-filled lines afford an attractive acting opportunity.)

Macduff. O horror, horror, horror! Tongue nor heart
Cannot conceive nor name thee. . . .
Confusion now hath made his masterpiece. (71)
Most sacrilegious murder hath broke ope
The Lord's anointed temple, and stole thence (73)
The life o' the building. . . . (74)
Awake, awake!
Ring the alarum bell. Murder and treason!
Banquo and Donalbain! Malcolm! Awake!
Shake off this downy sleep, death's counterfeit, (81)
And look on death itself! Up, up, and see
The great doom's image! Malcolm! Banquo!
As from your graves rise up, and walk like sprites, (84)
To countenance this horror. Ring the bell.
Macbeth. Here lay Duncan,
His silver skin laced with his golden blood, (117)

And his gashed stabs looked like a breach in nature
For ruin's wasteful entrance. There, the murderers,
<u>Steeped in the colors of their trade</u>, their daggers (120)
Unmannerly breeched with gore. Who could refrain
That had a heart to love, and in that heart
Courage to make love's known?
Macbeth, 2.3, 69-146

(MACDUFF'S third line, 'Confusion now hath made
his masterpiece' (71) indicates that he sees Duncan's
death as the worst thing to happen since the world
began.

Two lines later he says that the murder has broken
open 'The Lord's anointed temple' (73) and 'The life
o' the building.' (74) He's saying that both the King
and the temple are consecrated.

Did you note that Macduff called sleep, 'death's
counterfeit?' (81) I liked that imaginative noun.

Macduff, in the next-to-final line of his speech,
calls on Duncan's sons to 'As from your graves rise
up and walk like sprites' (84) to see the horror. The
wording cuts a little close to the bone. Since it's their
father's corpse they're being called on to view, using
'graves' rather than beds may be a rare case of Will
overplaying his hand.

Macbeth speaks some fervent poetry about slain Duncan: 'His silver skin laced with his golden blood,' (117) Note the apposite pairing of silver and gold.

Three lines later the bloody grooms lie, 'Steeped in the colors of their trade.' (120) "Steeped' is the ideal verb in that it suggests Duncan's servants were soaked in blood. Just before these lines, Macbeth tells them that in 'my fury' (111) he killed the grooms

Lady Macbeth enters to hear that Macbeth is saying too much. To distract and add faux innocence, she faints away and is carried offstage.

Before the scene ends, Banquo mentions 'undivulged pretense' (137) and 'treasonous malice.' (138) He knows that someone did the deed, but doesn't know why. But it was with malice. Given his soliloquy at the opening of act three, Banquo already surmises it's Macbeth

Duncan's sons fear being suspected, they also fear being killed, and ride off in different directions. Before departing, Donalbain says, 'The near in blood, the nearer bloody,' (146) or the closer in relationship to the King, the more likely to be murdered.)

* * *

(IN the final scene of act two, Ross talks to an old man about the murders nearby and in Macbeth's castle. Ross has a nice line when he says that although it is day, 'yet dark night strangles the traveling lamp,' (7) or sun.

They speak of the horses of the just-murdered Duncan breaking their stalls and turning wild. The old man reports, 'Tis said they eat each other.' (18)

Macduff joins them to tell that Duncan's sons have fled 'which puts upon them suspicion of the deed.' (36) We just heard that angle from Malcolm and Donalbain before they wisely bolted.

Ross observes that 'The sovereignty will fall upon Macbeth.' (30) Macduff answers that 'He is already named, and gone to Scone to be invested.' (31) The Fates are stirring the pot, and the witches are adding more animal parts.)

Macbeth, 2.4, 1-41

* * *

(ACT THREE opens in Forres, Scotland at Duncan's castle now occupied by King Macbeth. Banquo soliloquizes.

Macbeth enters the scene and verbally fences with Banquo.

Then Macbeth soliloquizes on how he fears Banquo and needs to kill him. Murderers enter, and, with Macbeth instructing, they lay plans for murder most foul.

But let's first study Banquo's soliloquy.)

Banquo. Thou hast it now. King, Cawdor, Glamis, all,
As the weird women promised, and I fear
Thou <u>play'dst most foully for 't.</u> (3) Yet it was said
<u>It should not stand in thy posterity,</u> (4)
<u>But that myself should be the root and father</u> (5)
<u>Of many kings.</u> If there come truth from them—
As upon thee, Macbeth, their speeches shine—
Why, by the verities on thee made good,
May they not <u>be my oracles as well</u> (9)
And set me up in hope? But hush, no more.
Macbeth, 3.1, 1-10

(BANQUO reflects on the weird sisters' prophecy and believes that in getting the kingship Macbeth, 'play'dst most foully for 't.' (3)

But the witches also said that 'It should not stand in thy posterity,' (4) meaning that Macbeth's sons will not succeed him.

'But that myself should be the root and father of many kings.' (5) In this line, Banquo reassures himself by repeating the witch's prediction that his sons will be kings.

Banquo goes on to say that the witches were right about Macbeth's fortunes, but they might 'be my oracles as well,' (9) which gives him more hope.

The Macbeth's enter with their train. Banquo and Macbeth exchange comments. Because Macbeth wants to kill Banquo and his son Fleance, his interest is in where they will be in the next few hours so he can post the murderers: 'Is 't far you ride?' (24) and 'Goes Fleance with you?' (36)

* * *

(Next, Macbeth in soliloquy, speaks to his anxiety and intentions.)

Macbeth. <u>To be thus is nothing.</u> (48)
<u>But to be safely thus.</u> Our fears in Banquo)
Stick deep, and in <u>his royalty of nature</u> (50)
Reigns that which would be feared. 'Tis much he dares,
And to that dauntless temper of his mind,
<u>He hath a wisdom that doth guide his valor</u> (52)
To act in safety. There is none but he
Whose being I do fear. And under him
My Genius is rebuked, as it is said
<u>Mark Antony's was by Caesar.</u> (57) He chid the sisters
When first they put the name of King upon me,

330

And bade them speak to him. Then prophetlike
They hailed him father to a line of kings.
<u>Upon my head they placed a fruitless crown</u> (61)
And put a barren scepter in my gripe,
<u>Thence to be wrenched with an unlineal hand</u>, (63)
No son of mine succeeding. If 't be so,
For Banquo's issue have I filed my mind,
For them the gracious Duncan have I murdered,
<u>Put rancors in the vessel of my peace</u> (67)
Only for them, and mine eternal jewel.
Given to the common enemy of man
To make them kings— the seed of Banquo kings!
Rather than so, come, fates, into the list,
And <u>champion me to the utterance</u>. (72)
Macbeth, 3.1, 49-72

('To be thus is nothing. (48) But to be safely thus.'
This means to Macbeth that what he is now is
nothing, and to be 'safely' King is everything.

By mentioning 'his royalty of nature' (50) Macbeth
acknowledges Banquo's kingly attributes, and that
makes his fears 'stick deep.'

Macbeth also accepts that Banquo is wise and
brave: 'He hath a wisdom that doth guide his valor.'
(52)

A few lines later, Macbeth feels that his genius is squelched by Banquo, much like 'Mark Antony's was by Caesar.' (57)

In *Antony and Cleopatra*, Octavius Caesar, nephew and adopted heir of Julius Caesar, had luck superior to Antony's. Cleopatra mentions Caesar's luck several times. Beyond that likelihood, Octavius Caesar, later the Roman emperor Augustus Caesar, was a better-formulated warrior.* Also, Mark Antony, once besotted with Cleopatra, was a shell of his former self. See more of Augustus Caesar in Shakespeare's late romance, *Cymbeline,* analyzed later in this book.

*As Louis Pasteur later observed, 'Fortune favors the prepared mind.' Baseball general manager Branch Richey said, "Luck is the residue of good design.' Alfred P. Sloan, former President of General Motors, said, 'The harder I work the luckier I get.' Octavius Caesar topped Mark Antony in following earlier versions of these maxims.

Back to Macbeth where he complains that 'Upon my head they placed a fruitless crown,' (61) making him a king without heirs to succeed him—'Thence to be wrenched with an unlineal hand,' (63) or to be taken away by someone other than a 'son of mine.' (64) 'Unlineal' in line (63) is a fitting adjective.

Later in the soliloquy, Macbeth complains the he has been defiled by the thought of Banquo's sons

332

succeeding him. He says that it has 'Put rancors in the vessel of my peace.' (67) A poetic line meaning that Macbeth's sense of peace curdled like acid.

Since they are next in line to be kings of Scotland, a rational man should be more worried about Duncan's sons succeeding. Macbeth's speech ranges between reality and paranoia because he believes the witch's prophesy that Banquo's sons will succeed him. As known, Banquo has a son named Fleance. As far as we know, the Macbeth's have no children.

In the last two lines, Macbeth wants to meet Fate on the tournament field, or 'list.' Overcome with hubris, and unsound of mind, Macbeth dares Fate to a fight to the death: 'champion me to the utterance.' (72) According to Elizabethan beliefs, picking fights with Fate is never a wise tactic.)

* * *

(NEXT, Macbeth meets with the murderers he's hired to kill Banquo and his son Fleance.)

Macbeth. Both of you
Know <u>Banquo was your enemy</u>. . . . (114)
So is he mine, and in such bloody distance
That every minute of his being thrusts
Against my near'st of life. . . .

333

Your spirits shine through you. (127) Within this hour at most
I will advise you where to plant yourselves,
Acquaint you with the perfect spy o' the time, (130)
The moment on 't. For 't must be done tonight,
And something from the palace, always thought (132)
That I require a clearness. And with him—
To leave no rubs or botches in the work—
Fleance his son, that keeps him company,
Whose absence is no less material to me
Than is his father's, must embrace the fate
Of that dark hour. . . .
It is concluded. Banquo, thy soul's flight,
If it find Heaven, must find it out tonight.
Macbeth, 3.1, 114-142

(Macbeth tells the murderers, who are convinced that they are killing Banquo for vengeance, 'Banquo was your enemy.' (114) Appealing to self-interest is usually salesworthy.

With 'Your spirits shine through you,' (127) Macbeth is buttering up the murderers by saying that their courage is visible.

Two lines later, Macbeth tells them, 'Acquaint you with the perfect spy o' the time.' (130) This distinct phrase means that he will send a messenger to tell the killers the precise time to pounce.

'And something from the palace, always thought that I require a clearness.' (132) Macbeth tells the murderers not to kill Banquo and Fleance too near the palace. He wants no impression left that he has anything to do with the murders.)

* * *

(MACBETH reports poetically to his wife on progress with their nefarious scheme. He leads off with a chilling snake metaphor for Banquo's pending murder and the need to finish him off.

We don't show it below in this passage, but Lady Macbeth intersperses dialogue such as, 'Gentle my lord, sleek o'er your rugged looks,' (26) to urge her disheveled and overheated husband to shape up and remain cool.)

Macbeth. We have scotched the snake, not killed it.
She'll close and be herself, whilst our poor malice
<u>Remains in danger of her former tooth</u>. (15)
<u>But let the frame of things disjoint, both the worlds</u>
<u>suffer</u>, (16)
Ere we will eat our meal in fear and sleep
In the affliction of these terrible dreams
That shake us nightly. Better be with the dead,
Whom we, to gain our peace, have sent to peace,

Than on the torture of the mind to lie
In restless ecstasy. Duncan is in his grave,
After life's fitful fever he sleeps well. (23)
Treason has done his worst. Nor steel, nor poison,
Malice domestic, foreign levy, nothing, (25)
Can touch him further. . . .
Oh, full of scorpions is my mind, dear wife! (36)
Thou know'st that Banquo and his Fleance lives. . . .
Ere the bat hath flown
His cloistered flight, ere to black Hecate's summons
(41)
The shard-borne beetle with his drowsy hums (42)
Hath rung night's yawning peal, there shall be done
A deed of dreadful note. . . . (43)
Come seeling night, (46)
Scarf up the tender eye of pitiful day, (47)
And with thy bloody and invisible hand
Cancel and tear to pieces that great bond
Which keeps me pale! Light thickens, and the crow
(51
Makes wing to the rooky wood,
Good things of day begin to droop and drowse
While night's black agents to their preys do rouse. (53)
Macbeth, 3.2, 13-53

(MACBETH concludes the marvelous snake metaphor with 'Remains in danger of her former tooth.' (15) This means that while Duncan's sons remain alive Macbeth's chances of keeping the crown are jeopardized.

Macbeth continues his hyperbolic tirade with, 'But let the frame of things disjoint, both the worlds suffer.' (16) He's saying that they face the absolute destruction of the universe.

Further on, after saying that Duncan 'sleeps well,' (23) or is dead, Macbeth says, 'Malice domestic, foreign levy, nothing can touch him further.' (25) I can't decide which I like better, "Malice domestic' or 'foreign levy.' I think, since it's so surprising, 'foreign levy' wins.

In the next line, 'Oh, full of scorpions is my mind' (36) reveals how Macbeth is lurching toward insanity.

Then with 'black Hecate's summons' (41) we're back to act one and references to the queen of witches. And now not only is the bat flying, so is the 'shard-borne beetle,' (42) both tied to the pending 'deed of dreadful note.' (43) Macbeth is in a sort of ecstasy of murder.

Further on we have 'Come seeling night,' (46) cleverly alluding to the practice of sewing shut hawks' eyelids during training. And doing this will cover and darken, or 'Scarf up the tender eye of pitiful day.' (47) 'Scarf up' sounds modern in the sense of gobbling food.

Macbeth goes on to say he is pale with fear and won't feel safe until Banquo and Fleance are dead. Then, the exceptionally poetic 'Light thickens, and the crow makes wing to the rooky wood.' (51)

This is quickly followed by Macbeth describing his hired killers' sanguinary purpose, 'While night's black agents to their preys do rouse. (53)

* * *

(In scene three, Macbeth's murderers are at their task: first killing Banquo, as he cries, 'Oh, treachery! Fly, good Fleance, fly, fly, fly!' (17)

Following the deed, one murderer says: 'There's but one down, the son is fled.' (19) Macbeth will not be happy to hear about that.)

* * *

(SCENE FOUR opens with a banquet hosted by the Macbeth's that includes, among others, the nobles Ross and Lennox. A key character is missing, and it's not Banquo.

At first, the Macbeth's put on a good face. Then a murderer enters to tell Macbeth that Banquo's 'throat is cut,' (16) but 'Fleance is 'scaped.' (18)

Macbeth. (Aside.) <u>Then comes my fit again</u>. (21) I had else been perfect,

Whole as the marble, founded as the rock,

As broad and general as the casing air.

<u>But now I am cabined, cribbed, confined</u>, (24) bound in

To saucy doubts and fears. (To murderer.) <u>But Banquo's safe?</u> (25)

Murderer. Aye, my good lord. <u>Safe in a ditch</u> he bides, (26)

<u>With twenty trenchèd gashes on his head</u>, (27)

The least a death to nature.

Macbeth. (Aside.) <u>There the grown serpent lies. The worm that's fled.</u> (29)

Hath nature that in time will venom breed,

No teeth for the present. Get thee gone. Tomorrow

We'll hear ourselves again.

Macbeth, 3.4, 16-29

(LIKE Julius Caesar, Macbeth is subject to fits: 'Then comes my fit again.' (21) Indications are that Caesar's fits were congenital, and that Macbeth's are brought on by stress.

   'But now I am cabined, cribbed, confined,' (24) an alliterative gem that means Macbeth feels trapped by 'doubts and fears' in a chain of events of his own making.

Macbeth asks, 'But Banquo's safe?' (25) He means is Banquo safely dead? The murderer answers that Banquo is 'Safe in a ditch' he bides, (26) with twenty trenchèd gashes on his head.'

The second aside opens with 'There the grown serpent lies. The worm that's fled.' (29) Banquo, the big snake, is accounted for, but the little snake, Fleance, has gotten away.)

* * *

(The murderers exit, and we're still at the banquet. In the full dialogue, which I hope you will read in your own copy of the play, Lady Macbeth chides her husband for not paying attention to the guests, 'To feed were best at home.' (35) She's saying that you can always get better food at home than at a state dinner. The only reason for coming is the pomp, and Macbeth is ignoring that.

He cheerfully agrees and starts to sit at table, but his chair is occupied by Banquo's ghost, which is invisible onstage to all others but Macbeth. The audience sees the ghost; otherwise the scene wouldn't work. The guests' confusion with Macbeth's speech informs the audience that the players can't see what they and Macbeth can see.

The fit is on Macbeth, as he asks the guests, 'Which of you have done this?' (47) And to Banquo's ghost he says, 'Never shake thy gory locks at me.' (50) Ross says, 'Gentlemen, rise. His Highness is not well.' (52)

Lady Macbeth tries to cover up Macbeth's behavior by saying, 'The fit is momentary.' (55) The guests sit down, but Macbeth believes Banquo's ghost is real, a presence who dares to look at 'what might appall the devil.' (59)

Lady M. pulls her husband aside:

Lady Macbeth. This is the very <u>painting</u> of your fear. (61)
This is the <u>air-drawn dagger</u> (62) which you said
Led you to Duncan.

(THE use of the word 'painting' in line one recalls a speech in 2.2, (53) in which Lady M. tells her husband that 'The sleeping and the dead are but as pictures.' The thought also connects nicely to the imaginary 'air-drawn dagger.'

Macbeth protests, 'Prithee see there! Behold! Look! Lo! How say you.' (68) The ghost exits, but Macbeth wonders how men can rise again 'With twenty mortal murders on their crowns.' (81) This line refers to the killers' report earlier in the scene that Banquo lies in a ditch 'With twenty trenchèd gashes on his head.' (27)

At Lady Macbeth's urging, her husband returns to his hosting role with a laughable, at least to the audience, toast to 'our dear friend Banquo, whom we miss.' (90) Like Alfred Hitchcock in his films, Will is a master at letting the audience in on a plot point while all or many of the characters in the show are oblivious. Hitch called it a MacGuffin. Here we have a MacGuffin in Macbeth. The opposite is often called a coup de theatre, where some dramatic event is known to everybody, as in 'Ding Dong! The witch is dead,' in the movie *The Wizard of OZ*.

Please forgive the missing accent marks in the word 'theatre' above. They keep slipping away like Banquo's ghost. But he's back, and Macbeth is spooked again.)

Macbeth. Avaunt! And quit my sight! Let the earth hide thee! (92)
Thy bones are marrowless, thy blood is cold,
Thou hast no speculation in those eyes
Which thou doth glare with. . . . (95)
What man dare, I dare.
Approach thou like the rugged Russian bear, (97)
The armed rhinocerous, or the Hyrcan tiger. (98)
Take any shape but that (102) and my firm nerves
Shall never tremble. Or be alive again,
And dare me to the desert (104) with thy sword.

(IN the first four lines, 92-95) Macbeth describes Banquo's imagined ghost.

In the next four lines, Macbeth lists fearsome creatures like a bear, rhinocerous and a tiger. (97-98) He'd rather face these than Banquo's ghost: 'Take any shape but that.' (99)

He says, you could 'dare me to the desert' (104) where no other human would be, than encounter the phantom again.

Banquo's ghost exits, the Macbeth's try to hold the party together, but Macbeth, who thinks others can also see Banquo's ghost, asks his guests how they can 'behold such sights and keep the natural ruby of your cheeks,' (115) or not change color with fear. Ross asks 'What sights, my lord?' (116) Lady M. recognizes that Macbeth is unfit for company and asks the guests to leave, which they do.)

* * *

(THERE'S no consoling Macbeth, as he continues the mad lecture about his fears, most of which now relate to Macduff, (125) who was not at the banquet but looms in Macbeth's mind.

Macbeth. It will have blood. They say blood will have blood.

Stones have been known to move and trees to speak. (122)

Augurs and understood relations have

By maggot pies and choughs and rooks (124) brought forth

The secret'st man of blood. . . .

There's not a one of them but in his house

I keep a servant feed. 132) I will tomorrow,

And betimes I will, to the weird sisters.

More shall they speak, for now I am bent to know

By the worst means, the worst. For mine own good (135)

All causes shall give way. I am in blood

Stepped in so far that I should wade no more, (137)

Returning were as tedious as go o'er.

Strange things I have in my head that will to hand, (139)

Which must be acted ere they may be scanned. . . .

Come, we'll to sleep. My strange and self-abuse

Is the initiate fear that wants hard use (143)

We are yet but young in deed. (144)

Macbeth, 3.4, 121-145

(IN the first few lines above, Macbeth talks of myths like stones that move and trees that talk. (122)

Then he muses about 'maggot pies and choughs and rooks,' (124) or birds with magical traits.

Two lines later, he tells Lady Macbeth 'I keep a servant feed.' (132) He has an informer who is in Macduff's employ. Macduff has now become a major player.

Three lines beyond that, Macbeth again expresses hubris by saying, 'For mine own good all causes shall give way.' (135)

'I am in blood stepped in so far that I should wade no more,' (136) 'Stepped' in blood fits well with 'wade.' Recall in 2.3, (120) where Macbeth describes Duncan's alleged murderers as being 'Steeped,' or soaked, 'in the colors of their trade.' Those little adjustments in the spelling of the two verbs makes the language of each sentence more visually rich.

Reread the couplet beginning, 'Strange things.' (139) I doubt Will composed this awkward syntax.

Finally, Macbeth says to Lady M. that they are new to this murder game and need more experience, or 'hard use.' (143) Then he rebrands them with, 'We are yet but young in decd.' (144) Hip audiences chuckle at this show of modesty from a pair of stone killers claiming unfamiliarity with murder.)

* * *

(THE three witches meet with a reproving Hecate. Witch One asks the witch of witches why she is vexed. The three underling witches get an earful from Hecate. Some excerpts follow.)

Hecate. How did you dare
To trade and traffic with Macbeth
In riddles and affairs of death,
And I, the mistress of your charms,
The close contriver of all harms,
Was never called to bear my part,
Or <u>show the glory of our art</u>? (9)
And, which is worse, all you have done
Hath been but <u>for a wayward son</u>, (11)
Spiteful and wrathful, who, as others do,
<u>Loves for his own ends, not for you.</u> . . . (13)
He <u>shall spurn fate</u>, (30) scorn death, and bear
His hopes 'bove wisdom, grace, and fear.
<u>And you all know security</u> (32)
<u>Is mortals' chiefest enemy.</u>
Macbeth, 3.5, 3-32

(HALFWAY through her scolding, Hecate asks why she wasn't called in to 'show the glory of our art.' (9) Like business, witchcraft is all about politics. Don't hold a meeting on new matters, like Macbeth's, and not involve the boss.

Moreover, Hecate tells them you did this 'for a wayward son' (11) who thinks only about himself and 'Loves for his own ends, not for you,' (13) another insight into Macbeth's character as evaluated by Hecate.

She also tells the witches that they've wasted their time on a loser who 'shall spurn fate.' (30)

Elizabethan-stage characters who ignore fate, like Macbeth is doing, end up in a bad place on Lady Fortune's wheel.

'And you all know security is mortals' chiefest enemy.' (32) People who think they are safe are the most vulnerable.)

* * *

(SCENE SIX, the last in act three, is expository from lines 1-48. Lennox and another lord meet at the palace in Forres. Lennox reviews the happenings to date, including the suspicion that Macbeth had Duncan and Banquo murdered.

We also learn that Banquo's son, Fleance, is living with Edward the Confessor, King of England. This places the action in mid-11th-Century.

Lennox also tells the lord that Macduff 'Is gone to pray the holy King, upon his aid.' (30) He wants the religiously devout King to send an army to help defeat Macbeth and is turned down, at least for now.

Following that information, and before the mission to England begins, the unnamed lord who's talking with Lennox summarizes the outcomes they seek.)

Lord. Give to our tables meat, sleep to our nights,
Free from our feasts and banquets <u>bloody knives,</u> (35)
Do faithful homage and receive free honors
All which we pine for now. And this report
Hath so exasperate the King that he
Prepares for some attempt at war.
Macbeth, 3.6, 34-39

(LINE TWO bolts out of the speech, like a great line from nowhere. The 'bloody knives' (35) ties to 'meat' in line one, but the true meaning is the murders of Duncan and Banquo and the wish to be free from further horrors. This brief speech neatly summarizes the situation in Scotland.

Following that, Lennox asks the lord, or 'Some holy angel, fly to the court of England' (45) and try to get a blessing in the form of an English army to help 'our suffering country under a hand accursed.' (48)

* * *

348

(ACT FOUR opens with the three onstage witches cavorting and cackling around a boiling cauldron while adding a slew of nasty things. The wickedly imaginative ingredients are worth a full read of the passage, but we'll name a few to whet your appetite. Pun intended.

The witch's brew bubbles in wait for Macbeth's visit. Just before he arrives, Hecate, the witch queen, adds a controversial couplet. But first, the stew's sickening constituents.)

Witch 2. <u>Fillet of a fenny snake,</u> (12)
In the caldron boil and bake.
Eye of newt and toe of frog,
Wool of bat and tongue of dog,
Adder's fork and blindworm's sting
Lizard's leg and howlet's wing.
For a charm of powerful trouble,
Like a Hell broth boil and bubble.
All. <u>Double, double toil and trouble,</u> (20)
Fire burn and caldron bubble. . . .
Hecate. <u>Oh, well done! I commend your pains,</u> (39)
And everyone shall share i' the gains.
And now about the caldron sing
Like elves and fairies in a ring,
Enchanting all that you put in.
Macbeth, 4.1, 12-43

(As said in the preliminary notes to this passage, we've included a sampling of the pot's abominable elements. Despite my protests at the awfulness of it all, I did like 'Fillet of a fenny snake,' (12) as best of list, with the adjective 'fenny' adding more gloom.

I also recommend for your additional reading some pot items we didn't include above, such as 'tooth of wolf' (22) and 'witch's mummy,' (23) or dead body.

Note the terrible sisters conclude the lists of cauldron ingredients with the indelible chant, 'Double, double toil and trouble. . . .' (20)

Hecate enters and sings a ditty (29) that is inappropriate for the three fates, and surely not written by Will. Some tin-eared poet must have snuck it into a copy of the play, and it stuck.

We're back to Will's creation when Witch Two says, 'By the pricking of my thumbs, something wicked this way comes,' (44) cueing the entering Macbeth's: 'How now, you secret, black, and midnight hags.' (46) You couldn't find three better adjectives to set up the noun 'hags.'

Macbeth then challenges the weird sisters, 'I conjure you, by that which you profess.' (50) Put differently, show me your magic arts.

Macbeth wants more prophecies. He needs to know what's coming: 'Call 'em, let me see 'em.' (63)

Witch One. <u>Pour in sow's blood that hath eaten</u> (64)
<u>Her nine farrow</u>, grease that's sweaten
<u>From the murderer's gibbet throw into the flame.</u> (66)

(YOU don't want to know what (64) and the next line means.

'From the murderer's gibbet throw into the flame.' (66) This is a dig at Macbeth. The witches predict that, as a killer, he'll hang from the gallows and then be burned.

The three witches then chant, 'Come high or low, thyself and office deftly show!' (67) The 'show' is an apparition of the armed head of Macduff rising through the cauldron.)

Apparition 1. Macbeth! Macbeth! Macbeth! Beware Macduff, (71)
Beware the Thane of Fife. Dismiss me. Enough.

(THE apparitions are actors' bodies, but the audience sees only the rising and descending heads. The cauldron has no bottom, and the ascent and descent is made through a trapdoor in the stage.

The stagecraft is chilling for the times, especially with rudimentary sound effects approximating thunder that precede the phantoms coming up out the witch's cauldron.

Next, the second specter, a child's bloody head, rises.)

Apparition 2. <u>Macbeth! Macbeth! Macbeth!</u> (77)
Macbeth. <u>Had I three ears, I'd hear thee.</u> (78)
Apparition 2. Be bloody, bold and, resolute, laugh to scorn
The power of man, <u>for none of woman born</u> (80)
Shall harm Macbeth.
Macbeth. Then live, Macduff. What need I fear of thee?
But yet I'll make assurance double sure,
And take a bond of fate. <u>Thou shalt not live,</u> (84)
That I may tell pale-hearted fear it lies,
And sleep in spite of thunder.
What is this
That rises like the issue of a king,
<u>And wears upon his baby brow the round</u> (87)
And <u>top of sovereignty.</u>
Apparition 3. (Crowned child holding a tree representing Malcolm, Duncan's son and heir apparent)
Be lion-mettled, proud, and take no care
Who chafes, who frets, or where conspirators are.
Macbeth shall never vanquished be until

Great Birnam Wood hath come to high Dunsinane
Hill (91)
Shall come against him.
Macbeth. That will never be.
Who can impress the forest, bid the tree
Unfix his earthbound root? Sweet bodements! Good!
Rebellion's head, rise never till the wood
Of Birnam rise, and our high-placed Macbeth (97)
Shall live the lease of nature, pay his breath
To time and mortal custom. Yet my heart
Throbs to know one thing. Tell me, if your art
Can tell so much. Shall Banquo's issue (102)
Reign in this kingdom? . . .
I will be satisfied. Deny me this,
And an eternal curse fall on you! Let me know.
Why sinks that cauldron? And what noise is this?
Macbeth, 4.1, 77-106

(APPARITION TWO, a bloody child, rises and calls
Macbeth three times: 'Macbeth! Macbeth! Macbeth!'
In what can only be a pun to cool the overheated
drama, Macbeth answers: 'Had I three ears, I'd hear
thee.' (78)

Apparition Two then tells Macbeth 'for none of
woman born' (80) will harm him. The line becomes
increasingly germane to the play's ultimate resolution.

Believing that Macduff was born of woman, Macbeth does not fear him. Just to be sure, he decides to kill him anyway: 'Thou shalt not live.' (84)

Macbeth says as he sees the child rising out of the cauldron: 'And wears upon his baby brow the round,' (87) meaning the child wears a crown, 'the top of sovereignty.'

Apparition three, conjuring Malcolm carrying a tree, tells Macbeth that he won't lose any battle until 'Great Birnam Wood hath come to high Dunsinane Hill,' (91) an oft-repeated line that is key to the resolution.

The phrase 'high-placed Macbeth' (97) and 'Macbeth shall live the lease of nature,' or enjoy a full life. This is another example of Macbeth's overweening pride, emphasized by speaking of himself in the third person.

Macbeth is desperate to know, 'Shall Banquo's issue (102) 'Reign in this kingdom?' The witches answered that question several acts earlier. Macbeth futilely asks for reassurance that it won't happen.

The witches each cry 'Show!' The cauldron sinks below the stage, the large trapdoor closes and eight small ones open. Using stiles, eight kings pop up and then down, but not before Macbeth comments on the entire line of apparitional kings. The last to descend holds a mirror. Banquo's ghost follows him.)

354

Macbeth. Thou art too like the spirit of Banquo. Down!
Thy crown does sear mine eyeballs. And thy hair,
Thou other gold-bound brow, is like the first. (113)
A third is like the former. (115) Filthy hags!
Why do you show me this? A fourth! Start, eyes!
What, will the line stretch out to the crack of doom? (117)
Another yet! A seventh! I'll see no more.
And yet the eighth appears, who bears a glass
Which shows me many more, and some I see (120)
That twofold balls and treble scepters carry. (121)
Horrible sight! Now I see 'tis true,
For the blood-bolstered Banquo smiles upon me, (123)
And points at them for his. What, is this so?
Witch 1. Aye, sir, all this is so. (125) But why
Stands Macbeth thus amazedly? (126)
Come Sisters, cheer we up his sprites, (127)
And show the best of our delights.
I'll charm the sir to give a sound
While you perform your antic round, (130)
That this great King may kindly say
Our duties did his welcome pay.
Macbeth. (Aside.) The castle of Macduff I will surprise,
Seize upon Fife, give to the edge o' the sword (151)
His wife, his babes, and all the unfortunate souls

<u>That trace him in his line</u>. (153) No boasting like a fool,
This deed I'll do before this purpose cool.
Macbeth, 4.1, 1-154

(DURING Macbeth's speech, as the apparitions appear and disappear, he comments several lines in, 'Thou other gold-bound brow, is like the first.' (113) and 'A third is like the former.' (115) Macbeth's saying that the second and third ghosts of kings also look like Banquo.

'What, will the line stretch out to the crack of doom?' (117) A nice phrase, especially when we expect 'dawn' to end the question. The construction also signals that no longer does time have meaning for Macbeth. He's caught in a whirlwind of conflicting emotions that confuse and overwhelm him.

To further shake Macbeth, the eighth specter carries a mirror reflecting the image 'Which shows me many more.' (120)

Macbeth sees other images of kings, some of which 'That twofold balls and treble scepters carry.' (121) This is a nod to King James 1, who the play was written and performed for. He united three countries: Scotland, England and Ireland under his rule.

Macbeth wonders why 'the blood-boltered Banquo smiles upon me?' (123) Witch One starts another song that tells Macbeth 'Aye, sir, all this is so.' (125)

In the next line, Witch One asks why 'Stands Macbeth thus amazedly?' (126) Would it cheer anyone to see the ghosts of eight kings followed by three hags singing and dancing.

Reread the six lines, starting with 'Come Sisters . . .' (127) that follow the one above. These should not be attributed to Will. Since so much sorcery is going on, perhaps Hecate is the author.

After the witches exit, Lennox, in dialogue not shown above, enters the scene and tells Macbeth that he didn't see them, in answer to his question, 'Saw you the weird sisters? (136) Of course, no one but Macbeth, the witches and the audience sees them. Lennox goes on to tell Macbeth that 'Macduff is fled to England.' (142)

Macbeth concludes scene one in an aside, telling the audience that he intends to go to Macduff's castle and 'give to the edge o' the sword' (151) to his wife and children and all others 'That trace him in his line.' (153)

Macbeth may not be someone we'd want to room with next semester. But we've got to give him credit for having constancy of purpose.)

* * *

(SCENE TWO of act four opens with Lennox at the Macduff castle reassuring his cousin, Lady Macduff, that her husband has not fled in fear to England. She's having none of it, feels abandoned, and tells her son that his father is dead, which he doesn't believe. 'If he were dead, you'd weep for him.' (61)

A messenger enters warning Lady Macduff of pending danger. She rejects it by saying, 'I have done no harm.' (74)

The messenger exits, and murderers enter. Lady Macduff exclaims, 'What are these faces?' (79) Will's murderers are always hideously ugly.

Murderer One asks, 'Where is your husband?' (80) and adds 'He's a traitor.' The precocious son says, 'Thou liest, thou shag-eared villain.' (82) The son's words, in the second-person singular, are insulting, and he is stabbed and dies, but not before urging his mother to run. She exits crying, 'Murder,' followed by the killers.)

* * *

(SCENE THREE is primarily exposition. Malcolm, Duncan's son and heir apparent meets in England

358

with Macduff. They lament what's happened to Scotland under Macbeth's rule. Malcolm wants to cry over it. Macduff takes an aggressive stance.)

Malcolm. Let us seek out some desolate shade, and there
Weep our sad bosoms empty.
Macduff. Let us rather
Hold fast the mortal sword, (3) and like good men
Bestride our downfall'n birthdom. Each new morn
New widows howl, new orphans cry, new sorrows (5)
Strike Heaven on the face, (6) that it resounds
As if it felt with Scotland and yelled out
Like syllable of dolor. (8)
Macbeth, 4.3, 1-8

(Macduff is having none of Malcolm's dithering. He wants to 'Hold fast the mortal sword,' (3) fight Macbeth and kill him.

Line four of Macduff's speech, 'New widows howl, new orphans cry, new sorrows,' (5) is nicely balanced and sets up 'Strike Heaven on the face.' (6) Hit so hard that the echo is heard in Scotland, 'Like syllable of dolor.' (8)

Malcolm doesn't fully trust Macduff, who later in the passage says, 'I am not treacherous.' (18) Malcolm answers with 'But Macbeth is.' (19)

Malcolm. Be not offended.
I speak not as in absolute fear of you.
I think our country sinks beneath the yoke.
It weeps, it bleeds, and each new day a gash
Is added to her wounds.
Macbeth, 4.3, 37-40

(MALCOLM continues by telling Macduff that thousands of English troops will march to Scotland to fight Macbeth, but it would open wounds and 'black Macbeth will seem as pure as snow.' (52)

Malcolm believes that he is unfit to be king, 'But I have none. The king-becoming graces.' (91) This self-effacing but artful phrase is followed by a vigorous Macduff pep talk.)

Macduff. Fit to govern!
No, not to live. O nation miserable!
With an untitled tyrant (104) bloody-sceptered,
When shalt thou see thy wholesome days again,
Since that the truest issue of thy throne (106)
By his own interdiction stands accursed,
And does blaspheme his breed. Thy royal father
Was a most sainted King. (109) The Queen that bore thee,
Oftener upon her knees than on her feet, (110)

Died every day she lived. Fare thee well!
These evils thou repeat'st upon thyself
Have banished me from Scotland. O my breast,
Thy hope ends here!
Malcolm. Macduff, this noble passion,
Child of integrity, hath from my soul
Wiped the black scruples, reconciled my thoughts
To thy good truth and honor. . . . (117)
Old Siward, with ten thousand warlike men, (134)
Already at a point, was setting forth.
Macbeth, 4.3, 52-135

(Macduff call Macbeth 'an untitled tyrant,' (104) and
names Malcolm, 'the truest issue of thy throne' (106)
the son of 'a most sainted King.' (109)

Recall that before assassinating him, Macbeth calls
Duncan a worthy King whose virtues 'Will plead like
angels trumpet-tongued,' 1.6, 17, against killing him.

Macduff further makes the case for Malcom's
investiture by saying that Malcom's mother, the
queen, was also a kind of saint who was 'Oftener upon
her knees than on her feet,' (110) and lived under
divine influence.

Malcolm is now convinced that Macduff is not one
of Macbeth's spies and is reconciled 'To thy good
truth and honor.' (117)

We skip to later in Malcolm's speech where he tells Macduff that 'Old Siward, with ten thousand warlike men,' (124) is ready to battle Macbeth. Siward is the English Earl of Northumberland. And contrary to earlier news from England, an English army is coming to help depose Macbeth.)

* * *

(Further on in the scene, Ross enters with dreadful news for Macduff.)

Ross. Let not your ears despise my tongue forever,
Which shall possess them with the heaviest sound
That ever yet they heard. . . .
Your castle is surprised, your wife and babes savagely slaughtered.
Macduff. Front to front
Bring thou this fiend of Scotland and myself,
<u>Within my sword's length set him.</u> (233) If he 'scape,
<u>Heaven forgive him too!</u> (234)
Macbeth, 4.3, 201-234

(MACDUFF answers the horrid news by saying he will fight Macbeth, 'Within my sword's length set him,' (233) and if he escapes, 'Heaven forgive him

362

too.' (234) He means that if he lets Macbeth gets away Heaven won't forgive him.

The die is cast, as Malcolm says, 'Our power is ready,' (236) and 'Macbeth is ripe for shaking.' (238) I see a quivering tree loaded with rotten fruit.)

* * *

(THE final act begins with a doctor and a gentlewoman attending a sleepwalking Lady Macbeth. Doctor: 'Look how she rubs her hands.' (30)

Gentlewoman. It is an accustomed action with her to seem thus washing her hands.
I have known her to continue in this a quarter of an hour. (32)
Lady Macbeth. Yet here's a spot. . . .
Out, damned spot! (39) Out, I say! One, two—why, then 'tis time to do 't. Hell is murky. (40) Fie, my lord, fie! A soldier and afeard? What need we fear who knows it, when none can call our power to account? Yet who would have thought the old man to have had so much blood in him? . . . (44)
The Thane of Fife had a wife. (47) Where is she now? What, will these hands ne'er be clean? No more of that, my lord, no more o' that.

You mar all this with starting . . . Here's the smell of
blood still. <u>All the perfumes of Arabia</u> (56) will not
sweeten this little hand. . . .
<u>Wash your hands,</u> (69) put on your nightgown, look
not so pale. I tell you yet again, Banquo's buried, he
cannot come out on 's grave. . . .
To bed, to bed, <u>there's knocking at the gate.</u> (73)
Come, come, come, come, give me your hand. What's
done cannot be undone. To bed, to bed, to bed.
Doctor. Foul whisperings are abroad. Unnatural deeds
Do breed unnatural troubles. <u>Infected minds</u> (80)
To their <u>deaf pillows</u> (81) will discharge their secrets.
Macbeth, 5.1, 30-81

(THE sleepwalking scene is an actor's dream, and one
of the most subtly theatrical in all of Will's plays.

'I have known her to continue in this a quarter of
an hour.' (32) The gentlewoman's observation brings
out the irony of Lady Macbeth's earlier comment to
her husband that 'a little water clears us of this deed.'

'Out, damned spot!' (39) is another timeless line
that branches to the following comment, 'Hell is
murky.' (40))

Between the two comments above, (39) and (40),
Lady M. counts 'One, two— why, then 'tis time to do
't.' She remembers the time of night when Duncan is
murdered.

Lady Macbeth's dream-thoughts ramble, as she speaks of Duncan's murder: 'who would have thought the old man to have had so much blood in him?' (44)

'The Thane of Fife had a wife,' refers to the murdered Lady Macduff. (47)

The 'All the perfumes of Arabia . . . ' (56) sentence is beautiful prose poetry.

The 'Wash your hands' (69) line reprises Lady Macbeth's advice to her husband after he returns from killing Duncan.

The sleepwalking dream recalls more from her haunted past with 'there's knocking at the gate.' (73) As said above, the knocking recollects the horror, and also supplies the audience, when they hear the knock, a break from the intensity.

I liked the doctor's insights from what he heard Lady Macbeth say in her sleepwalking dream, particularly 'infected minds' (80) and 'deaf pillows.' (81)

* * *

(IN scene two of act five, the Scots opposing Macbeth, together with 'English power,' (1) are on the battlefield near Dunsinane ready to fight. Malcolm is in the lead, and 'His uncle Siward and the good Macduff' (2) are with him.

Macbeth 'strongly fortifies' (12) Dunsinane. His opponents think he is mad and wonder if he feels 'His secret murders sticking to his hands.' (17) The verb 'sticking' astutely suggests blood.)
Macbeth, 5.2, 1-17

* * *

(SCENE THREE opens with Macbeth, the Doctor and servants in the castle at Dunsinane. Macbeth is unbalanced, but capable of waging battle.)

Macbeth. <u>Bring me no more reports, let them fly all.</u> (1)
Till Birnam Wood remove to Dunsinane
I cannot taint with fear. What's the boy Malcolm?
<u>Was he not born of woman?</u> (4) The spirits that know
All mortal consequences have pronounced me thus
'Fear not, Macbeth, <u>no man that's born of woman</u> (5)
Shall e'er have power upon thee.' Then fly, false thanes, (6)
<u>And mingle with the English epicures.</u>
The mind I swear by and the heart I bear
Shall never sag with doubt not shake with fear.
Macbeth, 5.3, 1-10

('Bring me no more reports, let them fly all.' (1) Macbeth has had enough bad news, and doesn't want to hear any more.

Once again, we hear the question, this time of Malcolm, 'Was he not born of woman?' (4) Macbeth knows the endgame approaches and is haunted by the witch's prophesies. Will is also preparing the audience for the twist in the denouement.

Then Macbeth reassures himself by repeating the witch's augury that he need fear 'no man that's born of woman.' (5) In his mind, this dismisses Malcolm as a threat.

And he says, 'Then fly, false thanes, and mingle with the English epicures.' (6) This can be read two ways: that the English soldiers are overfed, and that the Scots are traditionally envious of English food productivity compared to the relative barrenness of Scotland.

* * *

(Macbeth and Lady Macbeth's doctor are at Dunsinane Castle.

A terrified servant enters to report that 'There is ten thousand . . . Soldiers, sir.' (13) Getting another unwelcome 'report,' and disposed to blame the messenger, Macbeth calls him a fool and 'lily-livered,' (15) and orders him out with the seemly, 'Take thy face hence.' (18) Modern street version: Get out of my face.

In the long speech that follows, Macbeth reflects on the decline of his personal and royal power. He is talking to himself and also to the doctor.)

Macbeth. I have lived long enough. (22) My way of life
Is fall'n into the sear, the yellow leaf, (23)
And that which should accompany old age, (24)
As honor, love, obedience, troops of friends,
I must not look to have, but in their stead
Curses, not loud but deep, (27) mouth-honor, breath,
Which the poor heart would fain deny, and dare not.
. . .
Hang those that talk of fear. Give me mine armor.
(36)
How does your patient, Doctor?
Doctor. Not so sick, my lord,
As she is troubled with thick-coming fancies (38)
That keep her from her rest.
Macbeth. Cure her of that.
Canst thou not minister to a mind diseased,
Pluck from the memory a rooted sorrow,
Raze out the written troubles of the brain, (42)
And with some sweet oblivious antidote
Cleanse the stuffed bosom of that terrible stuff (43)
Which weighs upon the heart? . . .

368

Come, put my armor on, give me my staff. . . . (48)
I will not be afraid of death and bane
Till Birnam Forest come to Dunsinane. (60)
Macbeth, 5.3, 22-60

(After Macbeth bullies the frightened lad who brings news of the size of the English army, he vacillates between saying he can't die and his wish to die: 'I have lived long enough.' 22)

And 'My way of life is fall'n into the sear, the yellow leaf.' (23) It's possible, and reasonable to think, that 'way' in 'way of life' is a typo, and it was originally written as 'May' of life.

The use of 'sear' in the line above indicates that Macbeth feels wrinkled and shriveled 'And that which should accompany old age.' (24) 'Yellow leaf' in the same line also contrasts nicely with 'May' suggesting youth.

Rather than have friends he has 'Curses, not loud but deep.' (27) He knows everybody hates him. And here he achieves, or attempts to achieve, pathos.

Macbeth quickly bucks up: 'Hang those that talk of fear. Give me mine armor.' (36

After the doctor tells Macbeth that Lady M. is not sick but 'troubled with thick-coming fancies.' (38) Macbeth asks him why he can't, 'Raze out the written troubles of the brain' (42) and 'Cleanse the stuffed bosom of that terrible stuff which weighs upon the heart? (43) Nice poetry, but Macbeth is not talking much about his wife. In fact, as always, it's all about him and his own problems.

Go back and reread the passage noting the delightful 'sweet oblivious antidote' phrase between lines (42) and (43). Will takes three disparate words, combines them and delivers lyricism. Despite Macbeth's self-absorption, he loves his wife, is dependent on her, and wants her cured.

Again, Macbeth does an about-face and wants his armor. 'Come, put my armor on, give me my staff. . . . (48) And twelve lines later declares he has nothing to fear 'Till Birnam Forest come to Dunsinane.' (60) Are you beginning to suspect that, like us, the audience is ready for Birnam Wood to appear?)

* * *

(IN scene four, Malcolm, Macduff, Siward, Menteith, other lords and the army are in Birnam Wood not far from Dunsinane.

Siward asks 'What wood is this before us?' (2) Menteith answers, 'The wood of Birnam.' (3)

Malcolm orders, 'Let every soldier hew him down a bough, and bear 't before him.' (4) He goes on to

say that this will conceal 'The numbers of our host.'
(6)

Will sure knew how to set a scene.)
Macbeth, 5.4, 2-6

* * *

(IN scene five, we're back in Dunsinane castle. Macbeth talks with Seyton, one of his officers and soldiers.

Macbeth gets terrible news, reflects poetically and memorably on the futility of life and saddles up for the inevitable.)

Macbeth. Hang out our banners on the outward walls.
. . .
Our castle's strength
Will <u>laugh a siege to scorn</u>. (3) Here let them lie
Till famine and the ague eat them up. . . .
What is that noise?
Seyton. It is <u>the cry of women</u>, (8) my good lord.
(Exits.)
Macbeth. <u>I have almost forgot the taste of fears.</u> (9)
The time has been my senses would have cooled
To hear a night shriek, and my fell of hair
Would at a dismal treatise rouse and stir
As life were in 't. <u>I have supped full with horrors.</u> (13)

Direness, familiar to my slaughterous thoughts,
Cannot once start me.
Wherefore was that cry?
Seyton. (Reenters.) The Queen, my lord, is dead. (16)
Macbeth. She should have died hereafter. (17)
There would have been a time for such a word. (18)
Tomorrow, and tomorrow, and tomorrow (19)
Creeps in this petty pace from day to day,
To the last syllable of recorded time,
And all our yesterdays have lighted fools (22)
The way to dusty death. Out, out, brief candle!
Life's but a walking shadow, a poor player (24)
That struts and frets his hour upon the stage (25)
And then is heard no more. It is a tale
Told by an idiot, full of sound and fury,
Signifying nothing.
Messenger. (Enters.) Gracious, my lord,
I should report that which I say I saw, (31)
But not know how to do it. . . .
As I did stand my watch upon the hill,
I looked toward Birnam, and anon methought
The wood began to move.
Macbeth. If thou speak'st false,
Upon the next tree shalt thou hang alive (39)
Till famine cling thee. If thy speech be sooth,
I care not if thou dost for me as much. . . (41)
Fear not, till Birnam Wood

Do come to Dunsinane.' And now a wood
Comes toward Dunsinane. Arm, arm, and out!
If this which he avouches does appear,
There is nor flying hence nor tarrying here.
I 'gin to be aweary of the sun, (49)
And wish the estate o' the world were now undone.
Ring the alarum bell! Blow, wind! Come, wrack!
At least we'll die with harness on our back. (52)
Macbeth, 5.5, 1-52

(IN the first part of Macbeth's speech he says that his castle is strong enough to 'laugh a siege to scorn,' (3) once again, the surprising verb. It's also an example of Will's awareness of human nature. More often than not people facing violent death stand and fight back.

After Macbeth learns from Seyton that the noise he hears is 'the cry of women,' (8) he admits that he has become jaded: 'I have almost forgot the taste of fears.' (9)

Followed by the penetrating line, 'I have supped full with horrors.' (13)

Then the moving line, 'The Queen, my lord, is dead.' (16) Macbeth, who is 'supped full with horrors' seems unmoved, as he answers: 'She should have died hereafter,' (17) followed by 'There would have been a time for such a word.' (18) If he means that she would have died anyway, he is being callous. Or, if he means this is a bad time I cannot mourn her, he is bereft of feeling. He's likely saying that there should have been a better time. If so, Macbeth is due a little forgiveness, should you feel charitable.

One of the myriad components that make Shakespearean language so attractive is the multiple ways it can be interpreted.

Next, with the 'Tomorrow . . .' (19) speech we're rewarded with one of Will's finest creations. Macbeth is exhausted, totally cynical and brilliantly poetic. All the lines are marvelous. Some favorites: 'And all our yesterdays have lighted fools the way to dusty death,' 22) and 'Life's but a walking shadow, a poor player that struts and frets his hour upon the stage.' (24) The latter is a treasure for the onstage actor speaking the abiding lines.

The messenger enters to say, 'I should report that which I say I saw, but not know how to do it.' (31) He's saying, I can't believe what I just saw. Macbeth tells him that if he lies 'Upon the next tree shalt thou hang alive.' (39) But if his message is true, 'I care not if thou dost for me as much,' (41) or you can hang me, surprising levity given the circumstances.

Near the end of this speech, Macbeth, who's fed up with it all, as exemplified in the 'Tomorrow . . .' speech, wearily says, 'I 'gin to be aweary of the sun, and wish the estate o' the world were now undone.' (49) He'd just as soon be dead.

But once again he revives, wants the alarm rung and the wind to blow hard. 'Come, wrack! At least we'll die with harness on our back,' (52) or in full armor.)

* * *

(SCENE SIX is brief. Malcolm, Siward and his English troops are outside Dunsinane Castle. Malcolm orders the soldiers to discard the Birnam Wood branches they have been carrying to disguise their numbers.

Scene seven opens on the battlefield. Macbeth feels trapped by events and likens himself to a baited bear.

He remains obsessed with the 'born of woman' prophecy. The reference is expositional in the short speech that follows. It's also well-placed since the resolution of the divination is near.)

Macbeth. They have tied me to a stake, I cannot fly,
But bearlike I must fight the course. What's he
That was not born of woman? Such a one
Am I to fear, or none.
Macbeth, 5.7, 1-4

(MACBETH encounters Young Siward, son of the English army general, and kills him in a sword fight. Then, in an expository speech prior to his climactic fight with Macduff, Macbeth boasts:

Macbeth. Thou wast born of woman.
But swords I smile at, weapons laugh to scorn,
Brandished by man that's of a woman born.
Macbeth, 5.7, 12-14

(Macbeth exits, and Macduff enters to say that if Macbeth dies through 'no stroke of mine,' (15) then 'My wife and children's ghosts will haunt me still.' This explanatory bit frames Macduff's determination to kill Macbeth and sets up the ultimate clash.

Will didn't like to give audiences surprises. They are well prepared for resolution in the tragedy of Macbeth.)

* * *

(Now we near the point toward which the play has inexorably moved. Macbeth, trying to save what's left of his life and kingdom, and Macduff, aching for revenge, meet on the battlefield.)

Macbeth. <u>Why should I play the Roman fool</u> (1) <u>and die?</u>
<u>On mine own sword?</u> Whiles I see lives, the gashes
Do better upon them.
Macduff. (Enters.) Turn, hellhound, turn!
Macbeth. Of all men else I have avoided thee.
But get thee back, my soul is too much charged
With blood of thine already.
Macduff. I have no words.
<u>My voice is in my sword,</u> (8) thou bloodier villain
Than terms can give thee out! (Fight ensues.)
Macbeth. Thou losest labor.
As easy mayst thou the intrenchant air
With thy keen sword impress as make me bleed.
Let fall thy blade on vulnerable crests.
<u>I bear a charmèd life, which must not yield</u> (12)
<u>To one of woman born.</u>
Macduff. <u>Despair thy charm,</u> (13)
And let the angel whom thou still hast served
Tell thee Macduff was from his mother's womb
<u>Untimely ripped.</u> (15)
Macbeth. Accursèd be that tongue that tells me so,
For it hath <u>cowed my better part of man!</u> (18)
And be these juggling fiends no more believed
That palter with us in a double sense,
That keep the word of promise to our ear
And break it to our hope. <u>I'll not fight with thee.</u> (22)

Macduff. Then yield thee, coward,
And live to be the show and gaze o' the time.
We'll have thee, as our rarest monsters are,
Painted upon a pole, (26) and underwrit,
'Here may you see the tyrant.'
Macbeth. I will not yield,
To kiss the ground before young Malcolm's feet, (28)
And to be baited with the rabble's curse.
Though Birnam Wood be come to Dunsinane, (30)
And thou opposed, being of no woman born,
Yet I will try the last. Before my body
I throw my warlike shield. Lay on, Macduff, (33)
And damned be him that first cries 'Hold, enough!
Macbeth, 5.8, 1-34

(MACDUFF and Macbeth exit sword fighting.

Malcolm, Siward and others enter to say that young
Siward is dead and Macduff is missing.

Soon Macduff enters carrying Macbeth's head and
addresses Malcolm.)

Macduff. Hail, King! For so thou art. Behold where
stands
The usurper's cursèd head. (54 The time is free.
I see thee compassed with thy kingdom's pearl,
That speak my salutation in their minds,
Whose voices I desire aloud with mine:

Hail, King of Scotland.
All. Hail, King of Scotland!
Macbeth, 5.8, 55-58

(IN the first line of Macbeth's speech opening the final scene, he will not 'play the Roman fool.' (1) This alludes to the Roman practice of defeated military leaders falling on their swords, as did Marc Antony when defeated by Octavius Caesar in *Antony and Cleopatra.*

Several lines later, when Macduff enters and challenges Macbeth, he answers Macbeth with 'My voice is in my sword.' (8) Macduff is not at Macbeth's level as a poet, but he's a better swordsman.

After Macduff swings his sword and only hits air, Macbeth tells him, 'I bear a charmèd life, which must not yield to one of woman born.' (12) In other words, you're wasting your time trying to kill me, the fates are on my side.

Macduff quickly dispels Macbeth of that notion with, 'Despair thy charm,' (13) followed by revealing that he was 'Untimely ripped' (15) from his mother's womb, meaning he was delivered by Caesarean section.

This information shocks Macbeth who believes, thanks to the witch's prophesy, that he wouldn't yield 'To one of woman born.'

This disclosure, Macbeth says, 'cowed my better part of man,' (18) or made me afraid. He adds, 'I'll not fight with thee.' (22)

Macduff calls Macbeth a coward, wants to take him prisoner, and see him, 'Painted upon a pole,' (8) or have a sign made calling Macbeth a despot and have it displayed publicly.

Despite his worry about defying fate as prophesied by the weird sisters, Macbeth says he will not 'kiss the ground before young Malcolm's feet.' (28)

Cornered, fates against him, knowing that 'Birnam Wood be come to Dunsinane,' (30) and with nothing else to do, Macbeth utters another timeless line, 'Lay on, Macduff, and damned be him that first cries Hold, enough.' (33) It is Macbeth's last line of the play and probably of his life. They go offstage fighting.

Macduff reenters holding 'The usurper's cursèd head,' (55) and Malcolm is hailed as Scotland's King.)

SUMMARY

In the introduction, we asked who was responsible for the tragedy of *Macbeth* and listed three possibilities: Is it the fates represented by the Weird Sisters, Macbeth's character, Lady Macbeth, or all three?

By this time, I'm sure you will agree, the flaws in the Macbeth's characters are well established. Since Macbeth was dependent on his wife, he was susceptible to her murderous encouragement. Lady Macbeth's persuasive eloquence and challenges to her husband's manhood worked. She managed well the dark and bloody side, but once the deadly deeds were done she fell apart.

I've heard arguments that Macbeth was, like Brutus in Julius Caesar, a noble character gone wrong. The evidence suggests that Macbeth was ignoble. Moreover, he was a self-absorbed, subjective man who saw everything from his own viewpoint. It was all about him. Unlike Malcolm and Macduff, Macbeth had nothing to say about the good he could do for Scotland. Hecate said it best about Macbeth in 3.5, (13) 'Loves for his own ends . . .'

Beyond the character analyses, all of the weird sisters' prophesies came true. Ignore the fates at your peril In Elizabethan literature.

We've scrutinized an intricate masterpiece in which all the pieces fit, and the whole delivers a play of estimable structure. Some of the writing wasn't done by Will, but overall the text was lush with his great poetry. You know, I think I'll go back and read Macbeth again for the uncounted number of times.

Part Two

Plantagenet Plays

Richard 11; Henry 1V, Parts One and Two; Henry V; Henry V1, Parts One, Two, and Three; Richard 111

Note: The formatting for the thirteen plays that follow is slightly different from the just-completed three tragedies. For example, selected lines from key speeches are unnumbered but are underlined. Testing showed that these formatting differences posed little difficulty for readers of the 13 plays making up the remainder of the book.

KING RICHARD 11

High-stomached are they both, and full of ire,
In rage deaf as the sea, hasty as fire.'
Richard II, 1.1

(Nice poetry, with 'high-stomached' a colorful
substitute for haughty opponents.)

King Richard. Let's purge this choler without letting
blood;
    This we prescribe, though no physician;
    Deep malice makes too deep incision:
    Forget, forgive; conclude, and be agreed;
    Our doctors say this is no time to bleed.
Richard II, 1.1

(First signs of Richard's weakness, 'without letting
blood.'
    'Forget and forgive' are also used in King Lear,
4.7. I believe I saw variations on the phrase in one or
two other of Shakespeare's plays.

In modern-day vernacular, the expression is usually worded, 'forgive and forget.')

Mowbray. Myself I throw, dread sovereign, at thy foot:
My life thou shalt command, but not my shame:
The one my duty owes; but my fair name,
Despite of death, that lives upon my grave,
To dark dishonour's use thou shalt not have.
I am disgraced, impeached, and baffled here;
Pierced to the soul with <u>slander's venomed spear</u>,
The which no balm can cure but his heart-blood
Which breathed this poison . . .'
And I resign my gage, my dear dear lord,
The purest treasure mortal times afford
Earl of Northumberland. Is spotless reputation; that away,
Men are but <u>gilded loam or painted clay</u>
A jewel in a ten-times barred-up chest
Is a bold spirit in a loyal breast.
Mine honour is my life; both grow in one;
Take honour from me, and my life is done:
Then, dear liege, mine honour let me try:
In that I live, and for that I will die.
Richard II, 1.1

(Moving loyalty arguments to King Richard with premiums such as: 'slander's venomed spear' and 'gilded loam or painted clay.')

Duchess of Gloster. Hath love in thy old <u>blood</u> no life no living fire?
    Edward's seven sons, whereof thyself art one,
    Were as seven vials of his sacred <u>blood,</u>
    <u>Of seven fair branches springing from one root:</u>
    <u>Some of these</u> are dried by nature's course,
    <u>Some of those</u> branches by the Destinies cut;
    But Thomas, my dear lord, my life, my Gloster,
    One vial full of Edward's sacred blood,
    One flourishing branch of his most royal root,
    Is cracked, and all the precious liquor spilt;
    Is hacked down, and his <u>summer-leaves all faded,</u>
    By envy's hand and murder's bloody axe.
    Richard II, 1.2

(Catch the divergent uses of 'blood' in lines one and three.

    Line four 'Of seven fair branches springing from one root' triggers the rhythmical 'Some of these' and Some of those' in lines five and six.

    With 'summer-leaves all faded' Will continues his use of leaves as metaphorical devices. Leaves were used hauntingly in Sonnet 73, 'When yellow leaves, or none, or few, do hang Upon those boughs which shake against the cold, Bare ruined choirs where late the sweet birds sang.'

> *Bolingbroke*. Norfolk, so far as to mine enemy;
> By this time, had the king permitted us,
> One of our <u>souls had wandered in the air</u>,
> Banished this frail sepulchre of our flesh,
> As now our flesh is banished from this land:
> Confess thy treasons, ere thou fly the realm;
> Since thou hast far to go, bear not along
> The <u>clogging burden of a guilty soul</u>.
> *Mowbray*. No, Bolingbroke: if ever I were a traitor,
> My name be <u>blotted from the book of life</u>.
> Richard II, 1.3

(Bolingbroke admits that he's a traitor, but Norfolk doesn't go along. Read again the evanescent image of 'souls wandering in the air' later juxtaposed with the 'clogging burden of a guilty soul.'

I liked Mowbray's dramatic 'be blotted from the book of life.')

> *John of Gaunt*. Teach thy necessity to reason thus;
> There is <u>no virtue like necessity</u>.

Richard II, 1.3

(Another saying courtesy of Will. It even prompted a modern-day book title.)

Bolingbroke. 'O, who can hold a fire in his hand
By thinking on the <u>frosty Caucasus</u>?
Or cloy the hungry edge of appetite
By bare imagination of a feast?
Or <u>wallow naked in December snow</u>
By thinking on fantastic summer's heat?
O, no! the apprehension of the good
<u>Gives but the greater feeling to the worse:</u>
Full <u>sorrow's tooth</u> doth never rankle more
Than when it bites, but lanceth not the sore.'
King Richard II, 1.3

(Consider examples of creative juxtaposition in the first six lines, plus the stop-and-smile 'frosty Caucasus' and 'wallow naked in December snow.'

Will liked the Caucasus as metaphor for cold winters. He used it at least three times in his plays.

'Sorrow's tooth' also bit me.)

388

John of Gaunt. This royal throne of kings, this sceptered isle

This earth of majesty, this seat of Mars,

This other Eden; demi-paradise:

This fortress built by nature for herself

Against infection and the hand of war;

<u>This happy breed of men</u>, this little world;

<u>This precious stone set in the silver sea,</u>

<u>Which serves it in the office of a wall,</u>

<u>Or as a moat defensive to a house,</u>

<u>Against the envy of less happier lands:</u>

This blessed plot, this earth, this realm, this England.

Richard II, 2.1

(Beyond the burnished poetry, this passage may be the acme of patriotic speech on behalf of one's country; and, as we know, Will was a patriot.

'This happy breed of men' reminds us of 'We few, we happy few, we band of brothers' from the St. Crispin's Day speech in Henry V, 4.3, probably written about four years after Richard 11.

My favorite four lines, and the ones that have stayed with me since I first read the passage many years ago: 'This precious stone . . . lands.')

Northumberland. The <u>king</u> is not himself, but <u>basely led</u>

By <u>flatterers</u>; and what they will inform,

Merely in hate, against any of us all,

That will the <u>king</u> severely prosecute

'Gainst us, our lives, our children, and our heirs.

Ross. The <u>commons</u> hath be <u>pilled</u> with <u>grievous taxes</u>,

And <u>quite lost their hearts</u>: the nobles hath he fined

For ancient quarrels, and <u>quite lost their hearts</u>.'

'He hath not money for these Irish wars,

<u>His burdensome taxation notwithstanding</u>,

But by the robbing of the banished duke.'

King Richard II, 2.1

(Northumberland and Lord Ross are unhappy with King Richard.

We can easily substitute some current bosses and politicians for 'king' in lines one and four.

'Basely led by flatterers' points to Richard's narcissism and weakness.

Our children and grandchildren will pay for all this wasteful spending is the modern version of Ross's line-five language: 'His burdensome taxation notwithstanding.'

'Pilled' meant skinned in Elizabethan days, a fitting verb for 'grievous taxes.'

Check the balanced use of 'quite lost their hearts' for both common folk and nobles.)

Bushy. Each substance of a grief hath twenty shadows,
   Which show like grief itself, but are not so;
   For <u>sorrow's eye</u>, glazed with blinding <u>tears</u>,
   Divides one thing entire to many objects.'
King Richard II, 2.2

(Bolingbroke used 'sorrow's tooth' in 1.3. Both effective and especially in this neat reference, sorrow's eye,' to tears obscuring vision.)

Northumberland. I am a stranger here in Glostershire:
   These high wild hills and rough uneven ways
   Draw out our miles, and make them wearisome;
   And yet your <u>fair discourse hath been as sugar</u>,
   Making the hard way sweet and delectable.
Richard II, 2.3

(Northumberland congratulates Bolingbroke—future King Henry IV—on his gift of gab, which can also mean silver-voiced, 'your fair discourse hath been as sugar.'

The role would have nicely fit the legendary British actor Sir John Gielgud. Another legend, Sir Lawrence Olivier, once described Gielgud's voice as a 'silver trumpet muffled in silk.')

Northumberland. Here come the Lords of Ross and Willoughby,
<u>Bloody with spurring and fiery-red with haste</u>.'
Richard II, 2.3

(Since it was unlikely that Ross and Willoughby galloped on horseback across the Rose, or another theater's stage, Will helps audiences speed their imaginations. And rereading line 2 in the Northumberland quote above, we see how stimulating the imagery cues are.)

Captain of a Band of Welshmen The pale-faced moon looks bloody on the earth,
And <u>lean-looked prophets</u> whisper fearful change;
<u>Rich men look sad</u>, and <u>ruffians dance and leap</u>,
<u>The one in fear to lose what they enjoy</u>,
<u>The other to enjoy by rage and war</u>:

These signs forerun the death or fall of kings.
Farewell: our countrymen are gone and fled,
As well assured Richard their King is dead. (Exits.)
Richard II, 2.4

(Lean-looked or not, change is in the air.

Lines three, four and five speak of an age-old truism. Those that have it don't want to give it up, 'fear to lose what they enjoy.' Those that don't have it, 'ruffians dance and leap,' do the fighting.)

Salisbury. 'Ah, Richard, with the eyes of heavy mind,
I see thy glory, like a shooting star,
Fall to the base earth from the firmament!
The sun sets weeping in the lowly west,
Witnessing storms to come, woe, and unrest;
Thy friends are fled to wait upon thy foes;
And crossly to thy good all fortune goes.
Richard II, 2.4

(Will presumes that many audience members know what happened to King Richard. And for those that don't the hints are clear as to what's coming, 'I see thy glory like a shooting star . . .'

I liked, 'The sun sets weeping in the lowly west.'

'Crossly' in the last line means adversely in modern terms. I like crossly better.)

Bolingbroke. Myself,—a prince by fortune of my birth,
　Near to the king in blood, and near in love
　<u>Till you did make him misinterpret me,</u>
　Have stooped my neck under your injuries,
　And sighed my English breath in foreign clouds,
　<u>Eating the bitter bread of banishment;</u>
　Whilst you have fed upon my signories,
　Disparked my parks, and felled my forest-woods,
　From my own windows torn my household coat,
　Razed out my impress, leaving me no sign,
　Save men's opinions and my living blood,
　<u>To show the world I am a gentleman.</u>
　This and much more, much more than twice all this,
　Condemns you to the death.—See them delivered over
　To execution and the hand of death.
　Richard II, 3.1

(Bushy and Green pay with their lives for influencing King Richard ll in the banishment of Bolingbroke. See line three.

Among all the choice phrases in Bolingbroke's emotive speech, I found the line, 'To show the world I am a gentleman' perfectly worded and placed.

In Henry 1V, Part 2, Bolingbroke, later Henry lV, confessed his guilt over deposing Richard ll to his son, Prince Hal, later Henry V.)

King Richard. Discomfortable cousin! Knowest thou not
That when the searching eye of heaven is hid
Behind the globe that lights the lower world,
Then thieves and robbers range abroad unseen,
In murders and in outrange, boldly here;
But when, from under this terrestrial ball,
He fires the proud tops of the eastern pines,
And darts his light through every guilty hole,
Then murders, treasons, and detested sins,
The cloak of night being plucked from off their backs.
Stand bare and naked, trembling at themselves?
So when this thief, this traitor, Bolingbroke,
Who all this while hath reveled in the night,
Whilst we were wandering with the antipodes,
Shall see us rising in our throne, the east,
His treasons will sit blushing in his face,
Not able to endure the sight of day,

But self-affrighted tremble at his sin.
<u>Not all the water in the rough rude sea</u>
<u>Can wash the balm from an anointed king;</u>
The breath of worldly men cannot depose
The deputy elected by the Lord;
For every man that Bolingbroke hath pressed
To lift shrewd steel against our golden crown,
God for his Richard hath in heavenly pay
A glorious angel: then, if angels fight,
Weak man must fall; for heaven still guards the
right-
    <u>Cry woe, destruction, ruin, loss, decay;</u>
    <u>The worst is death; and death will have his day!'</u>
Richard II, 3.2

(King Richard believes that the divine rights of kings will save his crown, 'Not all the water in the rough rude sea Can wash the balm from an anointed king.'

Reread the beautiful final couplet. 'Cry woe . . .'' Reminds us 'Dog will have its day,' from Hamlet, 5.1. Which Will borrowed from Erasmus.

As eloquently described below, things are more desperate than Richard ever imagined: Bolingbroke not only had the arms and the men, he had women, children and old men ready to fight.

I'm reminded of Churchill's cautioning Stalin toward the end of World War II to consider the Pope's concerns regarding the occupation of heavily Catholic Eastern Europe. Stalin's cynical reply: 'How many divisions does the Pope have?')

Sir Stephen Scroop. 'Glad I am that your highness is so armed
  To bear the tidings of calamity.
  Like an unseasonable stormy day,
  Which make the silver rivers drown their shores,
  As if the world were all dissolved to tears;
  So high above his limits swells the rage
  Of Bolingbroke, covering your fearful land
  With hard bright steel, and hearts harder than steel.
  White-beards have armed their thin and hairless scalps
  Against thy majesty; and boys, with women's voices,
  Strive to speak big, and clap their female joints
  In stiff unwieldy arms against thy crown:
  The very beadsmen learn to bend their bows
  Of double-fatal yew against thy state;
  Yea, distaff women manage rusty bills
  Against thy seat: both old and young rebel,
  And all goes worse that I have power to tell.'

Richard II, 3.2

(As underlined above, Scroop tells the King that, led by Bolingbroke, the population, young, 'boys with women's voices' and old, 'white beards' stands ready to rebel.

No longer being on the morning side of the mountain myself, 'White-beards have armed their thin and hairless scalps' tickled me.)

King Richard. <u>Let's talk of graves, of worms, and epitaphs</u>;
    Make dust our paper, and with rainy eyes
    Write sorrow on the bosom of the earth.
    Let's choose executors, and talk of wills . . .
    All murdered:—for within <u>the hollow crown</u>
    That rounds the mortal temples of a king
    Keeps death his court; and there the antic sits,
    Scoffing his state, and <u>grinning at his pomp</u>;
    Allowing him a breath, a little scene,
    To monarchize, be feared, and kill with looks;
    Infusing himself with self and vain conceit,—
    As if this flesh, which walls about our life,
    Were brass impregnable; and humoured thus,
    Comes at the last, <u>and with a little pin</u>
    <u>Bores through his castle-wall, and farewell king!</u>

King Richard II, 3.2

(Line one, 'Let's talk of graves, of worms, and epitaphs' indicates that King Richard knows the game is up.

'The Hollow Crown,' is the name of a 2015 British television production starring, among others, Tom Hiddleston and Benedict Cumberbatch.

'And with a little pin . . . shows that Richard knows that despite all the trappings of his kingship, his enemies are 'grinning at his pomp' and can depose him.)

And my large kingdom for a little grave,
A little little grave, an obscure grave;—
Or I'll be buried in the king's highway,
Some way of common trade, where subjects' feet
May hourly trample on their sovereign's head;
For on my heart they tread now whilst I live;
And buried once, why not upon my head?
King Richard II, 3.3

(From the time Bolingbroke had King Richard's men Bushy and Green executed, Will shows the decline of a doomed king. Starting in King Richard's speeches in 3.2, the king goes through several stages of grief. He knows his reign is over in the speech mentioning 'graves, worms, and epitaphs.' Then, in 3.3, he talks bitterly of being 'buried in the king's highway' with subject's feet trampling on their sovereign's head.

In writing the part of a weak, impractical king who believes that his religious beliefs and inherent rights will save him, Will again shows superb character development. I recommend going back and rereading Bolingbroke's speech in 3.1 and on through the one above by King Richard.)

Carlisle. I speak to subjects and a subject speaks,
Stirred up by God, thus boldly for his king.
My Lord of Hereford here, whom you call king,
Is a <u>foul traitor</u>, to proud Hereford's king;
And if you crown him, let me prophesy,
The blood of English shall manure the ground,
And future ages groan for this foul act;
Peace shall go to sleep with Turk and infidels,
And in this seat of peace tumultuous wars
Shall kin with <u>kin and kind</u> with kind confound;
Disorder, horror, fear, and mutiny,
Shall here inhabit, and this land be called
<u>The field of Golgotha</u> and dead men's skulls.
Or, if you raise <u>this house against this house</u>,
It will the woefullest division prove

That ever fell upon this cursed earth,
Prevent, resist it, let it not be so,
Lest child, child's children, cry against you "Woe.!"
Northumberland. Well you have argued, sir; and, for your pains,
Of <u>capital treason</u> we arrest you here.'
King Richard II, 4.1

(The Bishop of Carlisle makes an impassioned, and, as it turns out, a dangerous speech on behalf of religious King Richard II. He also calls Lord Hereford, a title held by Bolingbroke, 'foul traitor.'

Note the line, 'Shall kin with kin and kind with kind confound.' Variations on these words were clichés in Will's day. When the king, who murdered his father and soon married his mother, refers to him as a cousin and a son, Hamlet replied, 'A little more than kin, and less than kind.' He let the king know, I have your number.

'The field of Golgotha' refers to the burial ground of Jesus.

Abraham Lincoln read Shakespeare. I wonder if the line, 'This house against this house' inspired his 'House divided' speech? 'A house divided against itself cannot stand.'

In the final two lines, Northumberland compliments Bishop Carlisle on a good argument that will cost him his head, 'capital treason.')

Bolingbroke. Our <u>scene</u> is altered from a serious thing,
    And now changed to <u>The Beggar and the King</u>.
    My dangerous <u>cousin</u>, let your mother in:
    I know she's come to pray for your foul sin . . .'
    <u>'Good aunt, stand up.'</u>
    Duchess. <u>'Nay, do not say stand up;</u>
    <u>But pardon first, and afterwards stand up.</u>
    An if I were thy nurse, thy tongue to teach,
    Pardon should be the first word of thy speech.
    I never longed to hear a word till now;
    Say pardon, king; let pity teach thee how:
    The word is short, but not so <u>short as sweet</u>;
    No word like pardon, for kings' mouths so meet.
    King Richard II, 5.3

(In line two, through Bolingbroke, Will refers to the legend of the African king who made a beggar his wife in several plays. Note also the theatrical reference to 'scene' and then to a different play.

The reference to 'cousin' in line three was also used in 'Hamlet' and other Elizabethan plays. It was a common term used among royals, whether they were related or not.

Then, in her riposte, the Duchess of York, after being told to stop kneeling, has a little language fun with her nephew Bolingbroke.

In the next-to-last line, a variation of the expression 'short and sweet' is used. The cliché predated Will.)

King Richard. As thoughts of things divine, are intermixed
With scruples, and do set the word against itself
Against the word:
As thus, Come, little ones; and then again,
It is as hard to come as for a camel
To thread the postern of a needle's eye.
Thoughts tending to ambition, they do plot
Unlikely wonders: how these vain weak nails
May tear a passage through the flinty ribs
Of this hard world, my ragged prison walls;
And, for they cannot, die in their own pride . . .
Ha, ha! keep time: how sour sweet music is
When time is broke and no proportion kept!
So it is in the music of men's lives.'
Richard II, 5.5

(Trapped in his prison dungeon, Richard II muses on his chances for an escape, even invoking, in lines five and six, Matthew 19:24.

In the last four lines, Richard laughs bitterly at the futility of keeping track of time in prison: 'time is broke.' Will had the ability to give poetic beauty to Richard's prison-bound grief.)

Variations on prisoner lamentations have come down through the ages in verse and song: 'If I had the wings of an angel.')

H. Percy. The grand conspirator, <u>Abbot of Westminster,</u>
<u>With clog of conscience and sour melancholy,</u>
<u>Hath yielded up his body to the grave;</u>
But here is Carlisle living, to abide
Thy kingly doom and sentence of his pride.
Bolingbroke. Carlisle, this your doom:
Choose out some secret place, some reverend room,
More than thou hast, and with it joy thy life.'
Exton. <u>Great king, within this coffin I prese</u>nt
Thy buried fear: herein all breathless lies
The mightiest of thy greatest enemies,
<u>Richard of Bordeaux, by me hither brought.'</u>

Boling. <u>Exton, I thank thee not</u>; for thou has wrought
A deed of slander, with thou fateful hand.
Upon my head and all this fateful land.'
Exton. From your own mouth, my lord, did I this deed.
Boling. They love not poison that do poison
Nor do I thee: though I did wish him dead,
<u>I hate the murderer, love him murdered.</u>'
King Richard II, 5.6

('With clog of conscience and sour melancholy,' the Abbot of Westminster and Bishop of Carlisle are executed for opposing Bolingbroke. Then, in a twist, the usurping King Henry is presented with the coffin containing the body of Richard II. And, in the final line, turns on the executioner, 'I hate the murderer, love him murdered.')

HENRY IV, PART ONE

King Henry. So shaken as we are, so wan with care,
For we a time for <u>frighted peace to pant,</u>
And breathe short-winded accents of new broils
To be commenced in strands far remote.
No more the thirsty entrance of this soil
Shall <u>daub her lips</u> with her own children's blood;
No more shall trenching war channel her fields,
Nor <u>bruise her flowerets</u> with the <u>armed hoofs</u>
Of hostile paces: those opposed eyes
Which, like the meteors of a troubled heaven,
All of one nature, of one substance bred,
Did lately meet in the <u>intestine shock</u>
And <u>furious close of civil butchery,</u>
Shall now, in well-beseeming ranks,
March all one way, and be no more opposed
Against acquaintance, kindred, and allies:
<u>The edge of war, like an ill-sheathed knife,</u>
<u>Shall no more cut his master.</u>
Henry IV, Part I, 1.1

(Formerly Bolingbroke, now Henry IV, usurped
the crown from King Richard II. Understandably, he

called for a halt to future wars. His guilt over the wrongful usurpation is told in a deathbed confession to his son, Prince Hal, late in Henry IV, Part Two.

I relished, 'frighted peace to pant,' 'daub her lips', and 'bruise her flowerets with armed hoofs.' 'Flowerets,' combined with 'hoofs' generates impressive imagery.

'Intestine shock' and 'furious close of civil butchery' are brilliant references to the horrors of hand-to-hand combat. It's likely that Will observed combat, or at least talked extensively with war veterans about it.

In the final two lines, 'The edge of war . . .' King Henry makes clear that he doesn't wish to suffer his predecessor's fate.)

King. In envy that my lord Northumberland
Should be the father to so blest a son,
A son who is the theme to honour's tongue;
Amongst a grove, the very straightest plant;
Who is sweet fortunes' minion and her pride:
Whilst I, by looking on the praise of him,'
See riot and dishonor stain the brow
Of my young Harry. O that it could be proved
That some night-tripping fairy had exchanged
In cradle-clothes our children where they lay,
And called mine Percy, his Plantagenet!

Then <u>I would have his Harry, and he mine.</u>
Henry IV, Part I, 1.1

(Northumberland, aka Henry Percy, like Henry IV, has a son named Henry, nicknamed Hotspur. The king doesn't have much use for his son Harry, aka Prince Henry and Hal, and wishes that Northumberland's son was his. Did you spot 'night-tripping fairy?')

Falstaff. Now, Hal, what time of day is it, lad?
Hal. Thou art so fat-witted with drinking of old sack, and <u>unbuttoning thee after supper</u>, and sleeping upon benches after noon, that thou has forgotten to demand that truly which thou wouldst truly know. What a devil hast though to do with the time of the day? Unless <u>hours</u> were cups of <u>sack</u>, and <u>minutes</u> <u>capons</u>, and cocks the <u>tongues of bawds</u>, and <u>dials</u> the signs of leaping houses, and the blessed <u>sun</u> himself a fair hot wench in <u>flame-coloured taffeta</u>, I see no reason why thou shouldst be so superfluous to demand the time of the day.
Henry IV, Part I, 1.1

(Now we are introduced, in all his excesses, to Sir John Falstaff, one of Will's greatest characters. Orson

Welles, in his later and weightier days, played Falstaff convincingly in his film 'Chimes at Midnight."

"Unbuttoning thee after supper' and 'flame-coloured taffeta' are notable imagery.

I liked the listing of Falstaff's favorite weaknesses: sack, capons, etc. to mock his asking the time of day.

In a segment from my novel *Discovering Will's Lost Years*, Will, at age 11, appears as an impromptu ingénue with a company of traveling players performing in Stratford. Frothingham, the lead player, is introduced as a possible model for Falstaff, and his assistant, Vegetarius, as a potential inspiration for Pistol.

In a later segment from the book, when Will first lived in London, he visited Robert Greene, a larger-than-life person, and a likely Falstaff prototype, who now lay dying. Greene, a popular satirical writer, had been critical of Will calling him 'an upstart crow' and a 'Shake-scene.' In the touching vignette, Will and Greene reconcile.

The fictional Falstaff had a history of other names and people who may have inspired his creation. But as Richard III said in the eponymous play, 'I go before my horse to market,' and let's continue the repartee between Falstaff and Hal.)

Falstaff. Marry, then, sweet wag, when thou art king, let not us that are squires of the night's body be called thieves of the day's <u>beauty</u>: let us be Diana's foresters, <u>gentlemen of the shade</u>, <u>minions of the moon</u>; and let men say we be men of good government, being governed, as the sea is, by our noble and chaste mistress the moon, under whose countenance we steal.'

Hal. 'Thou sayest well, and it holds well too; for the fortune of us that are the moon's men doth ebb and flow like the sea, being governed, as the sea is, by the moon. As, for proof, now: a purse of gold most resolutely snatched on Monday night, and most dissolutely spent on Tuesday morning; got with swearing <u>lay by</u>, and spent with crying <u>bring in</u>; now in as low an ebb as the foot of the ladder, and by and by in as high a flow as the ridge of the <u>gallows</u>.

Henry IV, Part I, 1.2

(Falstaff's pun of 'beauty' for 'booty' in line 2 is fun.

Neat pairing: 'gentlemen of the shade' and 'minions of the moon.'

In using 'lay by' and 'bring in,' Hal accuses Falstaff of robbing then using the loot to buy sack, and that low act will probably get him to the 'gallows.')

Falstaff. What sayest thou to a hare, or the melancholy of <u>Moor-ditch</u>?'

'Thou hast the most unsavoury similes, and art, indeed, the most comparative, rascallest,—sweet young prince,—but, Hal, I would to God thou and I knew where a commodity of <u>good names</u> were to be bought.

Henry IV, Part I, 1.2

(Falstaff kids Hal over mentioning, 'moor-ditch,' a smelly sewer.

The final 'good names' line sounds like the lament of a modern-day marketer.

Later in the scene, Falstaff tells Hal of meeting an old lord who talks wisely in the street. Hal responds: 'wisdom cries out in the streets, and no man regards it.' No one regarded street talk more than Will. He listened to everything and forgot nothing.

And after more bantering, Hal admires Falstaff's ability to switch easily between praying and purse-taking.)

Ned. 'Good morrow, sweet Hal. What says Monsieur Remorse? What says Sir John Sack-and-sugar? Jack, how agrees the devil and thee about thy soul, that thou soldest him on Good-Friday last for a cup of Madeira and a cold capon's leg?'

Hal. 'Sir John stands to his word, the devil shall have his bargain; for he was never yet a breaker of proverbs, <u>he will give the devil his due</u>.'

Henry IV, Part I, 1.2

(Ned Poins, a member of Falstaff's gang of bad boys, enters the scene to show that he also has Jack's number.

Hal responded and closed with yet another of Will's originals, 'he will give the devil his due.'

Poins then told Jack and Hal that he learned of pilgrims and traders riding to Canterbury with fat purses. Hal hesitated, then agreed to join the robbers saying, 'once in my days I'll be a madcap.'

After Falstaff exited the scene, Poins told Hal that they would not be there for the actual holdup, but after it happened they would rob Falstaff, Bardolph and the rest of the miscreants.

Poins left and Hal spoke alone. Reminder: Elizabethan characters always speak the truth, insofar as they know it, in soliloquy.)

Hal. I know you all, and will awhile uphold

The unyoked humour of your idleness:
Yet herein will <u>I imitate the sun,</u>
Who doth permit the base contagious clouds
To smother up his beauty from the world,
That, when he please again to be himself,
Being wanted, he may be more wondered at
<u>By breaking through the foul and ugly mists</u>
Of vapours that did seem to strangle him.
<u>If all the year were playing holidays,</u>
<u>To sport would be as tedious as to work;</u>
But when they seldom come, they wished-for
come,
And nothing pleaseth but rare accidents.
So, when this loose behavior I throw off,
<u>And pay the debt I never promised,</u>
By how much better than my word I am,
By so much shall I falsify men's hopes;
And, like bright metal on a sullen ground,
My reformation, glittering over my fault,
Shall show more goodly and attract more eyes
Than that which hath no foil to set it off.
I'll so offend, to make offence a skill;
<u>Redeeming time when men think least I will.</u>
Henry IV, Part I, 1.2

(The words are, of course, Shakespeare's, as he tells
the audience, especially those slow to catch on, that

413

Hal (Prince Henry) know what he's doing and will reform when he needs to. The speech is also designed to reduce some of the sting when Hal became king and rejects Falstaff.

'I imitate the sun' is a phrase I truly love. It's followed up by 'breaking through the foul and ugly mists' which Hal intends to do: 'Redeeming time when men think least I will.' Meaning, most of all, that he must prove to his father, King Henry, that he is worthy of succession. Earlier, King Henry wished that Hotspur, not Hal, was his son.

The reference in mid-speech to 'playing holidays' is yet another example of Will's capacity to produce universal truisms in useful contexts.

In the line, 'And pay the debt I never promised,' Hal pledges his intent to be a good king, which he became as Henry V.

And we move to Hotspur serving in the play as a dues ex machina.)

Hotspur. But I remember when the fight was done,
When I was dry with rage and extreme toil,
Breathless and faint, leaning upon my sword,
Came there a certain lord, neat, trimly dressed,
Fresh as a bridegroom; and his chin new reaped
<u>Showed like a stubble-land at harvest-home;</u>

He was perfumed like a milliner;
And 'twixt his finger and his thumb he held
A pouncet-box, which ever and anon
<u>He gave his nose</u>, and took it away again.
Henry IV, Part I, 1.3

(Will gave Hal's rival, Hotspur, good lines. Here, Hotspur delivers a satirical description of an Elizabethan fop wandering incongruously on the battlefield, reminiscent of a scene in 'War and Peace.'

'Stubble-land at harvest-home' is a nice way to describe a clean shave.

In the visual-rich last four lines, the dandy sniffed perfume. 'He gave his nose . . .' to hide the stench of rotting corpses.)

Worcester. 'Peace, cousin; say no more:
And now I will unclasp a secret book,
And to your quick-conceiving discontents
I'll read you matter deep and dangerous;
As full of peril and adventurous spirit
As to o'er walk a current roaring loud
On the unsteadfast <u>footing of a spear</u>.'
Hotspur. 'If he fall in, good-night! or <u>sink or swim</u>:
Send danger from the east unto the west,
So honour cross it from the north to south,

And let them grapple. O, the blood more stirs
To rouse a lion than to start a hare! . . .
By heaven, methinks it were an <u>easy leap</u>
<u>To pluck bright honour from the pale-faced moon</u>;
Or dive into the bottom of the deep,
Where fathom-line could never touch the ground,
And pluck up drowned honour by the locks.
Henry IV, Part I, 1.3

(Worcester tells the impetuous Hotspur to think before crossing a stream using a spear for a bridge. The caution came when Hotspur, in a previous speech, went on at length about how Bolingbroke, current King Henry IV, took the crown from Richard II.

As was his wont, Hotspur launched into another description of how he thought crossing the stream on a spear was no big deal, 'sink or swim,' another phrase that fell into the vernacular. Or any challenge, was an 'easy leap,' like, 'plucking honour from the pale-faced moon,' a marvelous phrase. And Hotspur did this in language that contained vivid and vigorous imagery. Will was a master of fitting names to characters' personas. Hotspur was also one of his best poets.

Later, in the same scene, Hotspur tells of meeting with Henry IV, 'this king of smiles.'

Then: 'Why, what a candy deal of courtesy this fawning greyhound did proffer me,' meaning that he thought the king was being hypocritical.)

Falstaff. I am the veriest varlet that ever chewed with a tooth. Eight yards of uneven ground is three-score and ten miles a-foot with me; and the stony-hearted villains know it well enough: a plague upon it, <u>when thieves cannot be true to one another</u>. <u>Whew!</u>—a plague upon you all! Give me my horse, you rogues; give me my horse and be hanged.'
Hal. Peace, ye fatguts! lie down, and listen if thou canst hear the tread of travelers.
Falstaff. <u>Have you any levers</u> to lift me up again, being down?
Henry IV, Part I, 2.2

(Falstaff on his back curses his gang members for abandoning him at the bottom of a hill. He wishes a plague on them with the wry, 'when thieves cannot be true to one another.' One of his fellow robbers did whistle to Jack, and all he could muster was a 'Whew!'

Jack ignores Hal's order to be quiet and then Falstaff shows he has not lost his sense of humor by asking, 'Have you any levers. . ?')

Lady Percy. For what offence have I this fortnight been
   <u>A banished woman from my Harry's bed?</u>
   Tell me, sweet lord, what is it that takes from thee
   Thy stomach, pleasure, and thy golden sleep?
   Why dost though bend thine eyes upon the earth .
. .

   <u>And given my treasures</u> and rights of thee
   To thick-eyed musing and cursed melancholy?
   In thy faint slumbers I be thee have watched.
   And heard thee murmur tales of iron wars;
   Speak terms to manage of thy bounding steed;
   Cry, Courage!—to the field!—And thou hast talked
. . .

   Some heavy business hath my lord in hand,
   And I must know it, else he loves me not.
Hotspur. <u>'What, ho!'</u>
Henry IV, Part I, 2.3

(In the segment above, Lady Percy, Hotspur's young wife, complains that he thinks too much of wars and not enough of their bed, 'A banished woman from my Harry's bed?' 'And given my treasures . . .'

At the close of her plaintive speech, it's obvious that Hotspur hasn't heard a word of it, sees a servant enter and ask about his horse. 'What, ho!' He can't wait to buckle on his sword, mount the horse and race off to find someone to fight.)

Hal. 'That ever this fellow should have fewer words than a parrot, and yet the son of a woman! His industry is upstairs and downstairs; his eloquence the parcel of a reckoning. I am not yet of Percy's mind, the Hotspur of the north; he that kills me some six or seven dozen Scots at a breakfast, washes his hands, and says to his wife, Fie upon this quiet life! I want work. O my sweet Harry, says she, how many hast thou killed to-day? Give my roan horse a drench, says he; and answers, Some fourteen, an hour after,— a trifle, a trifle.

Henry IV, Part I, 3.1

(Hal cleverly mimicked Hotspur's reputation.)

Poins. Where hast thou been, Hal?
Hal. With three of four loggerheads amongst three or fourscore hogsheads. I have sounded the very base string of humility. Sirrah, I am sworn brother to a leash of <u>drawers</u>; and call them all by their Christian names, as <u>Tom, Dick and Francis</u>.

Henry IV, Part I, 2.4

('Every Tom, Dick and Harry' was in use during Shakespeare's time. In this scene in Eastcheap's Boar's Head Tavern, Francis, an apprentice, is named as one of a 'leash' or three, bartenders, or 'drawers', serving Hal, hence the name switch.)

Falstaff. What, upon compulsion? No, were I at the <u>strappado</u>, or all the racks in the world, I would not tell you on compulsion.

Hal. I'll be no longer guilty of this sin; this sanguine coward, this bed-presser, <u>this horse back-breaker</u>, this huge hill of flesh.

Falstaff. Away, you starveling, you elf-skin, you dried neat's tongue, bull's pizzle, you stockfish, <u>O for a breath to utter what is like thee</u>! you tailor's yard, you sheath, you bow-case, you vile standing-tuck.

Henry IV, Part I, 2.4

('Strappado,' hung by the wrists strapped behind the victim. Ouch!

Falstaff, caught in exaggerations and lies about a holdup, realizes that Hal knew the truth and lashes out. As always, portly Falstaff and slim Hal did a fair job of out-insulting each other. Falstaff even pauses and pleads for a breath so he can call more damnations down on Hal. Of course, it's all in fun, a version of the modern 'doing the dozens.' They really like each other, but it's theater, and the audience likes comic moments.)

Hal. That villainous abominable misleader of youth, Falstaff, that old white-bearded Satan.
Falstaff. If sack and sugar be a fault, God help the wicked! If to be old and merry be a sin, then many an old host that I know is damned; if to be fat be to be hated, then Pharaoh's leankine are to be loved. No, my good lord; banish Peto, banish Bardolph, banish Poins: but for sweet Jack Falstaff, kind Jack Falstaff, true Jack Falstaff, valiant Jack Falstaff, and therefore more valiant, being, as he, is old Jack Falstaff, banish not him thy Harry's company, banish not him thy Harry's company: banish plump Jack, and banish all the world.
Hal. I do. I will.
Henry IV, Part I, 2.4

(The exchange starts with Hal's usual insults. Falstaff senses a deeper problem and is willing to toss his entire gang overboard in order to save his own skin, before closing his case with a plea in which he repeats, 'banish not him thy Harry's company.' There was never created, in the history of literature, a more likable and convincing pious old fraud.

In the final line of the sequence, Hal answers Jack portentously, 'I do. I will.' And he eventually does.)

Glendower. <u>I can call spirits from the vasty deep.</u>
Hotspur. Why, so can I, so can any man;
But will they come when you call for them?
Henry IV, Part I, 3.1

Glendower. I can speak English as well as you;
For I was trained up in the English court,
Where, being but young, I framed to the harp
Many an English ditty, lovely well,
And gave the tongue a helpful ornament,
A virtue that was never seen in you.
Hotspur. Marry, and I am glad of it with all my heart
I had rather be a kitten and cry mew,
Than one of these <u>same meter ballad-mongers</u>;
I had rather hear a brazen candlestick turned;
Or a dry wheel grate on the axle-tree;
And that would set my teeth nothing on edge,
Nothing so much as <u>mincing poetry</u>:
'Tis like the forced gait of a <u>shuffling nag</u>.

(The two excerpts above came from a scene that shows the pomposity of Glendower, 'I can call spirits from the vasty deep' and the arrogance of Hotspur.

Since it also contains dialogue describing how they will divide up the land after they beat the army of Henry IV, the scene is well-worth reading in its entirety.

Will expresses his poetic prejudices in Hotspur's speech in the second excerpt. 'Same meter ballad-mongers' refers to rhyming in doggerel.

Hotspur closes his speech by comparing 'mincing poetry' with the 'shuffling nag' reference to a lame horse.)

King Henry. 'Thrice hath this Hotspur Mars in swathing-clothes,
  This infant warrior, in his enterprises
  Discomfited great Douglas; taken him once,
  Enlarged him, and made a friend of him,
  To fill the mouth of deep defiance up,
  And shake the peace and safety of our throne.
  And what say you to this? Percy, Northumberland,
  The Archbishop's grace of York, Douglas Mortimer,

Capitulate against us, and are up.
<u>But wherefore do I tell these news to thee?</u>
Hal. God forgive them that have so much swayed
Your majesty's good thoughts away from me!
<u>I will redeem all this on Percy's head,</u>
And, in the closing of some glorious day,
Be bold to tell you that I am your son;
When I will wear a garment all of blood,
And stain my favours in a bloody mask,
Which, washed away, shall scour my shame with it:
And that shall be the day, whenever it lights,
That this same child of honour and renown,
This gallant Hotspur, this all-praised knight,
And your unthought-of Harry chance to meet . . .
That I shall make this northern youth exchange
<u>His glorious deeds for my indignities.</u>
Percy is but my <u>factor</u>, good my lord,
<u>To engross up glorious deeds on my behalf;</u>
And I will call him to so strict account
That he shall render every glory up,
Yea, even the slightest worship of his time,
<u>Or I will tear the reckoning from his heart.</u>
This, in the name of God, I promise here.'
Henry IV, Part I, 3.2

(King Henry tells his son Prince Henry that civil war is brewing, 'shake the peace and safety of our throne.'

And then he asks why he is even telling Hal this: 'But wherefore do I tell these news to thee?'

As shown, he doesn't trust his son and thinks he may be in league with the enemy. Harry's powerful speech goes far in disabusing his father of this notion.

In speaking of, 'His glorious deeds for my indignities' through 'To engross up glorious deeds on my behalf,' Hal is saying: the more glorious Hotspur is, the more glorious it will be to kill him.

Note in the line between the two above, that Hal mentions that Percy is his 'factor,' meaning his agent. He plans to use Hotspur as a symbol, or device, in the enemy's defeat: 'I will redeem all this on Percy's head.')

Hotspur. Where is his son,
The nimble-footed <u>madcap</u> Prince of Wales,
And his comrades, that daffed the world aside,
And bid it pass?'
Vernon. All furnished; all in arms;
<u>All plumed like estridges, that wing the wind;</u>
Bated like eagles having lately bathed;
Glittering in golden coats, like images;

425

As full of spirit as the month of May,
And gorgeous as the sun at midsummer;
Wanton as youthful goats, wild as young bulls.
I saw young Harry,—with his beaver on,
His cuisses on his thighs, gallantly armed,—
Rise from the ground like feathered Mercury,
And vaulted with such ease into his seat,
As if an angel dropped down from the clouds,
To turn and wind a fiery Pegasus,
And witch the world with noble horsemanship.'
Hotspur. 'No more, no more; worse than the sun in
March,
This praise doth furnish agues. Let them come.
They come like sacrifices in their trim,
And to the fiery-eyed maid of smoky war,
All hot and bleeding we will offer them:
The mailed Mars shall on his altar sit,
Up to the ears in blood. I am on fire
To hear this rich reprisal is so nigh.
And yet not ours.—Come, let me taste my horse,
Who is to bear me, like a thunderbolt,
Against the bosom of the Prince of Wales:
Harry to Harry shall, hot horse to horse,
Meet, and never part till one drop down a corpse.
Henry IV, Part I, 4.1

(In line 2 of his speech, Hotspur calls Hal a 'madcap.' Earlier in the play, Hal refers to himself as a 'madcap.' Evidently, the term meant reckless, audacious, impulsive in Elizabethan times. The term was often used during Hollywood's golden age to describe a 'madcap heiress' deftly played by the likes of Jean Harlow and Carole Lombard.

As always, Hotspur is ready for a scrap and can't wait to take on Hal. The imagery from Vernon and Hotspur makes us see the two armies. The entire passage is worth rereading. At least read the underlined examples. My favorites: 'plumed like estridges,' 'witch the world with noble horsemanship,' 'turn and wind a fiery Pegasus,' 'fiery-eyed maid of smoky war.' Winning verb: 'witch.')

Worcester. For mine on part, I could be well content
To entertain the lag-end of my life in quiet hours
Henry IV, Part I, 5.1

(Worcester attempts to act as a mediator between the two sides poised for war, but is accused of going against King Henry. He opens a long-winded plea with a sighing, oldish comment he hopes will ease the king's anger.)

Hal. In both our armies there is many a soul
Shall pay full dearly for this encounter,
If once they join in trial. Tell your nephew,
The Prince of Wales doth join with all the world
In praise of Henry Percy: by my hopes,
This present enterprise set off his head,
I do not think a braver gentleman . . .
Yet this before my father's majesty,
I am content that he shall take the odds
Of his great name and estimation,
And will, to save the blood on either side,
Try fortune with him in a single fight.
Henry IV, Part I, 5.1

(In Hal's quest to avoid a full-scale war, he challenges Hotspur to a 'single fight.' But first he praises Hotspur, 'in praise of Henry Percy,' including the 'present enterprise set off his head,' meaning that the insurrection is the only mark against him.

King Henry sends Worcester back with the message which he passes on to 'a hare-brained Hotspur, governed by a spleen.' Hotspur answers.)

Hotspur. I will embrace him with a soldier's arm,
That he shall shrink under my courtesy.
Arm, arm with speed . . .

O gentleman, the time of life is very short!
To spend that shortness basely were too long.
If life did ride upon a dial's point,
Still ending at the arrival of an hour.
And if we live, we live to tread on kings;
If die, brave death, if princes die with us!
Henry IV, Part I, 5.2

Hal. I am the Prince of Wales; and think not, Percy,
To share with me in glory anymore:
Two stars keep not their motion in one sphere;
Nor can one England brook a double reign,
Of Harry Percy and the Prince of Wales.
Nor shall it, Harry, for the hour has come
To end the one of us; and would to God
Thy name in arms were now as great as mine!
(They fight.)
Hotspur. O, Harry, thou hast robbed me of my youth!
But that the earthy and cold hand of death
Lies on my tongue: No, Percy, thou art dust,
And food for . . .'
Hal. 'For worms, brave Percy: fare thee well, great heart!
Ill-weaved ambition, how much art thou shrunk!
What that this body did contain a spirit,

A kingdom for it was too small a bound;
But now two paces of the vilest earth
Is room enough: this earth that bears thee dead
Bears not alive so stout a gentleman.'
Henry IV, Part I, 5.4

(As so often is the case, as shown in the final line
above, the victor praises the vanquished.)

HENRY IV, PART TWO

Rumour. The still-discordant wavering multitude
Can play upon it. But what I need thus
My well-known body to anatomize
Among my household? Why is Rumour here?
I run before King Harry's victory;
Who, in a bloody field by Shrewsbury,
Hath beaten down young Hotspur and his troops,
Quenching the flame of bold rebellion
Even with the rebel's blood. But what mean I
To speak so true at first? My office is
To noise abroad that Harry Monmouth fell
Under the wrath of noble Hotspur's sword;
And that the king before the Douglas' rage
Stooped his anointed head as low as death.
This have I rumoured through the peasant towns
Between that royal field of Shrewsbury
And this worm-eaten hold of ragged stone,
Where Hotspur's father, old Northumberland,
Lies crafty-sick: the posts come tiring on,
And not a man of them brings other news
That they have learned of me: from Rumour's
tongues

They bring smooth comforts false, worse than true wrongs.

Henry IV, Part 2, 1.1

(Will uses Rumour as Prologue. Members of the audience, called 'my household' by Rumour in line 2 of this excerpt, may or may not have seen Henry IV, Part I. Then he asks, 'Why is Rumour here?' And then goes on to tell the truth, 'I run before King Harry's victory.'

Followed by telling his audience that his job or 'office' is to lie, or 'noise abroad that Harry Monmouth fell . . .'

Earlier in his speech, Rumour said, 'Upon my tongues continual slanders ride/Stuffing the ears of men with false reports.

He accuses old Northumberland of faking sickness, 'crafty-sick.'

In the next-to-last-line of Rumour's speech he mentions 'Rumour's tongues.' That is said because Rumour wears an appropriate costume, a garment decorated with tongues.)

Morton. Let heaven kiss earth! Now let not nature's hand
Keep the wild flood confined! Let order die!

And let this world no longer a <u>stage</u>
To feed contention in a <u>lingering act</u>;
But let one spirit of the first-born Cain
Reign in all bosoms, that, each heart being set
On bloody courses, the rude <u>scene</u> may end,
And darkness be the burier of the dead!
Henry IV, Part 2, 1.1

(It's no surprise that Will, whose life is writing for the theater, often refers to 'stages' and 'acts' as seen in lines three and four. In this case, 'lingering act' refers to an act featuring discord that appears to be without end.

    'Scene' is used in the next-to-last line.)

Chief Justice. Do you set down your name in the scroll of youth, that are written down old with all the characters of age? Have you not a moist eye? a dry hand? a yellow cheek? a white beard? a decreasing leg? an increasing belly? Is not your voice broken? your wind short? your chin double? your wit single? and <u>every part about you blasted with antiquity?</u> and will you yet call yourself young? Fie, fie, fie, Sir John.
Falstaff. My lord, I was born about three of the clock in the afternoon, with a white head, and something of a round belly. For my voice, I have lost it with hollaing

and singing of anthems. To approve my youth further, I will not; the truth is, I am only old in judgment and understanding; and he that will caper with me for a thousand marks, let him lend me the money, and have at him. For the box of the ears that the prince gave you, he gave it like a rude prince, and you took it like a sensible lord. I have checked him for it; and the young lion repents; marry, not in ashes and sackcloth, but in new silk and old sack.

Henry IV, Part 2, 1.2

(Earlier in the scene, the Chief Justice tells Falstaff, 'you live in great infamy' and 'You have misled the youthful Prince,' and 'You follow the Prince up and down like his ill angel,' a marvelous phrase. Falstaff, of course, blames Hal and argues that they are both in the vanguard of their youth.

My favorite line in the Chief Justice's speech: 'and every part about you blasted with antiquity?')

Bardolph. Yes, in this present quality of war;
Indeed, the instant action, a cause on foot,
Lives so in hope, as in early spring
We see the appearing buds; which, to prove fruit,
Hope gives not so much warrant, as despair
That frosts will bite them. When we mean to build,

We first <u>survey the plot</u>, then <u>draw the model</u>;
And when we see the figure of the house,
Then must we rate the cost of the erection;
Which, if we find outweighs ability,
What do we then but draw anew the model
In fewer offices, or at least desist
To build at all? Much more, in this great work
Which is almost to pluck a kingdom down
And set another up, should we survey
The plot of situation and the model,
<u>Consent upon a sure foundation</u>,
<u>Question surveyors</u>, know our own estate,
How able such a work to undergo,
To weigh against his opposite; or else,
<u>We fortify in paper and in figures</u>,
Using the names of men instead of men:
<u>Like one that draws the model of a house</u>
Beyond his power to build it; who, half through,
Gives over, and leaves his part-created cost
A naked subject to the weeping clouds,
And waste for churlish winter's tyranny.
Henry IV, Part 2, 1.3

(John Shakespeare, Will's father, bought and sold properties and likely built houses and other buildings. Will surely helped him, hence the knowledge.

As shown in the underlined phrases, the gist of the passage is, if you plan to go to war make certain, much like building a house, that your plans fit the scale of the intended action. And, if not, redo them lest you get caught out in the cold with a half-finished project.)

Falstaff. Away, you scullion! you <u>rampallian</u>! you <u>fustilarian</u>! I'll tickle your catastrophe.
Henry IV, Part 2, 2.

(Falstsff crammed two insults and a comical threat into one sentence with 'You rascal, you stinker, I'll tickle your fanny.')

Poins. My lord, I will steep this letter in sack, and make him eat it.
Hal. That's to make him <u>eat twenty of his words</u>.
Henry IV, Part 2, 2.2

(Possibly the origin of phrases referring to 'eating one's words.')

Lady Percy. There were two honour's lost, yours and your son's.

For yours, may heavenly glory it brighten it!
For his, it stuck upon him, as the sun
In the grey vault of heaven: and by his light
Did all the chivalry of England move
To do brave acts: he was, indeed, the <u>glass</u>
Wherein the noble youth did dress themselves:
He had no legs that practiced not his gait;
And speaking thick, which made his nature blemish,
Became the accents of the valiant;
For those that could speak low and tardily
Would turn their own perfection to abuse
To seem like him: so that in speech, in gait,
In diet, in affections of delight,
In military rules, humours of blood,
He was the mark and <u>glass</u>, copy and book,
That <u>fashioned</u> others. And him, O wondrous him!
O miracle of men! him did you leave,
Second to none, unseconded by you,
To look upon the hideous god of war
In disadvantage; to abide a field
Where nothing but the sound of Hotspur's name
Did seem defensible: so you left him.
Never, O never, do his ghost the wrong
To hold your honour more precise and nice

With others than with him! let them alone:
The marshal and the archbishop are strong:
Had my sweet Harry but half their numbers,
To-day might I, hanging on Hotspur's neck,
Have talked of Monmouth's grave.
Henry IV, Part 2, 2.3

(Lady Percy, Hotspur's loving wife delivers a stunning epitaph. She uses 'glass' and 'fashioned' in the same sentence. Earlier, in line 8, she referred to 'glass' as a mirror.

Ophelia, referring to Hamlet, speaks of 'The glass of fashion and the mould of form' in Hamlet, 3.1

Like innumerable phrases by Shakespeare, 'Glass of fashion' fell into the language. The 20th-Century photographer and chronicler of taste, Cecil Beaton, used the phrase as the title of his classic book.)

Doll. They say Poins has a good wit.
Falstaff. He a good wit? hang him, baboon! his wit is as thick as Tewksbury mustard; there is no more conceit in him than is in a mallet.
Doll. Why does the prince love him so, then?

Falstaff. Because <u>their legs are both of a bigness</u>; and he plays at quoits well; and eats conger and fennel; and <u>drinks off candles' ends for flapdragons</u>; and rides the wild mare with the boys; and jumps upon joined stools; and swears with a good grace; and wears his boot very smooth, like unto the sign of the leg; and breeds no bate with the telling of <u>discreet stories</u>; and such other gambol faculties he has, that shows a weak mind and an able body, for which the prince admits him: for the prince himself is such another; the weight of a hair will turn the scales between their avoirdupois.

Henry IV, Part 2, 2.4

(Doll Tearsheet, a perfect whore's name, and Falstaff talk of gang-member Poins, a favorite of Hal's.

Note the reference to 'Tewksbury mustard' in line two. Tewksbury is a town close to Stratford, and is also a like-named Boston, Massachusetts suburb.

'Drinks off candles' ends for flapdragons' is a drinking sport in which a lighted candle floats in a drink. The idea is to drink it off without getting burned.

Falstaff says that Poins and Hal have well-shaped legs and both tell 'discreet stories.')

K. Henry. How many thousand of my poorest subjects
   Are at this hour asleep! O sleep, O gentle sleep,
   Nature's soft nurse, how have I frighted thee.
   That no more wilt weigh my eyelids down,
   And steep my senses in fotgetfulness?
   Why, rather, Sleep, liest thou in smoky cribs,
   Upon <u>uneasy pallets</u> stretching thee,
   And hushed with <u>buzzing night-flies</u> to thy slumber,
   Than in the perfumed chambers of the great,
   Under high canopies of costly state,
   And lulled with sounds of sweetest melody?
   O thou dull god, why liest thou with the vile
   In loathsome beds, and leavest <u>the kingly couch</u>
   A <u>watch-case or a common alarum bell?</u>
   Wilt thou upon the high and <u>giddy mast</u>
   Seal up the ship-boys eyes, and rock his brains
   In cradle of the imperious surge,
   And in the visitation of the winds,
   Who take the ruffian billows by the top,
   Curling their monstrous heads, and hanging them
   With deafening clamour in the slippery shrouds,
   That, with the hurly, death itself awakes?
   Canst thou, O partial Sleep, give thy repose
   To the wet sea-boy in an hour so rude,

And in the calmest and most stillest night,
With all appliances and means to boot,
Deny it to a king? Then, happy low, lie down!
<u>Uneasy lies the head that wears a crown.</u>
Henry IV, Part 2, 3.1

(The build appealing to restful sleep right through to the famous last line is brilliant.   The poor, living in huts on rough mattresses, 'uneasy pallets' and buzzed by flies sleep fine, but I, the king, in comfortable quarters don't sleep much at all. In fact, I'm like a 'watch-case or a common alarum bell,' always on the alert.

The quick shift to a ship boy high in the 'giddy mast,' who can also sleep well as a happy low-born, while I am denied. Will likes the verb 'giddy.' He uses it often, once, I believe, in 'The Tempest,' and 'Richard 111' referring to slipping on the giddy hatches. Like his knowledge of soldiering, Will also spent time at sea, and some of that in wild storms.

'Uneasy lies the head that wears a crown' is an oft-quoted lament that also applies to CEO's of modern corporations who fail to make their numbers or coaches who have more losses than wins.

Later in the scene, King Henry cries, 'O God! that one might read the book of fate and see the revolution of the times.' How fortunate it would be if all of us could do that, especially in these times characterized by the rapidity of change.)

Shallow. O, Sir John, do you remember since we lay all night in the windmill in St. George's Fields? . . . Ha, it was a merry night. And is <u>Jane Nightwork</u> alive? . . .
Silence. That's fifty-five year ago.
Shallow. Ha, Cousin Silence, that though hadst seen that that this knight and I have seen! Ha, Sir John, said I well?
Falstaff. We have heard the <u>chimes at midnight</u>, Master Shallow.
Henry IV, Part 2, 3.2

(I forgot that Jane Nightwork was a contender when I said that Doll Tearsheet was the perfect whore's name.

As said earlier, 'Chimes at Midnight' is the title of an Orson Welles film in which a rotund Welles plays Falstaff admirably.)

Westmoreland. Out of the <u>speech of peace</u>, that bears such grace,
Into the harsh and boisterous <u>tongue</u> of war;
Turning your <u>books</u> to graves, your <u>ink</u> to blood,

Your <u>pens</u> to lances, and your <u>tongue divine</u>
<u>To a loud trumpet and a point of war.</u>'
Henry IV, Part 2, 4.1

Note how the 'speech of peace' is cleverly transmuted into 'tongue of war' and 'tongue divine into a loud trumpet and a point of war.')

(In close-to-home metaphors, Will turns the tools of his trade, 'books, ink, pens,' into instruments of war.

Mowbray. Being mounted and both roused in their seats,
Their neighing coursers daring of the spur,
<u>Their armed staves in charge, their beavers down,</u>
<u>Their eyes of fire sparkling through sights of steel,</u>
And the loud trumpet blowing them together.
Henry IV, Part 2, 4.1

(Dickens may have thinking of lines three and four when he advised writers to: 'Make me see!)

Hastings. 'My lord, our army is dispersed already.
<u>Like youthful steers unyoked</u>, they take their courses
East, west, north, south, or <u>like a school broke up,</u>

Each <u>hurries toward his home and sporting place</u>.
Henry IV, Part 2, 4.1

(Will never forgot his school days in Stratford, 'like a school broke up.')

K. Henry. <u>Where is the crown?</u> Who took it from my pillow? . . .
<u>The prince hath taken it hence</u>, Go, seek him out. . . .

See, sons, what things you are!
How quickly nature falls into revolt
When gold becomes her object!
For this the foolish over-careful fathers
Have broke their sleep with thoughts, their brains with care,
Their bones with industry;
For this they have engrossed and piled up
The cankered heaps of strange-achieved gold;
For this they have been thoughtful to invest
Their sons with arts and martial exercises.
When, like the bee, culling from every flower
The virtuous sweets,
Our thighs packed with wax, our mouths with honey,
We bring it to the hive: and, like the bees,

444

Are murdered for our pains . . .

Hal. Coming to look on you, thinking you were dead,

And dead almost, my liege, to think you were,
I spake unto the crown as having sense,
<u>And thus upbraided it</u>:
Accusing it, I put it on my head,
To try with it, as with an enemy
That had before my face murdered my father.
K. Henry. Come hither, Harry, sit thou by my bed;
And hear, I think, the very latest counsel
That ever I shall breathe. God knows, my son,
<u>By what by-paths and indirect crooked ways</u>
I met this crown: and I myself know well
How troublesome it sat upon my head.
<u>To thee it shall descend with better quiet,</u>
<u>Better opinion, better confirmation.</u>
For all the soil of the achievement goes
With me into the earth.
Henry IV, Part 2, 4.4

(The unwell King Henry lies in his bed barely breathing. Prince Hal mistakenly thinks he's dead and takes the crown from the pillow. He tries it on with distaste because he didn't want his father to die. The king awakes and accuses Hal of being disrespectful and premature. Hal explains what he did and why, apologizes and is forgiven.

The king, as Bolingbroke, usurped the crown, 'by what by-paths and indirect crooked ways' from Richard II. King Henry tells Hal that he will inherit with 'better quiet, better opinion, better confirmation.')

Falstaff. What wind blew you hither, Pistol?

Pistol. Not the <u>ill wind which blows no man to good</u>

Under which king, bezonian? speak or die.

Shallow. Under King Harry.

Pistol. Harry the fourth? or fifth?

Shallow. Harry the fourth.

*Pisto*l. A foutre for thine office,

Sir John, thy tender lambkin now is king;

Harry the fifth's the man. I speak the truth:

When Pistol lies, do this; and <u>fig me</u>, like

The bragging Spaniard.

Falstaff. What! is the old king dead?

Pistol. <u>As nail in door</u>: the things I speak are just. . .

.

Falstaff. I am <u>fortune's steward</u>. . . . . I know the young king is sick for me. Let us <u>take any man's horses</u>; the laws of England are at my commandment.

Happy are they which have been my friends; and woe
unto my Lord Chief-Justice!
Henry IV, Part 2, 5.3

(Both clichés, 'ill wind that blows no good' and
'dead as a doornail,' predate Shakespeare.

'Fig me' is an insult that also preceded
Elizabethan times. In the gesture, the thumb is placed
between the index and middle finger and jabbed
toward the recipient.

Falstaff's closing speech is loaded with self-
importance: 'fortune's steward' means he can do
anything he wants with the goods at his disposal.

Therefore, 'take any man's horses,' And my
friends are lucky and my enemies, like the Chief
Justice, are in trouble.

Falstaff, full of misguided hope and imagined
new power, rides off to meet Hal, the new King
Henry V.

In an example of Will's sense of structure, he
sets up Falstaff's pending downfall. You may recall, in
Henry IV, Part 1 Falstaff's concern that he will be
banished once Hal (Prince Henry) becomes king. Hal
answered, 'I do. I will.')

Falstaff. But to stand stained with travel, and sweating with desire to see him, thinking of nothing else, putting all affairs else in oblivion, as if there was nothing else to be done but to see him. . . .

God save thou royal grace, King Hal! My royal Hal!
. . .

God save thee, my sweet boy! . . .

My king! My jove, I speak to thee, my heart!

King Henry V. I know thee not, old man. Fall to thy prayers;

How ill white hairs become a fool and jester!

I have long dreamed of such a kind of man,

So surfeit-swelled, so old, and so profane,

But, being awaked, I do despise my dream . . .

For God doth know, so shall the world perceive,

That I have turned away my former self;

So will I those that have kept me company.

Falstaff. Do not grieve at this. I shall be sent for in private to him. Look you, he must seem thus to the world. Fear not your advancements, I will be the man yet that shall make you great.

Henry IV, Part 2, 5.5

(Sadly, even pathetically, Falstaff, unlike Hal, fails to see the break with the past, even with the crushing, 'I know thee not, old man'

And so that his gang doesn't see him in defeat, he invents his own reality. 'I shall be sent for in private to him.' And, 'I will be the man yet that shall make you great.')

Prince John. I will lay odds, that ere this year expire,
We bear our <u>civil swords</u> and native fire
As far as France: I heard a bird so sing,
Whose music, to my thinking, pleased the king.
Henry IV, Part 2, 5.5

(Will, through Prince John, Hal's brother, lets the audience know that the 'civil swords,' the ones used in the recent civil wars, will now be used in France. The stage is set for the play, 'Henry V.')

HENRY V

PROLOGUE

Chorus. O for a <u>muse of fire</u> that would ascend
The brightest <u>heaven of invention,</u>
A kingdom for a <u>stage</u>, princes to <u>act</u>
And monarchs to behold the swelling <u>scene</u>!
Then should the warlike Harry, like himself,
Assume the port of Mars, and at his heels,
Leashed in like hounds, should famine, sword, and
fire
Crouch for employment. But pardon gentles all,
The flat unraised spirits that have dared
On this <u>unworthy scaffold</u> to bring forth
So great an object this <u>cockpit hold</u>
The <u>vasty fields of France</u>? Or may we <u>cram</u>
Within this <u>wooded O</u> the very casques
That did affright the air at Agincourt?
Henry V, Prologue

(The 'muse of fire' in line one is language written
to inspire the audience's imagination. It's also ironic
that the Globe Theatre later burned to the ground

when the 'heaven of invention' painted on the cloth ceiling caught fire during a performance.

The lines that follow ask the audience to imagine that the upcoming battles on 'the vasty fields of France' will take place within this 'unworthy scaffold,' or 'cockpit,' or 'wooded O,' a reference to The Globe, or other round-shaped theatres.

Incidentally, Shakespeare was instrumental in getting the original Globe built in 1599.

I'm sure you noticed the underlined 'stage, 'act' and 'scene.'

Throughout, Chorus is telling the audience in the little theatre to suspend disbelief and 'cram' the 'vasty fields of France' near Agincourt into their imaginations. Will, who was known in his day as a good businessman, is doing a bit of selling here. In elegant language to boot.)

Canterbury. The king is full of grace and fair regard
. . .

The courses of his youth promised it not.
The breath no sooner left his father's body
But that his wildness, mortified in him,
Seemed to die too. Yea, at that very moment,
Consideration, like an angel, came,
And whipped the offending Adam out of him,

Leaving his body as a paradise,
To envelop and contain celestial spirits.
Ely. The strawberry grows underneath the nettle,
And wholesome berries thrive and ripen best
Neighbored by fruit of baser quality.
Henry V, 1.1

(Like other histories, Will closely based this play on Holinshed's Chronicles, which, in that particular history, was a hagiography to Henry V.

Canterbury is surprised that Hal turned out so well given that 'The courses of his youth promised it not.' Then he gets into a hagiography of his own saying that Hal's 'wildness' seemed to 'die too.' 'Leaving his body as a paradise' containing 'celestial spirits.'

Ely makes his point that 'wholesome berries' like Hal thrive when they grow alongside 'fruit of baser quality.' I wonder who he had in mind.

Following the passages above, the bishops of Canterbury and Ely go on to praise how well-lettered: 'never was such a sudden scholar made the new king is', and how unlikely that is, given his former 'companies unlettered, rude, and shallow.' How, they wonder, could this recent playboy turn overnight into a great man?)

King Henry. <u>May I with right and conscience make</u> this claim?

Canterbury. Go, my dread lord, to your great grandsire's tomb,

From whom you claim; invoke his warlike spirit,
And your great-uncle's, Edward the Black Prince,
Who on the French ground played a tragedy,
Making defeat on the full power of France,
While his most mighty father on a hill
Stood smiling to behold his lion's whelp
Forage in blood of French nobility.
Oh noble English, that could entertain
With half their forces the full pride of France
And let another half standing by,
<u>All out of work and cold for action</u>!
Ely. <u>You are their heir; you sit upon their thro</u>ne;
The blood and courage that renowned them
Runs in your veins; and my <u>thrice-puissant liege</u>
In the very May-morn of his youth,
Ripe for exploits and mighty enterprises.
Henry V, 1.2

(Young king Henry asks whether he can by birthright lay claim to be the King of France. The bishops of Canterbury and Ely reassure him that he can. In justifying that position, Canterbury goes off on a long discourse of intricate French history mentioning Charlemagne, his son Pippin, and a host of other monarchs and finishes with the passage above describing the Black Prince's 14th-Century defeat of the French. Reminder: I included only a late portion of that speech. Because it's almost comical in its mazelike detail, you may want to find and read the earlier sixty or so of Canterbury's lines.

Did Will know all this French history? Likely not, and he probably lifted most of it from Holinshed's Chronicles. This was common practice among Elizabethan authors.

I delighted in Canterbury's final line, 'All out of work and cold for action!' He refers to the French army standing by unready to fight.

Ely's 'thrice-puissant liege' also gives pause and brings a smile. I'll bet the actors pronounce that stagy line 'trippingly on the tongue,' trills and all. It means that the King's might, thanks to his noble heritage, his uncle the black Prince and others, is three times what he needs)

(Following the Canterbury and Ely pep talks, Harry, in the next scene, finds that going to war in France could be the easy part. But what he might find in England upon his return is more complicated, as in 'defend against the Scot.')

King Henry. We must not only arm to invade against the French,
   But lay down our proportions to <u>defend</u>
   <u>Against the Scot</u>, who will make road upon us
   With all advantages . . .
   We do not mean the coursing snatchers only,
   But fear the main intendment of the <u>Scot</u>,
   Who hath been still a <u>giddy neighbor</u> to us;
   For you shall read that my great-grandfather
   Never went with his forces into France
   But that the <u>Scot</u> on his unfurnished kingdom
   Came pouring, <u>like a tide into a breach</u>,
   With ample and brim fulness of his force;
   Galling the gleaned land with hot essays,
   Girding with grievous siege castles and towns;
   That England, being empty of defence,
   Hath shook and trembled at the ill neighbourhood.
   Canterbury. The king of Scots; whom she did send
to France,
   To fill King Edward's fame with prisoner kings,
   And make her chronicle as rich with praise
   As is the ooze and bottom of the sea
   With sunken wreck and sumless treasuries.
   Westmoreland. But there's saying, very old and true,

If that you will France win,
Then with Scotland first begin:
For once the eagle England being in prey,
To her unguarded nest the <u>weasel Scot</u>
Comes sneaking, and so <u>sucks her princely eggs</u>;
Playing the mouse in absence of the cat,
To tear and havoc more than she can eat.
Canterbury. As many arrows, loosed several ways,
Fly to one mark;
As many several ways meet in one town;
As many fresh streams meet in one salt sea;
As many line close in the dial's centre:
So many a thousand actions, once afoot,
End in one purpose, and be all well borne
Without defeat, Therefore, to France, my liege.
Divide your happy England into four;
Whereof you take one quarter into France,
And you withal make all Gallia shake.
King Henry. Either our history shall with full mouth
Speak freely of our acts, or else our grave,
Like Turkish mute, shall have a tongueless mouth,
Not worshipped like a waxen epitaph . . .
What treasure, uncle?
Exeter. <u>Tennis-balls, my liege</u>.
King Henry. We are glad the Dauphin is so pleasant
with us;
His present and your pains we thank you for:

When we have matched our rackets to these balls,
We will, in France, by God's grace, play a set
Shall strike his father's crown into the hazard.
Tell him he hath made a match with such a
wrangler
That all the courts of France will be disturbed
With chases . . .
But tell the Dauphin, I will keep my state;
Be like a king, and show my sail of greatness,
When I do rouse me in my throne of France:
For that I have laid by my majesty,
And plodded like a man for working-days;
But I will rise there with so full a glory
That I will dazzle all the eyes of France,
Yea, strike the Dauphin blind to look on us.
And tell the pleasant prince this mock of his
Hath turned his balls to gun-stones; and his soul
Shall stand sore charged for the wasteful vengeance
That shall fly with them; for many a thousand
widows
Shall this his mock out of their husbands;
Mock mothers from their sons, mock castles down;
And some are yet ungotten and unborn
That shall have cause to curse the Dauphin's scorn.
Chorus. Now all the youth of England are on fire,
And silken dalliance in the wardrobe lies:
Now thrive the armourer's, and honour's thought

457

Reigns solely in the breast of every man:
They sell the pasture now to buy the horse;
Following the mirror of all Christian kings,
With winged heels, as English mercuries,
For now sits Expectation in the air;
And hides a sword from hilts unto the point
With crowns imperial, crowns and coronets,
Promised to Harry and his followers.
The French, advised by good intelligence
Of this most dreadful preparation,
Shake in their fear; and with pale policy
Seek to divert the English purposes.
O England! Model to thy inward greatness
Like little body with a mighty heart,
What mightst thou do, that honour would thee do,
Were all thy children kind and natural!
But see thy fault! France hath in thee found out
A nest of hollow bosoms, which he fills
With treacherous crowns; and three corrupted men,
    One, Richard Earl of Cambridge; and the second,
    Henry Lord Scroop of Masham; and the third,
    Sir Thomas Grey, knight, of Northumberland,
Have, for the guilt of France, O guilt indeed!
Confirmed conspiracy with fearful France;
And by their hands this grace of kings must die,
If hell and treason hold their promises,

Ere he take ship for France, and in Southampton.
Linger your patience on; and we'll digest
The abuse of distance, while we force a play.
The sum is paid; the traitors are agreed;
The king is set from London; and the scene
Is now transported, gentles, to Southampton,
There is the play-house now, there you must sit:
And thence to France we will convey you safe,
And bring you back, charming the narrow seas
To give you gentle pass; for, if we may,
We'll not offend one stomach with our play.
But, till the king come forth, and not till then,
Unto Southampton do we shift our scene.
Henry V, 1.2

(King Henry uses 'giddy neighbor' referencing the Scots. As said earlier, we've all known giddy neighbors. Giddy persists as one of Will's favorite adjectives.

Westmoreland's the 'weasel Scot' sucking the princely eggs is good.

'Tennis-balls, my liege.' King Henry is not amused by the Dauphin's gift of tennis balls. He launches into clever tennis metaphors that show his determination to make the Dauphin pay for his mocking and assumption that Harry is still the wastrel.

'When we have matched our rackets to these balls.'

'Shall strike his father's crown into the hazard.'

'And tell the pleasant prince this mock of his hath turned his balls to gun-stones.'

The tennis balls' scene is among the most famous in the Shakespeare canon.

The Chorus provides a bridge to Act Two. 'They sell the pasture now to buy the horse' indicates to the audience that the people are behind Harry.

Chorus names three English traitors Earl, Scroop and Grey, to die. 'France hath in thee found out' informs that the traitors have told France of the pending invasion.

Then, Chorus invites the audience to Southampton, 'There is the play-house now.'

Following that, Chorus reassures the audience that they will be transported safe home, 'And bring you back, charming the narrow seas,' meaning the English Channel. These are stage directions for the audience.

Note: In some versions of Henry V, Chorus leads off Act Two as Epilogue to Act One.

Imagine the Elizabethan audience in the small round theatre living the patriotic action: the groundlings shouting out, and the dandies sitting on the edge of the stage and in the boxes above commenting with cynical barbs. Will kept the action fast-paced to hold the focus on the play and not the distractions.

As we wrote in the novel, 'Larceny of Love' people who believe that acting is easy should think again. Especially when looking back to the Elizabethan stage, when often 'quite athwart goes all decorum,' using Will's phrase about the baby beating the nurse from 'Measure for Measure,' 1.3

(As Chorus predicted, the English traitors, Scroop, Grey and Earl, are found out and brought before King Henry V.)

King Henry. Treason and murder ever kept together,
As two yoke devils sworn to either's purpose,
Working so grossly in natural cause
That admiration did not hoop at them.
But thou, 'gainst all proportion, didst bring in
Wonder to wait on treason and on murder . . .
For this revolt of thine, methinks, is like
Another fall of man. Their faults are open.
Arrest them to the answer of the law,
And God acquit them of their practices!
. . . You have conspired against our royal person,

Joined with an enemy proclaimed, and from his coffers

Received the golden earnest of our death.

Wherein you would have sold your King to slaughter,

His princes and his peers to servitude,

His subjects to oppression and contempt,

And his whole kingdom into desolation.

Touching our person seek we no revenge,

But we are Kingdom's safety must so tender,

Whose ruin you have sought, that to her laws

We do deliver you. Get you therefore hence,

Poor miserable wretches, to your death . . .

Now, lords, for France, the enterprise whereof

Shall be to you, as us, like glorious.

We doubt not of a fair and lucky war,

Since God so graciously hath brought to light

This dangerous treason lurking in our way

To hinder our beginnings. We doubt not now

But every rub is smoothed on our way.

Then forth, dear countrymen. Let us deliver

Our puissance into the hand of god,

Putting it straight in expedition.

Cheerly to sea, The signs of war advance.

No King of England if not King of France.

Henry V, 2.2

(Note in the first two lines that Henry V says that treason and murder are 'yoked' together, as, in this instance, they surely are.

Then King Henry tells the conspirators that they have 'Received the golden earnest of our death.' In other words, they took money from the French coffers, and 'sold your King to slaughter.'

But, Henry goes on to say, 'Touching our person seek we no revenge,' but your seditious actions jeopardized the Kingdom, and for that you will die.

In the final two lines of his speech, Henry V makes his ambitious purposes clear. 'No King of England if not King of France.')

(We learn of Falstaff's fate, then learn that his old gang's goals in France don't quite match Harry's.)

Pistol. No, for my manly heart doth yearn.
Bardolph, be blithe. Nym, rouse thy vaunting veins.
Boy, bristle thy courage up, for Falstaff he is dead,
And we must yearn therefore.
Bardolph. Would I were with him, wheresome'er he is, either in Heaven or in Hell!
Hostess Quickly. Nay, sure he's not in hell. He's in Arthur's bosom, if ever a man went to Arthur's bosom. A' made a finer end and went away an it had

been any christom child. A' parted even just between twelve and one, even at the turning o' the tide. For after I saw him <u>fumble with the sheets</u>, and play with flowers, and smile upon his fingers' ends, I knew there was but one way. For his nose was as sharp as a pen, and a' <u>babbled of green fields</u>. "How now, Sir John!" quoth I. "What man! Be o' good cheer." So a' cried out "God, God, God!" three or four times. Now I, to comfort him, bid him a' should not think of God, I hoped there was no need to trouble himself with any such thoughts yet. So a' bade me lay more clothes on his feet. I put my hand into the bed and felt them, and they were as cold as any stone. Then I felt to his knees, and they were as cold as any stone, and so upward and upward, and all was as cold as any stone.

Nym. They say he cried out of sack.

Hostess. Aye, that a' did.

Bardolph. And of women.

Hostess. Nay, that a' did not.

Boy. Yes, that a' did, and said they were devils incarnate.

Hostess. A' could never abide carnation. 'Twas a color he never liked.

Boy. A' said once, the devil would have him about women.

464

Hostess. A' did in some sort, indeed, handle women, but then he was rheumatic, and talked of the whore of Babylon.

Boy. Do you not remember, a' saw a flea tick upon Bardolph's nose, and a' said it was a black soul burning in hell-fire!

Bardolph. Well, the fuel is gone that maintained that fire. That's all the riches I got in his service.

Nym. Shall we shog? The king will be gone from Southampton.

Pistol. Come, let's away. My love, give me thy lips.
Look to my chattels and my movables.
Let senses rule, the word is "Pitch and pay."
Trust none,
For oaths are straws, men's faiths are wafer cakes,
And holdfast is the only dog, my duck.
Therefore, Caveto be thy counselor,
Go, clear thy crystals. Yokefellows in arms,
Let us to France, like horseleeches, my boys,
To suck, to suck, the very blood to suck!
Henry V, 2.3

(This scene, designed as an informative interlude between the scenes of heavy drama, plays out in Hostess Quickly's Eastcheap tavern. The hostess, who is Pistol's wife, touchingly describes Falstaff's death: 'babbled of green fields.' 'Fumble with the sheets' indicates that death was imminent. By 'Arthur's bosom' she means to say Abraham's bosom.

The end of Falstaff? Nay, he's right back in Henry V111. But there he lacks his old wit and spirit.

Pistol tells his wife to use common sense and accept no credit, 'pitch and pay' while he is away.

The gang's banter following Hostess Quickly's requiem for Falstaff is written to give the groundlings in the pit a little comic relief. And it also tees up Pistol's lifting, off-to-France 'the very blood to suck' speech. And the 'suck' alludes to their intent to loot.)

(We go to Chorus introducing Act Three, where we finally get to France and open with the first of several great wartime speeches by Henry V. But first, let's look at several Chorus devices Will uses to get the audience in the proper expectation, and while examining those we can admire the inspired language.)

Chorus. Thus with imagined wing our swift scene flies
    In motion of no less celerity
    Than that of thought. Suppose that you have seen
    The well-appointed King at Hampton Pier
    Embark his royalty, and his brave fleet

With young silken streamers the Phoebus_fanning.
Play with your fancies, and in them behold
Upon the hempen tackle ship boys climbing.
Hear the shrill whistle which doth order give . . .
Holding due course to Harlfleur. Follow, follow.
Grapple your minds to sternage, of this Navy,
And leave your England, as dead midnight still,
Guarded with grandsires, babies, and old women .
. .

Suppose the Ambassador from the French comes back,
Tells Harry that the king doth offer him
Katherine his daughter, and with her, to dowry,
Some petty and unprofitable dukedoms.
The offer likes not. And the nimble gunner
With linstock now the devilish cannon touches,
And down goes all before them. Still be kind,
And eke out our performance with your mind.
Henry V. 3. Prologue

(I believe that Will's use of Chorus as Prologue in Henry V is a surpassing technique. And it is most effective in helping audiences anticipate the ensuing battles with the French forces. And painting pictures for the audience in the 'little O.'

'Play with your fancies' and 'grapple your minds to sternage' are motivating. The use of the navy terms 'grapple' and 'sternage' is apt.

'And eke out our performance with your mind' is a clever way to ask the audience to play a part in augmenting the drama.

Talented writers and directors of any era know that the audience is a character, or at least active participant in a stage production. Similarly, the camera is potentially a character in film. Truffaut, Spielberg, Ford, Lean and Hitchcock brilliantly use the camera as constituent in the storytelling. The same is true of clever television directors.)

(The first of several heroic speeches.)

King Henry. <u>Once more into the breach</u>, dear friends, once more;
   Or <u>close up the wall up with our English dead!</u>
   In peace there's nothing so becomes a man
   As modest stillness and humility:
   But when the blast of war blows in our ears,
   Imitate the action of the tiger;
   Stiffen the sinews, summon up the blood.
   Disguise fair nature with hard-favoured rage;
   Then lend the eye a terrible aspect . . .

I see you <u>stand like greyhounds in the slips,</u>
Straining upon the start. <u>The game's afoot</u>:
Follow your spirit; and upon this charge
<u>Cry, God for Harry! England! And Saint George!</u>
Henry V. 3.1

(Hearing those great lines, you see the English soldiers 'stand like greyhounds in the slips.' And know that 'The game's afoot.')

(In an abrupt shift, Will confirms what we already suspected, that the priorities of former Falstaff gang members Nym, Bardolph and Pistol differ markedly from King Henry's goals in the French expedition. The Boy describes their antics)

Boy. As young as I am, I have observed these three swashers. I am boy to them all three: but all they three, though they would serve me, could not be man to me; for, indeed, three such antics do not amount to a man. For Bardolph, he is white-livered and red-faced; by the means whereof 'a faces it out, but fights not. For Pistol, he hath a killing tongue and a quiet sword; by the means whereof 'a breaks words and keeps whole weapons, For Nym, he hath heard that men of few words are the best men; and therefore he scorns to say his prayers lest 'a should be thought a coward . . .

They will steal anything, and call it purchase. Bardolph stole a lute-case, bore it twelve leagues, and sold it for three halfpence. <u>Nym and Bardolph are sworn brothers in filching</u>; and in Calais they stole a fire-shovel: I knew by that piece of service the men would carry coals. They would have me as familiar with men's pockets as their gloves or handkerchers: which makes much against my manhood, if I should take from another man's pocket to put into mine; for it is plain pocketing up of wrongs. I must leave them and seek some better service: their villainy goes against my weak stomach, and therefore I must cast it up.

Henry V. 3.1

(Will, ever the change-of-pace master, transports the audience from King Henry's lofty rhetoric to the base doings of a pack of rascals. And Will uses a boy to cue the audience: 'Nym and Bardolph are sworn brothers in filching.'

The technique is also contrapuntal. In this and numerous other instances, Will recognizes that many in the audience, especially the groundlings, need some comic relief, and they won't be content to sit through heavy weather for two hours.)

(And then, in a twist, we learn that Bardolph and Nym are sentenced to death by hanging and that the Boy's speech is not so comic after all. In fact, his speech is portentous.

Pistol and Fluellen talk of Bardolph's fate and Fortune's fickle wheel.)

Pistol. Bardolph, a soldier, firm and sound of heart,
And of buxom valor, hath, by cruel fate
And giddy <u>Fortune's furious fickle wheel</u>,
That goddess blind
That stands upon that rolling restless stone.
Fluellen. By your patience, Aunchient Pistol. Fortune is painted blind, with a muffler afore her eyes, to signify to you that Fortune is blind. And she is painted also with a wheel to signify to you, which is the moral of it, that she is turning, and inconstant, and mutability, and variation. And her foot, look you, is fixed upon a spherical stone, which rolls, and rolls, and rolls. In good truth, the poet makes a most excellent description of it. Fortune is an excellent moral.

Pistol. Fortune is Bardolph's foe, and frowns on him,
For he hath <u>stolen a pax</u>, and hanged must 'a be.

471

A damned death!
Henry V. 3.6

(Pistol segways from praising his friend Bardolph to damning him for stealing a pax, or the container for holding the sanctified wafer, from a church. The two-faced Pistol, named as a villain by the Boy, escapes the fate of Bardolph and Nym.

The idea of Fortune's Wheel traces to antiquity, and is mentioned by Cicero and Chaucer, among many others. It was usually depicted as an actual wheel upon which a deity makes fateful decisions, which often appear capricious. Pistol excuses his behavior based on the evidence that he is not chosen to die.)

(Chorus introduces us to 'A little touch of Harry in the night.')

Chorus. Now entertain conjecture of a time
<u>When creeping murmur and the poring dark</u>
Fills the wide vessel of the universe.
From camp to camp, through the <u>foul womb of
night</u>
The hum of either army stilly sounds,
That the fixed sentinels almost receive

472

The secret whispers of each other's watch:
Fire answers fire, and through their paly flames
Each battle see the other's umbered face:
Steed threatens steed, in high and boastful neighs
Piercing the night's dull ear; and from the tents
The armourer's, accomplishing the knights,
With busy hammers closing rivets up,
Give dreadful note of preparation . . .
So many horrid ghosts. O, now, who will behold
The royal captain of this ruined band
Walking from watch to watch, from tent to tent . .
.

A little touch of Harry in the night
And so our scene must to the battle fly;
Where, O for pity! we shall much disgrace
With four or five most ragged foils,
Right ill-disposed in brawl ridiculous,
The name of Agincourt.
Henry V, 4. Prologue

(The Prologue prepares us for the pivotal battle of Agincourt. It also describes Harry visiting the troops in the night. Many lines are memorable: 'creeping murmur and the poring dark' in line two and 'foul womb of night' in line four.

'Brawl ridiculous' in the next-to-last line is congruent language.)

(Scene One of Act Four follows, and here Harry (King Henry), in disguise, talks with his fighting men where he learns and teaches with the ever-mouthy and cocky Pistol and three soldiers, Bates, Court and Williams, we have not yet met.)

Pistol. Discuss unto me; art thou officer?
Or art thou base, common, and popular?
King Henry. I am a gentleman of a company.
Pistol. Trailest thou the puissant pike?
King Henry. Even so. What are you?
Pistol. As good a gentleman as the emperor.
King Henry. Then you are a better than the king?
Pistol. The king's a bawcock and a heart of gold
<u>A lad of life, an imp of fame</u>. . .
Court. Brother John Bates, is that not the morning which breaks yonder?
Bates. I think it be: but we have no great cause to desire the approach of day.
Williams. <u>We see yonder the beginning of the day, but I think we shall never see the end of it.</u> Who goes there?
King Henry. A friend.
Williams. Under what captain serve you?
King Henry. Under Sir Thomas Erpingham.

Williams. A good old commander and a most kind gentleman.

Henry V, 4.1

(The initial dialogue among the three soldiers is believable in its fatalism. This is how soldiers talk before a battle. For example, modern British-speak of troops anticipating a fight the next day: 'We're for it tomorrow.' Or the American: 'If your numbers up, your numbers up.'

In my original work of fiction, 'Discovering Will's Lost Years,' two of the contemporary characters discuss the scene with Court, Bates and Williams and mention that in the Kenneth Branagh production of Henry V,' Michael Williams, 'We see yonder . . .' was played by an actor named Michael Williams. He is the late husband of Judi Dench, who was also in the film.

Pistol's, 'A lad of life, an imp of fame' is wonderful writing.)

(Williams and King Henry argue, and Williams threaten to give the disguised King a 'box on the ear' until Bates intercedes.)

*Bate*s. 'Be friends, you English fools, be friends.

We have French quarrels enow, if you could tell how to reckon.

King Henry. Indeed, the French will bet us twenty crowns to one they will beat us, for they bear them on their soldiers. But <u>it is no English treason to cut French crowns</u>, and tomorrow the King himself will be a clipper. (Exit soldiers.)

Upon the King! Let us our lives, our souls,
Our debts, our careful lives,
Our children, and our sins lay on the King!
We must bear all . . .
That playest so subtly with a King's repose,
I am King that find thee, and I know
'Tis not the balm, the scepter and the ball,
The sword, the mace, the crown imperial,
The intertissued robe of gold and pearl,
The farced title running 'afore the King,
The throne he sits, nor the tide of pomp
That beats on the high shore of this world
No, not all these, thrice-gorgeous ceremony,
Not all these laid in bed majestical,
<u>Can sleep so soundly as the wretched slave.</u>
Henry V, 4.1

(King Henry says that even though he can illegally clip parts off French coins, it isn't treasonous to do so: 'it is no English treason to cut French crowns.'

476

After the soldiers exit, the King lists the emblems of his office and remarks that they do not offer the solace of sleep that is given to common folk, 'Can sleep so soundly as the wretched slave.'

The passage is reminiscent of the 'uneasy lies the head that wears the crown' speech by his father in Henry IV, Part Two, 3.1.

Will wrote much of sleep and the lack thereof. Hamlet in Hamlet, 2.2: 'Oh God, I could be bounded in a nutshell and count myself a king of infinite space, were it not that I have bad dreams.

(The French brim with pre-battle confidence and over-egged rhetoric.)

Constable. <u>Hark, how our steeds for present service neigh!</u>

Dauphin. Mount them, and make incision in their hides,

That their hot blood may spin in English eyes,

And dout them with superfluous courage, ha!

Rambures. What, will you have them weep our horse's blood?

How shall we, then, behold their natural tears?

Messenger. The English are embattled, you French peers.

Constable. <u>To horse, you gallant princes! Straight to</u>
<u>ho</u>rse!

Do but behold yon poor and starved band,
And your fair show shall suck away their souls,
Leaving them but the shales and husks of men.
There is not work enough for all our hands;
Scarce blood enough in all their sickly veins
To give each naked curtle-axe a stain,
That our French gallants shall to-day draw out,
And sheathe for lack of sport: let us but blow on
them,
The vapour of our valour will overturn them.

Grandpree. Why do you stay so long, my lords of
France?

Yond island carrions, desperate of their bones,
Ill-favouredly become the morning field:
Their ragged curtains poorly are let loose,
And our air shakes them passing scornfully:
Big Mars seems bankrupt in their beggared host,
And faintly through a rusty beaver peeps:
<u>The horsemen sit like fixed candlesticks,</u>
With torch-staves in their hand; and their poor
jades
Lob down their heads, dropping the hides and hips.
The gum down-roping from their pale-dead eyes,
And in their pale dull mouths <u>the gimmel-bit</u>
<u>Lies foul with chewed grass,</u> still and motionless;

And their executors, the knavish crows,
Fly over them, all impatient for their hour.
<u>Description cannot suit itself in words</u>
<u>To demonstrate the life of such a battle</u>
In life so lifeless as it shows itself.
Henry V, 4.2

(Since Constable's line one ranks up there in corniness with 'Hark I hear the cannons roar,' it must be difficult for contemporary actors to read it with a straight face. Also, did Will write the line? I believe that Will, like many Elizabethan writers was a heavy collaborator. This was particularly evident in 'Two Gentleman of Verona,' 'Henry VI,' and 'Richard the Third,' where he likely had help from Kit Marlowe. The OED has given Marlowe a co-writing credit for Henry VI. Finally, line one of the speech may have not been written at all, but rather ad-libbed by an actor and included in a quarto. We'll never know, but it's always fun to think about the possibilities.

The speeches do have some useful imagery: 'The horsemen sit like fixed candlesticks' and 'the gimmel-bit lies foul with chewed grass . . .'

'Description cannot suit itself in words to demonstrate the life of such a battle' is surely an author's lament to his audience and another call for them to exercise their imaginations.)

(Now we revisit one of Will's best and most-quoted speeches.)

Henry V. This day is called the Feast of Saint Crispian:
   He that outlives this day, and comes safe home,
   Will stand a tip-toe when this day is named,
   And rouse him at the name of Crispian.
   He that shall live this day, and see old age,
   Will yearly on the vigil feast his neighbors,
   And say, Tomorrow is Saint Crispian:
   Then he will strip his sleeve and show his scars,
   And say, these wounds I had on Crispin' day.
   Old men forget; yet all shall be forgot,
   But he'll remember with advantages
   What feats he did that day: then shall our names,
   Familiar in their mouths as household words,
   Harry the King, Bedford and Exeter,
   Warwick and Talbot, Salisbury and Gloster,
   Be in their flowing cups freshly remembered.
   The story shall the good man teach his son;
   And Crispin Crispian shall ne'er go by,
   From this day till the ending of the world,
   But we in it shall be remembered,
   <u>We few, we happy few, we band of brothers;</u>

For he to-day that sheds his blood with me
Shall be my brother; be he ne'er so vile,
This day shall gentle his condition:
And gentlemen in England now a-bed
Shall think themselves accursed they were not here,
And hold their manhoods cheap while any speaks
That fought with us upon Saint Crispin's day.
Henry V, 4.3

(It's difficult to read, or hear aloud in a play, 'We few, we happy few, we band of brothers' without getting a tingle. The finest reading of the speech I've heard, among many stirring ones, was by the British actor Laurence Harvey with the Old Vic touring company in a Boston stage performance of Henry V, with a youthful Judi Dench playing Katherine, Henry's future wife.

Beyond his powerful stage appearances, Harvey was also a movie actor of note: 'Room at the Top' and 'The Manchurian candidate' were two notable roles.)

King Henry. What is this castle called that stands hard by?
Montjoy. They call it Agincourt.
King Henry. Then call we this <u>the field of Agincourt,</u>
<u>Fought on the day of Crispin Crispianus.</u>

481

Fluellen. Your grandfather of famous memory, an't please your majesty, and your great-uncle Edward the Black Prince of Wales, <u>as I have read in the chronicles,</u> fought a most brave battle here in France.

King Henry. They did, Fluellen.

Henry V, 4.7

(We have the identification of the battle's location, 'Agincourt,' and the reiteration of the historical relevance of 'Saint Crisipin's day.'

Through a character, Will speaks his own thoughts in Fluellan's next-to-last line, 'as I have read in the chronicles,' because he read it in the chronicles.

Chorus. <u>How London doth pour out her citizens!</u>
The mayor and all his brethren, in best sort,
<u>Like to the senators of the antique Rome,</u>
With all the plebeians swarming at their heels,
Go forth and fetch their <u>conquering Caesar</u>:
As, by a lower but by loving likelihood,
Were now <u>the general</u> of <u>our gracious empress,</u>
<u>As in good time he may, from Ireland coming,</u>
<u>Bringing rebellion broached on his sword.</u>
Henry V, 5. Prologue

(In lines one and two of the Act Five Prologue, Chorus anticipates King Henry's triumphant return to England from France. 'How London doth pour out its citizens.' 'Like to the senators of antique Rome.' And, in the next three lines, compares his victory with the 'conquering Caesar.' I wonder whether Will's play, 'Julius Caesar' was in the works around the same time as Henry V, hence the Caesar mention.

Then, in a contemporary reference in the last three lines, Chorus contrasts those earlier jubilations with the Earl of Essex, 'the general' coming back to England from wars in Ireland and fomenting rebellion against, 'our gracious empress,' Queen Elizabeth I, 'Bringing rebellion broached on his sword,' for which he lost his head.)

(We find victorious Harry in the French King's palace acting beneficently and wooing the defeated King's daughter Katharine.)

King Henry. And while thou livest, dear Kate, take a fellow of plain and uncoined constancy, for he perforce must do thee right, because he hath not the gift to woo in other places. For these fellows of infinite tongue that can rhyme themselves into ladies' favors, they do always reason themselves out again.

What! A speaker is but a prater, a rhyme is but a ballad. A good leg will fall, a straight back will stoop, a black beard will turn white, a curled pate will grow bald, a fair face will wither, a full eye will wax hollow. But a good heart, Kate, is the sun and the moon, or rather the sun and not the moon, for it shines bright and never changes, but keeps his course truly. If thou would have such a one, take me. And take me, take a soldier, take a King. And what sayest thou then to my love? Speak, my fair, and fairly, I pray thee.

Katharine. Is it possible dat I sould love de enemy of France?

King Henry. No, it is not possible you should love the enemy of France, Kate. But in loving me you should love the friend of France, for I love France so well that I will not part with a village of it, I will have it all mine. And, Kate, when France is mine and I am yours, then yours is France and you are mine. . . . Put off your maiden blushes, avouch the thoughts of your heart with the looks of an empress. Take me by the hand and say, "Harry of England I am thine" Which word thou shalt no sooner bless my ear withal but I will tell thee aloud "England is thine, Ireland is thine, France is thine, and Henry Plantagenet is thine," who, though I speak it before his face, if he be not fellow with the best king, thou shalt find the best king of good fellows. Come, your answer in broken music, for thy voice is music and thy English broken. Therefore, queen of all, Katharine, break thy mind to me in <u>broken </u>English, wilt thou have me?

Katharine. Dat is as it sall please de roi mon pere.

Henry V, 5. 2

(I mentioned above that I saw Laurence Harvey as Henry V and Judi Dench as Katharine in a stage performance. They played this delightful scene lightly, smiling and chuckling during the punning on 'broken' in the last four lines.)

Chorus. <u>Thus far, with rough and all-unable pen,</u>
<u>Our bending author hath pursued the story,</u>
<u>In little room confining mighty men,</u>
<u>Mangling by starts the full course of their glory.</u>
Small time, but in that small most greatly lived
This star of England. Fortune made his sword,
By which the world's best garden he achieved,
And of it left his son imperial lord.
Henry the Sixth, <u>in infant bands crowned king</u>
Of France and England, did this King succeed,
Whose state so many had the managing
<u>That they lost France and made his England bleed.</u>
Which oft our stage hath shown, and, for their sake
In your fair minds let this acceptance take.

Henry V, 5. Epilogue

(In the first four lines of the Epilogue, Will bows
to the audience for telling the story of Henry V
roughly in segments, 'mangling by starts . . .' I'm sure
the audiences of his time and later forgave his 'all-
unable pen.'

Then, in the ensuing lines, we learn that Henry
VI inherits the crown, 'in infant bands crowned king.'
from his father, and that things do not go smoothly,
'That they lost France and made his England bleed.')

HENRY VI, PART ONE

Bedford. Hung be the heavens with black, yield day to night!

Comets, importing change of time and states,

Brandish your crystal tresses in the sky,

And with them scourge the bad revolting stars

That have consented unto Henry's death!

Henry the Fifth, too famous to live long!

England never lost a king of so much worth.

Gloster. England never had a king until his time.

Virtue he had, deserving to command:

His brandished sword did blind men with his beams;

His arms spread wider than a dragon's wings;

His sparkling eyes, replete with wrathful fire,

More dazzled and drove back his enemies

Than mid-day sun fierce bent against their faces.

What should I say? His deeds exceed all speech:

He ne'er lift up his hand but conquered.

Exeter. We mourn in black: why mourn we not in blood?

Henry is dead, and never shall revive:

Upon a wooden coffin we attend;

And death's dishonourable victory

We with our stately presence glorify,
Like captives bound to a triumphant <u>car</u>.
Henry VI, Part I, 1.1

(In the opening of Henry V1, his father Henry the
Fifth's death is mourned and exalted, 'England never
lost a king of so much worth.'

'Car' in the final line refers to the chariot of a
mythological God to which the mourners are
figuratively attached.)

Henry the Fifth's tomb is in the floor of
Westminster Abbey. When I saw it, I stopped,
thought and was moved.)

(Back to Henry Vl and the continuing wars in
France, with Joan La Pucelle, aka Joan of Arc, leading
the French charge.)

Joan La Pucelle. <u>Assigned am I to be the English
scourge</u>.
This night the siege assuredly I'll raise:
<u>Expect Saint Martin's summer, halcyon days</u>,
Since I have entered these wars.
Glory is <u>like a circle in the water</u>,
<u>Which never ceaseth to enlarge itself</u>,
Till by broad spreading it disperse to naught.

With Henry's death the English circle ends;
Dispersed are the glories it included.
Now am I like that proud insulting ship
Which <u>Caesar and his fortune</u> bare at once.
Henry VI, Part I, 1.2

(Joan La Pucelle, aka Joan of Arc, predicts that she
will end English control of France, 'Assigned am I to
be the English scourge.' And it will be like a warm, fall
feast day, 'Expect Saint Martin's summer, halcyon
days.' We also learn that Joan has no self-doubts.

Joan also announces that her entrance into the
wars will spread France's glory like 'a circle in the
water,' a lovely comparison.

Caesar's triumphs are invoked again, 'Caesar and
his fortune.' It's likely that Will was thinking about or
drafting his play 'Julius Caesar.'

When someone mentioned Joan of Arc to
Gracie Allen, she said, "They laughed at her, but she
built it anyway.")

(Talbot, the English warrior, meets in single
combat with Joan.)

Talbot. Where is my strength, my valour, and my
force?

Our English troops retire, I cannot stay with them;

A woman clad in armour chaseth them.

Here, here she comes.

I'll have a bout with thee;

Devil or Devil's dam, I'll conjure thee:

Blood will I draw on thee, thou art a witch,

And straightaway give thy soul to him thou servest.

Pucelle. Come, come, 'tis only I that must disgrace

thee.

Talbot. Heavens, can you suffer hell so to prevail?

My breast I'll burst with straining of my courage,

And from my shoulders crack my arms asunder,

But I will chastise this high-minded strumpet.

Pucelle. Talbot, farewell: thy hour is not yet come:

I must go victual Orleans forthwith.

Overtake me if thou canst; I scorn thy strength.

Go, go, cheer up thy hunger-starved men;

Help Salisbury to make his testament:

This day is ours, as many more shall be.

Talbot. My thoughts are whirled like a potter's

wheel;

I know not where I am nor what I do:

A witch by fear, not force, like Hannibal

Drives back our troops, and conquers as she lists:

So bees with smoke and doves with noisome

stench

Are from their hives and houses driven away.

The called us, for our fierceness, English dogs;
Now like to whelps we crying run away.
Henry VI, Part I, 1.5

(In line seven of the passage, Talbot talks of drawing the <u>witch </u>Joan's blood. It was believed at the time that taking blood from witches* rendered them harmless.

Following their indecisive sword fight, Joan scorns Talbot and leaves to retake Orleans. Talbot vows, even though his arms are aching, to 'chastise this high-minded strumpet,' but soon confesses that 'I know not where I am nor what I do.' It is a worth rereading, marvelously well-constructed exchange, and, particularly in Talbot's case, very human and very male with its degrading terms 'witch and 'strumpet.'

*In Tennessee Williams' masterful screenplay, he describes the night that the fragile Blanche DuBois arrives in New Orleans and waits for a streetcar named Desire: 'The night is windy, and the moon three-quarters full and the clouds are low and filmy like the torn garments of witches.')

*Charle*s. 'Tis Joan, not we, by whom the day is won;
For which I will divide my crown with her;
And all the priests and friars in my realm

491

Shall in procession sing her endless praise.
A statelier pyramis to her I'll rear
Than Rhodope's of Memphis ever was:
In memory of her when she is dead,
Her ashes in an urn more precious
Than the rich jeweled coffer of Darius,
Transported shall be at high festivals
Before the kings and queens of France.
No longer on Saint Denis will we cry,
But Joan La Pucelle shall be France's saint.
Come in, and let us banquet royally,
After this golden day of victory.
Henry VI, Part I, 1.5

(Will's references, such as 'Rhodope' from Greek mythology, 'Darius,' the Persian King, and 'Denis,' patron saint of Paris again confirms his astonishing erudition cultivated through tireless reading in the classics, inexhaustible research, photographic memory and willingness to borrow from his predecessors.

Note the accurate prediction that 'Joan La Pucelle shall be France's saint.' She was canonized in the early 19th-century.)

Talbot. This happy night, the Frenchmen are secure,

Having all day caroused and banqueted:
Embrace we, then, this opportunity,
As fitting best to quittance their deceit,
Contrived by art and baleful sorcery.
Bedford. Coward of France! how much he wrongs his fame,
Despairing of his own arm's fortitude,
<u>To join with witches and the help of hell.</u>
Henry VI, Part I, 2.1

(The English, led by the redoubtable Talbot, are about to scale the French walls, catch them in their beds and send them fleeing into the night.

Bedford's last line, 'To join with witches and the help of hell' reinforces the prejudiced belief of the times that a woman who fights as well as Joan must be a witch.)

(In the next lines, Talbot, who sent the French scurrying, doesn't want to parley with them, and especially with Joan of Arc.)

Talbot. But, lords, in all our bloody massacre,
I muse <u>we meet not</u> with the Dauphin's grace,
His new-come champion, virtuous <u>Joan of Arc</u>,
Nor any of his false confederates.

(A comic interlude with a twist follows, as Talbot bends his rule and agrees to meet with the French Countess of Auvergne who compare herself to Tomyris a sixth-century warrior queen.

Given Talbot's battlefield reputation, 'Great is the rumour of this dreadful knight the countess expects 'Hercules' or a 'second Hector a great Troy fighter. Instead, she finally meets Talbot and calls him a 'weak and withed shrimp.')

Countess. The plot is laid: if all things fall out right,
I shall as famous be by this exploit
As Scythian <u>Tomyris</u> by Cyrus' death.
<u>Great is the rumour of this dreadful knight,</u>
And his achievements of no less account:
Fain would mine eyes be witness with mine ears,
To give their censure of these rare reports . . .
What! Is this the man?
Is this the scourge of France?
Is this the Talbot, so much feared abroad
That with his name the mothers still their babes?
I see report is fabulous and false:
I thought I should have seen some <u>Hercules</u>,
A <u>second Hector</u>, for his grim aspect,

And large proportion of his strong-knit limbs.
Alas, this is a child, a silly dwarf!
It cannot be this <u>weak and writhled shrimp</u>
Should strike such terror to his enemies.
Henry VI, Part I, 2.3

(In the dialogue that follows, Talbot tells the countess that he is Talbot, but only part of him has arrived, 'but a shadow of myself,' and then he brings in his soldiers: 'These are his substance, sinews, arms, and strength.'

The countess caves: 'pardon my abuse: I find thou art no less than fame hath bruited.'

Many people initially underestimated the diminutive Napoleon Bonaparte, and also Joseph Stalin who was five-three in his shoes.)

(In this London-based scene, snippets of acid-tongued dialogue between representatives of the houses of York, white-rose, and Lancaster, red-rose, anticipate the destructive Wars of the Roses.

And we meet Richard Plantagenet, later Richard 111 and son of Richard of York.)

Richard Plantagenet. Since you are tongue-tied and so loth to speak,

495

In dumb significants proclaim your thoughts:
Let him that is a true-born gentleman,
And stands upon the honour of his birth,
If he suppose that I have pleaded truth,
From off this brier pluck a white rose with me.
Somerset. Let him that is no coward nor no flatterer,
But dare maintain the party of the truth,
Pluck a red rose off this thorn with me.
Warwick. I love no colours; and, without all colour
Of base insinuating flattery,
I pluck this white rose with Plantagenet.
Suffolk. I pluck this red rose with young Somerset
And say withal, I think he held the right.
Vernon. Stay, lords and gentlemen, and pluck no more
Till you conclude that he upon whose side
The fewest roses are cropped from the tree
Shall yield the other in the right opinion.
Vernon. Then, for the truth and plainness of the case,
I pluck this pale and maiden blossom here,
Giving my verdict on the white rose side.
Somerset. Prick not your finger as you pluck it off,
Lest, bleeding, you do paint the white rose red,
And fall on my side so, against your will.
Plantagenet. Hath not thy rose a canker, Somerset?
Somerset. Hath not thy rose a thorn, Plantagenet?

Plantagenet. And, by my soul, this pale and angry rose,

As cognizance of my <u>blood-drinking hate</u>,
Will I forever, and my faction, wear,
Until it wither with me to my grave,
Or flourish to the height of my degree.
Suffolk. Go forward and be <u>choked with thy ambition</u>!
Warwick. Will I upon thy party wear this rose:
And here I prophesy, this brawl to-day,
Grown to this faction, in the Temple-garden,
Shall send, between the red rose and the white,
<u>A thousand souls to death and deadly night</u>.
Henry VI, Part I, 2.4

(Richard Plantagenet's 'my blood-drinking hate' is portentous, as is Suffolk's 'choked with thy ambition.' Will crammed a lot of history into this grating exchange.

Warwick's 'A thousand souls to death and deadly night' in the final line of the passage vastly underestimates the lives lost in the ensuing civil wars, popularly known as the Wars of the Roses.)

(Pucelle, aka Joan of Arc, and Talbot, the English warrior, are at it again.)

Bedford. O let no words, but deeds, revenge this treason!

Pucelle. What will you do, <u>good gray-beard</u>? break a lance,

<u>And run a tilt at death within a chair?</u>

Talbot. <u>Foul fiend of France, and hag of all despite,</u>

Encompass'd with thy lustful paramours!

Becomes it thee to taunt his valiant age

And twit with cowardice a man half dead?

Damsel, I'll have a bout with you again,

O else let Talbot perish with this shame.

Pucelle. Are ye so hot, sir? Yet, Pucelle hold thy peace;

<u>If Talbot do but thunder, rain will follow.</u>

Henry VI, Part I, 3.2

(Bedford, brought into the scene unwell in a chair, is taunted by Pucelle. Enraged, Talbot insults and challenges Pucelle, who answers calmly.

Throughout the plays, the men tend to deal in hyperbolic and sexist slurs. In the passage above, Talbot uses 'foul fiend' and 'hag' to lambaste Pucelle. Earlier, it was 'witch' and 'strumpet.')

The women's disparagements lean more toward belittlement, as in 'graybeard' just above, and 'If Talbot do but thunder, rain will follow.'

However, Countess Auvergne put down Talbot with 'silly dwarf' and 'weak and writhled shrimp.' Or maybe it's simply Will writing women in dudgeon in less-harsh language. That said, I thought that the digs on Talbot by the Countess were priceless.)

(Exeter's complaints below sounds much like the travails of modern government, with 'discord,' 'shouldering' and 'factitious bandying.')

Exeter. This <u>jarring discord</u> of nobility,
This <u>shouldering of each other</u> in the court,
This <u>factious bandying of their favourites</u>,
But that it does presage some ill event.
'Tis much when <u>sceptres are in children's hands</u>;
But more when envy breeds unkind division;
There comes the ruin, there begins confusion.
Henry VI, Part I, 4.1

(With 'sceptres are in children's hands' in line five, Exeter alludes to the youthful Henry VI.)

York. Damsel of France, <u>I think I have you fast</u>:
Unchain your spirits now with spelling charms,
And try if they can gain your liberty.

A goodly prize, fit for the devil's grace!
See how the ugly witch doth bend her brows,
As if, with Circe, she would change my shape!
Pucelle. Chang'd to a worser shape thou canst not be.
York. O, Charles the Dauphin is a proper man;
No shape but his can please your dainty eye.
Pucelle. A plaguing mischief light on Charles and thee!
And may ye both be suddenly surpris'd
By bloody hands, in sleeping on your beds!
York. Fell, banning hag; enchantress hold thy tongue!
Pucelle. I pr'ythee, give me leave to curse awhile.
York. Curse, miscreant, when thou comest to the stake.

Henry VI, Part I, 5.3

(More insults for Joan of Arc on being captured by the English, including comparing her to 'Circe,' the mythical goddess of sorcery.

Pucelle's French compatriots have fled, and she is under threat to be burned alive, 'I think I have you fast,' 'comest to the stake.')

(Next, we meet Margaret, daughter of the King of Naples and future wife of Henry VI. Meanwhile, she is Suffolk's prisoner, and he, already married, is playing paramour.)

Suffolk. My hand would free her, but my heart says no.
As plays the sun upon the glassy streams,
Twinkling another counterfeited beam,
So seems this gorgeous beauty to mine eyes.
Fain would I woo her, yet I dare not speak:
I'll call for pen and ink, and write my mind:
Fie, De-la-Poole! Disable not thyself;
Hast not a tongue? Is she not her thy prisoner?
Wilt thou be daunted at a woman's sight?
Ay, beauty's princely majesty is such,
Confounds the tongue, and makes the senses rough.

Margaret. Say, Earl of Suffolk, if thy name be so,
What ransom must I pay before I pass?
For I perceive I am thy prisoner.

Suffolk. How canst thou tell she will deny thy suit
Before thou make a trial of her love?

Margaret. Why speak'st thou not? what ransom must I pay?

Suffolk. She's beautiful, and therefore to be woo'd;
She is a woman, therefore to be won.

(Will keeps his audiences guessing. He switches from Joan of Arc headed for the stake to the farcical scene with Suffolk, the hapless would-be lover, speaking in asides while trying to woo Margaret, who says later in the vignette: 'He talks at random; sure, the man is mad.'

Richard de la Pole was an early 16th-Century Yorkist pretender to the crown.

In a character-development tip to the audience, Will has the casual, but tough, Margaret asking offhand, 'Say, Earl of Suffolk . . .'

'Wooed' and 'won' in the last two lines was also used in Richard III, 1.2. Both times in preposterous situations. Here, the clueless Suffolk.* Richard, angling and murdering to become king, successfully courted a woman whose husband he has just murdered, and she knows it.

*Knowing he can't have Margaret, Suffolk plays a political card and fixes it so that Margaret marries King Henry.

You can almost hear Will's brain whirring, as he pivots from a noble's silly flirtation into creating Margaret, about to become the wife of a king, and one of Will's most formidable female characters.

(Speaking of strong women, in the exchange that follows, Pucelle, aka Joan of Arc, rejects her surrogate peasant father. Then she weaves a convoluted tale, first of her virginity then of the child she claims to be carrying.)

Pucelle. Peasant, avaunt! You have suborn'd this man,
Of purpose to obscure my noble birth.
Shepherd. 'Tis true, I gave a noble to the priest
The morn that I was wedded to her mother.
Kneel down and take my blessing, good my girl.
Wilt thou not stoop? Now cursed be the time
Of thy nativity! I would the milk
Thy mother gave thee when thou suck'dst her breast
Had been a little ratsbane for thy sake!
Or else, when thou didst keep my lambs a-field,
I wish some ravenous wolf had eaten thee!
Dost thou deny thy father, cursed drab?
O, burn her, burn her! Hanging is too good.
York. Take her away; for she hath liv'd too long,
To fill the world with vicious qualities.
Pucelle. First let me tell you whom you have condemn'd:
Not me begotten of a shepherd swain,

But issu'd from the progeny of kings;
Virtuous and holy; <u>chosen from above,</u>
<u>By inspiration of celestial grace,</u>
To work exceeding miracles on earth.
I never had to do with wicked spirits:
But you, that are <u>polluted with your lusts,</u>
Stain'd with the guiltless blood of innocents,
Corrupt and tainted with a thousand vices,
Because you want the grace that others have,
You judge it straight a thing impossible
To compass wonders but by help of devils.
No, misconceived! <u>Joan of Arc hath been</u>
<u>A virgin from her tender infancy,</u>
Chaste and immaculate in very thought;
Whose maiden blood, thus rigorously effus'd,
Will cry for vengeance at the gates of heaven.
York. Ay, ay: away with her to execution!
Warwick. And hark ye, sirs; because she is a maid,
Spare no fagots, let there be enow:
Place barrels of pitch upon the fatal stake,
That so her torture may be shortened.
Pucelle. Will nothing turn your unrelenting hearts?
Then, Joan, discover thy infirmity,
That warranteth by law to be thy privilege.
<u>I am with child,</u> ye bloody homicides:
Murder not, then, the fruit within my womb,
Although ye hale me to a violent death.

York. Now heaven forfend! the holy maid with child!

Warwick. The greatest miracle that e'er ye wrought:
Is all your strict preciseness come to this?

York. She and the Dauphin have been juggling:
I did imagine what would be her refuge.

Warwick. Well, go to; we will have no bastards
Especially since Charles must father it.

Pucelle. You are deceiv'd; my child is none of his:
It was Alencon that enjoyed my love.

York. Alencon! that notorious Machiavel!
It dies, an if it had a thousand lives.

Pucelle. O, give me leave, I have deluded you;
Twas neither Charles nor yet the duke I named,
But Reignier, King of Naples, that prevail'd.

Warwick. A married man! That's most intolerable.

York. Why, here's a girl! I think she knows not well
There were so many whom she may accuse.

Warwick. It's sign she hath been liberal and free.

York. And yet, forsooth, she is a virgin pure.
Strumpet, thy words condemn thy brat and thee:
Use no entreaty, for it is in vain.

Pucelle. Then lead me hence; with whom I leave my curse:
May never glorious sun reflex his beams
Upon the country where you make abode;
But darkness and the gloomy shade of death

505

Environ you, till mischief and despair
Drive you to break your necks or hang yourselves?
York. Break thou in pieces and consume to ashes,
Thou foul accursed minister of Hell!
Henry VI, Part I, 5.4

(This passage can be taken apart line by line to
derive meaning. I've reread it over and over and
discussed it with friends and colleagues, all of whom
have differing opinions. Does Pucelle expect mercy
for being a holy virgin? Or not seeing that working
why does she name two lovers as the father of the
child she claims to be bearing, one of whom is the
redoubtable Margaret's father? Is she playing York
and Warwick in a quest for mercy? It ranks as one of
literatures greatest sales pitches, even though it didn't
work. Pucelle's, 'polluted with your lusts,' is a gem.
The bitter father's 'ratsbane' line wasn't bad either. I
have no idea why Will wrote the episode this way, but
it's brilliant and an appealingly scandalous topic for
discussion, dissension and possibly fistfights.)

506

HENRY VI, PART TWO

(And now Margaret is Queen. As promised, she is one of Will's most enthralling women. The young King is smitten.)

King Henry. I can express no kinder sign of love
Than this kind kiss. O Lord that lends me
Lend me a heart replete with thankfulness!
For thou hast given me, in this beauteous face,
A world of earthly blessings to my soul,
If sympathy of love unite our thoughts.
Queen Margaret. Great King of England, and my gracious Lord,
The mutual conference that my mind hath had,
By day, by night, waking and in my dreams,
<u>In courtly company or at my beads,</u>
With you, my alder-liefest sovereign,
Makes me the bolder to salute my king.
With ruder terms, such as my wit affords
And over-joy of heart doth minister.
King Henry. Her sight did ravish; but her grace in speech,
Her words y-clad with wisdom's majesty,

Makes me from wondering fall to weeping joys;
Such is the fullness of my heart's content.
Lords, with one cheerful voice welcome my love.
Henry VI, Part Two, 1.1

(I like Margaret's juxtaposition of 'courtly company
or at my beads.'
We'll soon see how cheerful the 'lords' are.)

Gloucester.   Shall   Henry's   conquest,   Bedford's
vigilance,
    Your deeds of war, and all our counsel die?
    O peers of England, shameful is this league!
    Fatal this marriage! cancelling your fame,
    Blotting your names from books of memory,
    Razing the characters of your renown.
    Defacing monuments of conquer'd France,
    Undoing all, as all had never been!
    Henry VI, Part Two, 1.1

(Henry VI, with Suffolk doing the maneuvering,
traded two French dukedoms to Reignier, King of
Naples for his daughter Margaret's hand in marriage.
The English nobles aren't happy about it.

Recall that Joan Pucelle named Reignier as one of the alleged fathers of the baby she claimed to be carrying

Reminder: Gloucester, aka Duke Humphrey, is young King Henry's uncle and Protector. He speaks in the first four lines above of his distaste for the marriage and its implications for advantage, but he speaks for many of his peers. In effect, he asks, 'Since everything we worked for in France is falling apart, what should we do? Since Gloucester is the heir apparent, his apprehension is well-founded.)

(Next, in sharp contrast, Richard, Duke of York, as always, expounds for himself and states exactly what he intends to do and how he will do it. We must say that the man has knowledge and know-how.)

York. Anjou and Maine are given to the French;
Paris is lost; the state of Normandy
Stands on a tickle point, now they are gone:
Suffolk concluded on the articles;
The peers agreed; and Henry was well pleas'd
To change two dukedoms for a Duke's fair daughter . . .
A day will come when York shall claim his own;
And therefore I will take the Nevils' parts,

And make a show of love to proud Duke Humphrey,
And when I spy advantage, <u>claim the crown,</u>
For that's <u>the golden mark I seek to hit:</u>
Nor shall proud Lancaster usurp my right,
Nor hold the sceptre in his <u>childish fist,</u>
Nor wear the diadem upon his head,
<u>Whose church-like humours fit not for a crown.</u>
Then, York, be still awhile, till time do serve:
Watch thou and wake, when others be asleep,
To pry into the secrets of the state;
Till Henry, surfeiting in joys of love
With his new bride and England's dear-bought queen,
And Humphrey with the peers be <u>fall'n at jars:</u>
Then will I raise aloft the milk-white rose,
With whose sweet smell the air shall be perfum'd;
And in my standard bear the arms of York,
To grapple with the house of Lancaster;
And, force perforce, I'll make him yield the crown,
Whose bookish rule hath pull'd fair England down.
Henry VI, Part Two, 1.1

(You likely know who York is. You're right, father of George, who will become Duke of Clarence in the play *Richard 111*. Edward who will become king for a short time. And the cleverest and most diabolical son, his namesake, Richard, who will become Richard 111.

'Anjou and Maine are given to the French,' refers to French provinces given up by Henry Six with more in the offing.

'Stands on a tickle point' in line three of York's speech tickled me.

'Nevils' parts' refers to York's mother Cecily Neville.

'Claim the crown' and 'golden mark I seek to hit' from York do not lack specificity.

'Childish fist' alludes to Henry's youth.

'Churchlike humours' makes reference to the young King's reliance on prayer rather than strong leadership, or being too church-like to be an effective sovereign.

'Fall'n at jars' means that Humphrey, the Duke of Gloucester, will fall out with animus, but meanwhile the Duchess, his wife Eleanor, has her own plans.)

Duchess. Follow I must; I cannot go before
While Gloucester bears this base and humble mind.
Were I a man, a duke, and next of blood,
I would remove these tedious stumbling blocks,
And smooth my way upon their headless necks:

And, being a woman, I will not be slack
To play my part in fortune's pageant.
Henry VI, Part Two, 1.2

'Smooth my way upon their headless necks' from
the Duchess is a line worthy of the scheming York.
'Headless necks' competes with 'severed heads.' I like
the imaginativeness of the former.

The Duchess is tough, and she will step up and play
her part in court action.)

(Next, we learn that young Queen Margaret is as
restless, impatient and ambitious as the Duchess of
Gloucester.)

Queen Margaret. My lord of Suffolk, say, is this the
guise,
   Is this the fashion in the court of England?
   Is this the government of Britain's isle,
   And this the royalty of Albion's king?
   What, shall King Henry be a pupil still,
   Under the surly Gloucester's governance?
   Am I a queen in title and in style,
   And must be made a subject to a duke?
   I tell thee, Poole, when in the city Tours
   Thou rann'st a tilt in honour of my love,

And stol'st away the ladies hearts of France,
I thought King Henry had resembled thee
In courage, courtship and proportion:
But all his mind is bent to holiness,
To number Ave-Maries on his beads:
His champions are the prophets and apostles;
His weapons, holy saws of sacred writ;
His study is his tilt-yard, and his loves
Are brazen images of canoniz'd saints.
I would the college of the cardinals
Would choose him pope, and carry him to Rome,
And set the triple crown upon his head:
That were a state fit for his holiness . . .
Not all these lords do vex me half so much
As that proud dame, the lord protector's wife.
She sweeps it through the court with troops of
ladies,
More like an empress than Duke Humphrey's wife:
Strangers in court do take her for the queen:
She bears a duke's revenues on her back,
And in her heart she scorns our poverty:
Shall I not live to be aveng'd on her?
Contemptuous base-born callet as she is,
She vaunted 'mongst her minions t' other day
The very train of her worst wearing gown
Was better worth than all my father's lands
Till Suffolk gave two dukedoms for his daughter.

(Margaret refers in line four to 'Albion's king. Albion is from the ancient Greek, and is the oldest name for England.

In line nine she refers to Suffolk as 'Poole.' The surnames of several earls of Suffolk was Poole, or Pole, and often written as the full name de la Poole, or Pole. Margaret mentions that Poole ran a joust, or tilt, in honor of her love for Henry. Then, a few lines later, she uses 'tilt-yard' as a metaphorical slight for Henry's non-combatant religious study.

Margaret is not only unhappy with Henry's pious behavior, 'to number Ave-Maries on his beads.' She also loathes the imperious Duchess of Gloucester, whom she calls a 'base-born callet,' or French court jester.

To appease Margaret, Suffolk tells her:
'So, one by one, we'll weed them all at last,
And you yourself shall steer the happy helm.'

(Next, the Duchess of Gloucester arranges a séance. Interestingly, the conjuror is named Bolingbroke, who we saw, is the surname of the Duke of Hereford, who became Henry IV after deposing Richard II.

Margery, or Mother Jourdain, is the witch. Even a spirit rises and speaks. Like tossing flour, or flowers red and white, into the mixture, the plot thickens.)

Bolingbroke. Mother Jourdain, be you prostrate, and grovel on the earth; John Southwell, read you; and let us to our work.

Duchess. Well said, my masters; and welcome all.
To this <u>gear</u>, the sooner the better.

Bolingbroke. Patience, good lady; wizards know their times:
Deep night, dark night, the silent of the night,
The time of night when Troy was set on fire;
The time when <u>screech-owls cry and bandogs howl</u>,
And spirits walk, and ghosts break up their graves,
That time best fits the work we have in hand.
Madam, sit you, and fear not: whom we raise
We will make fast within a hallow'd verge. . . .

Spirit. Ask what thou wilt: that I had said and done!

Bolingbroke. First of the King: What shall of him become?

Spirit. The duke yet lives that Henry shall depose;
But him outlive, and die a violent death.

Bolingbroke. What fate awaits the duke of Suffolk?

Spirit. By water shall he die and take his end.

Bolingbroke. What shall befall the Duke of
Somerset?

Spirit. Let him shun castles;
Safer shall he be upon the sandy plains
Than where castles mounted stand.
Have done, for more I can hardly endure.
Bolingbroke. Descend to darkness and the burning
lake!
False fiend, avoid!
(York and Buckingham enter.)
York. <u>Lay hands upon these traitors and their trash.</u>
. . .

Buckingham. Away with them! let them be clapped
up close,
And kept asunder. You, madam, shall with us. . . .
(Exit Duchess guarded.)
Henry VI, Part Two, 1.4

(The 'gear' that the Duchess refers to is the
business at hand.

'Bandogs' are mastiffs who roam at night
guarding against interlopers.

York, the ultimate pragmatist, has no truck with
ritual, 'Lay hands upon these traitors and their trash,'
especially the kind that can adversely affect him. He
also knows he can get at the Duke of Gloucester by
apprehending his wife.

516

Will is a master of eerie scenes, made perfection in Macbeth and Hamlet. I'll wager that less-sophisticated Elizabethan audience members quaked when they heard: 'screech-owls cry and bandogs howl.')

(Buckingham lets King Henry know of the previous mischievous sorcery.)

Buckingham. Such as my heart doth tremble to unfold.
A sort of naughty persons, lewdly bent,
Under the countenance and confederacy
Of Lady Eleanor, the protector's wife,
The ringleader and head of all this rout,
Have practiced dangerously against your state,
Dealing with witches and with conjurers:
Whom we have apprehended in the fact;
Raising up wicked spirits from under ground,
Demanding of King Henry's life and death,
And other of your highness' privy council;
As more at large your grace shall understand.
Henry VI, Part Two, 2.1

(Line two in this speech is my favorite: 'A sort of naughty persons, lewdly bent.')

(York tells Warwick and Salisbury why, by lineage and through a tortuous tale, he should be king.)

York. Edward the Third, my lords, had seven sons:
The first, Edward the Black Prince, Prince of Wales;
The second, William of Hatfield, and the Third,
Lionel Duke of Clarence; next to whom
Was John of Gaunt, the Duke of Lancaster . .
Edward, the Black Prince died before his father,
And left behind him Richard, his only son,
Who, after Edward the Third's death reign'd as king . . .
Henry VI, Part Two, 2.2

(The lengthy exchange continues with Warwick and Salisbury contributing fawningly to the historical recitation, likely lifted from Holinshed. They conclude that York, aka Richard Plantagenet, deserves the crown, as they declare in unison, 'Long live our sovereign Richard, England's king!'
To which he replies:
York. We thank you, lords. But I am not your king
Till I be crowned, and that my <u>sword be stain'd</u>
<u>With heart-blood of the House of Lancaster</u> . . .)

518

Henry VI, Part Two, 2.2

(The hard-headed York knows, as the Wars of the Roses heads toward an inevitable showdown, that bloodshed, 'sword be stain'd,' in battles with the House of Lancaster, not proclamations, will win him the crown. 'Heart-blood is worth noting. It's called going for the kill.))

(Watched by her unsympathetic husband, the Duchess of Gloucester is marched through the streets escorted by officers.)

Duchess. Mail'd up in shame, with <u>papers on my back</u>,
   And follow'd with a rabble that rejoice
   To see my tears and hear my deep-felt groans.
   The ruthless flint doth cut my tender feet,
   And when I start, the envious people laugh,
   And bid me advised how I tread. . . .
   As he stood by whilst I, his forlorn duchess,
   Was made a wonder and a pointing-stock
   To every rascal idle follower.
   <u>Be thou mild and blush not at my shame,</u>
   <u>Nor stir at nothing till the axe of death</u>
   <u>Hang over thee, as, sure it will.</u>

Henry VI, Part Two, 2.4

('Papers on my back' refers to Elizabethan-age criminals who wore on their backs papers describing their crimes.

In the final three lines, the Duchess advises her husband, the Duke, that he won't be unperturbed for long, 'axe of death', is sure to get his attention.)

(The Duchess' prophecy begins to take shape, as King Henry asks Suffolk why his uncle the Duke of Gloucester is not in attendance.)

Suffolk. Well hath your highness seen into this duke;
And, had I first been put to speak my mind,
I think I should have told your grace's tale.
The duchess by his subornation,
Upon my life, began her devilish practices:
Or, if he were not privy to those faults,
Yet, by reputing of his high descent,
As next the king he was successive heir,
As such high vaults of his nobility,
Did instigate the <u>bedlam</u> brain-sick duchess
By wicked means to frame our sovereign's fall.
<u>Smooth runs the water where the brook is deep</u>;
And in his simple show he harbors treason.

The <u>fox</u> barks not when he would steal the <u>lamb</u>.
No, no, my sovereign; Gloucester is a man
Unsounded yet and full of deep deceit.
Henry VI, Part Two, 3.1

('Bedlam' was an Elizabethan London hospital for the reputedly insane. Cruel, revolting and counterproductive treatments like forced vomiting, designed to purge the insanity, were the norm.

'Smooth runs the water where the brook is deep,' like the more contemporary, 'still water runs deep,' are both derivations of a Latin saying that predated Shakespeare.)

(Despite Suffolk's warning, the inexperienced King Henry is unconvinced of Gloucester's disloyalty. Queen Margaret attempts to persuade him otherwise.)

King Henry. Our kinsman Gloucester is as innocent
From meaning treason to our royal person,
As is the <u>sucking lamb</u> or harmless dove:
The duke is virtuous, mild and too well given
To dream on evil or to work my downfall.
Queen Margaret. Ah, what's more dangerous than this fond affiance!
Seems he a dove? his feathers are but borrow'd,

For he's dispos'd as the hateful raven:
Is he a <u>lamb</u>? his skin is surely lent him,
For he's inclined as is the ravenous <u>wolf</u>.
Who cannot steal a shape that means deceit?
Take heed, my lord; the welfare of us all
Hangs on the cutting short that fraudful man.
Henry VI, Part Two, 3.1

(Suffolk introduces the 'lamb' metaphor and pairs it with 'fox' in the previous speech. King Henry, in his naiveté, uses 'sucking lamb' to protest Gloucester's innocence. The Queen goes Suffolk one better by matching 'lamb' and 'wolf.'

(In the presence of the king, York learns from Somerset that all the conquered French territories are lost. King Henry responds that it is, 'Cold news, but God's will be done!'

York answers in an aside.)

York. <u>Cold news</u> for me; for I had hope of France
As firmly as I hope for fertile England.
Thus are my <u>blossoms blasted in the bud,</u>
And caterpillars eat my leaves away;
But I will remedy this gear ere long,
Or sell my title for a glorious grave.

Henry VI, Part Two, 3.1

(As said in the Introduction, Will likes the 'bud' metaphor, often associated with 'canker.' 'Blossoms' and 'blasted' are ideal here in the context of York's hopes.

(Surrounded by his enemies, Gloucester blames them while making his case to the king.)

Gloucester. Ah, gracious lord, these days are dangerous:
　　Virtue is choked with vile ambition,
　　And charity chased hence by rancor's hand;
　　Foul subordination is predominant,
　　And equity exiled your highness' land.
　　I know their complot is to have my life;
　　And if my death might make this island happy,
　　And prove the period of their tyranny,
　　I would expend it with all willingness:
　　<u>But mine is made the prologue of their play;</u>
　　For thousands more, that yet suspect no peril,
　　Will not conclude their plotted tragedy.
　　<u>Beaufort's red sparkling eyes blab his heart's malice,</u>
　　And Suffolk's cloudy brow his stormy hate;

Sharp Buckingham unburthens with his tongue
The envious load that lies upon his heart;
And dogged York, that reaches at the moon,
Whose overweening arm I have plucked back,
By false accuse doth level at my life:
And you, my sovereign lady, with the rest,
Causeless have laid disgraces on my head,
And with your best endeavor have stirr'd up
My lifest liege to be my enemy:
Aye, all of you have laid your heads together
Myself had notice of your conventicles
And all to make away my guiltless life.
I shall not want false witness to condemn me.
Nor store of treasons to augment my guilt;
The ancient proverb will be well effected:
'A staff is quickly found to beat a dog.'
Henry VI, Part Two, 3.1

(The King gives in to Gloucester's opponents, and he is led away under guard. Before that, Gloucester utters some sharp turns of the phrase: 'But mine is made the prologue of their play,' 'Beaufort's red sparkling eyes blab his heart's malice,' 'And dogged York, that reaches at the moon.'

In the first example, 'prologue of their play' shows that Will's mind is brimming with playwriting. This is early in his touring company and London-based career. It is a period of enormous productivity, where he finishes up The Comedy of Errors, The Two Gentlemen of Verona, Titus Andronicus, the three parts of Henry VI, with Marlowe's help, and is likely hard at work on Richard III.

Gloucester even takes on Queen Margaret: 'And you, my sovereign lady . . .' In the interest of persuading the madly in love king, he should have omitted those lines.

(Regarding Gloucester's unwise gaffe,* the Queen, after the King exits the scene, answers Gloucester by calling for his death.

*'A gaffe is when a politician speaks the truth.' - Michael Kinsley.)

Queen Margaret. Free lords, <u>cold</u> snow melts with the sun's hot beams.
<u>Henry my lord is cold in great affairs,</u>
<u>Too full of foolish pity,</u> and Gloucester's show
Beguiles him, as the mournful crocodile
With sorrow snares relenting passengers,
Or as the snake roll'd in a flowering bank
With <u>shiny checker'd slough,</u> doth sting a child
That for the beauty thinks it excellent.
Believe me, my lords, were none more wise than I

And yet herein I judge mine own with good
<u>This Gloucester should be quickly rid the world</u>
To rid us from the fear we have of him.
Henry VI, Part Two, 3.1

(The slick Margaret tells the assembled lords that even though her husband, the king, is soft she isn't. The lords then argue about the best way to get rid of Gloucester.

Much enjoyed the uses of 'cold' in lines one and two and later in the speech with the snake's, 'shiny checker'd slough.')

(A messenger from Ireland enters the scene to report a new uprising that 'being green, there is great hope of help.' The lords argue about who should lead the relief army, and they settle on York.)

Cardinal Beaufort. My Lord of York, try what your fortune is.
The uncivil <u>kernes</u> of Ireland are in arms,
And temper clay with blood of Englishmen:
To Ireland you will lead a band of men,
Collected choicely, from each county some
And try your hap against the Irishmen?
York. <u>I will, my lord, so please his majesty</u> . . .

My brain more busy than the laboring spider
Weaves tedious snares to trap mine enemies.
Well, nobles, well, 'tis politicly done,
To send me packing with a host of men:
I fear me you but warm the starved snake,
Who, cherish'd in your breasts, will sting your
hearts.
'Twas men I lack'd, and you will give them me:
I take it kindly; yet be well assured
You put sharp weapons in a madman's hands.
While I in Ireland nourish a mighty band.
I will stir up England some black storm
Shall blow ten thousand souls to heaven or hell;
And this fell tempest shall not cease to rage
Until the golden circuit on my head,
Like to the glorious sun's transparent beams,
Do calm the fury of this mad-bred flaw,
And, for a minister of my intent,
I have seduced a headstrong Kentishman,
John Cade of Ashford,
To make commotion, as full well he can,
Under the title of John Mortimer.
In Ireland have I seen this stubborn Cade
Oppose himself against a troop of Kernes,
And fought so long, till that his thighs with darts
Were almost like a sharp-quilled porcupine;
And, in the end being rescued, I have seen

527

Him caper upright like a <u>wild Morisco,</u>
Shaking the bloody darts as he his bells.
Full often like a shag-hair'd crafty kerne,
Hath he conversed with the enemy,
And undiscover'd come to me again,
And given me notice of their villainies.
The devil here shall be my substitute;
For that John Mortimer, which is now dead,
In face, in gait, in speech, he doth resemble:
By this I shall perceive the common's mind,
How they affect the house and claim of York.
Say he be taken, rack'd and tortured,
I know no pain they can inflict upon him
Will make him say I moved him to those arms.
Say that he thrive, as 'tis great like he will,
Why, then from Ireland come I with my strength,
<u>And reap the harvest which that rascal sow'd;</u>
<u>For Humphrey being dead, as he shall be,</u>
<u>And Henry put apart, the next for me.</u>
Henry VI, Part Two, 3.1

(As you likely know or assumed, 'Kernes,' mentioned by Beaufort in line two, are Irish groups, usually, and in this case certainly, fighting men.

In line one of his speech, York agrees to lead the relief army, and likes the fact he's been given 'sharp weapons in a madman's hands,' which likely means

528

Jack Cade, to stir up a 'black storm.' York is not shy about wanting the 'golden circuit' on his head. I enjoy all the euphemisms for the crown in the plays: 'golden round,' 'diadem,' 'garland.'

York sees the proposed mutiny as an opportunity while away to mount a rebellion at home using the notorious Jack Cade as his surrogate. There is no hard-historical evidence that York stirred up the true Jack Cade Rebellion, in which his gang marched on London, only to be thrown out by the citizens. But it's a good plot device by Will, especially since Cade adopted the alias John Mortimer and York had Mortimer ancestry.

'Wild Morisco' refers to dancers of the time who wore bells and often danced energetically. Later, the name became 'Morris Dancers.'

Delighted by, 'And reap the harvest which that rascal sow'd,' followed by the York-style, sonnet-like, but ominous-sounding and predictive, couplet of the final two lines. 'For Humphrey being dead . . .')

(When young and weak King Henry learns from Suffolk of his Uncle Gloucester's death he faints, and they fear he is dead. Somerset says, 'Wring him by the nose.' That would surely get a live person's attention. Upon his revival, Suffolk tries to comfort Henry.)

King Henry. What, doth my Lord of Suffolk comfort me?

Came he right now to sing a raven's note,
Whose dismal tune bereft my vital powers;
And thinks he that the chirping of a wren,
By crying comfort from a hollow breast,
Can chase away the first-conceived sound?
Hide not thy poison with such sugar'd words;
Lay not thy hands on me; forbear, I say;
Their touch affrights me as a serpent's sting.
Thou baleful messenger, out of my sight!
Upon thy eye-balls murderous tyranny
Set in grim majesty, to fright the world.
Look not upon me, for thine eyes are wounding:
Yet do not go away: come, <u>basilisk</u>,
And kill the innocent gazer with thy sight;
For in the shade of death I shall find joy;
In life but double death, now Gloucester's dead.
Henry VI, Part Two, 3.2

(The king calls Suffolk 'basilisk' four lines before the speech ends. Basilisks are snakes from the legends. Both their gaze and their sting are reputed to cause death.

Following Gloucester's death, the various lords accuse each other of doing the deed. Meantime, Cardinal Beaufort has also died.)

(Despite Queen Margaret's protests, Suffolk ends up on a ship under guard going to exile in France along with other prisoners. The captain and a mate named Walter Whitmore attempt to extract ransoms from the captives. Before getting to the point, the captain goes off on a wonderful introductory harangue.)

> *Captain.* The gaudy, blabbing and remorseful day
> Is crept into the bosom of the sea;
> And now loud-howling <u>wolves</u> arouse the <u>jades</u>
> That drag the tragic melancholy night;
> Who, with their drowsy, slow and flagging wings,
> Clip dead men's <u>graves</u>, and from their misty jaws
> Breathe foul contagious darkness in the air.
> Therefore bring forth the soldiers of our prize;
> For, whilst our pinnace anchors in the Downs,
> <u>Here shall they make their ransom on the sand,</u>
> Or with their blood stain this discolour'd shore.
> Master, this prisoner freely give I thee;
> And thou that art his mate, make boot of this;
> The other, Walter Whitmore, is thy share.

Suffolk. Look on my George; I am a gentleman:
Rate me at what thou wilt, thou shalt be paid.
Whitmore. And so am I; my name is Walter
Whitmore.

How now! How starts'st thou? What, doth death
affright?
Suffolk. Thy name affrights me, in whose sound is
death.

A cunning man did calculate my birth,
And told me that by water I should die:
Yet let not this make thee be bloody-minded;
Thy name is Gaultier, being rightly sounded.
Whitmore. Gaultier or <u>Walter</u>, which it is, I care not:
Never did base dishonor blur our name
But with the sword we wiped away the blot . . .
Suffolk. Stay, Whitmore; for thy prisoner is a prince,
The Duke of Suffolk, <u>William de la Pole</u>.
Whitmore. Speak, captain, <u>shall I stab the forlorn
swain</u>?
Captain. <u>First let my words stab him</u>, as he hath me.
Suffolk. Base slave, thy words are blunt, and so art
thou.
Captain. Convey him hence and on our longboat's
side
<u>Strike off his head</u>.
Suffolk. Thou darest not, for thy own.
Captain. Yes, Pole.

Suffolk. Pole!

Captain. Pool! Sir Pool! Lord!

Aye, kennel, puddle, sink; whose filth and dirt

Troubles the silver spring where fertile England drinks.

Nor will I dam up this thy yawning mouth,

For swallowing the treasure of the realm:

The lips that kiss'd the queen shall sweep the ground;

And thou that smiledst at good Duke Humphrey's death

Against the senseless winds shalt grin in vain,

Who in contempt shall hiss at thee again:

And wedded be thou to the hags of hell,

For daring to affray a mighty lord

Unto the daughter of a worthless king,

Having neither subject, wealth, nor diadem.

By devilish policy art thou grown great,

And like ambitious Sylla, overgorged

With gobbets of thy mother's bleeding heart.

By thee Anjou and Maine were sold to France,

The false revolting Normans through thee

Disdain to call us lord, and Picardy

Hath slain their governors, surprised our forts,

And sent the ragged soldiers wounded home.

The princely Warwick, and the Nevils all,

Whose dreadful swords were never drawn in vain,

533

As hating thee, are rising up in arms:
And now the house of York, thrust from the crown
By shameful murder of a guiltless king,
And lofty proud encroaching tyranny,
Burns with revenging fire; whose hopeful colours
Advance our half-faced sun, striving to shine,
Under the which is writ 'Invitis nubibus.'
The commons here in Kent are up in arms:
And, to conclude, reproach and beggary
Is crept into the palace of our king,
And all by thee. Away! convey him hence.
Henry VI, Part Two, 4.1

(The captain's initial speech transitions from the sea in line two into 'wolves', 'horses' (jades) and 'graves' in lines three through six, but it all works.

The Spirit in the Duchess of Gloucester's séance predicted Suffolk's death by water; and, as prophesied, a man named 'Walter' Whitmore removed his head.

Note the reference to 'Sylla,' a Roman general and statesman from the first-century, B.C.

I especially liked the three lines below from the captain's final speech:
'Against the senseless winds shalt grin in vain,
Who in contempt shall hiss at thee again:
And wedded be thou to the hags of hell . . .'

(Scene two of Act Four switches to Blackheath where Jack Cade, Dick Butcher and other mob members are in the midst of their rebellion.

Cade brags on his background: 'My mother a Plantagenet.'

Dick Butcher, in asides, that must have had the groundlings rolling around, shoots them all down: 'I know her well; she was a midwife.'

Cade's speech below reminds me of the false promises of many contemporary politicians.)

Cade. Be brave, then; for your captain is brave, and vows reformation. There shall be in England seven halfpenny loaves sold for a penny: the three-hooped pot shall have ten hoops; and I will make it a felony to drink small beer: all the realm shall be in common; and in Cheapside shall my palfrey go to grass: and when I am king, as king I will be.

All. God save your majesty!

Cade. I thank you, good people: there shall be no money; all shall eat and drink on my score; and I will apparel them all in one livery, that they may agree like brothers and worship me their lord.

Dick. The first thing we do, let's kill all the lawyers.
Henry VI, Part Two, 4.2

(In my Amazon book 'Discovering Will's Lost Years,' Will apprentices to two Stratford lawyers one of whom is a fool. Mary Shakespeare, Will's mother, asks him how the work is going:

'The days in court are best. I prompt him as needed, as he is slow of memory and wit. I have given him measure for measure. Business lags, and he is sharp-tongued offending me and those who seek his counsel. He has talked of moving to Birmingham. I would not miss him, nor would his dwindling clientele.'

'We must not make a scarecrow of the law,
Setting it up to fear the birds of prey,
And let it keep one shape till custom make it
Their perch, and not their terror.'
Measure for Measure, 2.1

(Cade spouts amusing nonsense about learning. And before he starts the speech below, Cade refers to himself as Lord Mortimer.)

Cade. Thou has most traitorously <u>corrupted the youth of the realm by erecting a grammar school</u>: and whereas, before, our forefathers had no other books but the score and the tally, thou hast caused printing to be used, and, contrary to the king, his crown and dignity, thou has built a paper-mill. It will be proved to thy face that thou hast men about thee that usually <u>talk of a noun and a verb, and such abominable words as no Christian ear can endure to hear.</u>

Henry VI, Part Two, 4.8

(This light, satirical passage has drawn many observations. Here's another: Will benefited enormously from grammar school Latin and instruction in the classics. However, being gifted and creative, he must often have been bored to distraction by repetition and inept reciting by less-able and younger classmates. They sat on hard benches from six in the morning until six at night, speaking only in Latin, with lessons beaten into them, both literally and figuratively. With that kind of discipline, it is no wonder that Will could later sit and write for hours on end, with deeply calloused fingers stained with ink.

But, being Will, good-natured and easy, he pokes fun at it all, particularly the small minds that see no utility in education: 'talk of a noun and a verb, and such abominable words as no Christian ear can endure to hear.')

(Jack Cade's rebellion has been quashed, and he hides in the woods dreaming of salads.)

Cade. Fie on ambition! fie on myself, that have a sword, and yet am ready to famish! These five days have I hid me in these woods and durst not peep out, for all the country is laid for me; but now am I so hungry that if I might have <u>a lease of my life</u> for a thousand years I could stay no longer. Wherefore, on a brick wall I have climbed into this garden, to see if I can eat grass, or pick a sallet another while, which is not amiss to cool a man's stomach this hot weather. And I think this word 'sallet' was born to do me good: for many a time, but for a sallet, my brain-pan had been cleft with a brown bill; and many a time, when I have been dry and bravely marching, it has served me instead of a quart pot to drink in; and now the word sallet must serve me to feed on.
Henry VI, Part Two, 4.10

(Will writes even the supposed bad guys in ways that make them human and, in some instances, likable. Cade's willingness to trade, 'a new lease on life' for some food, like a salad, is funny.

He has stumbled into the garden of a gentleman named Alexander Iden who first challenges Cade, then agrees to feed him. Cade, being Cade, challenges

Iden and threatens to kill him and his five men leaving them all 'as dead as a door nail.' They fight and Cade dies. And Act Four ends with a comical skit that resolves the Jack Cade legend and gives us two clichés for the ages.

(Act Five opens with York back in England and in fighting form. The scene may well have been inspired by the 1578 return of Essex from Ireland and his failed coup against Queen Elizabeth the First.)

York. From Ireland thus comes York to gain his right,
   And pluck the crown from feeble Henry's head:
   Ring, bells, aloud; burn, bonfires, clear and bright,
   To entertain great England's lawful king.
   Ah, sancta majestas, who would not buy thee dear?
   Let them obey that know not how to rule;
   This hand was made to handle nought but gold.
   I cannot give due to my words,
   Except a sword of scepter balance it:
   A scepter shall it have, have I a soul,
   On which I'll toss the flower-de-luce of France.
   Henry VI, Part Two, 5.1

(In line five, York says that 'sancta majestas,' or the sacred and royal prerogative of kings, is worth any price.

He goes on to say that words are not enough, and he will use a scepter to toss the symbol, flower-de-luce,' of France.)

(Alexander Iden brings the head of Jack Cade to King Henry, and he is knighted and rewarded.

Opposing forces challenge the king, but he, 'Can we outrun the heavens? is bucked up by the steely Queen Margaret, 'What are you made of? You'll nor fight nor fly.'

We end the quotes from Act Five with a speech by Young Clifford whose father has just been killed by York. The son is a member of King Henry's party and a Lancaster.)

Young Clifford. My heart is turn'd to stone: and while 'tis mine,
  It shall be stony. York not our old men spares;
  No more will I their babes: tears virginal
  Shall be to me even as the dew to fire,
  And beauty that the tyrant oft reclaims
  Shall to my flaming wrath be oil and flax.
  Henceforth I will not have to do with pity:

Meet I an infant of the house of York.,
Into as many gobbets will I cut it
As <u>wild Medea young Absyrtus did</u>:
In cruelty will I seek out my fame.
Henry VI, Part Two, 5.2

(In one version of Greek mythology, Medea killed her brother and cut him into pieces.

York wins the battle of St. Alban's, and he and his followers are off to London to find King Henry.)

HENRY VI, PART THREE

(King Henry agrees to 'reign in quiet' and let York act as regent. This does not make Queen Margaret happy after Henry tells her that they, 'enforc'd me.

  She divorces Henry from their table and bed.)

Queen Margaret. <u>Enforc'd thee</u>! Art thou king, and will be forc'd?
  I shame to hear thee speak. Ah, timorous wretch!
  Thou hast undone thyself, thy son, and me;
  And given unto the house of York such head
  As thou shalt reign by their sufferance.
  To entail him and his heirs unto the crown,
  What is it, but to make thy sepulcher,
  And creep into it far before thy time?
  Warwick is chancellor and lord of Calais;
  Stern Falconbridge commands the narrow seas;
  The duke is made protector of the realm;
  And yet shalt thou be safe? such safety finds
  The trembling lamb environed with wolves.
  Had I been there, which am a silly woman,
  The soldiers should have toss'd me on their pikes
  Before I would have granted to that act.

But thou preferr'st thy life before thine honour:
And seeing thou dost, I here divorce myself
Both from thy table, Henry, and from thy bed,
Until that act of parliament be repeal'd,
Whereby my son is disinherited.
The northern lords that have forsworn thy colours
Will follow mine, if once they see them spread;
And spread they shall be, to thy foul disgrace,
And utter ruin of the house of York.
Thus do I leave thee. Come, son, let's away;
Our army is ready; come, we'll after them.
Henry VI, Part Three, 1.1

(Henry asks his son Edward to stay, and he refuses telling his father that he will see him 'when I return with victory from the field.'

(Margaret is well-equipped with an army of twenty-thousand men, and the Duke of York knows he is beaten.)

York. The army of the queen hath got the field:
My uncles both are slain in rescuing me;
And all my followers to the eager foe
Turn back, and fly, like ships before the wind,
Or lambs pursued by hunger-starved wolves.

My sons, God know what hath bechanced them:
But this I know, they have demean'd themselves
Like men born to renown by life or death.
Three times did Richard make a lane to me;
And thrice cried, Courage, father! fight it out!
And full as oft came Edward to my side,
With purple fanchion painted to the hilt
In blood of those that had encounter'd him:
And when the hardiest warriors did retire,
Richard cried, Charge! and give no foot of ground!
And cried, A crown, or else a glorious tomb!
A sceptre, or an earthly sepulchre!
With this, we charg'd again: but, out, alas!
We bodged again; as I have seen a swan
With bootless labour swim against the tide,
And spend her strength with over-matching waves.
Ah, hark! the fatal followers do pursue;
And I am faint, and cannot fly their fury:
And were I strong, I would not shun their fury:
The sands are number'd that make up my life;
Here must I stay, and here my life must end.
Queen Margaret. Where are your mess of sons to
back you now?
The wanton Edward and the lusty George?
And where's that valiant <u>crook-back prodigy,</u>
<u>Dicky</u>, your boy, that with his grumbling voice
Was wont to cheer his dad in mutinies?

544

York. She-wolf of France, but worse than wolves of France,

Whose tongue more poisons than the adder's tooth!

<u>How ill-seeming is it in thy sex.</u>

To triumph like an <u>Amazonian trull,</u>

Upon their woes whom fortune captivates . . . !

Thou art as opposite to every good

As the antipodes are unto us,

Or as the south to the Septentrion.

<u>O tiger's heart wrapped in a woman's hide!</u>

Queen Margaret. Off with his head, and set it on York gates;

So York may overlook the town of York.

Henry VI, Part Three, 1.4

(York's beaten, 'The army of the queen . . .'

We have 'lambs' and 'wolves' again. Will loves the metaphor.

We know who the 'crook-back prodigy, Dicky,' is.

York doesn't like being beaten in battle by a woman, 'How ill-seeming,' especially by an 'Amazonian trull' or prostitute.

The indelible 'tiger's heart' highlights York's speech.

Clifford stabs York, and just to make sure Margaret also stabs him, plus she also wants his head off for display. That's called getting in the last word.)

(The Wars of the Roses continues. In a face-to-face verbal confrontation, Margaret lets 'crook-back prodigy, Dicky,' Richard Plantagenet, know, in choice words, what she thinks of him.)

Queen Margaret. But thou art neither like thy sire nor dam;
But like a foul misshapen stigmatic,
Mark'd by the destinies to be avoided,
As venom toads, or lizards' dreadful stings
Henry VI, Part Three, 2.2

(Back to the battles. The York's are losing, and Richard tells his ally Warwick to buckle down and revenge his brother's death.)

Richard. Ah, Warwick, why hast thou withdrawn thyself?
Thy brother's blood the thirsty earth hath drunk,
Broach'd with the steely point of Clifford's lance;
And in the very pangs of death he cried,

Like to a dismal clangor heard from far,
Warwick, revenge! brother, revenge my death!
So, underneath the belly of their steeds,
That stain'd their fetlocks in his smoking blood,
The noble gentleman gave up the ghost.
Warwick. Then let the earth be drunken with our
blood:
I'll kill my horse, because I will not fly.
Why stand we like soft-hearted women here,
Wailing our losses, whiles the foe doth rage;
And look upon, as if the tragedy
Were played in jest by counterfeiting actors?
Here on my knee I vow to God above
I'll never pause again, never stand still,
Till either death hath closed these eyes of mine
Or fortune given me measure of revenge.
Edward. O Warwick, I do bend my knee with thine;
And in this vow do chain my soul to thine!
And ere my knee rise from the earth's cold face
I throw my hands, mine eyes, my heart to thee,
Thou setter-up and plucker-down of kings . . .
George. Yet let us all together to our troops
And give them leave to fly that will not stay;
And call them pillars that will stand to us;
And if we thrive, promise such rewards
As victors wear at the Olympian games.
Henry VI, Part Three, 2.3

(In Richard's speech on York's death, he tells how 'gave up the ghost,' another phrase still in use.

Warwick's 'let the earth be drunken with our blood' is notable, as is 'played in jest by counterfeiting actors.'

Richard's brother, Edward, later Edward IV, rewards us with 'Thou setter-up and plucker-down of kings.' I nearly broke into a round of applause when I first read that line.

George, soon to be Duke of Clarence, dips into antiquity with the 'Olympian games' reference. Note: The games were held in Greece for 12 consecutive centuries through the fourth-century A.D. The modern Olympics began in 1896.)

(Richard and his enemy, Clifford, meet on the battlefield to settle scores.)

Richard. Now, Clifford, <u>I have singled thee alone</u>:
Suppose this <u>arm</u> is for the Duke of York,
And this for Rutland; both bound to revenge,
Wert thou environ'd with a grazen wall.
Clifford. Now, Richard, I am with thee here alone:
<u>This is the hand that stabbed thy father York;</u>
And this the <u>hand</u> that slew thy brother Rutland;

And here's the <u>heart</u> that triumphs in their death,

And cheers these <u>hands</u> that slew thy sire and brother

To execute the like upon thyself;

And so, have at thee!

('I have singled thee alone' reminds us of Hal and Hotspur fighting an individual battle in Henry IV, Part 1.

They fight, but Clifford retreats when Warwick enters the scene.)

Richard. Nay, Warwick, single out some other chase;

For I myself will hunt this wolf to death.

Henry VI, Part Three, 2.4

(We're reminded in this passage that Will writes for playing, not reading. And this is a tempting scene for actors, particularly Elizabethan actors, where they can point to 'arms' and 'hearts' and 'hands' while mimicking the action. As we read earlier in this book, in Hamlet's instruction to the players, many period actors were not shy with the histrionics. And Will, through Hamlet's instruction to the players, makes clear the style of acting he prefers. 'Do not saw the air . . .'

(King Henry sits on a molehill wistfully commenting on the battle surging to and fro, 'sways it' and wishing for a simpler shepherd's life, 'a homely swain,' in the final line.)

King Henry. Now <u>sways it</u> this way, like a mighty sea
    Forc'd by the tide to combat with the wind;
    Now <u>sways it</u> this way, like a mighty sea
    Forc'd to retire by fury of the wind:
    Sometime the flood prevails, and then the wind;
    Now one the better, then another best;
    Both tugging to be victors, breast to breast,
    Yet neither conqueror nor conquer'd:
    So is the equal poise of this fell war.
    <u>Here on this molehill will I set me down.</u>
    To whom God will, there be the victory!
    <u>For Margaret my queen, and Clifford too,</u>
    <u>Have chid me from the battle;</u> swearing both
    They prosper best of all when I am thence.
    Would I were dead! if God's good will were so;
    For what in this world but grief and woe?
    O God! methinks it were a happy life
    To be no better than <u>a homely swain</u>.
    Henry VI, Part Three, 2.5

(As Will wrote in 'Twelfth Night,' 'Some are born great . . .' but not this hapless king whose warrior queen orders him off the battlefield, 'chid me from the battle.')

(The king is bathed in pathos, as fathers and sons suffer unbearable tragedy. We begin with a son and his father's corpse and end with a father carrying his son's dead body.)

Son. <u>Ill blows the wind that profits nobody</u>.
This man, whom hand to hand I slew in fight,
May be possessed with some store of crowns;
And I, that haply take them from him now,
May yet ere night yield both my life and them
To some man else, as this dead man doth me.
Who's this? O God! <u>It is my father's face,</u>
<u>Whom in this conflict I unawares hath kill'd.</u>
O heavy times, begetting such events!
From London by the king was <u>I press'd forth</u>:
My father, being the Earl of Warwick's man,
Came on the part of York, <u>press'd by his master</u>;
And I, who at his hands receiv'd my life,
Have by my hands of life bereaved him.
Pardon me, God, I knew not what I did!

And pardon father, for I knew not thee!
My tears shall wipe away these bloody marks;
And no more words till they have flow'd their fill.
King Henry. O piteous spectacle! O bloody times!
Whilst lions war, and battle for their dens,
Poor harmless <u>lambs</u> abide their enmity.
Weep, wretched man, I'll aid thee tear for tear;
And let our hearts and eyes, like civil war,
Be blind with tears, and break o'ercharged with grief.
   Father. Thou that so stoutly resisted me.
Give me thy gold, if thou hast any gold;
For I have bought it with an hundred blows.
<u>But let me see: is this our foeman's face?</u>
<u>Ah, no, no, no, it is mine only son!</u>
Ah, boy, if any life be left in thee,
Throw up thine eye! see, see what showers arise,
<u>Blown with the windy tempest of my heart,</u>
Upon thy wounds, that kill mine eye and heart!
O pity, God, this miserable age!
What stratagems, how fell, how butcherly,
Erroneous, mutinous, and unnatural,
This daily quarrel daily doth beget!
<u>O boy, thy father gave thee life too soon,</u>
<u>And hath bereft thee of thy life too late!</u>
   King Henry. The red rose and the white are on his face,

The fatal colours of our striving houses:
The one his purple blood right well resembles;
The other his pale cheeks, methinks, presenteth:
Wither one rose, and let the other flourish;
If you contend, a thousand lives must wither.
Henry VI, Part Three, 2.5

(Will's disdain for war is shown in this famous and heart-rending scene. But as Thomas Hardy wrote: 'War makes rattling good history.'

The son who mistakenly killed his father says, 'by the king was I press'd forth.' His father happened to be one of Warwick's men, the son became involved, and tragedy ensued.

'Windy tempest of my heart' helps express the father's grief at having killed his only son.

Neither of those slain was recognizable in the muck and confusion of close combat. 'It is my father's face, Whom in this conflict I unawares hath kill'd.'

Possibly a little levity may help after those gruesome orations. Forms of the 'Ill wind' mention in line one of the son's speech predate Shakespeare. Variations on the theme are used humorously about musical instruments, like the oboe and bassoon that are difficult to play: 'Winds nobody plays good.'

Clifford is killed. King Henry flees to Scotland and Queen Margaret to France.

Edward York usurps the crown becoming Edward IV. He appoints his brother Richard, Duke of Gloster and his brother George, Duke of Clarence.

Following amusing repartee that includes the brother's asides, King Edward asks the widow Lady Grey to be 'my love.' And she responds:

'I am too mean to be your queen,
And yet too good to be your concubine.'
So far, I like Lady Grey.'

Former King Henry is captured and imprisoned in the Tower. And we can't forget that he has a son named Edward, who is potentially a king. Nowadays, the announcement would be: We are approaching a turbulent zone, please fasten your seatbelts.)

(In soliloquy, Gloster, previously called Richard Plantagenet, is no less ambitious for the crown, but now with the seas getting rougher, he wonders whether he can navigate his way to port. And before you curse my cliché read on.)

Gloster. Ay, Edward will use women honorably.
Would he were wasted, marrow, bones, and all,
That from his loins no hopeful branch may spring,
To cross me from the golden time I look for!
And yet, between my soul's desire and me,

The lustful Edward's title buried,
Is Clarence, Henry, and his young son Edward,
And all the unlook'd for issue of their bodies,
To take their rooms, ere I can place myself:
A cold premeditation for my purpose!
Why, then, I do but dream on sovereignty,
And spies a far-off shore where he would tread;
Wishing his foot were equal with his eye;
And chides the sea that sunders him from thence
Saying he'll lade it dry to have his way:
So do I wish the crown, being so far off;
And so I chide the means that keep me from it;
And so I say I'll cut the causes off,
Flattering me with impossibilities.
My eyes too quick, my heart o'erweens too much,
Unless my hand and speech could equal them.
Well, say there is no kingdom, then, for Richard;
What other pleasures can the world afford?
I'll make my heaven in a lady's lap,
And deck my body in gay ornaments,
And witch sweet ladies with my words and looks.
O miserable thought! And more unlikely
Than to accomplish twenty golden crowns!
Why, love forswore me in my mother's womb:
And, for I should not deal in her soft laws,
She did corrupt frail nature with some bribe,
To shrink mine arm like a wither'd shrub;

To make an envious mountain on my back,
Where sits deformity to mock my body;
To shape my legs of an unequal size;
To disproportion me in every part,
Like to a chaos, or an unlick'd bear-whelp
That carries no impression like the dam.
And am I, then, a man to be belov'd?
O monstrous fault, to harbor such a thought!
Then, since this world affords no joy to me
But to command, to check, to o'erbear such
As are of better person than myself,
I'll make my heaven to dream upon the crown,
And whiles I live to account this world but hell,
Until my misshap'd trunk that bears this head
Be round empaled with a glorious crown.
And yet I know not how to get the crown,
For many lives stand between me and home:
And I, like one lost in a thorny wood,
That rents the thorns, and is rent with the thorns,
Seeking a way, and straying from the way;
Not knowing how to find the open air,
But toiling desperately to find it out,
Torment myself to catch the English crown:
And from that torment I will free myself,
Or hew my way out with a bloody axe.
Why, I can smile, and murder while I smile;
And cry content to that which grieves my heart;

And wet my cheeks with artificial tears,
And frame my face to all occasions.
I'll drown more sailors than the mermaid shall;
I'll slay more gazers than the basilisk;
I'll play the orator as well as <u>Nestor</u>;
Deceive more slily than Ulysses could;
And, <u>like a Sinon, take another Troy</u>:
I can add <u>colours to the chameleon</u>;
Change shapes with Proteus for advantages;
<u>And set the murderous Machiavel to school</u>;
Can I do this, and cannot get a crown?
Tut, were it further off, <u>I'll pluck it down</u>.
Henry VI, Part Three, 3.2

(Will prepares Richard Plantagenet, now Gloster, well to become Richard III. In this electrifying speech, written for an actor like Will's contemporary Richard Burbage, or Lawrence Olivier in the 20th-century. Gloster enumerates in ten early lines all the obstacles to the crown, 'the golden time,' and how might overcome them, including murdering several relatives and their offspring: 'A cold premeditation for my purpose!'

Then he gets realistic: 'My eyes too quick, my heart o'erweens too much,' and figures that doing all that is improbable, so he decides to become a lady's man: 'And witch sweet ladies with my words and looks.' But no, he has too many physical faults to be a lover: 'love forswore me in my mother's womb.' And then the self-aware description of his deformities.

So, first he laments the distance between his current state and his goal, 'Until my missap'd trunk' and 'me and home,' or crown.

Then he returns to scheming and congratulates himself on his ability to do what is needed to snatch the crown: 'hew my way out with a bloody axe,' and smile while he murders.

In his litany of planned evil, Gloster even likens himself to 'Nestor' the sagacious King in the Odyssey.

'And, like a Sinon, take another Troy' refers to the Greek soldier in the Aeneid who fools the Trojans into believing that the wooden horse is a gift, prompting the saying: 'Beware of Greeks bearing gifts.'

Amidst all the bragging, Gloster uses the chameleon to show how cannily he can change colors. The subtext here is that the chameleon is a lizard which perfectly fits Gloster's persona.

Amongst all the bragging about how clever he is, Gloster says he can 'set the murderous Machiavel to school,' and teach him a thing or two. Talk about chutzpah.

Will knows human nature and catalogs it perfectly in timeless poetry. This is storytelling at its best: set the plot, dress the characters' language appropriately, add a touch of humor within the outrageousness of it all, and cause the audience to ask themselves, 'Can this crazy, odd-looking Gloster actually pull this off?' 'I'll pluck it down.' You can see the attendees of Henry VI, Part Three pouring in to see Richard III.

(Mighty Warwick dies in battle, but not before a lamenting speech.)

Warwick. These eyes, that now are dimm'd with death's black vail,
  Have been as piercing as the mid-day sun,
  To search the secret treasons of the world:
  The wrinkles in my brow now fill'd with blood,
  Were liken'd oft to kingly sepulchres;
  For who liv'd king, but I could dig his grave?
  And who durst smile when Warwick bent his brow?
  Lo, now my glory smear'd in dust and blood!
  My parks, my walks, my manors that I had,
  Even now forsake me; and all of my lands
  Is nothing left me but my body's length!

Why, what is pomp, rule, reign, but earth and dust!
And, live we how we can, yet die we must.
Henry VI, Part Three, 5.2

(In Warwick's dying reminiscences, he boasts: 'For who liv'd king, but I could dig his grave?' To back this claim, we're reminded of York's son and future King Edward calling Warwick, 'Thou setter-up and puller-down of kings' in 2.3.

Warwick realizes that his power and possessions don't do him much good now: 'nothing left me but my body's length!' The speech's closing, sonnet-like couplet is worth rereading.)

(Self-crowned King Edward, brother of Gloster and Clarence, all sons of the now-dead Duke of York, is pleased with how the civil war is going against the House of Lancaster.

But while usurped King Henry languishes in the tower, his wife Queen Margaret has not been shilly-shallying in France.)

King Edward. Thus far our fortune keeps an upward course,
    And we are grac'd with wreaths of victory.
    But in the midst of this bright shining day

I spy a black, suspicious threatening cloud,
That will encounter with our glorious sun
Ere he attain his his easeful western bed:
I mean, my lords, those powers that the queen
Hath rais'd in Gallia have arriv'd our coast,
And, as we hear, march on to fight with us.
Henry VI, Part Three, 5.3

(Margaret has thirty thousand men. However, the ship is swamped en route from France, half are lost, and she loses the battle near Tewksbury. Her son Prince Edward, not to be confused with King Edward, is caught and suffers a trifecta of finality through stabbings in turn by Edward, Clarence and Gloster. Since the prince was an obstacle to Gloster's campaign for the crown, we're sure that he was happy to lend a hand: 'And there's for twitting me for perjury.' It sounds almost electronic-age.

Margaret is captured, asks to be killed, and Gloster, no surprise, offers to do it, 'Why should she live, to fill the world with words?'

King Edward intercedes: 'Hold, Richard, hold; for we have done too much,' and Margaret is taken to the Tower. Before leaving, she curses the murderers.)

Queen Margaret. And I will speak, that so my heart may burst.

Butchers and villains! bloody cannibals!

How sweet a plant that you have untimely cropp'd!

You have no children, butchers! If you had,

The thought of them would have stirr'd up remorse:

But if you ever chance to have a child,

Look in his youth to have him so cut off

As <u>deathsmen</u>, you have rid this sweet young price.

Henry VI, Part Three, 5.3

(I doubt that anything, including filicide, would stir up remorse in Gloster.

'Deathsmen,' applied to the three killers, strikes me as a unique and appropriate plural.

Margaret unsheathes her sword asking Clarence to use it on her. He refuses.

King Edward asks, 'Where's Richard gone?'

Clarence answers: 'To London, all in post; and, as I guess, to make a bloody supper in the Tower.'

'Bloody supper' caught my attention, as my eyes lingered on the phrase.)

(Gloster, Richard lll to be, confronts King Henry in the Tower.)

King Henry. But wherefore dos't thou come? Is't for my life?

Gloster. Think'st thou I am an executioner?

King Henry. And thus I prophecy, that many a thousand . . .

Shall rue the hour that ever thou wast born

The owl shrieked at thy birth, an evil sign;

The night-crow cried, aboding luckless time;

Dogs howl'd, and hideous tempest shook down trees;

The raven rook'd her on the chimney's top

And chattering pies in dismal discords sung

Thy mother felt more than a mother's pain,

And yet brought forth less than a mother's hope,

To wit,

An indigest deformed lump,

Not like the fruit of such a goodly tree.

Teeth hadst thou in thy head when thou wast born,

To signify thou cam'st to bite the world:

And if the rest be true which I have heard,

Thou cam'st——

Gloster. I'll hear no more: die, prophet, in thy speech:

For this, amongst the rest, was I ordain'd . . .

If any spark of life be yet remaining,

Down, down to hell and say I sent thee thither . . .

Indeed, 'tis true that Henry told me of;

For I have often hard my mother say
<u>I came into this world with my legs forward:</u>
Had I not reason, think ye, to make haste,
And seek their ruin that usurp'd our right:
The midwife wonder'd; and the women cried,
<u>O, Jesus bless us, he is born with teeth!</u>
And so I was, which plainly signified
That I should snarl, and bite, and play the dog.
Then, since the heavens have shap'd my body so,
Let hell make crook'd my mind to answer it.
<u>I have no brother, I am like no brother;</u>
And this word love, which graybeards call divine,
Be resident in men like one another,
And not in me: I am myself alone.
Clarence, beware; thou keep'st me from the light:
But I will sort a pitchy day for thee;
For I will buzz abroad such prophecies
That Edward shall be fearful of his life:
And then, to purge his fear, I'll be thy death.
King Henry and the prince his son are gone:
<u>Clarence, thy turn is next, and then the rest;</u>
Counting myself but bad till I be best.
I'll throw thy body in another room,
And triumph, Henry, in thy day of doom.
Henry VI, Part Three, 5.6

564

(Not taking any chances, Gloster stabs Henry again, 'If any spark of life.'

Then he agrees with Henry's insults: 'tis true that Henry told me of,' even quoting
the midwife at birth, 'O, Jesus bless us, he is born with teeth!' I've never seen the line played, but imagine that any good actor would follow the line with a large grin and a long take. I also liked, 'I came into this world with my legs forward.'

In Gloster, here's a Will creation who really understands and is comfortable with himself: 'I have no brother, I am like no brother.'

Characters keep topping themselves with insults flung at Gloster: 'indigest deformed lump' and 'thou cam'st to bite the world' from King Henry are two of my favorites from this passage.

With Henry's murder, Gloster knocks down another hurdle, 'Henry and the prince his son are gone,' and announces trusting Clarence's pending demise, 'Clarence, thy turn is next.'

Will, the undisputed master of the Elizabethan stage soliloquy, leads off the next play we quote from with one of his best introductory speeches.)

RICHARD III

(Note: As said earlier, soliloquizers always tell the absolute truth, as far as the characters know it, in Shakespeare or most Elizabethan playwriting. Soliloquies are, of course, dramatic devices told at the stage apron. No person would ever really say it.)

Gloster. Now is the winter of our discontent
Made glorious summer by this <u>sun of York</u>,
And all the clouds that lowered upon our house
In the deep bosom of the ocean buried.
Now are our brows bound with victorious wreaths,
Our bruised arms hung up for monuments,
Our stern alarums changed to merry meetings,
Our dreadful marches to delightful measures.
Grim-visaged war hath smoothed his wrinkled front,
And now, instead of mounting barbed steeds
To fright the souls of fearful adversaries,
He <u>capers nimbly</u> in a lady's chamber
To the <u>lascivious pleasing of a lute</u>.
But I that am not shaped for sportive tricks,
Nor made to court an <u>amorous looking-glass</u>;

I, that am rudely stamped and want love's majesty
To strut before a wanton ambling nymph;
I, that am curtailed of this fair proportion,
Cheated of feature by dissembling nature,
Deformed, unfinished, sent before my time
Into this breathing world, scarce half made up,
And that so lamely and unfashionable
That dogs bark at me as I halt by them
Why, I, in this weak piping time of peace,
Have no delight to pass away the time,
Unless to spy my shadow in the sun
And discant on mine own deformity,
And therefore, since I cannot prove a lover,
To entertain these fair well-spoken days,
I am determined to prove a villain
And hate the idle pleasures of these days.
Plots have I laid, inductions dangerous,
By drunken prophecies, libels, and dreams,
To set my brother Clarence and the king
In deadly hate the one against the other.
And if King Edward be as true and just
As I am subtle, false and treacherous,
This day should Clarence closely be mewed up,
About a prophecy, which says that G
Of Edward's heirs the murderer shall be.
Dive, thoughts, down to my soul, here Clarence
comes.

Richard III, 1.1, 1-42

(This play is in many ways a continuation of Henry VI. Gloster picks up his plotting where he left off in Part Three.

But here the writing is even better, with superb poetry, but not yet, even in structure, at the ethereal Hamlet, King Lear level. Not to complain, Richard III is riveting theater that even with its nearly four-hour length keeps audiences sitting upright, leaning in and focused.

'Sun of York,' second line, has two meanings: Richard, or Gloster, is the son of the Duke of York. He is also the shining sun of the House of York, at least in his own mind.

Regarding other lines, four gems stick: 'capers nimbly,' 'lascivious pleasing of a lute,' 'amorous looking-glass,' meaning he can't look into a mirror and have it like him, 'weak piping time of peace,' when shepherds at rest blow pipes.

If anyone in the audience has doubts about Gloster's intentions, the following line should dispel them: 'I am determined to prove a villain.' This was further confirmed as he congratulated himself on being 'subtle, false and treacherous.')

(Brakenbury, Warder of the Tower, came in to tell Gloster and Clarence that the king forbids private conferences. Gloster answers, and Clarence is led off followed by Lord Hastings who is also imprisoned.

'Shore's wife' is married to a London merchant and is King Edward's mistress.)

Gloster. You may partake of anything we say:
We speak no treason, man; we say the king
Is wise and virtuous; and his noble queen
Well struck in years, fair, and not jealous;
We say that <u>Shore's wife</u> hath a pretty foot,
A cherry lip, a bonny eye, a passing pleasing tongue;
And the queen's kindred are made gentlefolks:
How say you, sir? Can you deny all this?
Brakenbury. With this, my lord, myself have naught to do.
Gloster. Not to do with Mistress Shore? I tell thee, fellow,
He that doth naught with her, excepting one,
Were best to do it secretly alone.
(Clarence and Brakenbury leave.)
Gloster. Go, tread the path that thou shalt ne'er return,
<u>Simple, plain Clarence! I do love thee so</u>
<u>That I will shortly send thy soul to heaven,</u>

If heaven will take the present at our hands.
But who come here? The new deliver'd Hastings .

He cannot live, I hope; and must not die
Till George be pack'd with posthorse up to heaven.
I'll in, to urge his hatred more to Clarence,
With lies well steel'd with weighty arguments;
And, if I fail not in my deep intent,
Clarence hath not another day to live:
Which done, God take King Edward to his mercy,
And leave the world for me to bustle in!
For then I'll marry Warwick's youngest daughter:
What though I killed her husband and her father?
The readiest way to make the wench amends
Is to become her husband and her father:
The which will I; not all so much for love
As for another secret close intent,
By marrying her, which I must reach unto.
But yet I run before my horse to market:
Clarence still breathes; Edward still lives and reigns:
When they are gone, then must I count my gains.
Richard III, 1.1

(Anyone wanting a proper definition of cynical should reread this passage.

With a frigid heart and no conscience, Gloster speaks of his brother: Simple, plain Clarence! I do

570

love thee so/ That I will shortly send thy soul to heaven.'

'Leave the world for me to bustle in.' 'Bustle' is the ideal verb for a malevolent schemer planning to marry Lady Anne whose husband and his father Gloster has recently killed.

But wait, Gloster tells himself, 'I run before my horse to market.' His brothers, Clarence and Edward, still live. 'When they are gone, then must I count my gains.' Don't get ahead of yourself. Get the family executions done and marry Anne before celebrating.)

(Lady Anne accompanies the open coffin of her dead husband's father, King Henry VI. She is confronted by Gloster who stops the hearse after threatening the attending guard.

Despite being preposterous and tipping the line into implausibility, the scene, thanks to Will's brilliant writing and a necessary suspension of audience disbelief, somehow works.

And work it did in Laurence Olivier's 1955 film adaptation of Richard III. Estimable strength was added by Claire Bloom, John Gielgud, Cedric Harwicke and Ralph Richardson in key roles. The music was among moviemaking's top scores.

Bloom and Olivier were sensational in the scene
that follows.)

Anne. Set down, set down your honorable load,
If honor may be shrouded in a hearse,
Whilst I obsequiously lament
The untimely fall of virtuous Lancaster.
Poor key-cold figure of a holy King!
Pale ashes of the House of Lancaster,
Thou bloodless remnant of that royal blood!
Be it lawful that I invoke thy ghost
To hear the lamentations of poor Anne,
Wife to thy Edward, to thy slaughtered son,
Stabbed by the selfsame hands that made these
wounds!
Lo, in these windows that let forth thy life
I pour the helpless balm of my poor eyes.
Cursed be the hand that made these fatal holes!
Cursed be the heart that had the heart to do it! . . .
Behold this pattern of thy butcheries.
O gentlemen, see, see! Dead Henry's wounds
Open their congealed mouths and breathe afresh.
Blush, blush thou lump of foul deformity,
For 'tis thy presence that exhales this blood
From cold and empty veins where no blood dwells;
Thy deed, inhuman and unnatural,
Provokes this deluge most unnatural.

572

O God, which this blood mad'st, revenge his death!

O earth, which this blood drink'st, revenge his death!

Either heaven with lightning strike the murderer dead,

Or earth, gape open wide and eat him quick,
As thou dost swallow up this good King's blood,
Which his hell-governed arm hath butchered!
Gloster. Lady, you know no rules of charity,
Which renders good for bad, blessings for curses.
Anne. Villain, thou know'st no law of God or man.
No <u>beast</u> so fierce but knows some touch of pity.
Gloster. I know none, and therefore am no <u>beast</u>.
Anne. Oh, wonderful when devils tell the truth!
Gloster. More wonderful when angels are so angry.

. . .

Your beauty was the cause of that effect;
To undertake the death of all the world,
So that I might live one hour in your sweet bosom.

. . .

Lo, here I lend thee this sharp-pointed sword;
Which if thou please to hide in this true breast,
And let the soul forth that adoreth thee,
I lay it naked to thy deadly stroke,
And humbly beg the death upon my knee.
Nay, do not pause; for I did kill King Henry,
But 'twas thy beauty that provoked me.

Nay, now dispatch; 'twas I that stabbed young Edward,
But 'twas thy heavenly face that set me on.
Take up the sword again, or take up me.
Anne. Arise, dissembler: thou I wish thy death,
I will not be thy executioner. (Exits.)
Gloster. Was ever woman in this humor woo'd?
Was ever woman in this humor won?
I'll have her, but I will not keep her long.
What! I, that killed her husband and his father,
To take her in her heart's extremest hate,
With curses in her mouth, tears in her eyes,
The bleeding witness of her hatred by
Having God, her conscience, and these bars against me,
And I nothing to back my suit at all
But the plain Devil and dissembling looks,
And yet to win her, all the world to nothing!
Ha!
Hath she forgot already that brave Prince,
Edward, her lord, whom I, some three months since,
Stabbed in my angry mood at Tewksbury?
A sweeter and a lovelier gentleman,
Framed in the prodigality of nature,
Young, valiant, wise, and no doubt right royal,
The spacious world cannot again afford.

And will she yet debase her eyes on me,
That cropped the golden prime of this sweet Prince
And made her widow to a woeful bed
On me, who all not equals Edward's moiety?
On me, that halt an am unshapen thus?
My dukedom to a beggarly denier,
I do mistake my person all this while.
Upon my life, she finds, although I cannot,
Myself to be a marvelous proper man.
I'll be at charges for a looking-glass,
And entertain some score or two of tailors,
To study fashions to adorn my body.
Since I am crept in favor with myself,
I will maintain it with some little cost.
But first I'll turn yon yellow in his grave
And then return lamenting to my love.
Shine out, fair sun, till I have bought a glass,
That I may see my shadow as I pass.
Richard III, 1.2

(In Elizabethan days, curses were thought to come true. In Anne's first speech, she curses the murderer of her husband and his father several times and knows that Gloster killed them both, 'stabbed by the self-same hands,' and 'Blush, blush thou lump of foul deformity.'

Excellent wordplay is found in Gloster and Anne's 'beast' exchange.

Gloster offers Anne his 'sharp-pointed' sword to stab him and revenge his murder of her husband and father-in-law. Gloster places the sword point against his chest and asks Anne to use it, she moves to kill him twice and then drops the sword. 'I will not be thy executioner.' Gloster knows he has won and offers her a ring which she puts on. In the Olivier film, Richard III, Anne goes into her home, and Richard follows her.

Then the famous 'Was ever woman . . .'

Followed by his plans to get rid of her, 'I will not keep her long.'

Gloster is so proud of himself he announces that he'll be 'at charges for a looking glass.'

And the preposterous, 'Shine out fair sun . . . where he will use his newly-purchased mirror to ogle his shadow.)

(The illness of King Edward IV, Gloster's brother, continues. Queen Elizabeth, nee Lady Grey, Edward's wife, enters the scene and comments on matters of succession. As she speaks to her brother, Lord Rivers, and her son, Lord Grey by a previous marriage, she is rightfully concerned that should her husband die their young son will become Edward V, and Gloster will be his protector.)

> *Queen Elizabeth.* Oh, he is young, and his minority
> I put into the trust of Richard Gloucester,
> A man that loves not me, nor none of you.
> *Rivers.* Is it concluded that he shall be Protector.
> *Queen Elizabeth.* It is determined, not concluded yet.
> But so it must be if the King miscarry.

(Gloucester enters and the Queen remarks on his ill intentions toward her family: 'The ground of your ill-will, and to remove it.')

> *Gloster.* I cannot tell. The world is grown so bad,
> That wrens make prey where eagles dare not perch:
> Since every Jack became a gentleman,
> There's many a gentle person made a Jack.

(In Richard's typical doubletalk when confronted, he says, don't blame me, the world is gone so mad that even wrens are predators where eagles dare not go. And an ordinary man (Jack) and a more privileged man can trade places.

Former Queen Margaret enters the scene like one of the fates or a chorus. She has lost the battle, but not her clever, bitter and vitriolic tongue. She curses all in attendance, including Queen Elizabeth. But first she goes after Gloster.)

Queen Margaret. Out devil! I remember them too well.
  Thou slewest my husband Henry in the Tower.
  And Edward, my poor son, at Tewksbury. . . .
  Hear me, you <u>wrangling pirates</u>, that fall out
  In sharing that which you <u>pilled from me</u>!
  Which of you trembles not that looks on me?
  If not that, I being queen, you bow like subjects,
  Yet that, by you deposed, you quake like rebels?
  O gentle villain, do not turn away.
Gloster. Foul wrinkled witch, which mak'st thou in my sight?
Margaret. What! Were you snarling all before I came,
  Ready to catch each other by the throat,
  And turn you all your hatred now on me?
  Did York's dead curse prevail so much with Heaven
  That Henry's death, my lovely Edward's death,
  Their kingdom loss, my woeful banishment,
  Could all but answer for that peevish brat?
  Can curses pierce the clouds and enter Heaven?
  Why then, give way, dull clouds, to my quick curses!

If not by war, <u>by surfeit die your King</u>,
As ours by murder, to make him a King!
Edward thy son, which is now Prince of Wales,
For Edward, my son, which was Prince of Wales,
Die in his youth by like untimely violence!
Thyself a Queen, for me that was a Queen,
Outlive thy glory, like my wretched self!
Long mayst thou live to wail thy children's loss,
And see another, as I see thee now,
Decked in thy rights, as thou art stalled in mine!
Long die thy happy days before thy death,
And after many lengthened hours of grief,
Die neither mother, wife, or England's Queen!
Rivers and Dorset, you were standers-by,
And so wast thou, Lord Hastings when my son
Was stabbed with bloody daggers. God, I pray Him
That none of you may live your natural age,
<u>But by some unlook'd accident cut off</u>!

Gloster. Have done thy charm, thou hateful withered hag!

Queen Margaret. Thou elvish-marked, abortive rooting hog!
Thou that wast sealed in thy nativity
<u>The slave of nature and the son of hell!</u>
Thou slander of thy mother's heavy womb!
Thou loathed issue of thy father's loins!
Thou rag of honor! Thou detested-

Gloster. <u>Margaret.</u>

Margaret. <u>Richard!</u>

Queen Elizabeth. <u>Thus have you breathed your curse against yourself.</u>

Margaret. Poor painted Queen, vain flourish of my fortune!

Why strew'st sugar on that <u>bottled spider</u>

Whose deadly web ensnareth thee about?

Fool, fool! Thou whet'st a knife to kill thyself.

The tine will come for that thou shalt wish for me

To help thee curse that poisonous <u>bunchbacked toad</u> . . .

Live each of you the subjects of his hate,

And he to yours, <u>all of you to God's!</u>

Gloster. But then I sigh, and with a piece of Scripture

Tell them that God bids us do good for evil.

And thus I clothe my naked villainy

<u>With old odd ends stolen out of Holy Writ,</u>

And seem a saint when I most play the devil.

But, soft! <u>Here come my executioners.</u>

Richard III, 1.3

(In Margaret's line-four tirade 'You wrangling pirates' is fitting before the next line, 'pilled from me,' of. She uses 'pilled' meaning pillaged.

'By surfeit die your King' is apt since Edward IV did die of overindulgence.

'Die in his youth by like untimely violence!' is another curse that will come true, since, like Margaret's son, Edward V does die.

Among all of the aspersions Margaret casts at Gloster, 'The slave of nature and the son of hell!' jumps off the page as an inventive disparagement. Gloster, she says, was stained at birth with his malformations.

When Gloster and Queen Margaret exchange each other's names: 'Margaret,' 'Richard' they are in the process of directly cursing each other. Queen Elizabeth picks up on this: 'Thus have you breathed your curse against yourself.'

'Bottled spider' and 'bunchbacked toad' refer to the deformity of Gloster's spine, making his rounded shape resemble a bottle. Additional meanings could be construed, like hunchbacked as a synonym for 'bunchbacked.'

In Margaret's final line, 'all of you to God's!' she assumes the role of one of God's executioners. It elevates the play from mere melodrama. Gloster has his own take on religion with 'old odd ends stolen out of Holy Writ' and 'Here come my executioners.')

(Clarence, imprisoned in the Tower, tells his keeper, Brakenbury, of a dream. Since it includes his brother Gloster, the dream, no surprise, is frightening and ill-omened.)

Clarence. Methought that I had broken from the Tower,
    And was embark'd to cross to Burgundy;
    And, in my company, my brother Gloster;
    Who from my cabin tempted me to walk
    Upon the hatches: thence we look'd toward England,
    And cited up a thousand heavy times,
    During the wars of York and Lancaster,
    That had befallen us. As we pac'd along
    Upon the giddy footing of the hatches,
    Methought that Gloster stumbled; and in falling,
    Struck me, that thought to stay him, overboard
    Into the tumbling billows of the main.
    O Lord! methought what pain it was to drown!
    What dreadful noise of water in mine ears!
    What sights of ugly death within mine eyes!
    Methought I saw a thousand fearful wrecks;
    A thousand men that fishes gnaw'd upon;
    Wedges of gold, great anchors, heaps of pearl,
    Inestimable stones, unvalu'd jewels,
    All scatter'd in the bottom of the sea:

Some lay in dead men's skulls; and in those holes
Where eyes did once inhabit there were crept,
As 'twere in scorn of eyes, reflecting gems,
That woo'd the slimy bottom of the deep,
And mock'd the dead bones that lay scatter'd by. .
 . .

O, then began the tempest to my soul!
I pass'd, methought, the melancholy flood
With that grim ferryman which poets write of,
Unto the kingdom of perpetual night.
The first that there did greet my stranger soul
Was my great father-in-law, renowned Warwick;
Who cried aloud, What scourge for perjury
Can this dark monarchy afford false Clarence?
And so he vanish'd: then came wandering by
A shadow like an Angel with bright hair
Dabbled in blood; and he shriek'd out aloud,
Clarence is come, false, fleeting, perjur'd Clarence,
That stabb'd me in the field by Tewksbury;
Sieze on him, Furies, take him to your torments!
With that, methought, a legion of foul fiends
Environ'd me, and howled in mine ears
Such hideous cries that, with the very noise,
I trembling wak'd, and for a season after
Could not believe but that I was in hell,
Such terrible impression made my dream.

(Think back to the ending of the previous scene, when Gloster said, 'Here come my executioners.' Well, come they did to stab Clarence.)

First Murderer. Take that, and that: if all this will not do,
I'll drown you in the <u>malmsey-butt </u>within.
Richard III, 1.4

(The sense-appealing 'giddy footing of the hatches,' 'woo'd the slimy bottom of the deep,' and 'a thousand men that fishes gnaw'd upon' are worth rereading for context.

The 'grim ferryman' refers to Charon in Greek mythology. He ferried the dead across the River Styx to Hades.

In the 1939 film, "Tower of London, loosely based on Richard III, the actor Vincent Price, playing Clarence, was drowned in a malmsey-butt. In the Hollywood version, it was a large barrel filled not with sweet wine but with Coca Cola.)

(At the opening of Act Two, sickly King Edward is happy because court members seem to be settling their differences. Then Gloster shows up.)

King Edward. Is Clarence dead? The order was reversed.

Gloster. But he, poor soul, by your first order died.
And that a <u>winged Mercury</u> did bear.
Some <u>tardy cripple</u> bore the countermand,
That came too lag to see him buried.
God grant that some, less noble and less loyal,
Nearer in bloody thoughts but not in blood,
Deserve not worse than wretched Clarence did,
And yet go current from suspicion!
Richard III, 2.1

(As always, Gloster is ready with a head-scratching, don't-blame-me-you-gave-the-order, and difficult-to-refute answer.

He counterpoints 'winged Mercury,' the mythological messenger of the gods, with 'tardy cripple,' no doubt subtly referring to himself.'

We've all met people like Gloster, especially in business, but none near so crafty. Dealing with them is like trying to win in Las Vegas. I read of a man who grew up in Vegas, left at 16 and didn't come back for many years. Upon returning and riding into the city from the airport, he saw a billboard announcing, 'We pay 97 cents on every dollar.' He thought: *Now that's my kind of town.*

(Will writes for actors, but more important he writes for audiences. He uses dialogue to refresh where we've been, where we are, and where we are going in the play. In the following extracts chosen for their relevance and language, Queen Elizabeth, husband of King Edward IV who is now dead, commiserates with the Duchess of York, mother to Edward IV, murdered Clarence, and Gloster.)

Queen Elizabeth. Ah, who shall hinder me to wail and <u>weep</u>,
To chide my fortune, and torment myself?
I'll join with black despair against my soul,
And to myself become an enemy.
Duchess of York. But now <u>two mirrors of his princely semblance</u>
<u>Are crack'd in pieces</u> by malignant death,
And I for comfort have but one false glass,
Which grieves me when I see my shame in him.
Thou art a widow; yet thou art a mother,
And hast the comfort of thy children left:
But death hath snatched my husband from mine arms,
And pluck'd two crutches from my feeble hands,
Clarence and Edward. O, what cause have I,

Thine being but a moiety of my moan,
To overgo thy woes and drown thy cries? . . .
Was never a mother had so dear a loss!
Alas, I am the mother of those griefs!
Their woes are parcell'd, mine are general.
She for an Edward <u>weeps</u>, and so do I;
I for a Clarence <u>weeps</u>, so doth not she:
These babes for Clarence <u>weep</u>, and so do I;
I for an Edward <u>weep</u>, so do not they:
Alas, you three, on me, threefold distress'd,
Pour all your tears! <u>I am your sorrow's nurse,</u>
And I will pamper it with lamentation.
Richard III, 2.2

(I hope you enjoyed the 'two cracked mirrors' metaphor in the first three lines of the Duchess's speech as much as I did.

The 'weep' juxtapositions are nicely balanced.

And since the Duchess is talking with and to Clarence's children, 'I am your sorrow's nurse' is poignant.)

(Queen Elizabeth and the Duchess of York have just learned that Lord Rivers and Lord Grey, brother and son, respectively, of the Queen are prisoners and have been sent to Pomfret by Gloster. Pomfret is far north, and few who go there ever come back.)

Queen Elizabeth. Ah me, I see the <u>downfall of our house</u>!
 <u>The tiger now hath seized the gentle hind;</u>
 Insulting tyranny begins to jet
 Upon the innocent and aweless throne:
 Welcome, destruction, blood, and massacre!
 I see, as in a map, the end of all.
Duchess of York. Accurs'd and unquiet wrangling
 How many of you have mine eyes beheld?
 My husband lost his life to get the crown;
 And often up and down my sons were toss'd,
 For me to joy and weep their gain and loss:
 And being seated, and domestic broils
 Clean over-blown, themselves, the conquerors,
 Make war upon themselves; brother to brother,
 Blood to blood, self against self: O, preposterous
 And frantic outrage, end thy damned spleen;
 O let me die, to look on death no more.
Richard III, 2.4

(Queen Elizabeth is right on seeing 'the downfall of our house,' as Gloster is cleaning it out: 'The tiger now hath seized the gentle hind.'

It's interesting to contrast the 'downfall' line with the queen's lines from act one, scene three:
'Would all were well! But that will never be.
I fear our happiness is at the highest.')

(With the death of Edward IV, his son Edward, Prince of Wales, is slated to become Edward V. He is now in the hands of Gloster, his protector, who wants to get rid of him, but for now gives the Prince tainted advice.)

Prince. I want more uncles here to welcome me.
Gloster. Sweet Prince, the untainted virtue of your years
Hath not yet dived into the world's deceit.
No more can you distinguish of a man
Than of his outward show, which, God He knows,
Seldom or never jumpeth with the heart.
Those uncles which you want were dangerous;
You grace attended to their sugared words,
But looked not on the poison of their hearts.
God keep you from them, and from such false friends.
Prince. <u>God keep me from false friends! But they were none</u>.
Richard III, 3.1

(The Prince says my uncles were not false, are you?)

(The action shifts to the bloody Tower where
Gloster, accompanied by Buckingham his co-
conspirator, tells the Prince that he will be safe.)

Prince. Say, Uncle Gloster, <u>if our brother come,</u>
Where shall we sojourn till our coronation?
Gloster. Where it seems best unto your royal self.
If I may counsel you, some day or two
Your Highness shall repose yourself at the Tower.
Then where you please, and shall be thought most
fit
<u>For your best health and recreation.</u>
Prince. I do not like the Tower, of any place.
Did Julius Caesar build that place, my lord?
Buckingham. He did, my gracious lord, begin that
place,
Which since succeeding ages have re-edified.
Prince. Is it upon record, or else reported
Successively from age to age, he built it?
Buckingham. Upon record, my gracious lord.
Prince. But say, my lord, if it were not registered,
Methinks the truth should live from age to age
As 'twere retailed to all posterity,

590

Even to the general all-ending day.

Gloster. (Aside.) <u>So wise so young, they say, do never live long</u>.

Prince. And if I live until I be a man,

I'll win our ancient right in France again,

Or die a soldier, as I lived a king.

Gloster. (Aside.) <u>Short summers likely have a forward spring</u>.

Richard III, 3.1

('If our brother come,' means the Duke of York, who does come to the Tower, and is also young and doomed.

'For your best health and recreation' may be the most ominous in Gloster's catalog of counsel to the Prince. This is consummate evil talking. More follows.

The concluding Gloster aside, 'Short summers likely have a forward spring' posits that since the Prince developed rapidly he isn't likely to live long. Confirming Gloster's earlier aside, 'So wise so young, they say, do never live long,')

(Lords Rivers and Grey arrive at Pomfret in the north for their executions. Will gives Rivers a good parting speech, and we have a review of Queen Margaret's curses...)

591

Rivers. O Pomfret, Pomfret! O thou bloody prison,
Fatal and ominous to noble peers!
Within the guilty closure of thy walls
<u>Richard the Second here was hacked to death;</u>
And for more slander to thy dismal seat,
We give thee up our guiltless blood to drink.
Grey. Now Margaret's curse has fall'n upon our heads,
For standing by when Richard stabbed her son.
Rivers. Then cursed she Hastings, then cursed she Buckingham,
Then cursed she Richard. Oh, remember, God,
To hear her prayers for them, as now for us!
And for my sister and her princely sons,
<u>Be satisfied, dear God, with our true blood.</u>
Which, as thou know'st, unjustly must be spilt.
Richard III, 3.3

(In line four of Rivers' opening speech, he refers to 'Richard the Second here was hacked to death.'

In Henry IV, Part 2, 4.4, dying King Henry tells his son Prince Hal that he, as Bolingbroke, usurped the crown, 'by what by-paths and indirect crooked ways' from Richard II. And he hopes that Hal will have 'better quiet, better opinion, better confirmation.'

Back to Richard III, the play at hand: when Rivers pleads, 'Be satisfied, dear God, with our true blood,' he is hoping that God will not demand that his sister, Queen Elizabeth, die as well.

(Now on to Hastings' demise, with dialogue from Buckingham, Gloster and Hastings, who presumes to think he can speak for Richard on the crowning of a new king.)

Buckingham. Had you not come upon your <u>cue</u>, my lord,
    William Lord Hastings had pronounced your <u>part,</u>
    I mean, your voice, for crowning of the King.
Hastings. Marry, that with no man here he is <u>offended</u>
    For, were he, he had <u>shown it in his looks.</u>

(Gloster has just entered the scene. Note the stage use of 'cue' and 'part' in Buckingham's lines.
    Hastings doesn't know he's condemned because Gloster doesn't look offended, but his mood darkens.)

Gloster. I pray you all, tell me what they deserve
    That do conspire my death with devilish plots

Of <u>damned witchcraft</u>, and that have prevailed
Upon my body with their hellish charms?
Hastings. The tender love I bear your Grace, my
lord,
Makes me most forward in this noble presence
To doom the offenders, whatsoever they be.
I say, my lord, that they deserved death.
<u>*Gloster.*</u> Then be your eyes the witness of this ill.
See how I am bewitched. Behold, mine arm
Is like a blasted sapling, withered up.
And this is Edward's wife, that monstrous witch,
Consorted with that harlot strumpet Shore,
That by their witchcraft thus have marked me.
<u>*Hastings.*</u> If they have done this thing, my gracious
lord—
Gloster. If! Thou protector of this damned
strumpet,
Tellest thou me of "if"? Thou art a traitor.
Off with his head! Now, by Saint Paul I swear,
<u>I will not dine</u> until I see the same.
Hastings. Woe, woe for England! Not a whit for me,
For I, too fond, might have prevented this.
Stanley did dream the boar did raze his helm,
But I disdained it, and did scorn to fly.
Three time today my <u>foot-cloth horse</u> did stumble,
And startled when he looked upon the Tower,
As oath to bear me to the slaughterhouse.

Oh, now I want the priest that spake to me.
I now repent I told the pursuivant,
As 'twere triumphing at mine enemies,
How they at Pomfret bloodily were butchered
And I myself secure in grace and favor.
O Margaret, Margaret, now thy heavy curse
Is lighted on poor Hastings' wretched head!
Sir Richard Ratcliff. Dispatch, my lord. The Duke
would be at dinner.
Make a short shrift. He longs to see your head.
Hastings. O bloody Richard! Miserable England!
I prophesy the fearfull'st time to thee
That ever wretched age hath looked upon.
Come, lead me to the block, bear him my head.
They smile at me that shortly shall be dead.
Richard III, 3.4

(Gloster speaks of witchcraft in line three. As said earlier, Elizabethans believed in it. It appears from his writing that Will leaned toward humanism, so I wonder if he believed in witchcraft.

'Foot-cloth horse' refers to the decorative material draping the sides of a horse.

Gloster said, 'I will not dine' until Hastings head is off. Then, the well-named Ratcliff, one of his henchmen, tells Hastings, 'The Duke would be at dinner. Make a short shrift. He longs to see your head.' Appetizing combination, heads lopped off and dinner. 'Make a short shrift,' or be quick and say your prayers before you die, originated with Shakespeare. It became part of the language as a generic phrase for make quick work of it.

The egregious Ratlcliff was also at Pomfret when Lord Rivers spoke his lament. Ratcliff said: 'Make haste; the hour of death is expiate.' Since the condemned were being hastened to the block, the man was thoughtful to urge prayers.

(Gloster and Buckingham enter the Tower ready to fake a little fear. Gloster tells Buckingham to act jittery, 'Come , cousin . . .'

The Lord Mayor joins the scene, then Ratcliff with Lovel and Catesby, other conspirators.)

Gloster. <u>Come, Cousin, canst thou quake and change thy color,</u>
  Murder thy breath in middle of a word,
  And then begin again, and stop again,
  As if thou wert distraught and mad with terror?
Buckingham. Tut, I can <u>counterfeit the deep tragedian,</u>
  Speak and look back, and pry on every side,
  Tremble and start at wagging of a straw,

Intending deep suspicion. Ghastly looks
Are at my service, like enforced smiles,
And both are ready in their offices
At any time, to grace my stratagems.
Gloster. Look to the drawbridge there!
Buckingham. Hark! A drum.
Gloster. Catesby, o'erlook the walls.
Look back, defend thee, here are enemies.
Buckingham. God and our innocency defend and
guard us!

Gloster. Be patient, they are friends, Ratcliff and
Lovel.

Lovel. Here is the head of that ignoble traitor,
The dangerous and unsuspected Hastings.
Gloster. So dear I loved the man that I must weep.
I took him for the plainest harmless creature
That breathed upon this earth a Christian;
Made him my book, wherein my soul recorded
The history of all her secret thoughts.
So smooth he daubed his vice with show of virtue
That his apparent open guilt omitted
I mean, his conversation with Shore's wife,
He lived from all attainder of suspect.
Buckingham. Well, well, he was the covert'st
sheltered traitor
That ever lived.
Would you imagine or almost believe,

Were't not that, by great preservation,
We live to tell it to you, the subtle traitor
This day had plotted in the council house
To murder me and my good Lord of Gloucester.
Mayor. Now fair befall you! He deserved his death,
And you, my good lords both, have well proceeded,
To warn false traitors from the like attempts.
I never looked for better at his hands
After he once fell in with Mistress Shore.
Richard III, 3.5

(Having a known dislike for overacting, 'counterfeit the deep tragedian,' I'm sure Will enjoyed writing the lines for Gloster and Buckingham's little charade for the Lord Mayor.

Once Gloster mentioned 'Shore's wife,' he knew the Puritan-minded Lord Mayor was hooked.

With this success, Gloster sends his lickspittles off to rouse the populace to cry, 'God save Richard, England's royal King.' No one but Will could invent a more adept huckster than Richard Plantagenet.)

(With the help of Buckingham's artful deception, Gloster plays hard to get.)

Buckingham. Ah, ha, my lord, this prince is not an Edward!

He is not lolling on a <u>lewd day-bed</u>,
<u>But on his knees at meditation;</u>
Not dallying with a <u>brace of courtesans,</u>
But meditating with two deep divines;
Not sleeping, to engross his idle body,
<u>But praying, to enrich his watchful soul.</u>
<u>Happy were England would this gracious Prince</u>
<u>Take on himself the sovereignty thereof.</u>
But sure, I fear we shall ne'er win him to it.

Lord Mayor. Marry, God forbid His Grace should say us nay!

Buckingham. I fear he will.

Richard III, 3.7

(Clever juxtaposing of the dissolute Edward IV and his Mistress Shore with the mock-saintly Richard, who the gullible Lord Mayor believes doesn't really want the crown.

The rhetorical balancing of the opposing lines is hypnotic, especially to the Lord Mayor.

I wonder which actor in Will's company plays Buckingham? I hear a deep and soothing voice: 'But praying, to enrich his watchful soul,' with 'soul' drawn out, as the actor folds hands and lowers lids.

Nearly forgot, loved 'brace of courtesans.' Not a pair, but the more kindling 'brace.')

(Queen Elizabeth, the Duchess of York, Lady Anne and others arrive at the Tower to visit the little princes. They are refused entrance, on Gloucester's orders, by Brakenbury the Tower lieutenant.

Although it's good theater, Lord Stanley couldn't have entered the scene at a worse time, as he issues an unwanted invitation first to the Queen and then Lady Anne. As you recall, Anne is the woman wooed and won by Richard, as she attended her father-in-law's coffin knowing Richard stabbed him and her husband.)

Lord Stanley. Let me meet you, ladies, one hour hence,
   And I'll salute your Grace of York as mother
   And reverend looker-on of two fair queens.
   Come, madam, you must straight to Westminster,
   There to be crowned Richard's royal queen.
Queen Elizabeth. Ah, <u>cut my lace in sunder</u>, that my pent-up heart
   May have some scope to beat, or else I swoon
   With this dead-killing news!
Lady Anne. Despiteful tidings! O unpleasing news!

(Dorset, Elizabeth's son, enters.)

Dorset. Be of good cheer. Mother, how fares your grace?

Queen Elizabeth. O Dorset, speak not to me. Get thee hence!
Death and destruction dog thee at the heels.
Thy mother's name is ominous to children.
If thou wilt outstrip death, go cross the seas,
And live with Richmond, from the reach of Hell.
Go, hie thee, high thee from this slaughterhouse,
Lest thou increase the number of the dead,
And make me die the thrall of Margaret's curse,
Nor mother, wife, not England's counted Queen .

. .

Oh, ill-dispersing wind of misery!
O my accursed womb, the bed of death,
A cockatrice hast thou hatched to the world,
Whose unavoided eye is murderous!
Lady Anne. And I in all unwillingness will go.
O would to God that the inclusive verge
Of golden metal that must round my brow
Were red-hot steel, to sear me to the brain!
Anointed let me be with deadly venom,
And die ere men can say God save the Queen ! . . .
For yet one hour in his bed

Did I enjoy the golden dew of sleep,
But have been waked by his timorous dreams.
Besides, he hates me for my father Warwick,
And will, no doubt, shortly be rid of me.
Richard III, 4.1

(Queen Elizabeth's first words 'cut my lace in sunder' refers to the cinched-in waists of Elizabethan noblewomen. The lace, or string, pulled the girdle-like struts tight. In period dramas with ladies in distress prone to fainting or swooning, the phase 'cut my lace' became a cliché.

The Queen tells her son Dorset to 'live with Richmond.' The advice alludes to the Earl of Richmond who is in France preparing an army to invade and fight Richard.

This the first reference to Richmond in the play. Later in the scene, with intentional repetition, Will has the Queen say again to Dorset, 'Go thou to Richmond, and good fortune guide thee!'

The 'A cockatrice hast thou hatched to the world' phrase is the Queen admonishing herself for delivering Richard, a mythical rooster-headed dragon. Stirring language, but is that any way to talk about your son?

Lady Anne is having second thoughts about being Richard's queen, as she wishes that the crown was 'red-hot steel, to sear me to the brain.'

Tolstoy was right: 'All happy families are alike; each unhappy family is unhappy in its own way.')

(As with most everybody else still breathing, things are going downhill for Buckingham. For now, as is customary, he takes King Richard's hand as he ascends the throne.)

King Richard. Give me thy hand
<u>Thus high, by thy advice</u>
<u>And thy assistance, is King Richard seated.</u>
But shall we wear these honors for a day?
Or shall they last, and we rejoice in them?

(As Richard ascended the throne on Buckingham's hand, he acknowledges that Buckingham put him there:
'Thus high, by thy advice
And thy assistance, is Richard seated.')

(Next, Buckingham and King Richard exchange dialogue about Prince Edward, heir apparent to the throne, and his brother York who languish in the Tower.)

King Richard. O, bitter consequence,
That Edward still should live true noble Prince!
Cousin, thou wert not want to be so dull.
Shall I be plain? <u>I wish the bastards dead,</u>
And I would have it suddenly performed.
What sayest thou? Speak suddenly, be brief.
Buckingham. Your grace may do your pleasure.
King Richard. Tut, tut, thou art all ice, thy kindness freezeth.

Say, have I consent that they shall die?
Buckingham. Give me some breath, some little pause, my lord.

Before I positively speak herein.

(The King bites his lip in anger: 'High-reaching Buckingham grows circumspect.'

Lord Stanley enters to announce: 'Dorset's fled to Richmond.'

Resurrecting the punch line from an old joke, Richard thinks, *It's about time I stopped being Mister Nice Guy.*)

King Richard. Rumor it abroad
That, Anne, my wife, is sick and like to die.

I will take order for her keeping close.
Inquire me out some mean-born gentleman,
Whom I will marry straight to Clarence' daughter.
The boy is foolish, and I fear not him.
Look how thou dream'st! I say again, give out
That Anne my wife is sick, and like to die.
About it, for it stands me much upon
To stop all hopes whose growth may damage me.
Or else my kingdom stands on brittle glass.
Murder her brothers, and then marry her!
Uncertain way of gain! But I am in
So far in blood that <u>sin will pluck on sin</u>
<u>Tear-falling pity dwells not in this eye.</u>

(Richard doesn't need Buckingham anymore, as he finds someone else to kill the little princes, 'those bastards in the tower,' as he calls them.

Buckingham tries to make amends, but is tone-deaf, as he asks Richard for an earldom promised earlier. Richard repeatedly ignores the request. His mind is on Richmond preparing in France to invade and depose.

'Sin will pluck on sin' in the next-to last line shows that Richard understands that he is caught in a vicious circle.

'Tear-falling pity dwells not in this eye' means that it is too late to repent, he is too far in.)

King Richard. I do remember me, <u>Henry the Sixth</u>
<u>Did prophesy that Richmond should be King</u>
When Richmond was a little peevish boy.
A King! perhaps—
Buckingham. <u>My lord, your promise for the</u>
<u>earldom</u>—
King Richard. When I was last at Exeter,
The Mayor in courtesy showed me the castle,
And called it Rougemont. At which name I started,
Because a <u>bard of Ireland</u> told me once
I should not live long after I saw Richmond.
Buckingham. I am thus bold to put your grace in
mind
Of what you promised me.
King Richard. Betwixt thy begging and my
meditation.
<u>I am not in the giving vein today.</u>
Buckingham. Why then resolve me whether you will
or no.
King Richard. Thou troublest me; I am not in the
vein.
Buckingham. (Aside.) And is it thus? repays he me
my true service
With such deep contempt? Made I him King for
this?

Oh. Let me think on Hastings, and be gone
<u>To Brecknock while my fearful head is on!</u>
Richard III, 4.2

(Richard recited two dire prophecies concerning Richmond, one from Henry VI and another from the bard in Ireland.

Much of the previous dialogue leads up to the memorable, 'I am not in the giving vein today.'

In the Lawrence Olivier Richard 111 film, Sir Ralph Richardson played Buckingham. His delivery of 'To Brecknock while my fearful head is on' is memorable.)

(The murderer tells Richard of the Princes' deaths. Richard asks him to come back after supper, 'When thou shalt tell the process of their death.' Unlike Henry 1V, Richard does not 'hate the murderer.'

Next, he recounts his gains and becomes again, 'a jolly, thriving wooer.')

King Richard. <u>The son of Clarence I have pent up close;</u>
His daughter meanly I have matched in marriage;
<u>The sons of Edward sleep in Abraham's bosom,</u>
<u>And Anne my wife hath bid the world goodnight.</u>

For now I know the <u>Breton Richmond</u> aims
At young Elizabeth, my brother's daughter,
And by that knot, looks proudly o'er her crown,
To her I go, <u>a jolly thriving wooer.</u>

(Lines one through four constitute a census of
Richard's recent mayhem.

'Breton Richmond' is, like Henry VI, a
Welshman.

Richard, who can 'smile while he murders,' puts
on his happy face and goes courting. Who will be the
lucky lady?)

(Catesby, another member of Richard's homicidal
retinue, has been around, but not mentioned before
the next scene.)

Catesby. Bad news, my lord. Ely has fled to
Richmond,
And Buckingham, backed with hardy Welshmen,
Is in the field, and still his power increaseth.
King Richard. Ely with Richmond troubles me more
near
Than Buckingham and his rash-levied army.
Come, I have heard that fearful commenting
In <u>leaden servitor</u> to dull delay.

Delay leads impotent and <u>snail-paced beggary,</u>
The fiery expedition be my wing,
Jove's Mercury, and herald for a king!
Come, muster men. My counsel is my shield.
We must be brief when traitors brave the field.
Richard III, 4.3

('Leaden servitor' and 'snail-paced beggary' work well in successive lines and skillfully says that in war delay and slow-paced work will put you into servitude and even penury.)

(Three royal women, three furies, three fates talk of their woes.)

Queen Elizabeth. Ah, my poor princes! Ah, my tender babes!
<u>My unblown flowers, new-appearing sweets!</u>
If yet your gentle souls fly in the air,
And be not fixed in doom perpetual,
Hover about me with your airy wings
And hear your mother's lamentation.
Queen Margaret. Tell o'er your woes again by viewing mine.
I had an Edward, till a Richard killed him;
I had a husband, till a Richard killed him.

Thou hadst an Edward till a Richard killed him;

Thou hadst a Richard till a Richard killed him.

Duchess of York. I had a Richard too, and thou didst kill him;

I had a Rutland too, and thou didst kill him.

Queen Margaret. Thou hadst a Clarence too, and Richard killed him

From forth the kennel of thy womb hath crept

A hell-hound that doth hunt us all to death:

That dog that had his teeth before his eyes,

<u>To worry lambs and lap their gentle blood;</u>

That foul defacer of God's handiwork,

That reigns in galled eyes of weeping souls;

That excellent grand tyrant of the earth

<u>Thy womb let loose to chase us to our graves.</u>

Duchess of York. O Harry's wife, triumph not in my woes.

God witness with me, I have wept for thine.

Queen Margaret. Bear with me, I am hungry for revenge,

And now I cloy me with beholding it.

Thy Edward, he is dead, that killed my Edward;

The other Edward dead, to quite my Edward;

Young York, he is but boot, because both they

Matched not the high perfection of my loss;

Thy Clarence, he is dead, that stabbed my Edward,

<u>And the beholders of this frantic play,</u>

Th' adulterate Hastings, Rivers, Vaughan, Gray

Untimely smothered in their dusky graves.

Richard yet live, hell's black intelligencer,

Only reserved their factor to buy souls

And send them thither; but at hand, at hand

Ensues his piteous and unpitied end.

Earth gapes, hell burns, fiends roar, saints pray,

To have him suddenly conveyed from hence.

Cancel his bond of life, dear God, I plead,

That I may live and say, 'The dog is dead.'

Queen Elizabeth. O thou didst prophecy the time would come

That I should wish for thee to help me curse

That bottled spider, that foul, bunch-backed toad.

Queen Margaret. I called thee then vain flourish of my fortune;

I called thee then, poor shadow, painted queen,

The presentation of but what I was,

The flattering index of a direful pageant,

One heaved a-high to be hurled down below,

A mother only mocked with two fair babes,

A dream of what thou wast, a garish flag

To be the aim of every dangerous shot,

A sign of dignity, a breath, a bubble,

A queen in jest only to fill the scene.

Queen Elizabeth. O thou, well skilled in curses, stay awhile,

And teach me how to curse mine enemies.

Queen Margaret. Forbear to sleep the nights, and fast the days;

Compare dead happiness with living woe;

Think that thy babes were sweeter than they were,

And he that slew them fouler than he is.

Bett'ring thy loss makes the bad causer worse.

Resolving this will teach thee how to curse.

Queen Elizabeth. My words are dull. O quicken them with thine!

Queen Margaret. Thy woes will make them sharp and pierce like mine.

Duchess of York. Why should calamity be full of words?

Queen Elizabeth. <u>Windy attorneys to their client woes,</u>

Airy recorders of intestate joys,

Poor breathing orators of miseries.

Let them have scope. Though what they will impart

Help nothing else, yet do they ease the heart.

Richard III, 4.4

(In Queen Elizabeth's first speech, second line, 'My unblown flowers, new-appearing sweets' laments the princes who died young and never bloomed.

Margaret's second speech is loaded with inventive invective. 'Thy womb let loose to chase us to our graves' may be the best line, although, 'To worry lambs and lap their gentle blood' is worthy of our appreciation.

And Margaret chews the scenery in her third speech with, 'Earth gapes, hell burns, fiends roar, saints pray.' Did you catch her line, 'And the beholders of this frantic play' in her third speech? Will never forgets his audience. Loved the 'frantic' adjective.

Queen Elizabeth then delivers the paired metaphorical hit, 'That bottled spider, that foul, bunch-backed toad.' 'Bottled' means that Richard is shaped like a bottle.

Will doesn't forget the law: Queen Elizabeth's first line in her closing speech in this passage includes 'windy attorneys.' In 'Twelfth Night,' 3.4, a character is told to keep,' On the windy side of the law.'

Will's language of hate directed at Richard is extensive and impressive. It reminds me of a short story, I believe by Steve Allen, in which a man commits heinous crimes. For punishment, he is placed at second base at Yankee Stadium and hated to death by eighty-thousand people.

(Richard's train is intercepted by the royal women, one of which is his mother, the Duchess of York.)

Duchess of York. Thou toad, thou toad, where is thy brother Clarence?

And little Ned Plantagenet, his son?

Queen Elizabeth. Where is the gentle Rivers, Vaughan, Grey?

Duchess of York. Where is kind Hastings?

King Richard. A flourish, trumpets! Strike alarum, drums!

Let not the heavens hear these telltale women
Rail on the Lord's anointed: strike, I say!

Duchess of York. Either thou wilt die, by Gods' just ordinance,

Ere from this war thou turn a conqueror,
Or I with grief and extreme age shall perish
And never look upon thy face again.
Therefore take thee with my most heavy curse,
Which in the day of battle tire thee more
Than all the complete armor that thou wear'st!
My prayers on the adverse party fight,
And there the little souls of Edward's children
Whisper the spirits of thine enemies
And promise them success and victory.
Bloody thou art, bloody will be thine end.
Shame serves thy life and doth thy death attend.
Richard III, 4.4

(The most heartrending line in the previous passage is from Richard's mother, the Duchess of York, when she asks him where is 'little Ned Plantagenet' one of the princes murdered in the Tower.

As if Richard didn't have enough curses on him already, his mother lays another on him punctuated by the famous parting shot, 'Bloody thou art, bloody will be thine end.')

(Richard has declared that he intends to woo and wed Queen Elizabeth's daughter. Keep in mind that the Queen previously called him 'bottled spider' among other vituperations. Let's have a glimpse of how he pulls it off.)

King Richard. You speak as if that I had slain my cousins.

Queen Elizabeth. Cousins, indeed; and by their uncle cozen'd
Of comfort, kingdom, kindred, freedom, life
Whose hand soever lanc'd their tender hearts,
Thy head, all indirectly, gave direction:
No doubt the murderous knife was dull and blunt
Till it was <u>whetted on thy stone-hard heart,</u>
<u>To revel in the entrails of my lambs</u>

But that still use of grief makes wild grief
My tongue should to thy ears not name my boys
Till that my nails were anchor'd in thine eyes.
King Richard. If I did take the kingdom from your sons,
To make amends I'll give it to your daughter.
If I have killed the issue of your womb,
To quicken your increase I will beget
Mine issue of your blood upon your daughter. . . .
The liquid drops of pearls that you have shed
Shall come again, transformed to orient pearl,
Advantaging their loan with interest
Of ten-times double gain of happiness.
Go, then, my mother, to thy daughter go;
Make bold her bashful years with your experience;
Prepare her ears to hear a wooer's tale:
Put in her heart the aspiring flame
Of golden sovereignty; acquaint the princess
With the sweet silent hours of marriage joys . . .
Therefore, dear mother, I must call you so,
<u>Be the attorney of my love</u> to her:
Plead what I will be, not what I have been.
Queen Elizabeth. But thou didst kill my children.
King Richard. But in your daughter's womb I bury them:
Where, in that <u>nest of spicery</u>, they shall breed
Selves of themselves, to your recomfiture.

Queen Elizabeth. <u>Shall I go win my daughter to thy will?</u>

King Richard. And be a happy mother by the deed.

(Aside.) Relenting fool, and shallow changing woman.

Richard III, 4.4

('Whetted' and 'revel' are two marvelous verbs:

'Whetted on thy stone-hard heart,

'To revel in the entrails of my lambs.'

Richard's 'nest of spicery' makes you stop and reread, as does 'Be the attorney of my love.'

Actually, Queen Elizabeth 'Shall I go win my daughter to thy will?' is kidding Richard, and he falls for it.

If you don't have the play, find it and read it, not least because of the sharp and lengthy one-line exchanges between Richard and Queen Elizabeth. An example:

King Richard. 'Harp not on that string, madam. That is past.'

Queen Elizabeth. 'Harp on it still shall I till heartstrings break.'

Single-line bantering is called Stichomythia in ancient Greek plays. It features contrasting opposition, repetition and literary potency.)

(The Earl of Richmond, who has been in France preparing for invasion and war, is now in England with his allies and their armies. Here, just before the battle of Bosworth Field, he speaks with Blunt, Herbert, and others.)

Richmond. Fellows in arms, and my most loving friends,
  Bruised underneath the yoke of tyranny,
  Thus far into the bowels of the land
  Have we marched on without impediment.
  And here receive we from our father Stanley
  Lines of fair comfort and encouragement.
  The wretched, bloody, and usurping boar
  That spoiled your summer fields and fruitful vines
  Swills your warm blood like wash, and makes his trough
  In your emboweled bosoms, this foul swine
  Lies now even in the centre of this isle,
  Near to the town of Leicester, as we learn.
  From Tamworth thither is but one day's march.
  In God's name, cheerly on, courageous friends,
  To reap the harvest of perpetual peace
  By this one bloody trial of sharp war.
  Richard III, 5.2

(Lines three and four show the influence of Seneca on Shakespeare.

Like his mother, Richmond was from the House of Lancaster. However, his mother was married to Lord Stanley, a Yorkist, hence the mention of Lord Stanley in line five, and in line six, with the 'lines' or letters of 'encouragement.'

'Swills your warm blood like wash, and makes his trough' is paired up nicely with 'foul swine' in the next line.

'To reap the harvest of perpetual peace' in the next-to-last line is accurate because Richmond as King Henry VII did just that.)

(Several ghosts haunt King Richard on the eve of the battle of Bosworth Field. First is the ghost of Prince Edward, son of Henry the Sixth, who appears between the tents of Richard and Richmond. Only Richard hears the ghosts.)

Ghost. (To Richard.) Let me sit heavy on thy soul tomorrow!
Think how thou stab'dst me in my prime of youth
At Tewksbury. Despair, therefore, and die!

(*Ghost* to Richmond.) Be cheerful, Richmond, for the wronged souls
Of butchered princes fight in thy behalf.
King Henry's issue, Richmond, comforts thee.
Richard III, 5.3

(Review the balance of the three lines cursing Richard and three lines praising Richmond. This is archaic, again mimicking Seneca.

More ghosts of those murdered by Richard enter, with the same three-line balance. Clarence had the best line: 'I that was washed to death with fulsome wine,' a sagacious way of saying that you had me drowned in the malmsey-butt full of foul wine.)

(The ghosts disappear, Richard sits up as the dream ends and launches into peculiar introspection.)

King Richard. <u>Give me another horse. Bind up my wounds.</u>
<u>Have mercy, Jesu! Soft! I did but dream.</u>
O coward conscience, how dost thou afflict me!
The lights burn blue. It is now dead midnight.
Cold fearful drops stand on my trembling flesh.
What do I fear? Myself? There's none else by.
Richard loves Richard; that is, I am I.

620

Is there a murderer here? No. Yes I am.
Then fly. What, from myself? Great reason why,
Lest I revenge. What, myself upon my myself?
Alack, I love myself. Wherefore? For any good
That I myself have done unto myself?
Oh no! I rather hate myself
For hateful deeds committed by myself!
I am a villain, yet I lie, I am not.
Fool, of thyself speak well. Fool, do not flatter.
My conscience hath a thousand several tongues,
And every tongue brings in a several tale,
And every tale condemns me for a villain.
Perjury, perjury, in the highest degree,
Murder, stern murder in the dir'st degree,
All several sins, all used in each degree,
Throng to the bar, crying all "Guilty, guilty!"
I shall despair. There is no creature loves me,
And If I die, no soul shall pity me.
Nay, wherefore should they, since that I myself
Find in myself no pity to myself?
Methought the souls of all that I had murdered
Came to my tent, and every one did threat
Tomorrow's vengeance on the head of Richard.
Richard III, 5.3

(Lines two and three do show that for all his faults
Richard is a human.

He does admit his guilt with: 'Is there a murderer here? No. Yes I am.'

'Throng to the bar . . .' again shows Will's knowledge of the law and more evidence that he likely worked as a law clerk in Stratford during the 'lost years.'

'All several sins, all used in each degree' shows that Richard recognizes that he has committed all seven of the deadly sins.

As in most of Will's plays, recognition scenes come in Act Five.

The 'I shall despair' line signals Richard's belief that he no longer has God's mercy, and there is no hope at all. Not a winning attitude with a battle looming.)

(But Richard isn't done yet. First a fighting speech, and then he fights on foot looking for Richmond.)

King Richard. Fight, gentlemen of England! Fight, bold yeomen!
Draw, archers, draw your arrows to the head!
Spur your proud horses hard, and ride in blood. . .

.

A thousand hearts are great within my bosom. . . .
A horse! A horse! My kingdom for a horse.

Richmond. God and your arms be praised, victorious friends!

The day is ours, the bloody dog is dead. . . .
We will unite the white rose and the red.
Smile heaven upon this fair conjunction,
That long have frowned upon their enmity! . . .
Oh, now let Richmond and Elizabeth,
The true succeeders of each royal house,
By God's fair ordinance conjoin together.
Richard III, 5.3

(Richard's speech concludes scene three. Richmond's excerpts from scenes four and five finish the passage above.

The Wars of the Roses ends with Richard Plantagenet's death* at Bosworth Field in 1485, Richmond became King Henry VII and began the Tudor reign, which lasted until the death of Elizabeth I in 1603.

*King Richard's body was exhumed from under a parking lot on the site of a former church in Leicester, England near Bosworth Field. DNA analysis proved the skeleton was Richard's. The spine showed deformity, and the death blow fatally damaged the back of the skull. Ceremonial reburial was held at Leicester Cathedral in 2015.

Part Three

Five Additional Plays

Julius Caesar
Antony and Cleopatra
Cymbeline
Titus Andronicus
Pericles

JULIUS CAESAR

(The play is halfway between history and tragedy.

Caesar, Mark Antony, Brutus, Casca, Cassius, others enter a public square. It is mid-February the time of preparation for the feast of Lupercal. The Roman year begins in March.

The crowd exhorts Caesar to speak. He is interrupted several times by a soothsayer: 'Beware the ides of March.' All exit but Brutus and Cassius.

Brutus is the main character in the play. Caesar leaves early and not of his own volition.)

Brutus. What means this shouting? I do fear the people
Choose Caesar for their king.
Cassius. Aye, do you fear it?
Then must I think you would not have it so.
Brutus. I would not, Cassius, yet I love him well. . .

.

For let the gods so speed me as <u>I love</u>
<u>The name of honor</u> more than I fear death.
Cassius. I know that virtue be in you, Brutus,
As well as I do know your outward favor.

626

Well, honor is the subject of my story.
I cannot tell what you and other men
Think of this life, but for my single self
I had as lief not be as live to be
In awe of such a thing as I myself.
I was born free of Caesar; so were you.
We both have fed as well, and we can both
Endure the winter's cold as well as he. . . .
Ye gods! It doth amaze me
A man of such a feeble temper should
So get the start of the majestic world
And bear the palm alone.
Brutus. Another general shout!
I do believe that these applauses are
For some new honors that are heaped on Caesar.
Cassius. Why, man, he doth bestride the narrow
world
Like a Colossus, and we petty men
Walk under his huge legs and peep about
To find ourselves dishonorable graves.
Men at some time are masters of their fates.
The fault, dear Brutus, is not in our stars,
But in ourselves, that we are underlings.
Brutus and Caesar. What should be in that Caesar?
Why should that name be sounded more than
yours?
Write them together, yours is as fair a name.

Sound them, it doth become the mouth as well.
Weigh them, it as heavy. Conjure with 'em,
Brutus will start a spirit as soon as Caesar.
Now, in the names of all the gods at once,
Upon what meat doth this our Caesar feed
That he is grown so great?
Brutus. <u>What you have said
I will consider.</u> What you have to say
I will with patience hear, and find a time
Both meet to hear and answer such high things.
Julius Caesar, 1.2

(In Cassius' second speech of the passage he mentions, 'Endure the winter's cold as well as he.' By that he means that he saved Caesar from drowning in the cold Tiber.

The metaphor of Caesar as a 'Colossus' leads into Cassius' 'underlings' passage. Through clever language he's leading Brutus into seeing himself crawling around under Caesar's legs while heading toward a 'dishonorable grave.' Cassius is also telling Brutus that Caesar is too big for his britches.

Elizabethan villains like Cassius always say that they have freedom of choice: 'But in ourselves, that we are underlings.' They believe that they do what they do because they can: 'Men at some time are masters of their fates.'

Brutus is an honest man. He says, I love 'the name of honor' in his second speech, but he is also ambitious and, like Othello, gullible. As with Iago, Cassius is a master persuader, 'Well, honor is the subject of my story.'

Brutus is tempted and willing to hear more, 'What you have said I will consider.' As said above, since Caesar dies early in the play, Brutus has the main part.)

(Caesar enters and speaks of Cassius with Mark Antony.)

Caesar. <u>Let me have men about me that are fat;</u>
<u>Sleek-headed men, and such as sleep o' nights:</u>
<u>Yond Cassius has a lean and hungry look;</u>
<u>He thinks too much: such men are dangerous.</u>
Antony. Fear him not, Caesar, he's not dangerous.
He is a noble Roman, and well given.
Caesar. Would he were fatter! But I fear him not:
Yet if my name were liable to fear,
I do not know the man I should avoid
So soon as that spare Cassius. He reads much;
He is a great observer, and he looks
Quite through the deeds of men: <u>he loves no plays,</u>
As though dost, Antony; <u>he hears no music:</u>

Seldom he smiles; and smiles in such a sort
As if he mocked himself, and scorn'd his spirit
That could be mov'd to smile at anything.
Such men as he be never at heart's ease
Whiles they behold a greater than themselves;
And therefore are they dangerous
I rather tell thee what is to be fear'd
Than what I fear, for always I am Caesar.
Come to my right hand, for this ear is deaf,
And tell me truly what thou think'st of him.
Julius Caesar, 1.2

(Following the 'lean and hungry' classic lines, Will, a theater man to his toenails, labels the malefactor Cassius by saying, 'he loves no plays' and 'he hears no music.')

(Casca, Cassius and Brutus discuss Caesar's behavior after he repeatedly refused a crown from Mark Antony. Cicero is in attendance.)

Casca. And then he offered it the third time; he put it the third time by: and still, as he refused it, the rabblement hooted, and clapped their chapped hands, and threw up their sweaty night-caps, and uttered such a deal of stinking breath because Caesar had refused the crown, that it had almost choked Caesar; for he swooned, and fell down at it: and for mine own part I durst not laugh, for fear of opening my lips and receiving the bad air.

Cassius. But, soft, I pray you: what, did Caesar swoon?

Casca. He fell down in the market-place, and foamed at mouth, and was speechless.

Brutus. 'Tis very like he hath the falling sickness.

Cassius. Did Cicero say anything?

Casca. Ay, he spoke Greek.

Cassius. To what effect?

Casca. Nay, an I tell you that, I'll ne'er look you i' the face again: but those that understood him smiled at one another, and shook their heads; but, for mine own part, it was Greek to me.

Cassius. (Brutus and Casca depart.) Well, Brutus, thou art noble. Yet I see,

Thy honorable mettle may be wrought
From that it is disposed. Therefore it is meet
That noble minds keep ever with their likes,
For who so firm that cannot be seduced.
Caesar doth bear me hard, but he loves Brutus.
If I were Brutus now and he were Cassius,
He should not humor me. I will this night,
In several hands, in at his window throw,
As if they came from several citizens,

631

Writings, all tending to the great opinion
That Rome holds his name, wherein obscurely
Caesar's ambition shall be glanced at.
And after this let Caesar seat him sure,
For we will shake him, or worse days endure.
Julius Caesar, 1.2

(Casca's opening speech of this passage mentions that the rabble, 'uttered such a deal of stinking breath.' Will is not a supporter of the mob. He likes law and order and stable government.

Following Casca's description of Caesar's swoon in the marketplace, Brutus says ''Tis very like he hath the falling sickness,' which is colloquial for epilepsy.

Casca's 'it was Greek to me' is another phrase generally credited to Will that has fallen into the language. He probably didn't originate it since it was used by other authors of his time. There is also a Latin equivalent that predated all of them. Whatever the induction, it's all Greek to me.

It's possible Will was expressing a self-perceived shortcoming through Casca. Will's contemporary, the Elizabethan author Ben Jonson, said of Will that he had 'small Latin and less Greek.' Jonson couldn't resist a barb, but he also had high praise for Will: 'He was not of an age but for all time!

In his final soliloquy, Cassius tells how he now knows that he has swayed Brutus: 'For who so firm that cannot be seduced.' In soliloquy, Justice is done to the good qualities of good characters by bad characters.

Will is a consummate master of character development. This knack exhibits most excitingly in parts written for the likes of Iago and Cassius. Their subtle treachery shines with ingenuity. 'In several hands . . .' or, let Caesar think that there is an uprising, while it's only me, Cassius, fooling him into thinking so.)

(Roman history, at least the mythical side, indicates that natural upheavals occur when a great man is born or dies. Whether that actually happens is another thing, but it does enliven the dramatic arts.

Will stood this belief in natural omens on its head when Cassius says in 1.2, 'The fault, dear Brutus, is not in our stars . . .' Will's bad guys always deny the fates.

Cicero, a senator, enters the play and speaks to Casca. Who, as you know by now, is a conspirator against Caesar.)

Cicero. Good even, Casca. Brought you Caesar home?

Why are you breathless? And why stare you so?

Casca. Are you not moved, when all the sway of earth

Shakes like a thing unfirm? O Cicero,

I have seen tempests when the <u>scolding winds</u>

Have rived the knotty oaks, and I have seen

The <u>ambitious ocean</u> swell and rage and foam,

To be exalted with the threatening clouds.

But never till tonight, never till now,

Did I go through a tempest dropping fire.

Either there is a civil strife in Heaven,

Or else the world <u>too saucy for the gods</u>

Incenses them to send destruction. . . .

For I believe they are portentous things

Upon the climate that they point upon.

Cicero. Good night then, Casca. This disturbed sky

Is not to walk in.

Cassius. (Enters.) Those that have known the earth so full of faults.

For my part, I have walked about the streets,

Submitting me unto the perilous night,

And thus unbraced, Casca, as you see,

Have bared my bosom to the thunder stone.

And when the cross blue lightning seemed to open

The breast of Heaven, I did present myself

Even in the very aim and flash of it.

Casca. But wherefore did you so much tempt the heavens?

It is the part of men to fear and tremble
When the most mighty gods by token send
Such dreadful heralds to astonish us.

Cassius. Now, could I, Casca, <u>name to thee a man</u>
Most like this dreadful night
That thunders, lightens, <u>open graves</u>, and roars
As doth the lion in the Capitol
<u>A man no mightier than thyself or me</u>
In personal action, yet prodigious grown
And fearful, as these strange eruptions are.

Casca. <u>'Tis Caesar that you mean, is it not, Cassius?</u>

. . .

Indeed they say the Senators tomorrow
Mean to establish Caesar as a king.

Cassius. I know where I will wear this dagger then;
Cassius from bondage will deliver Cassius: . . .
That part of tyranny that I do bear,
I can shake off at pleasure. . . .
Come Casca, you and I will yet, ere day
<u>See Brutus at his house: three parts of him</u>
<u>Is ours already; and the man entire,</u>
<u>Upon the next encounter, yields him ours.</u>

Casca. O, he sits high in all the people's hearts:
And that which appear offence in us,

His countenance, like richest alchemy,
Will change to virtue and to worthiness.
Julius Caesar, 1.3

('Ambitious' in Casaca's 'ambitious ocean' is a marvelous attributive adjective that ties back nicely to 'scolding winds.'

'Too saucy for the gods' is a clever way of saying that the world is not delivering what the gods need, and they are getting their revenge through foul weather. Little wonder that actors love playing Shakespeare with all its lively language.

I liked 'open graves' as a creative way of saying that the rain is heavy.

Cassius tells how he walked in the storm, 'did present myself.' This sets up telling Casca that Caesar is 'a man no mightier than thyself or me.' Let's take him down a peg.

Cassius asserts that once the esteemed Brutus is part of the conspiracy, 'Upon the next encounter, yields him ours.'

To the thinking of the conspirators, base assassination becomes a loyal deed.)

(One of the particularities of Shakespeare's plays is that there are few surprises. There is also a tradition in Elizabethan drama that audiences should not be fooled. These conventions are the main reasons for soliloquies, as demonstrated in the Brutus speech that follows. As said before, characters delivering Elizabethan soliloquies speak the truth insofar as they know it.)

Brutus. It must be by his death and for my part
I know no personal cause to spurn in him,
But for the general. He would be crowned.
How that might change his nature, there's the question.
It is the bright day that brings forth the adder,
And that craves wary walking. Crown him? That.
And then, I grant, we put a sting in him,
That at his will he may do danger with.
The abuse of greatness is when it disjoins
Remorse from power; and to speak truth of Caesar,
I have not known when his affections swayed
More than his reason. But 'Tis a common proof
That lowliness is young ambition's ladder,
Whereto the climber-upward turns his face,
But when he once attains the utmost round,
He then unto the ladder turns his back,
Looks in the clouds, scorning the base degrees,
By which he did ascend. So Caesar may.
Then, lest he may, prevent. And since the quarrel

Will bear no color for the thing he is,
Fashion it thus: that what he is, augmented,
Would run to these and these extremities:
And therefore think him as a serpent's egg
Which hatched would as his kind grown
mischievous,
And kill him in the shell.
Julius Caesar, 2.1

('It is the bright day that brings forth the adder' and
'lowliness is young ambition's ladder' are favorites.

Reread the final four lines and the match of
'serpent's egg' and 'kill him in the shell.' Note the
vivid visual impact.

Brutus is one of Shakespeare's strangest lead
characters. Is he really a leader and great man? Clearly,
he's impressionable and bewildered by events.

'Fashion it thus: that what he is, augmented'
means we know what it is we're doing, but let's
enlarge it and see how it looks.)

(Next, Brutus further expresses his quandary in
another soliloquy.)

Brutus. Since Cassius did first whet me against
Caesar

I have not slept.
Between the acting of a dreadful thing
And the first motion, all the interim is
Like a phantasma or a hideous dream.
The genius and the mortal instruments
Are then in council, and the state of man,
Like to a little kingdom, suffers then
The nature of an insurrection. . . .
They are the faction. O conspiracy,
Sham'st thou to show thy dangerous brow to night,
When evils are most free? O, then, by day
Where wilt thou find a cavern dark enough
To mask thy monstrous visage? Seek none, conspiracy;
Hide it in smiles of affability:
For if thou hath thy native semblance on,
Not Erebus itself were dim enough
To hide thee from prevention.
Julius Caesar, 2.1

(Like Macbeth, Brutus doesn't sleep well, as the plot unfolds.

During 'all the interim,' or between the time when killing Caesar was first proposed and the actual doing of it has put Brutus in torment.

In saying, 'Not Erebus itself were dim enough,' Brutus fears that even dark hell, personified by

639

Erebus the God of Darkness in Greek mythology, won't prevent an unveiling of the plot before it happens.)

(The conspirators enter to weigh the effects of the pending assassination on other Roman leaders.

Cassius wants an oath, which Brutus refuses as a bad idea. It is his first mistake.

What to do about Cicero is argued. Metullus thinks that Cicero's age and reputation 'Will purchase us a good opinion.')

Brutus. O, name him not: let us not break with him;
For he will never follow anything
That other men begin.
Cassius. Mark Antony, so well beloved of Caesar,
Should outlive Caesar: we shall find of him
A shrewd contriver; and, you know, his means,
If he improve them, may well stretch so far
Let Antony and Caesar fall together.
Brutus. Our course will seem too bloody, Caius
Cassius,
To cut the head off and then hack the limbs,
Like wrath in death and envy afterwards;
<u>For Antony is but a limb of Caesar:</u>
Let us be sacrificers, but not butchers, Caius.

We all stand up against the spirit of Caesar;
And in the spirit of men there is no blood:
Oh that we then could come by Caesar's spirit.
And not dismember Caesar! But, alas,
Caesar must bleed for it! And, gentle friends,
Let's kill him boldly, but not wrathfully;
<u>Let's carve him as a dish fit for the gods,</u>
Not hew him as a carcass fit for hounds:
And let our hearts, as subtle masters do,
Stir up their servants to an act of rage,
And after seem to chide 'em. This shall make
Our purpose necessary, and not envious:
Which so appearing to the common eyes,
We shall be called purgers, not murderers.
And for Mark Antony, think not of him;
For he can do no more than Caesar's arm
<u>When Caesar's head is off.</u>
Julius Caesar, 2.1

('For Antony is but a limb of Caesar' is the answer to Cassius who wants to kill Antony along with Caesar. It is Brutus' second mistake.

'Let's carve him as a dish fit for the gods' is chilling and the most decorative line in the passage. Although, 'When Caesar's head is off' is competitive.

(Before the conspirators depart they debate on how to get Caesar to the Capitol. Decius says, "I can o'ersway him.'

During this conversation, stage directions indicate that a clock strikes, an anachronism since in Caesar's day no clocks struck in Rome.

On returning home, Portia, Brutus's wife, confronts him on his strange behavior of late.)

Portia. Is Brutus sick, and is it physical
To walk unbraced and suck up the humors
Of the dank morning? What, is Brutus sick,
<u>And will he steal out of his wholesome bed</u>
<u>To dare the vile contagion of the night,</u>
And tempt the rheumy and unpurgèd air
To add to his sickness? No, my Brutus;
You have some sick offense within your mind,
Which by the right and virtue of my place
I ought to know of. . . .
Brutus. Kneel not, gentle Portia.
Portia. I should not need if you were gentle Brutus.
Within the bond of marriage, tell me, Brutus,
It is excepted I should know no secrets
That appertain to you? Am I yourself
But, as it were, in sort or limitation.
To keep with you at meals, comfort your bed,

And talk to you sometimes? <u>Dwell I but in the suburbs</u>
  Of your good pleasure? If it be no more
  Portia is Brutus' harlot, not his wife.
  Julius Caesar, 2.1

(I read and reread the first six lines of Portia's heartfelt speech. 'And will he steal out of his wholesome bed to dare the vile contagion of the night,' popped out among several admirable phrases.

Later in the speech, 'Dwell I but in the suburbs,' is praiseworthy.

Brutus goes on to reassure Portia that he will tell her 'The secrets of my heart.')

(Like Portia, Caesar's wife, Calpurnia, senses menace. The scene opens with Caesar exclaiming: 'Thrice hath Calpurnia in her sleep cried out.')

Calpurnia. Caesar, <u>I never stood on ceremonies,</u>
Yet now they fright me. There is one within,
Besides the things that we have heard and seen,
Recounts most horrid sights seen by the watch.
A lioness hath whelped in the streets;
And graves have yawn'd and yielded up their dead;
Fierce fiery warriors fight upon the clouds,

In ranks and squadrons and right form of war,
Which drizzled blood upon the Capitol;
The noise of battle hurtled in the air,
Horses did neigh, and dying men did groan,
And ghosts did shriek and squeal about the streets.
O Caesar, these things are beyond all use,
And I do fear them! . . .
When beggars die there are no comets seen;
The heavens themselves blaze for the death of
princes.
    Caesar. The gods do this in shame of cowardice.
Caesar should be a beast without a heart
If he should stay at home today for fear.
No, Caesar shall not. Danger knows full well
That Caesar is more dangerous than he.
We are two lions littered in one day,
And I the elder and more terrible.
And Caesar shall go forth.
Julius Caesar, 2.2

('I never stood on ceremonies' in line one was used
as 'stand on ceremony' in Macbeth, and is the more
frequent modern usage. It usually means, let's be
informal and has become a well-used cliché.

    'And ghosts did shriek and squeal about the
streets,' a line in Calpurnia's description of her dream
filled with foreboding, repeats the period belief that

strange phenomena precede the death of a leader. 'When beggars die there are no comets seen; The heavens themselves blaze for the death of princes.'

Despite his vow, 'Caesar should be a beast without a heart/If he should stay at home today for fear.'

When he says in a personification of danger, 'That Caesar is more dangerous than he,' Caesar is speaking like a pompous idiot. It is amusing and pretentious then and now when people speak of themselves in the third person.

He is such a full-of-himself braggart: 'And I the elder and more terrible.' No wonder the conspirators want to get rid of him.

Calpurnia prevails, Caesar agrees: 'And for thy humor, I will stay at home.'

Remember, in 2.1 when the conspirators debate on how to get Caesar to the Capitol? Decius says, 'I can o'ersway him.' Enter, Decius, on cue, and Caesar tells him of Calpurnia's fear-filled dream.)

Decius. This dream is all <u>amiss interpreted</u>;
It was a vision fair and fortunate:
Your statue spouting blood in many pipes,
In which so many smiling Romans bath'd,
Signifies that from you great Rome shall suck
Reviving blood; and that great men shall press

For <u>tinctures, stains, relics, and cognizance.</u>
This by Calpurnia's dream is signified. . . .
And know it now, the Senate have concluded
<u>To give this day a crown to mighty Caesar.</u>
If you should send them word you will not come,
<u>Their minds may change.</u>
Caesar. How foolish do your fears seem now,
Calpurnia!
I am ashamed I did yield to them.
Give me my robe for I will go.
Julius Caesar, 2.2

(It's not included above, but Caesar also said, 'Whose end is purposed by the mighty gods?' He's fatalistic in asking, in effect, will this be good or bad? Hybris (now hubris) was the Greek goddess of arrogance and pride among many other unsavory behaviors. This is the tragic flaw in some heroes of Greek tragedy. When someone is too proud to believe in gods he always gets killed. Edmund is 'King Lear' is another example.

Decius' speech changing Caesars's mind about going to the Capitol is a lesson in the art of understated inducement. Unless Caesar comes to the Capitol to snatch the crown Decius dangles, 'Their minds may change,' a perfect line to close the sale. And off Caesar goes: 'Give me my robe for I will go.'

Decius also intimates that people will expect to receive gifts, 'tinctures' from Caesar. The speech also tells the audience that the gift-seekers may instead receive relics of his death. It is a beautifully-crafted speech. Go back to line one, 'amiss interpreted.' Could misinterpreted be a derivation?)

(Alone near the Capitol, Artemidorus, a Sophist, or teacher, reads from a document.)

Artemidorus. Caesar, beware of Brutus; take heed of Cassius; come not near Casca; have an eye to Cinna; trust not Trebonius; mark well Metellus Cimber; Decius Brutus loves thee not; thou hast wronged Caius Ligarius. There is but one mind in all these men, and it is bent against Caesar. If thou beest not immortal, look about you. Security gives way to conspiracy. The mighty gods defend thee!
"Thy lover, Artemidorus."
<u>Here will I stand till pass along,</u>
<u>And as a suitor will I give him this.</u>
My heart laments that virtue cannot live
Out of the teeth of emulation.
If thou read this, O Caesar, thou mayst live;
If not, the Fates with traitors do contrive.
Julius Caesar, 2.3

(By sorting out who's who and what they're up to, this soliloquy prepares the audience and makes them wonder whether Caesar will heed the written advice: 'Here will I stand till Caesar pass along, 'And as a suitor will I give him this.')

(Caesar arrives at the Capitol surrounded by conspirators to announce: 'The ides of March are come.'

Artemidus steps up with his paper: 'Delay not, Caesar. Read it instantly.' Caesar asks, 'What, is the fellow mad.'

In an apparent ruse to get close to Caesar, or further justify their point about his arrogance, Metellus Cimber seeks a pardon for his banished brother Publius. Brutus and Cassius also plead the case.)

Metellus. Is there no voice more worthy than my own,
To sound more sweetly in great Caesar's ear
For the repealing of my banish'd brother?
Brutus. I kiss thy hand, but not in flattery, Caesar,
Desiring thee that Publius Cimber may
Have an immediate freedom of repeal.

Cassius. Pardon, Caesar; Caesar, pardon:
As low as to thy foot doth Cassius fall,
To beg enfranchisement for Publius Cimber.
Caesar. I could well be moved if I were as you;
If I could pray to move, prayers would move me:
But I am constant as the northern star,
Of whose true-fix'd and resting quality
There is no fellow in the firmament.
The skies are painted with unnumber'd sparks,
They are all fire and everyone doth shine;
But there's but one in all doth hold his place:
So in the world, 'tis furnished well with men,
And men are flesh and blood, and apprehensive;
Yet in the number I do know but one
That unassailable holds on his rank,
Unshak'd of motion: and that I am he,
Let me a little show it even in this,
That I was constant that Cimber should be
banished,
And constant do remain to keep him so. . . .
Et tu, Brute? Then fall, Caesar!
Brutus. Grant that, and then death is a benefit:
So are we Caesar's friends, that have abridg'd
His time of fearing death. Stoop, Romans, stoop,
And let us bathe our hands in Caesar's blood
Up to the elbows and besmear our swords:
Then walk we forth to the market-place,

And waving our red weapons o'er our heads,

Let's all cry, Peace! freedom! and liberty!

Cassius. Stoop then, and wash. <u>How many ages hence</u>

<u>Shall this our lofty scene be acted over,</u>

<u>In states unborn and accents yet unknown!</u>

Julius Caesar, 3.1

(Additional entreaties from Metellus precede the scene-opening speech.

Caesar accuses Metellus with the image-rich 'base spaniel fawning.' He then tells Metellus 'Know, Caesar doth not wrong.' In other words, Caesar does not make mistakes, therefore your begging won't help, and your brother remains banished.

When Brutus says, 'I kiss thy hand, but not in flattery, Caesar' he is begging Caesar to recall Publius Cimber.

In 'King Lear,' the blind Gloucester senses Lear's presence on a cliff and wants to kiss his hand. Lear replies, 'Let me wipe it first, it smells of mortality.'

'I am constant as the northern star' is a well-placed metaphor and yet another example of Caesar's egomania. Not satisfied with that, Caesar announces that of all the men in the world that are 'Unshak'd of motion: and that I am he.'

The conspirators stab Caesar, with Casca leading off. When Brutus delivers the final thrust, Caesar asks in Latin, 'You, too, Brutus?'

Casca makes the case that killing Caesar 'Cuts off so many ears of fearing death.' Reread Brutus agreeing that they have shortened Caesar's 'time of fearing death.' It seems the killers believe there is nothing like helping out an old friend.

In the 'let us bathe our hands in Caesar's blood' scene, followed by 'Let's all cry, Peace! freedom! and liberty,' Brutus is trying to sell Caesar's murder as a sacrificial rite.

Brutus gets carried away when he bawls, 'How many times shall Caesar bleed in sport, meaning entertainment. This a bit callous and unworthy of Brutus' reputation, but let's give Brutus the benefit of the doubt. You don't get to kill the boss every day, although many of us think on it. It's also Will predicting that Caesar will be killed in future performances of the play.

Cassius' line 'Shall this our lofty scene be acted over' is Will again thinking like a playwright, recognizing that it is a stunning scene and predicting that it will be seen 'In states unborn and accents yet unknown.'

Ben Jonson was correct: Shakespeare is 'Not of an age but for all time!' Perhaps in his heart Will felt that way as well.)

(Mark Antony's servant enters to tell Brutus and the other assassins that Antony, although sad that Caesar is dead, wants to talk to Brutus who he loves. Antony hopes to 'safely come to him and be resolved,' or relieved of his qualms.

After the servant leaves, Brutus speaks to Cassius.)

Brutus. I know that we shall have him well to friend.
Cassius. I wish we may, but yet have I a mind
That fears him much, and <u>my misgiving</u> still
Falls shrewdly to the purpose.
Julius Caesar, 3.1

(Cassius, the shrewder and more able contriver, is unhappy with Brutus' proposition to meet with Mark Antony, and he believes that his doubts, 'my misgiving' always come true.)

(Antony enters and lets the assassins know what, in his opinion, they have done.)

Antony. O mighty Caesar, dost thou lie so low?
Are all thy conquests, glories, triumphs, spoils,
Shrunk to this little measure? Fare thee well.
I know not, gentlemen, what you intend,
Who else must be let blood, who else is rank.
If I myself, there is no hour so fit
At Caesar's death's hour, nor no instrument
Of half that worth as those your swords, made rich
With the most noble blood of all this world.
I do beseech ye, if you bear me hard,
Now, whilst your purpled hands do reek and smoke,
Fulfill your pleasure. Live a thousand years,
I shall not find myself so apt to die.
No place will please me so, no mean of death,
And here by Caesar, and by you cut off,
The choice and master spirits of this age.
Brutus. O Antony, beg not your death of us.
Though now we must appear bloody and cruel.
And by our hands and this our present act
You see we do. Yet see you but our hands
And this the bleeding business they have done.
Our hearts see you not. They are pitiful,
And pity to the general wrong of Rome,
As fire drives out fire, so pity pity,
Hath done this deed on Caesar.

(Mark Antony tells the assassins that if they want to let more blood, 'If I myself, there is no hour so fit,' so he might as well die 'here by Caesar.'

Brutus protests that they don't wish to kill Antony, and that he only sees their hands and the 'the bleeding business they have done.'

Antony takes each of the assassins bloody hands and says cynically, as though talking to Caesar, 'It would become me better' to be friends with your enemies.

Or, as The Godfather said in the eponymous film, 'Keep your friends close and your enemies closer.'"

Antony. Am I moreover suitor that I may
Produce his body to the market place,
And in the pulpit, as becomes a friend,
Speak in the order of his funeral.
Cassius. (Aside.) <u>You know not what you do. Do not consent</u>
<u>That Antony speak in his funeral.</u>
Know you how much the people may be moved
By that which he will utter?

(Brutus tells Cassius that he will speak first and 'It shall advantage us more than do us wrong.'

654

Cassius: 'I know not what may fall. I like it not.'

Brutus tells Antony to take Caesar's body, but 'You shall not in your funeral speech blame us.'

Cassius sees that letting Antony speak at Caesar's funeral is a mistake. Stating in an aside, but to Brutus abstractly and to the audience. 'You know not what you do.'

All but Antony exit, a moving and revealing soliloquy over Caesar's corpse follows.)

Antony. O, pardon me, thou bleeding piece of earth,
That I am meek and gentle with these butchers!
Thou art the ruins of the noblest man
That ever lived in the tide of times.
Woe to the hands that shed this costly blood!
Over thy wounds now do I prophesy,
Which like dumb mouths do ope their ruby lips,
To beg the voice and utterance of my tongue,
A curse shall light upon the limbs of men;
Domestic fury and fierce civil strife
Shall cumber all the parts of Italy;
Blood and destruction shall be so in use,
And dreadful objects so familiar,
That mothers shall but smile when they behold
Their infants quarter'd with the hands of war;
All pity chok'd with custom of fell deeds:
And Caesar's spirit ranging for revenge,

With Até by his side come hot from hell,
Shall in these confine with a monarch's voice
Cry Havoc, and let slip the dogs of war;
That this foul deed shall smell above the earth
With carrion men, groaning for burial.
Julius Caesar, 3.1

(Até is the mythological daughter of Zeus, and the Greek goddess of ruin.

'Cry Havoc, and let slip the dogs of war' promises that the revenge on Caesar's murder will be merciless and 'cumber all the parts of Italy.')

(Mark Antony asks a servant whether Octavius Caesar, Julius Caesar's nephew, is coming to Rome. When Antony learns that he is, he tells the servant to have Octavius to wait outside 'a dangerous Rome' until he gives the funeral oration and sees how the populace takes it.

Next, Brutus ascends to the pulpit to address the citizens. His speech is a masterpiece of the brittle stoic form of oration fittingly delivered in prose. The first part follows.)

Brutus. Be patient till the last.

Romans, countrymen, and lovers! hear me for my cause; and be silent, that you may hear: believe me for mine honour; and have respect to mine honour, that you may believe: censure me in your wisdom; and awake your senses, that you may the better judge. If there be any in this assembly, any dear friend of Caesar's, to him I say that Brutus' love to Caesar was no less than his. If, then, that friend demand why Brutus rose against Caesar, this is my answer, not that I loved Caesar less, but the I love Rome more. Had you rather Caesar were living, and die all slaves, than that Caesar were dead, to live all freemen. As Caesar loved me, I weep for him; as he was fortunate, I rejoice at it: as he was valiant, I honour him: but, as he was ambitious I slew him. . . .'

(Even though his speech is quiet, brief, and over the heads of the crowd, Brutus receives shouts of approval. Some citizens criticize Caesar: 'This Caesar was a tyrant.' Overall, the speech doesn't incite the mob to march.

Mark Antony enters with Caesar's body. Brutus tells the crowd to 'grace his speech' that 'By our permission is allowed to make.'

Antony's speech in verse is emotional and rabble rousing.)

657

Antony. Friends, Romans, countrymen, lend me your ears.

I come to bury Caesar, not to praise him.
The evil that men do lives after them,
The good is oft interred with their bones.
So let it be with Caesar. The noble Brutus
Hath told you Caesar was ambitious.
If it were so, it was a grievous fault,
And grievously hath Caesar answered it.
Here, under leave of Brutus and the rest,
For Brutus is an honourable man,
So are they all, all honourable men,
Come I to speak in Caesar's funeral.
He was my friend, faithful and just to me.
But Brutus says he was ambitious,
And Brutus is an honourable man.
He hath brought many captives home to Rome,
Whose ransoms did the general coffers fill?
Did this in Caesar seem ambitious?
When that the poor hath cried, Caesar hath wept:
Ambition should be made of sterner stuff.
Yet Brutus says he was ambitious,
And Brutus is an honourable man.
You did see that on the Lupercal
I thrice presented him a kingly crown,
Which he did thrice refuse. Was this ambition?
Yet Brutus says he was ambitious

658

And, sure, he is an <u>honourable</u> man.
I speak not to disprove what Brutus spoke,
But here I am to speak what I do know.
You all did love him once, not without cause.
What cause withholds you then to mourn for him?
O judgment, thou art fled <u>to brutish</u> beasts,
And men have lost their reason! Bear with me,
<u>My heart is in the coffin there with Caesar,</u>
And I must pause till it come back to me.
Julius Caesar, 3.2

(Antony cites Caesar's positive acts casting doubt on Brutus' accusations: 'ransoms did the general coffers fill.' And he matched that with the heartstring-pulling, 'When that the poor hath cried, Caesar hath wept.'

The charge that Caesar was ambitious is answered with the storied, 'Ambition should be made of sterner stuff.'

The repetition of 'honourable' forces the question of whether Brutus and the rest of the assassins really are honorable. And, was Caesar, as Brutus claimed, 'ambitious.'

'O judgment, thou art fled to brutish beasts' is a sharp poke at Brutus' name.

'My heart is in the coffin there with Caesar' is irresistible language for the increasingly restive mob.

The citizens are swayed, as one says, 'Marked ye
his words? He would not take the crown, therefore
'tis certain he was not ambitious' and another,
'There's not a nobler man in Rome than Antony.'

All are not yet convinced? A citizen cues
Antony: 'Now mark him, he begins again to speak.')

Antony. But yesterday the word of Caesar might
Have stood against the world. Now lies he there,
And none so poor to do him reverence.
O masters, if I were disposed to stir,
Your hearts and minds to mutiny and rage,
I should do Brutus wrong and Cassius wrong,
Who, you all know, are <u>honourable</u> men.
I will not do them wrong; I rather choose
To wrong the dead, to wrong myself and you,
Than I will wrong such <u>honourable</u> men.
But here's a parchment with the seal of Caesar,
I found it in his closet, 'tis his will.
Let but the commons hear this testament,
Which, pardon me, I do not mean to read,
<u>And they would go and kiss dead Caesar's wounds</u>
And dip their napkins in his sacred blood,
Yea, beg a hair of him for memory,
And dying, mention it within their wills,
Bequeathing it as a rich legacy
Unto their issue. . . .

Have patience, gentle friends. I must not read it,
It is not meet you know how Caesar loved you.
You are not wood, you are not stones, but men;
And, being men, hearing the will of Caesar,
It will inflame you, it will make you mad.
'Tis good you know not that you are his heirs,
For if you should, oh, what would come of it!
Citizens. We'll hear the will: read it, Mark Antony.
Antony. Will you be patient? Will you stay awhile?
I have o'ershot myself to tell you of it:
<u>I fear I wrong the honourable men</u>
<u>Whose daggers have stabb'd Caesar; I do fear it. . .</u>

You will compel me then to read the will?
Then make a ring about the corpse of Caesar,
And let me show you him that made the will.
Shall I descend? And will you give me leave? . . .
If you have tears, prepare to shed them now.
You all do know this mantle. I remember
The first time ever Caesar put it on.
'Twas on a summer's evening, in his tent,
That day he overcome the Nervii.
Look, in this place ran Cassius' dagger through.
See what a rent the envious Casca made.
Through this the well-belovèd Brutus stabbed,
And as he plucked his cursèd steel away,
Mark how the blood of Caesar followed it,

As rushing out of doors, to be resolved
If Brutus so unkindly knocked, or no.
For Brutus, as you know, was Caesar's angel.
Judge, O you gods, how dearly Caesar loved him!
This was the most unkindest cut of all,
For when the noble Caesar saw him stab,
Ingratitude, more strong than traitor's arms,
Quite vanquished him. Then burst his mighty
heart,
And, in his mantle muffling up his face,
Even at the base of Pompey's statue,
Which all the while ran blood, great Caesar fell.
Oh, what a fall was there, my countrymen!
Then I, and you, and all of us fell down,
Whilst blood treason flourished over us.
Oh, now you weep, and I perceive you feel
The dint of pity. These are gracious drops.
Kind souls, what weep you when you but behold
Our Caesar's venture wounded? Look you here,
Here is himself, marred, as you see, with traitors. .

. .

Good friends, sweet friends, let me not stir you up
To such a sudden flood of mutiny.
They that have done this deed are honorable
What private griefs they have, alas, I know not,
That made them do it. They are wise and
honorable,

662

And will, no doubt, with reasons answer you.
I come not friends, to steal away your hearts.
<u>I am no orator, as Brutus is,</u>
But, as you know me all, a plain blunt man
That love my friend; and that they know full well
That gave me public leave to speak of him.
For I have neither wit, nor words, nor worth,
Action, nor utterance, nor the power of speech,
To stir men's blood. I only speak right on,
I tell you that which you yourselves do know,
<u>Show you sweet Caesar's wounds, poor dumb</u>
<u>mouths,</u>
    <u>And bid them speak for me.</u> But were I Brutus,
And Brutus Antony, there were an Antony
Would ruffle up your spirits, and put a tongue
In every wound of Caesar that should move
The stones of Rome to rise in mutiny. . . .
    Citizen. (Among other shouts.) We'll burn the
house of Brutus.
    Antony. Why, friends, you go to do you know not
what.
    Wherein hath Caesar thus deserved your loves?
Alas, you know not. I must tell you, then,
You have forgot the will I told you of. . . .
Here is the will, and under Caesar's seal.
<u>To every Roman citizen he gives,</u>
<u>To every several man, seventy-five drachmas.</u>

Citizen. Most noble Caesar! We'll revenge his death.
Antony. Moreover, he left you all his walks,
His private arbors and new-planted orchards,
On this side Tiber. He hath left them you,
And to your heirs forever, common pleasures,
To walk abroad and recreate yourselves.
<u>Here was a Caesar! When comes such another?</u>
Citizen. Never, never. Come away, away!
We'll burn his body in the holy place,
And with the brands fire the traitors' houses!
Antony. (Aside.) Now let it work. <u>Mischief, thou art afoot,</u>
Take thou what course thou wilt.
Julius Caesar, 3.2

('And they would go and kiss dead Caesar's wounds' is Antony's first pass at generating pity. 'Oh, now you weep, and I perceive you feel' is the second.

Twice Antony tells the crowd that he feels he's wronged 'honourable men.' Obviously, the crowd doesn't seriously accept Antony's false humility.

''Tis good you know not that you are his heirs' shifts the crowd's emotions to greed and the desire to read the will.

Antony shows Caesar's wounds and names the stabber to engender anger. The last wound he shows is the one by Brutus who has been a 'commons' favorite. It's important, above all else, that Antony indict Brutus. Hence, 'This was the most unkindest cut of all.'

Antony goes on to tell the crowd that he is no orator like Brutus, thereby classifying himself as one of them. But if he were and did 'Show you sweet Caesar's wounds,' you might be incited to mutiny.

Mark Antony even incites the citizens' greed, with 'To every Roman citizen he gives, To every several man, seventy-five drachmas.'

And then Antony closes his reading of the will with 'Here was a Caesar! When comes such another? The mob is bent on mayhem, and Antony knows that his tactics have worked, 'Mischief, thou art afoot.'

A strange incident closes Act Three: Cinna, the poet walks in the Roman streets and is accosted by as mob. He tells them he is going to Caesar's funeral as a friend, but they accuse him of being a traitor, 'Tear him to pieces. He's a conspirator.' 'I am Cinna the poet.' 'Tear him for his bad verses.' Was Will poking fun with the last line? Anyway, Cinna is torn to pieces as a symbol of a Rome in chaos, and the plebians are off to burn the houses of Brutus, Cassius and the other assassins.)

(THE FIRST THREE ACTS are a closely-knit play that could be called Caesar's Fall. Then the play falls in two. Acts four and five are loose, cover two years of marching, then fighting ranging over the entire Roman Empire, including Rome, Asia Minor and Bulgaria.

Act Four opens with a meeting of the Second Triumvirate, Antony, Octavius Caesar and Lepidus. Brief excerpts follow.)

Antony. These many then shall die, their names are pricked.

Octavius. Your brother too must die. Consent you Lepidus?

Lepidus. I do consent. . . . Upon condition Publius shall not live,

Who is your sister's son, Mark Antony.

Antony. He shall not live. Look, with a spot I damn him.

Julius Caesar, 4.1

(The scene proves that the Triumvirate members are worse than Caesar, more selfish, ruthless, dictatorial, trading in death with close relations.

That said, Antony tells the Triumvirate, 'Brutus and Cassius are levying powers,' meaning they have gathered armies and are on the move.)

(Brutus speaks ill of Cassius.)

Brutus. Thou hast described
A hot friend cooling. Ever note, Lucilius,
When love begins to sicken and decay,
It useth an enforcèd ceremony.
<u>There are no tricks in plain and simple faith.</u>
<u>But hollow men, like horses hot at hand,</u>
Make gallant show and promise of their mettle,
But when they should endure the bloody spur,
They fall their crests and like deceitful jades
Sink in the trial.
Julius Caesar, 4.2

(I liked the simply put and perceptive, 'There are no tricks in plain and simple faith.'

'But hollow men, like horses hot at hand' is an effective comparison of jumpy horses to weak men who act ready for battle, but fail when it comes.)

(Brutus criticizes Cassius over his greed. They argue bitterly, resolve their differences and plot their actions against the Triumvirate.)

Brutus. Let me tell you, Cassius, you yourself

Are much condemned to have an itching palm,

To sell and mart your offices for gold

To undeservers.

Cassius. I an itching palm!

You know that you are Brutus that speaks this,

Or, by the gods, this speech were else your last.

Brutus. The name of Cassius honors this corruption,

And chastisement doth therefore hide his head. . .

.

Remember March, the ides of March remember.

Did not great Julius bleed for justice' sake?

What villain touched his body that did stab,

And not for justice? What, shall one of us,

That struck the foremost man of all this world

But for supporting robbers, shall we now

Contaminate our fingers with base bribes,

And sell the mighty space of our large honours

For so much trash as may be graspèd thus?

I had rather be a dog and bay the moon

Than such a Roman.

Cassius. Brutus, bait not me,

I'll not endure it. You forget yourself,

To hedge me in. I am a soldier, I,

Older in practice, abler than yourself

To make conditions.

Brutus. Hear me, for I will speak.
Must I give way and room to your rash choler?
Shall I be frighted when a madman stares? . . .
Go show your slaves how choleric you are,
And make your bondmen tremble. Must I budge?
Must I observe you? Must I stand and crouch
Under your testy humour? By the gods,
You shall digest the venom of your spleen,
Though it do split you; for, from this day forth,
I'll use you for my mirth, yea, for my laughter,
When you are waspish.
Cassius. Do not presume too much upon my love.
I may do that I shall be sorry for.
Brutus. You have done that you should be sorry for.
There is not terror, Cassius, in your threats,
For I am armed so strong in honesty
That they pass me by as the idle wind
Which I respect not.
Cassius. Come, Antony, and young Octavius, come,
Revenge yourselves alone on Cassius,
For Cassius is a a weary of the world;
Hated by the one he loves, braved by his brother,
Checked like a bondman, all his faults observed. . .

There is my dagger,
And here my naked breast; within, a heart
Dearer than Plutus' mine, richer than gold.

Brutus. Sheathe your dagger.
Be angry when you will, it shall have scope;
Do what you will, dishonor shall be humor.
<u>O Cassius, you are yokèd with a lamb</u>
<u>That carries anger as the flint bears fire,</u>
Who, much enforcèd, shows a hasty spark
And straight is cold again.
Julius Caesar, 4.3

(Brutus accuses Cassius of being greedy and having an 'itching palm.'

Or, by the gods, this speech were else your last' is Cassius' first threat to Brutus.

Brutus rejects the idea of taking bribes, 'I'd rather be a dog . . . than such a Roman.'

Cassius' next threat to Brutus: 'Have mind upon your health, tempt me no farther.'

'Go show your slaves how choleric you are' is Brutus' way of telling Cassius that he is acting like an oriental potentate.

'I'll use you for my mirth, yea, for my laughter' labels Cassius as a fool.

Cassius threatens to stab Brutus, 'I may do that I shall be sorry for.'

'You have done that you should be sorry for.' Brutus means that Cassius took bribes.

Cassius goes into hysterics, threatens suicide, 'And here my naked breast; within, a heart,' . . . 'Dearer than Plutus' mine, richer than gold.' Since Plutus is the Greek mythological god of wealth, it is not an apt metaphor for Cassius, accused of an 'itching palm,' to use.

Brutus ends the argument with, 'you are yokèd with a lamb . . . That carries anger as the flint bears fire.' Brutus says that he's really a softy who can't carry a grudge.)

(Brutus and Cassius make up and drink wine. His wife Portia killed herself Brutus tells Cassius.)

Brutus. No man bears sorrow better. Portia is dead.
Cassius. How 'scaped I killing when I crossed you so?
Oh, insupportable and touching loss!
Upon what sickness?
Brutus. Impatient of my absence,
And grief that young Octavius with Mark Antony
Have made themselves so strong; for with her death
The tidings came; with this she fell distract,
And, her attendants absent, swallow'd fire.
Julius Caesar, 4.3

('The tidings came' suggests that the same messenger bringing news of Portia's death also told Brutus that Octavius and Antony are on the march.

The traditional way of Romans committing suicide is swallowing fire.)

(Brutus decides that his armies will meet Antony's at Philippi in Macedonia. Cassius wants to wait until the enemy is tired out, but Brutus interrupts with a forceful speech.

Brutus. Under your pardon. You must note beside
That we have tried the utmost of our friends,
Our legions are brimful, our cause is ripe.
The enemy increaseth every day,
We, at the height, are ready to decline.
There is a tide in the affairs of men
Which taketh at the flood leads on to fortune;
Omitted, all the voyage of their life
Is bound in shallows and in miseries.
On such a full sea we are now afloat,
And we must take the current when it serves,
Or lose our ventures.
Julius Caesar, 4.3

('There is a tide in the affairs of men' is fatalistic. It says there is one chance, so take it at high tide, or you will be 'bound in shallows and in miseries.')

(Caesar's ghost appears as Brutus sits reading.)

Brutus. How ill this taper burns! Ha! Who come here?
It is the weakness of mine eyes
That shapes this <u>monstrous</u> apparition.
It comes upon me. Art thou anything?
Art thou some god, some angel, or some devil,
That makest my blood cold, and <u>my hair to stare</u>?
Speak to me what thou art.
Ghost. Thy evil spirit, Brutus.
Brutus. Why comest thou?
Ghost. To tell thee thou shalt see me at <u>Philippi</u>.
Julius Caesar, 4.3

(Ghosts in the tragedies tend to make accurate predictions.
'Monstrous' in line three means unnatural.
Vivid language in, 'my hair to stare.'
'Phillipi' was a major city in Macedonia in the late fourth-century B.C. It becomes significant for Brutus.)

(Cassius and Brutus say their goodbyes as they prepare for battle.)

Cassius. Coming from Sardis, on our former ensign
Two mighty eagles fell, and there they perched,
Gorging and feeding from our soldiers' hands,
Who to Philippi here consorted us.
This morning are they fled away and gone,
And in their steads do <u>ravens, crows and kites</u>
Fly o'er our heads and downward look on us,
As we were sickly prey. Their shadows seem
<u>A canopy most fateful</u>, under which
Our army lies, ready to give up the ghost. . . .
Now, most noble Brutus,
The gods today stand friendly, that we may,
Lovers in peace, lead on our days to age!
But since <u>the affairs of men rest still incertain</u>,
Let's reason with the worst that may befall.
If we do lose this battle, then is this
The very last time we shall speak together.
What are you then determinèd to do? . . .
Then, if we lose this battle,
<u>You are contented to be led in triumph</u>
<u>Through the streets of Rome?</u>

Brutus. No, Cassius, no. Think not, thou noble Roman,

That ever Brutus will go bound to Rome.
He bears too great a mind. But this same day
Must end that work the ides of March began,
And whether we shall meet again I know not.
Therefore our everlasting farewell take.
Forever and forever, farewell, Cassius!
Julius Caesar, 5.1

(Like ghosts in tragedies, omens also tend to come true, as with the eagles who flew away and were replaced by 'ravens, crows and kites' . . . 'A canopy most fateful.'

Cassius echoes Brutus' earlier 'There is a tide in the affairs of men' with his 'the affairs of men rest still incertain.'

Even though he earlier rejected suicide, Brutus dismisses Cassius' idea that he will be taken prisoner and 'go bound to Rome.'

And in the battle with Antony, he 'Must end that work the ides of March began.')

(Cassius sees the battle is lost and gives his servant, or more accurately his slave, a chance to free himself

675

from bondage by killing Cassius with the sword that helped murder Caesar.)

Cassius. In Parthia did I take thee prisoner,
And then I swore thee, saving of thy life,
That whatsoever I did bid thee do
Thou shouldst attempt it. Come now, keep thine oath.
Now be a free man, and <u>with this good sword</u>
<u>That ran through Caesar's bowels, search this bosom.</u>
Stand not to answer. Here, take thou the hilts,
And when my face is covered, as 'tis now,
Guide thou the sword. <u>Caesar, thou art revenged,</u>
Even with the sword that killed thee.
Julius Caesar, 5.3

(Knowing defeat is certain at Philippi, Brutus asks his friend Volumnius for a final favor. Volumnius refuses and Strato, a servant, fulfills the request.)

Brutus. <u>The ghost of Caesar hath appeared to me</u>
Two several times by night, at Sardis once,
<u>And this last night here in Philippi fields.</u>
I know my hour is come. . . .
Our enemies have beat us to the pit.

It is more worthy to leap in ourselves
Than tarry till they push us. Good Volumnius,
Thou know'st that we two went to school together.
Even for that love of old, I prithee
<u>Hold thy my sword hilts whilst I run on it. . . .</u>
(Volumnius exits. Brutus continues.)
I prithee, Strato, stay thou by thy lord.
Thou art a fellow of a good respect,
Thy life hath had some smatch of honor in it.
<u>Hold then my sword, and turn away thy face</u>
<u>While I do run upon it. . . .</u>
Caesar, now be still.
I killed not thee with half so good a will.
Julius Caesar, 5.5

(Before Volumnius exited, he refused to participate in Brutus' suicide by saying, 'That's not an office for a friend, my lord.'

Caesar's ghost predicted in 4.3, 'Thou shall see me at Philippi.' And since Elizabethan ghosts' predictions come true in Elizabethan tragedies, they also do here.)

(At the end of the tragedies, the winner almost always speaks well of the loser. Here, Mark Antony eulogizes Marcus Brutus.)

Antony. This was the noblest Roman of them all.
All the conspirators, save only he,
Did that they did in envy of great Caesar.
He only, in a general honest thought
And common good to all, made one of them.
His life was gentle, and the elements
So mixed in him that nature might stand up
And say to all the world. This was a man!
Julius Caesar, 5.5

ANTONY AND CLEOPATRA

(In this language-rich follow-up to 'Julius Caesar,' the Triumvirate of Mark Antony, Octavius Caesar and Lepidus divide the Roman Empire, following their victory at Phillipi.

Fresh from victory and living in luxury, Antony is gaga over Cleopatra, Queen of Egypt. Philo, a friend, comments on Antony's obsession.)

Philo. Nay, but this dotage of our general's
O'erflows the measure: those his goodly eyes,
That o'er the files and musters of the war
Have glow'd like plated Mars, now bend, now turn
The office and devotion of their view
Upon a tawny front: his captain's heart,
Which in the scuffles of great fights hath burst
The buckles of his breast, reneges all temper,
And it becomes the bellows and the fan
To cool a gypsy's lust. Look where they come:
Take but good note, and you shall see in him
The triple pillar of the world transform'd
Into a strumpet's fool: behold and see.
Antony and Cleopatra, 1.1

(Philo sees Antony's priorities switched from being an armored Mars in battle to devotion 'Upon a tawny front,' meaning Cleopatra's yellowish-brown forehead.

Antony, Philo reports, is without restraint and works 'To cool a gypsy's lust.'

Gypsies, a term derivative of Egypt, were thought to have come from that country.

Philo laments that one of 'The triple pillar,' or one of the victorious Triumvirate, namely Antony, has mutated 'Into a strumpet's fool.')

(Octavius Caesar sends orders, and Cleopatra tells Antony that he must leave. 'You must not stay here longer, your dismission Is come from Caesar.'

It looks like Octavius is no longer thinking of the Triple-Pillar' and is hell-bent on ruling the world.)

Antony. Let Rome in Tiber melt, and the wide arch
Of the rang'd empire fall! Here is my space.
Kingdoms are clay: our dungy earth alike
Feeds beast as man: the nobleness of life
Is to do thus; when such a mutual pair
And such a twain can do't, in which I bind,
On pain of punishment, the world to weet

<u>We stand up peerless.</u>
Antony and Cleopatra, 1.1

(Antony is so hung up he doesn't care what Octavius Caesar wants, and for that matter let the Roman Empire fall. 'Let Rome in Tiber melt . . .'

Antony and Cleopatra embrace following the phrase, 'when such a mutual pair.'

'We stand up peerless' means that their love is like no other, and Antony wants the world to know it.

Somebody once said, "I don't know what the question is, but the answer is sex.')

(ANTONY is away, and Cleopatra is all moony over him. Note the mention of 'serpent' and 'poison,' as Cleopatra speaks to her servant like a woman hopelessly in love.)

Cleopatra. O Charmian,
Where think'st thou he is now? Stands he or sits he?
Or does he walk? or is he on his horse?
O happy horse to bear the weight of Antony!
Do bravely, horse! For wott'st thou whom thou mov'st?
The demi-Atlas of this earth, the arm

And burgonet of men. He's speaking now,
Or murmuring, <u>Where's my serpent of old Nile</u>?
For so he calls me. Now I feed myself
<u>With most delicious poison</u>: think on me
That am with Phoebus' amorous pinches black,
And wrinkled deep in time? <u>Broad-fronted Caesar</u>,
When thou wast here above the ground I was
<u>A morsel for a monarch</u>: <u>and great Pompey</u>
<u>Would stand and make his eyes grow in my brow</u>;
There he would anchor his aspect and die
With looking on his life.
Antony and Cleopatra, 1.5

('Where's my serpent of old Nile' makes one think ahead with Will to Cleopatra's suicide.

'With most delicious poison' refers to mandrake, a sleeping potion.

The lucid, 'A morsel for a monarch' calls attention to Cleopatra's prior affair with Julius Caesar, 'Broad-fronted Caesar.'

And, thanks to Hollywood, who can forget Rex Harrison as Caesar, with Liz and Dick's illicit, true-life love-affair pulsating off the screen. Quick, cut my lace!

In her musings about Mark Antony, Cleopatra doesn't ask what he is thinking. But she did that earlier in 1.2 with, 'A Roman thought hath struck him,' meaning that she believed that Antony was thinking about Rome rather than her.

I wonder what would have happened had Reagan and Thatcher fallen for each other? Would steel-willed Maggie have convinced Ron, who was surely on the downside of his career, to give back the colonies?

Former French President Francois Mitterrand on Margaret Thatcher: 'The eyes of Caligula and the mouth of Marilyn Monroe.')

(The Roman general, Pompey, is a character in the play. In actuality, he was assassinated before reaching Egypt. Even though in the speech above, Cleopatra intimates that they were an item, 'and great Pompey would stand and make his eyes grow in my brow.' But this is show business, and let's not let facts get in the way of a better plot.

Will used history, and especially Plutarch, to create Antony and Cleopatra. As Emerson accurately wrote, 'There is properly no history, only biography.' And, through lustrous poetry, Will flavors biography with upraised entertainment.)

683

(Next, Pompey talks with his friend Menecrates about the warlike adventures of Octavius Caesar and Lepidus and the lovelike escapades of Antony and Cleopatra.)

Pompey. I shall do well:
The people love me, and the sea is mine;
My powers are crescent, and my auguring hope
Says it will come to the full. Mark Antony
In Egypt sits at dinner, and will make
No wars without doors: Caesar gets money where
He loses hearts: Lepidus flatters both,
Of both is flattered, but he neither loves
Nor either cares for him.
Menecrates. Caesar and Lepidus
Are in the field: a mighty strength they carry.
Pompey. He dreams: I know they are in Rome
together,
  Looking for Antony. But all the charms of love
  Salt Cleopatra, soften thy waned lip!
  Let witchcraft join with beauty, lust with both!
  Tie up the libertine in a field of feasts,
  Keep his brain fuming. Epicurean cooks
  Sharpen with cloyless sauce his appetite,
  That sleep and feeding may prorogue his honor
  Even to a lethed dullness.
  Antony and Cleopatra, 2.1

('Pompey saying, 'the Sea is mine' tells us that he possesses a mighty fleet.

The 'In Egypt sits at dinner' in line 5 is surely a euphemism for Mark Antony's frolicking with Cleopatra.

Silius, an army officer, tells Menecrates that Octavius Caesar is ready to fight. Pompey says they are in Rome 'Looking for Antony.'

In lines 3-6 in Pompey's second speech, there is a nice poetic pairing of 'Let witchcraft join with beauty, lust with both!' and 'Tie up the libertine in a field of feasts,'

Plus, Pompey knows that Antony is with 'Salt,' or libidinous Cleopatra, who will 'Keep his brain fuming' with a sauce he devours to the point of surrendering his honor to stupefaction.)

(Enobarbus, Roman politician, friend of Antony's, and later betrayer tells in rapturous poetry of Antony's first meeting Cleopatra. The idea for the passage, with some exact phrases used, was lifted from Plutarch. Will, as always, turns his extensive borrowings into magic.)

Enobarbus. When she first met Mark Antony she
pursed up his heart, upon the river of Cydnus. . . .
I will tell you.
The barge she sat in, like a burnished throne,
Burn'd on the water, the poop was beaten gold;
Purple the sails, and so perfumed
The winds were love-sick with them: the oars were
silver,
Which to the tune of flutes kept stroke, and
The water which they beat to follow faster,
As amorous of their strokes. For her own person,
It beggar'd all description: she did lie
In her pavilion, cloth-of-gold of tissue,
O'er picturing that Venus where we see
The fancy out-work nature: on each side her
Stood pretty dimpled boys, like smiling Cupids,
With divers-colour'd fans, whose wind did seem
To glow the delicate cheeks which they did cool,
And what they undid did. . . .
Her gentlewomen, like the Nereids,
So many mermaids tendered her i' the eyes,
And made their bends adorning: at the helm
A seeming mermaid steers: the silken tackle
Swell with the touches of those flower-soft hands
That yarely frame the office. From the barge
A strange invisible perfume hits the sense
Of the adjacent wharfs. The city cast

Her people out upon her; and Antony,
Enthron'd i' the market-place, did sit alone,
Whistling to the air; which, but for vacancy,
Had gone to gaze on Cleopatra too,
And made a gap in nature. . . .
Age cannot wither her, nor custom stale
Her infinite variety: other women cloy
The appetites they feed; but she makes hungry
Where she most satisfies: for vilest things
Become themselves in her; that holy priests
Bless her when she is riggish.
Antony and Cleopatra, 2.2

(Will wrote better plays than Antony and Cleopatra, but none with more musical and exotic language. This harmonic play floats above ground in a romantic cloud suffused with soft rainwater that never falls, but only moistens the erotic atmosphere.

Line 7 of the passage is so sensual that 'The winds were love-sick' from carrying perfume from the sails.

Even the water was 'amorous of their strokes' as the silver oars beat the water faster 'to the tune of flutes.'

It's worth rereading the famous lines 4 and 5.

The barges silver tackle 'Swell with the touches of those flower-soft hands' of mermaids and sea nymphs. The innuendo in this line does, paraphrasing Will's words, beggar all description.

Antony, sitting alone on the wharf, was so taken with the scene that he was 'Whistling to the air.'

Later in the scene, Agrippa, a friend of Octavius Caesar, calls Cleopatra a 'Royal wench,' who Julius Caesar made use of.

Menecrates, a friend of Pompey, declares that 'Antony must leave her utterly.'

Enobarbus rejects these thoughts with everlasting poetry in the lines:

'Age cannot wither her, nor custom stale
Her infinite variety.'

ENOBARBUS concludes by saying what we have already read. Men can't get enough of Cleopatra. When she's erotic or 'riggish', her actions deserve blessing, even from 'holy priests.' No wonder Antony's whistling.)

(Although Cleopatra's charms consume Antony, he does retain some political interest, and asks a soothsayer, 'Whose fortunes shall rise higher, Octavius Caesar's or mine?')

Soothsayer. Caesar's.
Therefore, O Antony, stay not by his side.
Thy demon, that thy spirit which keeps thee, is
Noble, courageous, high, unmatchable,
Where Caesar is not. But near him thy angel
Becomes a fear, as being o'erpowered. Therefore,
Make space enough between you. . . .
If thou dost play with him at any game,
Thou art sure to lose, and, of that natural luck,
He beats thee 'gainst the odds. Thy luster thickens
When he shines by. I say again, thy spirit,
Is all afraid to govern near him,
But he away, is noble.
Antony and Cleopatra, 2.3

(IN THE tragedies, soothsayers and their kind usually portend accurately. Antony's ministering angel works to his advantage, but the angel's powers weaken when Octavius Caesar is present: 'Becomes a fear, as being o'erpowered.'

Don't play any games with Caesar, the soothsayer warns in line nine, because, 'Thou art sure to lose.'

'Thy luster thickens' and 'When he shines by' in lines 10 and 11 is a pleasing contrast. And as the verb-master Will shows, 'shines' is the perfect verb in this place.)

(A playful Cleopatra tosses off amusing innuendo.)

Cleopatra. Give me some music, music, <u>moody food</u>
Of us that <u>trade in love</u>.
Antony and Cleopatra, 2.5

(IN WILL'S memorable speeches, the characters are always given arresting phrases like 'moody food' and 'trade in love' to gloss the whole.

'Music' and 'food' are also echoed in Orsino's 'If music be the food of love, play on' in Twelfth Night, 1,1.

Bored, an unserious Cleopatra suggests billiards and then fishing to her maid Charmian.)

Cleopatra. Give me mine angle, we'll to the river. There,
<u>My music playing far off</u>, I will betray
<u>Tawny-finned fishes</u>. My bended hook shall pierce
Their slimy jaws, and as I draw them up,
I'll think <u>every one an Antony</u>,
And say, Ah, ha! You're caught.
Charmian. 'Twas merry when

You wagered on your angling, when your diver
Did <u>hang a salt fish on his hook</u>, which he
With fervency drew up.
Cleopatra. That time, oh times!
I laughed him out of patience, and that night
I laughed him into patience. And the next morn,
<u>Ere the ninth hour, I drunk him to his bed,</u>
Then put my tires and mantles on him whilst
I wore his sword Philippan.
Antony and Cleopatra, 2.5

(In line 2, 'My music playing far off' reminds us that, music, like water, imbues the play.

Earlier, Cleopatra was described as tawny, and here we have 'Tawny-finned fishes.' And each one she catches will remind her of Antony.

Knowing that 'salt' means lustful in Elizabethan terms, 'hang a salt fish on his hook' cues Cleopatra's, 'Ere the ninth hour, I drunk him to his bed.' Where she dressed Antony in her clothes and strapped on the sword he fought with at Philippi.

As a former television director, I thought about how I would shoot that kinky encounter and keep it R-rated.)

(In a model kill-the-messenger episode, miscommunication tilts Cleopatra's lighthearted mood to homicide. A messenger enters. He keeps trying to tell Cleopatra that Antony is not dead but is well. She first praises, then, not liking his acidulous expression, berates the messenger.)

Cleopatra. Oh, from Italy!
<u>Ram thou fruitful tidings in mine ears,</u>
That long time have been barren. . . .
Antonius dead! If thou say so, villain,
Thou kill'st thy mistress. But well and free,
If thou so yield him, there is gold, and here
<u>My bluest veins to kiss, a hand that kings</u>
<u>Have lipped, and trembled kissing. . . .</u>
Why there's more gold.
But, sirrah, mark, we use
To say the dead are well. Bring it to that,
The gold I give thee will I melt and pour
Down thy ill-uttering throat. . . .
But there's no goodness in thy face. If Antony
Be free and healthful, so tart a favor
To trumpet such good tidings! If not well,
Thou should'st come like a Fury crowned with snakes,
Not like a formal man. . . .
I have a mind to strike thee ere thou speak'st'

Yet if thou say Antony lives, is well,
Or friends with Caesar or not captive to him,
I'll set thee in a shower of gold and hail
Rich pearls upon thee.

(In the midst of his reassurances that Antony is
both well and friends with Caesar, the poor devil adds
a 'But yet, madam.')

Cleopatra. I do not like "<u>But yet</u>." It does allay
The good precédence. Fie upon <u>But yet</u>!
"But yet" is a jailer to bring forth
Some monstrous malefactor, Prithee, friend,
Pour out the pack of matter to mine ear,
The good and bad together. He's friends with
Caesar,
In state of health thou say'st, and thou say'st free.

(THE impolitic messenger goes on to report that
he didn't say that Antony is free. That, 'He's bound to
Octavia' 'For the best turn i' the bed.' Moreover, 'he's
married to Octavia.')

Cleopatra. (Knocks him to the ground.) The most
infectious pestilence upon thee. . . .
(Hits him again.) Horrible villain! Or I'll spurn
thine eyes

Like balls before me, I'll unhair thy head. (She whips him.)
Thou shalt be whipped with wire, and stewed in brine,
Smarting in lingering pickle. . . .
Rogue, thou hast lived too long.
Antony and Cleopatra, 2.5

(Cleopatra caps her tirade by bringing out a knife. The messenger runs off stage.)

Several phrases stand out: 'Ram thou fruitful tidings in mine ears.'

And if the messenger brings good news, she will offer 'My bluest veins to kiss, a hand that kings' have trembled over. Little question that the young messenger is nonplussed.

'Smarting in lingering pickle' and 'stewed in brine' is rich visualization for open wounds that are 'whipped with wire' for not pleasing the Queen of the Nile.)

(Octavius Caesar is in Alexandria. Antony prepares to fight him. In the style of Antony and Cleopatra, there is time for another night of revelry.)

Antony. If from the field I shall return once more

694

To kiss these lips, I will appear in blood:
I and my sword will earn our chronicle: . . .
I will be treble-sinew'd, hearted, breath'd,
And fight maliciously: for when mine hours
Were nice and lucky, men did ransom lives
Of me for jests; but now I'll set my teeth,
And send to darkness all that stop me. Come,
Let's have another gaudy night: call to me
All my sad captains, fill our bowls; once more
Let's mock the midnight bell.
Cleopatra. It is my birthday.
I had thought to have held it poor; but since my lord
Is Antony again, I will be Cleopatra.
Antony and Cleopatra, 3.13

(Despite protestations like, 'And fight maliciously' in line 5, and the 'Cry Havoc, and let slip the dogs of war' from 'Julius Caesar,' Antony has turned to jelly. As evidenced in the curiously modern, off-hand, 'nice and lucky.'

I like Antony's seamless segue from 'send to darkness all that stop me' to 'Let's have another gaudy night' in lines 8 and 9.' Will constantly surprises with inverse phrases conveying conflicted feelings.

'Let's mock the midnight bell' in Antony's final line reminds me of the rowdy and witty Falstaff who would gladly join the party. 'We have heard the chimes at midnight, Master Shallow.' *Henry Four, Part Two*, 3.2

Although Antony slips from warrior to love slave, his paramour is always up for a dalliance: 'I will be Cleopatra' is her closing line in this passage.)

(Antony ignores the soothsayer's advice not to battle Caesar and Cleopatra's counsel to avoid fighting Caesar at sea.

Antony now believes that Cleopatra deceives him and joins with Caesar. He speaks to his friend Eros, a fitting name in this love-drenched and erotic play.)

Antony. All is lost;
This foul Egyptian hath betrayed me:
My fleet hath yielded to the foe; and yonder
They cast their caps up, and carouse together
Like friends long lost. Triple turn'd whore! 'tis thou
Hast sold me to this novice; and my heart
Makes only wars on thee. Bid them all fly;
For when I am reveng'd upon my charm,
I have done all. Bid them all fly; begone.
O sun, thy uprise shall I see no more:
Fortune and Antony part here; even here

Do we shake hands. All come to this! The hearts
That spaniel'd me at heels, to whom I gave
Their wishes, do discandy, melt their sweets
On blossoming Caesar; and this pine is bark'd
That overtopp'd them all. Betray'd I am:
O this false soul of Egypt! this grave charm,
Whose eye beck'd forth my wars and call'd them
home;
Whose bosom was my crownet, my chief end,
Like a right gipsy, hath, at fast and loose,
Beguil'd me to the very heart of loss.
What, Eros, Eros!
Ah, thou spell! Avaunt!
(Cleopatra enters just before the line above, speaks
one line and exits.)
Cleopatra. Why is my lord enrag'd against his love?
Antony. Vanish; or I shall give thee thy deserving,
And blemish Caesar's triumph. Let him take
And hoist thee up to the shouting Plebeians:
Follow his chariot, like the greatest spot
Of all thy sex; most monster-like . . .
The shirt of Nessus is upon me: teach me,
Alcides, thou mine ancestor, thy rage:
Let me lodge Lichas on the horns o' the moon;
And with those hands, that grasp'd the heaviest
club,
Subdue my worthiest self. The witch shall

To the young Roman boy she hath sold me, and I
fall
Under this plot: she dies for 't. Eros, ho!
Antony and Cleopatra, 4.12

(With 'Triple-turned whore!' in line 5, Antony believes that Cleopatra has tricked three men, Julius Caesar, Pompey and now himself. 'Triple-turned' is a notable compound modifier of the noun 'whore.'

'Fortune and Antony part here,' dooms Antony for he disdains fate. You can't do that in Elizabethan literature and survive.

'Like a right gipsy . . .' has Antony blaming Cleopatra for his troubles. Probably true, but it labels him as weak.

In line 15, 'this pine is bark'd' has Antony complaining that his enemies have stripped the skin off his body.

In an inventive metaphor near the end of his speech, Antony is so mad that he wants to 'lodge Lichas on the horns o' the moon.' Lichas is the aide who inadvertently destroyed Hercules by bringing him a poisoned shirt. Before dying, Hercules chucked Lichas into the ocean then killed himself to end his pain. It is another sterling example of literate Will adapting a mythological tale and, for his times, modernizing it.)

(In the next scene, 4.13, Cleopatra orders her servant, Mardian the eunuch, to 'go tell him I have slain myelf.'

In 4.14, Mardian tells Antony that Cleopatra's last words were 'Antony! Most noble Antony!'

After much guilt-ridden back and forth, Antony asks his friend Eros to kill him. Eros can't bear that and kills himself.

Antony says, 'I will be a bridegroom in my death,' and falls on his sword. He doesn't die and asks to be taken to Cleopatra.

In scene 4.15 below, Antony is carried into Cleopatra's chamber.)

Cleopatra. O sun,
Burn the great sphere thou mov'st in! darkling stand
The varying shore of the world.
Antony. I am dying, Egypt, dying; only
Here I importune death awhile, until
Of many thousand kisses the poor last
I lay upon thy lips.
Cleopatra. But come, come, Antony
Help me, my women, we must draw thee up; . . .
<u>Here's sport indeed</u>! How heavy weighs my lord!

Our strength is all gone into heaviness,
That makes the weight: had I great Juno's power,
The strong-wing'd Mercury should fetch thee up,
And set thee by Jove's side, Yet come a little,
Wishers were ever fools, O, come, come, come;
And welcome, welcome! die where thou hast liv'd:
Quicken with kissing: had my lips that power,
Thus would I wear them out. . . .
No, let me speak; and let me rail to high
That the false housewife Fortune break her wheel,
Provok'd by my offence. . . .
Noblest of men woo't die?
Hast thou no care of me? shall I abide
In this dull world, which in thy absence is
No better than a sty? O, see, my women,
The crown O' the earth doth melt. My lord!
O, wither'd is the garland of the war,
The soldier's pole is fallen: young boys and girls
Are level now with men: the odds are gone,
And there is nothing left remarkable
Beneath the visiting moon. . . .
Our lamp is spent, it's out! Good sirs take heart:
We'll bury him; and then, what's brave, what's
noble,
Let's do it after the high Roman fashion,
And make death proud to take us.
Antony and Cleopatra, 4.15

(In line three of her second speech in this passage, Cleopatra use of 'Here's sport indeed!' while lifting the dying Antony is unusual since she is not at play. However, the usage is consistent with the spirited Cleopatra.

'Juno' in Roman mythology, is the wife of 'Jove,' another name for Jupiter. Cleopatra wishes for Juno's power so she could save the dying Antony.

Line 13 has 'the false housewife Fortune break her wheel.' Fortune's wheel is used throughout Shakespeare. Here Will uses 'false housewife' giving—forgive me—the modifier more spin.

'The soldier's pole is fallen' in line 21 is a fresh alternative to polar, or guiding star.)

In the last lines of her speech, Cleopatra discusses burying Antony and offers, 'Let's do it after the high Roman fashion.'

From floating into Antony's gaze: 'The barge she sat in, like a burnished throne' to her lover's death, Cleopatra understands royalty's trappings.)

(Octavius Caesar learns of Antony's death from Dercetas, a former friend of Antony's.

Reminder: Octavius is Julius Caesar's nephew, and after his uncle's assassination joined with Antony to defeat the assassins Brutus and Cassius at Phillipi.

Along with Lepidus, they formed the Triumvirate.

Now Caesar defeats Antony and rules Egypt.)

Dercetas. (Carries Antony's sword.) I am call'd Dercetas;
    Mark Antony I serv'd, who best was worthy
    Best to be serv'd: whilst he stood up and spoke,
    He was my master; and I wore my life
    To spend upon his haters. If thou please
    To take me to thee, as I was to him
    I'll be to Caesar; if thou pleasest not,
    I yield thee up my life. . . .
    I say, O Caesar, Antony is dead.
Caesar. The breaking of so a great a thing should make
    A greater crack: the round world
    Should have shook <u>lions</u> into civil <u>streets,</u>
    And <u>citizens </u>to their <u>dens</u>. The death of Antony
    Is not a single doom; in the name lay
    <u>A moiety of the world.</u>
Dercetas. He is dead, Caesar;
    Not by a public minister of justice,
    Nor by a hired knife; but that self hand

Which writ his honour in the acts it did
Hath, with the courage which the heart did lend it,
Splitted the heart. This is his sword;
I robb'd the wound of it; behold it stain'd
With his most noble blood.
Caesar. Look you sad, friends?
The gods rebuke me, but it is tidings
To wash the eyes of kings. . . .
O Antony!
I have follow'd thee to this. But we do lance
Diseases in our bodies: I must perforce
Have shown to thee such a declining day
Or look on thine; we could not stall together
In the whole world: but yet let me lament,
With tears as sovereign as the blood of hearts,
That thou, my brother, my competitor
In top of all design, my mate in empire,
Friend and companion in the front of war,
The arm of mine own body, and the heart
Where mine his thoughts did kindle, that our stars,
Unreconcilable, should divide
Our equalness to this. Hear me, good friends,
But I will tell you at some meter season.
Antony and Cleopatra, 5.1

(Lines three and four of Caesar's first speech of the
passage bemoan the fact that Antony's death is so

703

earth-shattering that it should have caused rioting. In clever juxtaposition, Will has lions in the streets and citizens in dens.

'A moiety of the world' in line six of the same speech, means that Antony's death is not just one person, but a large slice of the world.

'I robb'd the wound of it' in the next-to-last line of Dercetas' second speech is expressive writing. I probably would have written for the Dercetas character: 'I pulled the sword out,' missing the imaginative 'robbed' and the sympathy-inducing 'wound.'

'To wash the eyes of kings' in line three of Caesar's second speech is a more literate way of saying kings cried.

'Tears' and 'hearts' in the line 10 sentence are nicely balanced and moving. Like Antony praised Brutus in death, so does Octavius, pouring it on with 'brother,' 'mate,' and more.

Following the lionizing of Antony, reread the last several lines of the passage to pick out words like 'stars,' 'unreconcilable' and 'equalness,' as Caesar describes how the world is not big enough for both he and Antony.)

(CLEOPATRA speaks to her attendants. At this point in her life, where she is planning suicide, Cleopatra wants her son to succeed her.)

Cleopatra. My desolation does begin to make
A better life. 'Tis paltry to be Caesar;
Not being Fortune, he's but Fortune's knave,
A minister of her will: and it is great
To do that thing that ends all other deeds:
Which shackles accidents and bolts up change;
Which sleeps, and never palates more the dug,
The beggar's nurse and Caesar's.
Antony and Cleopatra, 5.2

(CLEOPATRA believes in line three that Octavius Caesar has been 'Fortune's knave' or lucky.

In line seven, sleep, or death, is better than eating 'dug,' or dung, like Caesar and beggars.)

Proculeius, a friend of Caesar's, enters to reassure Cleopatra of Caesar's good intentions. Cleopatra continues.)

Cleopatra. Antony did tell me of you, bade me to trust you; but
I do not greatly care to be deceiv'd,

That have no use for trusting. If your master
Would have a queen his beggar, you must tell him
That majesty, to keep decorum, must
No less beg than a kingdom: if he please
To give me conquer'd Egypt for my son,
He gives me so much of mine own as I
Will kneel to him with thanks.
Antony and Cleopatra, 5.2

(Cleopatra is told that she won't have to kneel to Caesar, but his men take her prisoner.

Distraught, she attempts to stab herself, is disarmed and continues speaking.)

Cleopatra. Shall they hoist me up,
And show me to the shouting varletry
Of censuring Rome? Rather a ditch in Egypt
Be gentle grave unto me! rather on Nilus' mud
Lay me stark nak'd, and let the water-flies
Blow me into abhorring! rather make
My country's high pyramids my gibbet,
And hang me up in chains!
Antony and Cleopatra, 5.1

(CLEOPATRA fears being taken to Rome and paraded before 'shouting varletry,' or slaves.

She'd rather 'a ditch in Egypt' be her grave, or 'high pyramids' her gallows.)

(IN a grand poetic eulogy, Cleopatra speaks eloquently of Antony.)

Cleopatra. His face was as the heavens; and therein stuck
A sun and moon, which kept their course, and lighted
The little O, the earth. . . .
His legs bestrid the ocean: his rear'd arm
Crested the world: his voice was propertied
As all the tunèd spheres, and that to friends;
But when he meant to quail and shake the orb,
He was as rattling thunder. For his bounty,
There was no winter in't; an autumn 'twas
That grew more by reaping: his delights
Were dolphinlike; they show'd his back above
The element they liv'd in: in his livery
Walk'd crowns and crownets; realms and islands were
As plates dropp'd from his pocket.
Antony and Cleopatra, 5.2

('His legs bestrid the ocean,' recalls Cassius in 'Julius Caesar,' 1.2. 'Like a Colossus he doth bestride he narrow world,' describing Caesar's influence on the Roman Empire.

'As all the tunèd spheres' means that Antony's voice was musical.

'That grew more by reaping' in line six has Will's imagination out of Africa and back in Stratford.

That Antony's pleasures were 'dolphinlike' suggests that he was a lover above all men.

'Walk'd crowns and crownets' shows Cleopatra's belief that royals were Antony's retainers.

In the wonderful 'As plates dropp'd from his pocket,' Cleopatra says that Antony was so large that kingdoms and geography dropped like shiny coinage from his pocket.)

(AS the play spirals to its end, Caesar arrives to take inventory. Cleopatra is betrayed by her treasurer who discloses that she has held back 'Enough to purchase what you have made known.'

Caesar tells her that he is 'no merchant to make prize with you.' In addition to not being there to calculate the value of her holdings, Caesar also says that 'we remain your friend.'

Caesar leaves and Cleopatra complains to her servants. Iras, one of her attendants, answers with a classic line. 'The bright day is done . . .' showing that she knows the game is up.

Cleopatra declares her wish for immortality and prepares to die from the bite of a poisonous snake.)

Cleopatra. He words me, girls, he words me, that I should not,
Be noble to myself.
Iras. Finish, good lady. <u>The bright day is done,
And we are for the dark.</u>
Cleopatra. Give me my robe, put on my crown; I have
<u>Immortal longings</u> in me: now no more
The juice of Egypt's grape shall moist this lip:
Yare, Yare, good Iras; quick. Methinks I hear
Antony call; I see him rouse himself
To praise my noble act; I hear him mock
The luck of Caesar, which the gods give men
To excuse their afterwrath. Husband, I come:
Now to that name my courage prove my title!
I am fire and air; my other elements
I give to baser life. So, have you done?
Come then, and take the last warmth of my lips.
Farewell, kind Charmian; Iras, long farewell.
Have I the aspic in my lips? Dost fall?

If thou and nature can so gently part,
The stoke of death is a lover's pinch,
Which hurts and is desir'd. Dost thou lie still?
If thus thou vanishes, thou tell'st the world
It is not worth leave-taking.
Charmian. Dissolve, thick cloud and rain; that I may
say
   The gods themselves do weep!
Cleopatra. This proves me base:
If she first met the curlèd Antony,
He'll make demand of her, and spend that kiss
Which is my Heaven to have. Come thou mortal
wretch,
   With thy sharp teeth this knot intrinsicate
   Of life at once untie: poor venomous fool,
   Be angry and dispatch. O couldst thou speak,
   That I might hear thee call great Caesar ass
unpolicied! . . .
   Dost thou not see my baby at my breast
   That sucks the nurse asleep? . . .
   As sweet as balm, as soft as air, as gentle: O
Antony!
   Antony and Cleopatra, 5.2

CYMBELINE

(THE PLAY is complex and challenging to work through, but well worth it. I will attempt to provide overall insight, but the intent of this book is to enjoy and analyze the key speeches.

Imogen, daughter of King Cymbeline of Britain by a previous marriage, is unhappy with her evil stepmother the current queen. Imogen speaks of her fears to Posthumus to whom she is secretly married and from whom she will soon be forcefully separated.)

Imogen. Dissembling courtesy! How fine this tyrant
Can tickle where she wounds! My dearest husband,
I something fear my father's wrath; but nothing,
Always reserv'd my holy duty, what
His rage can do on me. You must be gone;
And I shall here abide the hourly shot
Of angry eyes; not comforted to live,
But that there is this jewel in the world
That I may see again. . . .
Look here, love;
This diamond was my mother's: take it, heart;

711

But keep it till you woo another wife,
When Imogen is dead.
Cymbeline, 1.1

('Can tickle where she wounds' in line two captures
the double-dealings of the stepmother queen.

In the last line, Imogen prophecies her own
death.

Following Imogen's plaintive speech to her
husband, King Cymbeline storms in with fatherly
greetings to Imogen and Posthumus, of whom he
disapproves: 'Thou art poison to my blood.'

And later in the scene, he wishes Imogen would
give 'A drop of blood a day; and, being aged,' she will
'Die of this folly!' It seems that dad is a hard case.)

(Imogen again complains about her father and
stepmother below.

Then Iachimo, friend of Philario, who is friend
to Posthumus (stay with me) comments on Imogen
and then directly comes to the point of his
speechmaking.)

Imogen. A father cruel and a step-dame false;
A foolish suitor to a wedded lady.
Iachimo. (Aside.) All of her that is out of door

If she be furnish'd with a mind so rare,
She is alone the Arabian bird; and I
Have lost the wager. Boldness be my friend!
Arm me, audacity, from head to foot!
Or, like the Parthian, I shall flying fight!
Rather directly fly. . . .
Had I this cheek to bathe my lips upon; this hand,
whose touch
Whose every touch, would force the feeler's
To the oath of loyalty; this object, which
Takes prisoner the wild motion of mine eye, . . .
Slaver with lips as common as the stairs
That mount the Capitol; . . . then bo-peeping in an
eye
Base and unlustrous as the smoky light
That's fed with stinking tallow, it were fit
That all the plagues of hell should at one time
Encounter such revolt.
Cymbeline, 1.6

(IN line three of his speech, 'She is alone the
Arabian bird' shows Iachimo's admiration of Imogen.

Cleopatra in 'Antony and Cleopatra,' 3.2 calls
Antony, 'O thou Arabian bird!'

I like Will's personalization of brawny nouns, as
in the line five use of audacity: 'Arm me, audacity,
from head to foot!'

'Had I this cheek to bathe my lips upon' and 'Slaver with lips' is hilarious.

We also have 'bo-peeping in an eye.' Bo-peep is a game played with babies. But, the phrase might also refer to bowling. Don't ask. Possibly Will feels that if he is writing a complicated play, he may as well do it with intricate language.

Iachimo calls Imogen's husband, Posthumus, an itinerant when he says he is 'More noble than that runagate to your bed.'

Imogen calls Iachimo, 'a saucy stranger.' She will report him to her father who, if he sees fit, will cook him 'As in a Romish stew.')

(IMOGEN sleeps in her bedchamber. Iachimo crawls out of a trunk, comments on her beauty, takes a bracelet from her wrist, and goes back into the trunk as the farcical scene ends.

I've heard colleagues describe Cymbeline as a tragedy. I don't think so. I believe the play defies labeling. The humorist Garrison Keillor said, 'Most tragedy is misunderstood comedy.')

Iachimo. How bravely thou becom'st thy bed! fresh lily!

And whiter than the sheets! That I might touch!
But kiss; one kiss! Rubies unparagon'd,
How dearly they do't! 'tis her breathing
That perfumes the chamber thus; the flame o' the
taper
Bows toward her, and would underpeep her lids,
To see the enclosed lights, now canopied
Under these windows, white and azure, lac'd
With blue of heaven's own tinct. But my design
To note the chamber: <u>I will write all down</u>:
Such and such pictures; there the window such
The adornment of her bed; the arras, figures,
Why, such and such; and the contents o' the story,
. . .
Come off, come off;
<u>As slippery as the Gordian knot was hard!</u>
'Tis mine; <u>and this will witness outwardly,</u>
As strongly as the conscience does within,
<u>To the madding of her lord</u>. On her left breast
<u>A mole cinque-spotted</u>, like the crimson drops
I' the bottom of a cowslip. Here's a voucher
Stronger than ever law could make: this secret
Will force him think that I have <u>pick'd the lock,</u>
<u>The treasure of her honour</u>. No more. To what
end?
<u>Why should I write this down, that's riveted,</u>
<u>Screw'd to my memory?</u>

(This is easy thinks Iachimo, not an intractable problem like the proverbial 'Gordian knot.' Nice juxtaposition.

In line ten of this disturbing scene, Iachimo is so taken with the sleeping Imogen and her bedchamber that he promises himself, 'I will write all down.'

As he slips a bracelet from Imogen's wrist, he comments in line 16, 'and this will witness outwardly.' Iachimo will use the bracelet, plus a 'cinque-spotted mole' he sees, to convince Posthumus that Imogen has been unfaithful.

As said above, Will not only finds the right verb, he also uses verb forms in unusual and creative ways. For example, in line 18 Iachimo knows that what he has taken and seen will lead 'To the madding of her lord.'

'Pick'd the lock' matches well the criminal act Iachimo is performing.

'The treasure of her honour' is familiar. Will used it often in referring to chastity. Perhaps best in Hamlet when Laertes counsels his sister, Ophelia, not to succumb to Hamlet's advances. Little does he now that she already has.

The weird Iachimo has a few more lines before crawling back into his trunk. The last ones included above begin with 'Why should I write this down.' This prompted me to wonder whether Will was thinking of his own astonishing memory. Given the vast range of topical references throughout his works, it's likely that even back in his boyhood Will rarely forgot anything he heard, saw or read.)

(JUST when we thought that the stepmother queen and the appalling Iachimo were the villains of the piece, out comes the execrable Cloten, son of the pernicious queen and her former husband. And we add that to the imbroglio.

Imogen was supposed to marry Cloten. As we know, she secretly married the now-banished Posthumus. As expected, Cloten fancies Imogen. From Iachimo's quirky bedchamber scene, to the equally strange occurrence that follows. In this play, Will writes for a festival of dirty minds.

Next, as Imogen sleeps nearby, Cloten speaks of her to a lord.)

Lord. Your lordship is the most patient man in loss, the most coldest that ever turned up ace.
Cloten. It would make any man cold to lose. . . .

Winning will put any man into courage. If I could get this foolish Imogen, I should have gold enough. . . .

I would this music would come: I am advised to give her music o' mornings; they say it will penetrate. . . .

(Musicians enter, and Cloten continues.) Come on; tune: if you can penetrate her with your fingering, so; we'll try with tongue too: if none will do, let her remain; but I'll never give o'er. First, a very excellent good-conceited thing; after a wonderful sweet air, with admirable rich words to it, and then let her consider.

Song. Hark, hark! the lark at heaven's gate sings, . .
.

Cloten. So, get you gone. If this penetrate, I will consider your music the better: If it do not, it is a vice in her ears; which horse-hairs and calves' guts, nor the voice of unpaved eunuch to boot, can never amend.

(King Cymbeline and his Queen enter.) *Cymbeline.* Attend you here the door of our stern daughter? Will she not forth?

Cloten. I have assailed her with music, but she vouchsafes no notice.

Cymbeline. The exile of her minion is too new;
She hath not yet forgot him: some more time
Must wear the print of his remembrance out,

718

And then she's yours.

Cloten. (Aside.) I know her women are about her: what

<u>If I do line one of their hands</u>. 'Tis gold
Which <u>buys admittance</u>; oft it doth; yea, and makes
<u>Diana's rangers</u> false themselves, yield up
Their deer to the stand o' the stealer; and 'tis gold
Which make true man kill'd and saves the thief;
Nay, sometimes hangs both thief and true man: what
Can I not do and undo? I will make
<u>One of her women lawyer to me</u>: for
I yet not understand the case myself.
Cymbeline, 2.3

(IN line two of Cloten's aside, he believes that 'If I do line one of their hands' he can use gold to 'buys admittance' to Imogen through one of her servants.

He likens Imogen's attendants to one of 'Diana's rangers,' or assistants to the mythological goddess of the hunt. The cynical Cloten believes that gold will buy anything, including deer protected by a goddess.

Failing that tactic, Cloten will make 'One of her women lawyer to me' to better learn how to get to Imogen.

Later in the scene, Cloten offers gold to one of Imogen's ladies. Imogen overhears and responds:

'You lay out too much pains for purchasing but trouble.')

(IMOGEN realizes that the bracelet stolen by Iachimo is missing. She tells Pisanio, a close friend of Posthumus, of her fears.)

Imogen. Last night 'twas on mine arm; I kiss'd it:
I hope it be not gone to tell my lord
That I kiss aught but he.
Cymbeline, 2.3

(POSTHUMUS is back in town and staying with his friend Philario. Iachimo shows up to tell Posthumus of his dalliance with Imogen. He displays Posthumus' ring, the bracelet and a detailed description of Imogen's bedchamber, including a tapestry that told the story of 'Cleopatra meeting Antony;' the 'Cydnus River in Turkey;' and a 'chimney piece' depicting 'chaste Dian,' a Roman goddess of the hunt, bathing.')

Iachimo. Your lady is one of the fairest I have look'd upon. . . .
I'll make a journey twice as far, to enjoy
A second night of such sweet shortness which

720

Was mine in Britain; for the ring is won. . . .
Posthumus. The stone's too hard to come by.
Iachimo. Not a whit,
Your lady being so easy.
Posthumus. If you can make't apparent
That you have tasted her in bed, my hand
And ring is yours: if not, the foul opinion
You had of her pure honour gains or loses
Your sword or mine, or masterless leaves both
To who shall find them.
Iachimo. Sir, my circumstances,
Being so near the truth as I shall make them,
Must first to induce you to believe: whose strength
I will confirm with oath; which I doubt not
You'll give me leave to spare when you shall find
You need it not. . . .
First, her bedchamber,
Where, I confess, I slept not; but profess
Had that was well worth watching, it was hang'd
With tapestry of silk and silver; the story
Proud Cleopatra, when she met her Roman,
And Cydnus swell'd above the banks . . .
The chimney
Is south the chamber; and the chimney-piece
Chaste Dian bathing: . . .
The roof o' the chamber
With golden cherubins is fretted: her andirons,

I had forgot them, were two winking cupids
Of silver, each on one foot standing, nicely
Depending on their brands. . . .
(Shows bracelet.) I beg but leave to air this jewel;
see!
And now 'tis up again: It must be married
To that your diamond; I'll keep them. . . .
She stripp'd it from her arm; I see her yet;
Her pretty action did outsell her gift,
And yet enrich'd it too: she gave it to me, and
She priz'd it once . . .
If you seek
For further satisfying, under her breast,
Worth the pressing, lies a mole, right proud
Of that most delicate lodging: by my life
I kiss'd it; and it gave me present hunger
To feed again, though full. You do remember
This stain upon her? . . .
Will you hear more?
Posthumus. Spare your arithmetic: never count the
turns;
Once, and a million!
Cymbeline, 2.4

(In his lying tale of having slept with Imogen,
Iachimo recites to Posthumous details of the room in
which he spied on the sleeping Imogen. He mentions

the tapestry that told the story of 'Cleopatra meeting Antony.' The next line of 'Cydnus swelling above her banks' is geographically questionable since Cleopatra met Antony in Egypt and the Cydnus River is in Turkey. I'm quibbling, let's give Will some literary license.

Philario is skeptical of Iachimo's story and urges Posthumus, who accepts the lies, to be patient.

Posthumus want to kill Imogen, "O that I had her here to tear her limbmeal.'

(AS you likely know, the action of the play takes place in 1st-Century Britain.

In the opening scene of Act Three, Cymbeline, the Queen and Cloten talk with Caius Lucius, a Roman general, who speaks for Augustus Caesar, current ruler of the Roman empire. Octavius Caesar, from Antony and Cleopatra, is now elevated to Augustus.

Lucius tells them that the tribute of three-thousand pounds a year, levied earlier by Julius Caesar on Cassibelan, Cymbeline's uncle, has not been recently been paid. Cloten rejects the idea: 'Britain is a world by itself; and we will nothing pay for wearing our own noses.'

For Cymbeline's benefit, the Queen lays out some history of unsuccessful Roman wars on Britain in admirable poetry.

Cloten follows with a polite, but firm brush-off to General Lucius.)

Queen. Remember, sir, my liege,
The kings, your ancestors; together with
The natural bravery of your isle, which stands
As Neptune's park, ribbed and paled in
With rocks unscaleable and roaring waters;
With sands that will not bear your enemies' boats,
But suck them to the top-mast. A kind of conquest
Caesar made here; but not made here his brag
Of came, and saw, and overcame: with shame,
The first that ever touch'd him, he was carried
From off our coast, twice beaten; and his shipping,
Poor ignorant baubles! on our terrible seas,
Like egg-shells mov'd upon their surges crack'd
As easily 'gainst our rocks: for joy whereof
The fam'd Cassibelan, who was once at point,
O, giglot fortune! To master Caesar's sword,
Made Lud's town with rejoicing fires bright
And Britons strut with courage.
Cloten. Come there's no more tribute to be paid: our kingdom is stronger that it was at that time; and, as I said, there is no more such Caesars: other of them

may have crooked noses; but to owe such straight
arms, none. . . .

We have yet many among us can gripe as hard as
Cassibelan: I do not say I am one; but I have a hand.
Why tribute? why should we pay tribute? If Caesar can
hide the sun from us with a blanket, or put the moon
in his pocket, we will pay him tribute for light; else,
sir, no more tribute, pray you now. . . .

His majesty bids you welcome. Make pastime with
us a day or two, or longer: if you seek us afterwards in
other terms, you shall find us in our salt-water girdle:
if you beat us out of it, it is yours; if you fall in the
adventure, our crows shall fare the better for you; and
there's an end.

Cymbeline, 3.1

(LINE four of the queen's speech calls Britain
'Neptune's park,' a sharp-witted way of saying that the
Roman god of the seas uses their island as a park.

A few lines later, the queen then tells of how
Caesar couldn't brag, 'Of came, and saw, and
overcame' in his attempted conquests of Britain,
clearly spoofing Veni, vidi, vici.'

He was 'From off our coast, twice beaten.' And,
in a crisp metaphor, the queen reports that Julius
Caesar's ships, 'Like egg-shells mov'd upon their
surges crack'd.'

'Cassibelan,' also known as Cassivellaunus, fought against Julius Caesar's second war against British forces in the first-century A.D. He came close to winning 'once at point,' but was betrayed by supposed allies and lost.

'Made Lud's town with rejoicing fires bright' in the next-to-last line of the queen's speech alludes to one version of the designation for ancient London named after mythical King Lud.

Cloten's 'other of them may have crooked noses' prompts us to think of Roman noses. I once thought I had a nice nose until I was about 16 when my mother told me: 'Richard, your nose is inclining toward the Roman.' I immediately abandoned my misguided plans to try my luck in Hollywood.

'If Caesar can hide the sun from us with a blanket, or put the moon in his pocket' reminds us that Will has Cloten speaking in prose. This line, with a few adjustments, is certainly verse-worthy.

Cloten invites Lucius and his master Caesar Augustus to repeat Julius Caesar's attempts to invade Britain from the sea with the 'you shall find us in our salt-water girdle.' Now that's enterprising language.

(Guiderius and Arviragus, sons of Cymbeline, enter their cave in Wales with a lord named Belarius. And, we have a twist.)

Belarius. A goodly day not to keep house, with such
Whose roof's as low as ours! Stoop, boys:
Instructs you how to adore the heavens, and bows
you
To a morning's holy office: the gates of monarchs
Are arch'd so high that giants may jet through
And keep their impious turbans on, without
Good-morrow to the sun. Hail, thou fair heaven!
We house i' the rock, yet use thee not so
As prouder livers do.
Arviragus. What should we speak of
When we are old as you" when we shall hear
The rain and wind beat dark December, how,
In this our pinching cave, shall we discourse
The freezing hours away? We have seen nothing:
We are beastly; subtle as the fox for prey;
Like warlike as the wolf for what we eat:
Our valour is to chase what flies; our cage
We make a quire, as doth the prison'd bird,
And sing our bondage freely.
Belarius. O, boys, this story
The world may read in me: my body's mark'd
With Roman swords; and my report was once

First with the best of note: Cymbeline lov'd me;
And when a soldier was the theme, my name
Was not far off: then was I as a tree
Whose boughs did bend with fruit: but in one night
A storm or robbery, call it what you will,
Shook down my mellow hangings, nay, my leaves,
And left me bare to weather. . . .
My fault being nothing, as I have told you oft.
But that two villains, whose false oaths prevail'd
Before my perfect honour, swore to Cymbeline
I was confederate with the Romans: so
Follw'd my banishment; and this twenty years
This rock and these demesnes have been my world.
. . .

(The boys leave to meet Belarius later. He
continues in soliloquy.)
How hard it is to hide the sparks of nature!
These boys know little they are sons to the king;
Nor Cymbeline dreams that they are alive.
They think they are mine: and though train'd us
thus meanly.
In the cave wherein they bow, their thoughts do hit
The roofs of palaces; and nature prompts them,
In simple and low things, to prince it much
Beyond the trick of others. . . .
Hark, the game is rous'd!
O Cymbeline! heaven and my conscience knows

Thou didst unjustly banish me: whereon,
At three and two years old, I stole these babes;
Thinking to bar thee of succession, . . .
Myself, Belarius, that am Morgan call'd,
They take for natural father. The game is up.
Cymbeline, 3.3

(THE descriptive 'Are arch'd so high that giants may jet through' of line five expertly contrasts the cave's low ceiling with the palaces of monarchs. The imagery is finished nicely by saying that the giants can even jet through without knocking off their 'impious,' or unholy, turbans.

Did you note 'Jet through' from four centuries ago? Some verbs have a long life.

Arviragus, one of the two boys living in the cave with Belarius, expects to remain in what Belarius called the 'house i' the rock' listening to 'The rain and wind beat dark December,' 'In this our pinching cave,' until he is as old as Belarius.

Aviragus' 'Beat dark December' recalls the impact of Ishmael's, 'damp, drizzly November in my soul' in Chapter One of Moby Dick.

Belarius describes his fall from grace in line nine of his second speech: 'Shook down my mellow hangings, nay, my leaves,' followed by, 'And left me bare to weather' bring to mind lines from Sonnet 73: 'When yellow leaves, or none, or few do hang.'

These 'demesnes' refers to the properties, in addition to the cave, owned by Belarius.

Later in the speech, when Belarius reveals that the boys are not his, but the sons of Cymbeline, he says in soliloquy: 'How hard it is to hide the sparks of nature! Their thoughts hit 'The roofs of palaces; and nature prompts them.' They don't know their heritage, but it's in them.)

(Posthumus, tricked by Iachimo into believing that Imogen has been unfaithful, orders his servant Pisanio to kill her. Pisanio can't bring himself to do it: 'Since I receiv'd command to do this business I have not slept one wink.'

Pisanio suggests that Imogen disguise herself as a man, go to Rome, live near Posthumus and become his friend.

Hey, if Hollywood can get you to suspend disbelief, surely Will can convince you to do it as well.)

Imogen. Do thou thy master's bidding: when thou see'st him,
A little witness my obedience: look!
I draw the sword myself: take it, and hit

The innocent mansion of my love, my heart:
Fear not; 'tis empty of all things but grief:
Thy master is not there; who was indeed
The riches of it: do his bidding; strike.
Thou mayst be valiant in a better cause;
But now thou seem'st a coward. . . .
The lamb entreats the butcher: where's thy knife?
Thou art too slow to do thy master's bidding,
When I desire it too.
Pisanio. I'll give him but notice you are dead, and
send him
Some bloody sign of it; for 'tis commanded
I should do so: for you shall be miss'd at court,
And that will well confirm it. . . .
If you'll back to the court.
Imogen. No court; no father; nor no more ado
With that harsh, noble, simple nothing,
That Cloten, whose love-suit hath been to me
As fearful as a siege.
Cymbeline, 3.4

(Imogen calls her heart the appealing 'innocent mansion of my love' when she asks Pisanio to stab her.

'The lamb entreats the butcher: where's thy knife?' is made fine with the verb 'entreats,' which is typically associated with acts less chilling than murder.

731

Similarly, using 'simple nothing' to describe Cloten makes his fatuous behavior toward Imogen more appalling. Especially since his silly courting is 'fearful as a siege.'

With a loathsome step-brother like Cloten, and a father who collaborates with him, no wonder Imogen doesn't want to go back to court. Like Lear, Cymbeline gets his filial priorities askew.

As she prepares to assume disguise, Pisanio tells Imogen, 'You must forget to be a woman.'

Imogen replies in her usual determined way, 'This attempt I am a soldier to.' Imogen is one of a long line of Will's estimable women.

(AFTER Pisanio lies to him that Imogen is dead, Cloten vows to kill Posthumus.

Meantime, Imogen in disguise has found the cave in Wales that houses her step-brothers Aviragus and Guiderius. They believe her to be a boy named Fidele.

Soon Cloten arrives wearing Posthumus' clothes. He and Guiderius fight, and Cloten's head is cut off.

Aviragus enters carrying the body of Imogen, aka Fidele. He and Guiderius think she/he is dead.)

Aviragus. The bird is dead
That we have made so much on. I had rather
Have <u>skipp'd from sixteen years of age to sixty</u>,
To have turn'd my leaping time into a crutch,
Than have seen this.
Guiderius. Why, he but sleeps:
If he be gone he'll make his grave a bed;
With female fairies will his tomb be haunted,
And worms will not come to thee.
Arviragus. With fairest flowers,
<u>While summer lasts</u> and I live here, Fidele,
<u>I'll sweeten thy sad grave</u>: thou shalt not lack
The flower that's like thy face, pale primrose, nor
The leaf of eglantine, whom not to slander,
Out-sweeten'd not thy breath: the Ruddock would
With charitable bill, O bill, sore shaming
Those rich-left heirs that <u>let their fathers lie</u>
<u>Without a monument!</u> bring thee all this;
Yea, and furr'd moss besides, when flowers are
none,
To winter-ground thy corpse.
Guiderius. (Sings.) Fear no more the heat o' the sun,
Nor the furious winter's rages;
Thou thy worldly task hast done,
Home art gone, and ta'en thy wages:
<u>Golden lads and girls all must,</u>
<u>As chimney sweepers, come to dust.</u>

(THE two boys grew fond of Fidele, aka Imogen. Aviragus, in his first speech, would rather have 'skipp'd from sixteen years of age to sixty' and missed his best years than to see Fidele dead.

In his second speech of the passage, Aviragus says that 'While summer lasts' 'I'll sweeten thy sad grave' with flowers. Being a boy of nature, he compares the charitable Robin's bill to wealthy heirs who 'let their fathers lie' in graves Without a monument!'

As Belarius said earlier, the boys have deep thoughts, and Will catches them poetically.

And then Guiderius shares his feelings for Fidele with a song ending with the enduring couplet, 'Golden lads . . .'

(BELARIUS enters carrying Cloten's body. Guiderius says, 'We have done our obsequies: come, lay him down.'

Belarius speaks poetically, and he and the two boys leave.

Imogen awakens, and soon she sees Cloten's headless body dressed in Posthumus' clothes.)

Belarius. Here's a few flowers; but 'bout midnight, more:

The herbs that have on them cold dew o' the night
Are strewing fitt'st for graves. Upon their faces.
You were as flowers, now wither'd: even so
These herblets shall, which we upon you strew.
Come on, away: apart upon our knees.
The ground that gave them first has them again:
Their pleasures here are past, so is their pain.
Imogen. For so I thought I was a cave-keeper,
And cook to honest creatures: but 'tis not so,
'Twas but a bolt of nothing, shot at nothing,
Which the brain makes of fumes: our very eyes
Are sometimes, like our judgments, blind.
Good faith,
I tremble still with fear: but if there be
Yet left in heaven as small a drop of pity
As a wren's eye, fear'd gods, a part of it!
The dream's here still: even when I wake it is
Without me, as within me; not imagin'd, felt.
A headless man! The garments of Posthumus!
I know the shape of 's leg: this is his hand;
His foot mercurial; his martial thigh;
The brawns of Hercules: but his Jovial face
Murder in heaven? How! 'Tis gone.
Pisanio,
All curses madded Hecuba gave the Greeks,

And mine to boot; be darted on thee! Thou,
Conspir'd with that irregulous devil, Cloten,
Hast here cut off my lord to write and read
Be henceforth treacherous ! Damn'd Pisanio
Hath with his forg'd letters, damn'd Pisanio,
From this most bravest vessel of the world
Struck the main-top! <u>O Posthumus! alas,</u>
<u>Where is thy head?</u> where's that? Ay me! where's
that?
Pisanio might have kill'd thee at the heart,
And left thy head on. How should this be? Pisanio?
'Tis he and Cloten: malice and lucre in them
Have laid this woe here. O 'tis pregnant, pregnant!
The drug he gave me, which he said was precious
And cordial to me, have I not found it
Murderous to the senses? That confirms it home
This is Pisanio'd deed and Cloten's: O!
Give colour to my pale cheek with thy blood,
That we the horrider may seem to those
Which chance to find us: O, my lord, my lord!
Cymbeline, 4.2

(IT'S worth rereading the imaginative verse in
Belarius' opening speech of the passage:

'The herbs that have on them cold dew o' the night
Are strewings fitt'st for graves.'

736

Similarly, lines eight and nine of Imogen's rending speech:

'Yet left in heaven as small a drop of pity
As a wren's eye,' are beautiful.

Imogen also mentions 'Hecuba,' the Queen of Troy in Greek mythology during the Trojan War, who gave birth to many children, including the warriors Hector and Paris. Hecuba is also mentioned in *Hamlet*. Hamlet asks one of the players to recite a scene, which he does with such emotion that Hamlet asks himself: 'What's Hecuba to him, or he to Hecuba,/That he should weep for her?'

I've heard that the London Globe Theatre put on an adaptation of Cymbeline in 2016, and they called it Imogen. Since she, not King Cymbeline, is the star of the play, it's a good title choice.

I'm wondering how they played it. Did the actress playing Imogen stay straight-faced when she asked Cloten's headless body, clad in Posthumus' clothes?

'O Posthumus! alas,
Where is thy head?'

(Of course, deadpan often works well in absurdist, or jump-the-shark sketches. In 4.3, Pisanio, servant to Posthumus and accomplice to Imogen in her adoption of disguise, meets with Posthumus and tells him he knows nothing of Imogen's whereabouts. Despite the Roman legions on Briton's shores and having no word from his master Posthumus, Pisanio remains optimistic:

All other doubts, by time let them be clear'd:
Fortune brings in some boats that are not steer'd.

(I suspect that Will had fun writing this plausibility-stretching and occasionally charade-like play. But will the audiences, a good quantity of whom have probably not read or seen the play, get it. Perhaps some laughs from the cognoscenti will cue them. I confess, as I wrote down many lines and then analyzed them, that I smiled and chuckled a lot, often, I'm sure, inappropriately.

Among Will's late plays, Cymbeline is the most fanciful. We need Polonius to designate the genre: tragic-comic? romantic-tragic? Whatever the label or none, we are happy. And given the elegant poetry and the preternatural Imogen, one of Will's great female creations, the play is a captivating treat.

This book is about Will's great speeches, and beyond this point I have no more to list. Your additions to 'Cymbeline' and other plays in the book are welcome @rnoyes1.

Be assured that by the end of Act Five the plot resolves, recognition occurs, families reunite and lovers find bliss.)

TITUS ANDRONICUS

(THE Roman General Titus Andronicus fights the invading Goths and 'With honour and with fortune is return'd' to Rome.

Tamora, Queen of the Goths and captive of Titus, pleads for her sons' lives, and in particular Alarbus, her oldest son.)

Tamora. Victorious Titus, rue the tears I shed,
A mother's passion for her son:
And if thy sons were ever dear to thee,
O, think my son to be as dear to me! . . .
Andronicus, stain not thy tomb with blood:
Wilt thou draw near the nature of the gods?
Draw near them, then, in being merciful:
<u>Sweet mercy is nobility's true badge.</u>

(Putative emperor Saturninus loves Tamora and frees her sons.

In a neat plot device, Tamora's secret lover is Aaron the moor, an able poet and a bad guy.

Note the last line in Tamora's speech above. She appeals to Titus' better angels. We'll see how that works out.)

Aaron. Now climbeth Tamora <u>Olympus' top</u>,
<u>Safe out of Fortune's shot</u>; and sits aloft,
Secure of thunder's crack or lightning's flash;
Advanc'd above pale envy's threatening reach.
And when the golden sun salutes the morn,
And, having gilt the ocean with his beams,
<u>Gallops the zodiac in his glistering coach</u>,
And overlooks the highest-peering hill;
So Tamora:
Upon her will doth earthly honour wait,
And virtue stoops and trembles at her frown.
Then, Aaron, arm thy heart and fit thy thoughts
To mount aloft with thy imperial mistress,
And mount her pitch, who thou in triumph long
Hast prisoner held, fetter'd in amorous chains,
And faster bound to Aaron's charming eyes
<u>Than is Prometheus tied to Caucasus</u>.
Away with slavish weeds and servile thoughts!
I will be bright, and shine in pearl and gold,
To wait upon this new-made empress.
To wait, said I? to wanton with this queen,
This goddess, this <u>Semiramis</u>, this nymph,
This siren, that will charm Rome's Saturnine,

And see his shipwreck and his commonweal's.
Titus Andronicus, 2.1

(Aaron confirms he's a villain when he advises Tamora to 'climb Olympus' top safe out of fortune's fate.'

LINE seven's 'Gallops the zodiac in his glistering coach' contains three superb word choices: the verb 'Gallops,' the noun 'zodiac' and the adjective 'glistering.' I also refer you back to the previous, verb-rich, lines that lead up this poetic gem.

Who but Will would attempt a speech with a phrase like 'Prometheus tied to Caucasus' in line 17? For sure, contrasting the heavens and a Russian land region works contextually. He also used the Caucasus cleverly in Richard 11:

'O, who can hold a fire in his hand By thinking on the frosty Caucasus?'

Given the reputation of the legendary Semiramis, female Babylonian leader, likened to an Amazon, I question why Aaron, in the third line from the bottom, uses her as an example with which to extol Tamora?)

(AS we read earlier, Tamora's son Alarbus was sacrificed on orders from Titus Andronicus. Her two remaining sons Demetrius and Chiron enter quarreling over who will win Titus' daughter Lavinia. And we must not forget that Bassianus, brother to Saturninus, is in love with Lavinia. Like a match between unfamiliar teams, this play needs a scorecard.

Aaron listens to the bickering over Lavinia. In an aside, he calls out: 'Clubs, clubs! these lovers will not keep the peace.' I hope that actors playing Aaron will say this line with a smile, contributing some levity to this bloody fray. If an actor, who is also a director, speaks the line he or she may inadvertently yell out: 'Props, props!

Chiron says that 'a thousand deaths' would he propose 'to achieve her.'

Aaron asks. To achieve her! How?' And his question leads to a speech that answers that question and includes two lines that will be familiar to readers or audiences of Richard III.

That speech is followed by Aaron offering contemptible advice to Demetrius and Chiron.)

Demetrius. Why mak'st thou it so strange?
She is a woman, therefore may be woo'd;
She is a woman, therefore may be won;
She is Lavinia, therefore must be lov'd.
Aaron. That which you cannot as you would achieve,

You must perforce accomplish as you may.
Take this of me, <u>Lucrece was not more chaste</u>
Than this Lavinia, Bassianus' love.
A speedier course than lingering banishment
Must we pursue, and I have found the path.
My lords, a solemn hunting is in hand;
There will the lovely Roman ladies troop:
The forest-walks are wide and spacious;
And many unfrequented plots there are
<u>Fitted by kind for rape and villainy:</u>
Single you thither, then, this dainty doe,
<u>And strike her home by force if not by words:</u>
This way, or not at all, stand you in hope. . . .
The emperor's house is like the <u>house of fame,</u>
The palace full of tongues, of eyes, and ears:
The woods are ruthless, dreadful, deaf, and dull;
There speak and strike, brave boys, and take your
turns;
There serve your lust, shadow'd from heaven's eye,
And <u>revel in Lavinia's treasury.</u>
Titus Andronicus, 2.1

(Demetrius' mention of 'a woman woo'd and won'
recalls Gloster's speech in *Richard 111*, 1.2, 226-227

THE inclusion of 'Lucrece was not more chaste' in
line three of Aaron's speech recalls Will's poem, *The
Rape of Lucrece,* and sets the stage for unsavory

references such as the final line's 'revel in Lavinia's treasury' and other debauched counsel in the text that immediately precedes it.

The 'house of fame' may refer to an earlier poem by Geoffrey Chaucer.)

(AARON buries a bag of gold under a forest tree. Tamora joins him.

Following that exchange, the lovers Bassianus and Lavinia enter, followed by Tamora's sons, Demetrius and Chiron, who stab Bassianus.

Demetrius dumps Bassianus into a pit, and Chiron drags Lavinia away.

Aaron reenters with Quintus and Martius, sons of Titus Andronicus. They discover the hole containing Bassianus' body.

The degenerate scene contains sublime poetry, and I will comment on some examples in the summary of the passage.)

Aaron. He that had wit would think that I had none.
To bury so much gold under a tree,
And never after to inherit it.
Let him that thinks of me so abjectly
Know that this gold must coin a stratagem,
Which cunningly effected, will beget

A very excellent piece of villainy:
And so repose, sweet gold, for their unrest
That have their alms out of the empress' chest.
Tamora. My lovely Aaron, wherefore look'st thou sad
When everything doth make a gleeful boast?
The birds chant melody on every bush;
The snake lies rolled in the cheerful sun;
The green leaves quiver with the cooling wind
And make a chequer'd shadow on the ground:
Under their sweet shade, Aaron, let us sit,
And, whilst the babbling echo mocks the hounds,
Replying shrilly to the well-tun'd horns,
As if a double hunt were heard at once, . . .
And curtain'd with a counsel-keeping cave,
We may, each wreathed in the other's arms,
Our pastimes done, possess a golden slumber;
Aaron. Madam, though Venus governs your desires,
Saturn is dominator over mine:
What signifies my deadly-standing eye
My silence and my cloudy melancholy,
My fleece of wooly hair that now uncurls
Even as an adder when she doth unroll
To do some fatal execution?
No, madam, there are no venereal signs,
Vengeance is in my heart, death in my hand,

Blood and revenge are hammering in my head.
Hark, Tamora, the empress of my soul,
Which never hopes more heaven than rests in thee,
This is the day of doom for Bassianus:
His Philomel must lose her tongue to-day;
Thy sons make pillage of her chastity,
And wash their hands in Bassianus' blood.

Tamora. (To her sons.) Have I not reason, think
you, to look pale and wan?

These two (Bassianus and Lavinia) have 'tic'd me
hither to this place:
A barren detested vale you see it is;
The trees, though summer, forlorn and lean,
O'ercome with moss and baleful mistletoe:
Here never shines the sun; here nothing breeds,
Unless the nightly owl or fatal raven:
And when they showed me this abhorred pit
They told me, here at dead time of the night
A thousand fiends, a thousand hissing snakes,
Ten thousand swelling toads, as many urchins,
Would make such fearful and confused cries
As any mortal body hearing it
Should straight fall mad or else die suddenly.
No sooner had they told this hellish tale
But straight they told me they would bind me here
Unto the body of a dismal yew,
And leave me to this miserable death:

And then they call'd me foul adultress,
Lascivious Goth and all the bitterest terms
That ever ear did hear to such effect:
And had you not by wondrous fortune come,
The vengeance on me had they executed.
Revenge it, as you love your mother's life,
Or be ye not henceforth call'd my children.
Lavinia. (After Bassianus is stabbed.)
When did the tiger's young one teach the dam?
O, do not learn her wrath, she taught it thee;
The milk thou suck'dst from her did turn to
marble;
Even at thy teat thou hadst thy tyranny.
Yet every mother breeds not sons alike:
Do thou entreat her show a woman pity. . . .
'Tis true, the raven doth not hatch a lark:
Yet I have heard, O, could I find it now!
The lion, mov'd with pity, did endure
To have his princely paws par'd all away:
Some say that ravens foster forlorn children,
The whilst their own birds famish in their nests:
O, be to me, though thy hard heart say no,
Nothing so kind, but something pitiful!
Tamora. Farewell, my sons: see that you make her
sure:
Ne'er let my heart know merry cheer indeed
Till all the Andronici be mad away.

Now will I hence to seek my lovely moor,
And <u>let my spleenful sons this trull deflower</u>.
Quintus. What, art thou fallen! What subtle hole is
this
Whose mouth is cover'd with rude-growing briers,
<u>Upon whose leaves are drops of new-shed blood</u>
<u>As fresh as morning's dew distill'd on flowers?</u>
A very fatal place it seems to me.
Titus Andronicus, 2.3

(LINES five and six in Tamora's first speech:

'The green leaves quiver with the cooling wind
And make a chequer'd shadow on the ground'

These lines render surpassing visualization with the
dancing shadows mirroring the leaves moving in the
breeze.

In her final line, Tamora mentions a hoped-for
intimate encounter with Aaron: 'Our pastimes done,
possess a golden slumber.' He has other things on his
mind in the first two lines of his first speech:

'Madam, though Venus governs your desires,
Saturn is dominator over mine.'

749

Even though Tamora is ruled by Venus, the goddess of love and sex, for the moment Aaron acts under Saturn who has various functions.

For example, a few lines later, 'Even as an adder when she doth unroll' signals that Aaron is preparing for mayhem. The line also echoes line four in Tamora's first speech, 'The snake lies rolled in the cheerful sun.'

To further confirm his murderous intentions, Aaron goes on to say: 'there are no venereal signs.' In this case, 'venereal' means that he is not interested in the sex act, rather 'Vengeance is in my heart.'

In her second speech of this sequence, Aaron has exited and Tamora has been joined by her two sons. In front of Bassianus and Lavinia, who arrived earlier, Tamora lies about being enticed to a bad place with thousands of fiends, snakes and 'Ten thousand swelling toads.' I admired Will's idea of including rather benign toads with fiends and snakes. I relished even more the 'swelling' as we envision a veritable army of little toad chests billowing and retracting. Will sure had fun with language.

After Tamora's sons stab Bassianus to death, Lavinia pleads for her life. In line seven's 'Tis true, the raven doth not hatch a lark' she doesn't anticipate that Tamora's sons will 'show a woman pity.' The raven metaphor is reprised a few lines later: 'Some say that ravens foster forlorn children,' but it doesn't help her as Bassianus' body is flung into a pit and Lavinia is dragged off.

As said in the preamble to this scene, Titus' sons find Bassianus' body in the hole.

As Quintus spies the 'rude-growing briers' covering the opening he delivers the most poetic and perturbing lines of the section:

Upon whose leaves are drops of new-shed blood
As fresh as morning's dew distill'd on flowers?

(THE horror continues: Titus' sons fall into the pit containing Bassianus' body, can't get out, are found, charged with the murder and face execution. Despite Titus' protestations, the emperor Saturninus says, "Let them not speak a word, the guilt is plain.'

After murdering Bassianus and raping Lavinia, Tamora's sons, Chiron and Demetrius, cut out Lavinia's tongue and chop off her hands, 'And if thy stumps will let thee play the scribe,' so she cannot report their crimes.

Next, Titus' brother Marcus sees Lavinia in her anguish. Reminder: Lavinia is Titus' daughter.)

Marcus. Speak, gentle niece, what stern ungentle hands
  Have lopp'd and hew'd, and made thy body bare
  Of her two branches, those <u>sweet ornaments</u>
  <u>Whose circling shadows kings have sought to sleep</u>
<u>in,</u>
  And might not gain so great a happiness
  As have thy love? Why dost thou not speak to me?
  Alas, a crimson river of warm blood,
  <u>Like to a bubbling fountain stirr'd with wind,</u>
  Doth rise and fall between thy rosed lips,
  Coming and going with thy honeyed breath.
  But sure some Tereus hath deflowered thee,
  And lest though shouldst detect him, cut thy
tongue.
  Ah, now thou turn'st away thy face for shame! . . .
  O, had the monster seen those lily hands
  <u>Tremble, like aspen leaves, upon a lute,</u>
  <u>And make the silken strings delight to kiss them.</u>
  Titus Andronicus, 2.4

(Is it possible to overcome the dreadful subject matter and consider the poetry? Let's try, and start with lines three and four where Marcus calls Lavinia's hands 'sweet ornaments' 'Whose circling shadows kings have sought to sleep in.' 'Circling shadows' is alone fitting language, and particularly apt as Will refers to Lavinia's missing hands.

'Like to a bubbling fountain stirr'd with wind' four lines later is descriptive, as we visualize blood foaming at Lavinia's lips with each breath she takes.

Given the shimmering light reflecting off sun-drenched and breeze-blown aspens, 'Tremble like aspen leaves, upon a lute' in the line before last is poetic.

Marcus' speech is nicely finished with 'And make the silken strings delight to kiss them.')

(TITUS grovels and wails to the Tribune's guarding Martius and Quintus before they are marched off to execution.

Then Titus debates with Lucius, his remaining son, on what can be done to free them. In this emotional conversation, a phrase is used that recalls a similar one from another of Will's plays.

But first, see a debt to Chaucer in Titus' speech that immediately follows.)

Titus. For these, good tribune's, <u>in the dust I write</u>
My heart's deep languor and my soul's sad tears:
Let my tears stanch the earth's dry appetite;
My sons' sweet blood will make it shame and blush.

O earth, I will befriend thee more with rain,
That shall distill from these two ancient ruins,
Than youthful April shall with all his showers:
In all his drought I'll drop upon thee still;
In winter, with warm tears I'll melt the snow,
And keep eternal spring-time on thy face,
So thou refuse to drink my dear sons' blood.
O reverend tribunes! O gentle aged men!
Unbind my sons, reverse the doom of death;
And let me say, that never wept before,
My tears are now prevailing orators.
Lucius. O noble father, you lament in vain:
The tribunes hear you not, no man is by;
And you recount your sorrows to a stone.
Titus. Therefore, I tell my sorrows to the stones;
Why, though they cannot answer my distress,
Yet in some sort they are better than the tribunes,
For that they will not intercept my tale:
When I do weep they humbly at my feet
Receive my tears, and seem to weep with me;
And were they but attired in grave weeds
Rome could afford no tribune like to these.
A stone is soft as wax, tribunes more hard than
stones;
A stone is silent, and offendeth not;
And tribunes with their tongues doom men to
death.

But wherefore stand'st thou with thy weapon
drawn?

Lucius. To rescue my two brothers from their
death:
For which attempt the judges have announc'd
My everlasting doom of banishment.
Titus. O happy man! they have befriended thee.
Why, foolish Lucius, dost thou not perceive
That <u>Rome is but a wilderness of tigers</u>?
Tigers must prey; and Rome affords no prey
But me and mine: how happy art thou, then,
From these devourers to be banished!
Titus Andronicus, 3.1

(IN line one, I found forlorn the phrase 'in the dust
I write' as Titus lay prostrate and begging for mercy
for his condemned sons.

As triggered in the comments above, in lines
seven and eight of Titus' first speech,

'Than youthful April shall with all his showers:
In all his drought I'll drop upon thee still;'

Owes a debt to Chaucer's initial lines in the
Prologue of the Canterbury Tales:

'Whan that Aprille with his shoures soote

The droghte of Marche hath perced to the roote,'

Even in Chaucer's Middle English, the comparison is unmistakable. Will didn't go to university, but he devotedly read the masters and forgot little.

In the final line of Titus' first speech, after using 'tears' three time before, he closes with the poignant phrase, 'My tears are now prevailing orators.' Nice.

Similarly, after Lucius tells his father, 'And you recount your sorrows to a stone,' Titus uses 'stones' or 'stone' four times to amplify his frustration with trying to win mercy from the Tribunes. Diacope is a useful rhetorical device.

Reread the passage to observe that 'doom' is used twice to contrasting effect in the Titus/Lucius interchange: 'reverse the doom of death,' and 'My everlasting doom of banishment.' Here we learn that in order to save his brothers from death, Lucius must accept banishment for life.

Titus responds by telling his son that he's better off being banished since 'Rome is but a wilderness of tigers.' A like phrase was used by Shylock in The Merchant of Venice, 3.1: 'I would not have given it for a wilderness of monkeys.'

(MARCUS and Lavinia, Titus' brother and daughter, enter.)

Titus. Speak, my Lavinia, what accursed hand
Hath made thee handless in thy father's sight?
What fool hath added water to the <u>sea</u>,
Or brought a fagot to <u>bright-burning Troy</u>?
My grief was at the height before thou cam'st;
And now, like <u>Nilus</u>, it disdaineth bounds.
<u>Give me a sword, I'll chop of my hands too</u>;
For they have fought for Rome, and all in vain; . . .
<u>For now I stand as one upon a rock,</u>
<u>Environ'd with a wilderness of sea;</u>
Who marks the waxing tide grow wave by wave,
Expecting ever when some envious surge
Will in his brinish bowels swallow him.
This way to death my wretched sons are gone;
Here stands my other son, a banish'd man;
And here my brother, weeping at my woes:
But that which gives my soul the greatest spurn
Is dear Lavinia, dearer than my soul.
Had I but see thy picture in this plight
It would have madded me: what shall I do
Now I behold thy lively body so?
Thou has no hands to wipe away thy tears,
Nor tongue to tell me who hath martyr'd thee:
Thy husband he is dead; and for his death

Thy brothers are condemn'd, and dead by this.

Aaron. (Enters.) Titus Andronicus, my lord, the emperor

Sends thee this word, that if thou love thy sons,
Let Marcus, Lucius, or thyself, old Titus,
Or any of you, <u>chop off your hand</u>
And send it the king: he for the same
Will send thee hither both thy sons alive;
And that shall be the ransom for their fault.

Titus. O gracious emperor! O gentle Aaron!
<u>Did ever raven sing so like a lark</u>
That gives sweet tidings of the sun's uprise?
With all my heart I'll send the emperor
My hand:
Good, Aaron, wilt thou help to <u>chop it off</u>? . . .
Good Aaron, give his majesty my hand:
Tell him it was a hand that warded him
From thousand dangers; bid him bury it; . . .
As for my sons, say I account of them
As jewels purchas'd at an easy price;
And yet dear too, because I bought mine own.

Aaron. I go, Andronicus: and for thy hand
<u>Look by and by to have thy sons with thee</u>:
(Aside.) <u>Their heads I mean</u>, O, how this villainy
Doth <u>fat</u> me with the very thoughts of it!
Let fools do good, and fair men call for grace,
Aaron will have his soul black like his face.

Messenger. Worthy Andronicus, ill art thou repaid
For the good hand thou sent'st the emperor.
Here are the heads of thy two noble sons;
And here's thy hand, in scorn to thee sent back,
<u>Thy griefs their sports, thy resolution mock'd</u>
That woe is to me to think upon thy woes,
More than remembrance of my father's death.
Lucius. Farewell, Andronicus, my noble father,
The woefull'st man that ever liv'd in Rome:
Farewell, proud Rome; till Lucius come again,
He leaves his pledges dearer than his life:
Farewell, Lavinia, my noble sister; . . .
If Lucius live, he will <u>requite your wrongs</u>,
And make proud Saturnine and his empress
Beg at the gates, like <u>Tarquin</u> and his queen.
<u>Now will I to the Goths, and raise a power</u>
<u>To be reveng'd on Rome and Saturnine.</u>
Titus Andronicus, 3.1

(IN lines three, four and six of his first speech, and after seeing mutilated Lavinia, Titus uses the sea, burning Troy, and the Nile in flood to describe the depths of his trauma. Will also uses these locutions to frame Titus' desperation, and have him say, 'Give me a sword, I'll chop of my hands too.' This build is worth rereading.

Then, with a one-line break, we have:

759

'For now I stand as one upon a rock,
Environ'd with a wilderness of sea;'

This is purposely or inadvertently biblical. And again, we have 'wilderness,' this time out of the jungle with tigers and monkeys and now alone, trapped on a rock, in the uncharted sea. It's one of an endless medley of language originals from Will.

After the detestable Aaron requests, on behalf of the emperor, that Titus, 'chop off your hand,' Titus says, 'Did ever raven sing so like a lark.' Will uses the contradistinction of 'raven' and 'lark' in several of his works. It's intriguing that Titus uses 'raven.' Does he suspect that Aaron was involved in the murder of Bassianus and the framing of Titus' sons?

Probably not, since Titus invites Aaron to 'chop it off,' which he does. Aaron leaves with the bloody ransom, assures Titus to 'Look by and by to have thy sons with thee,' and says in an aside, 'Their heads I mean.' I love the way Will generates malefactors with no redeeming qualities. He even gives them great verbs like 'fat' me.

The messenger who brings Titus' severed hand and his sons decapitated heads characterizes the behavior of the emperor and his court with the meritorious 'Thy griefs their sports, thy resolution mock'd.'

In the final speech of the passage, Titus' son Lucius gallantly vows to 'requite your wrongs' for his father and sister Lavinia. He is up for a fight and pledges:

'Now will I to the Goths, and raise a power
To be reveng'd on Rome and Saturnine.'

No way will Lucius, Titus' son, let the would-be emperor Saturnine reign. He'll beg at the gates like 'Tarquin' the last king of Rome, a tyrannical ruler who was over- thrown leading to the establishment of the Roman Republic around 510 B.C.)

(WILL keeps his characters in character and dealing with their frailties whether they understand them or not. In this passage, members of Titus' family sit for a meal.

Despite chiding from his brother Marcus, Titus, in his own heavy-handed, but well-meaning and spirited way, encourages his daughter Lavinia to buck up and deal with her damaged body.

We also meet Titus' precocious grandson, young Lucius.)

Titus. When thy poor heart beats with outrageous beating,
   Thou canst not strike it thus to make it still.
   <u>Wound it with sighing, girl; kill it with groans;</u>
   <u>Or get some little knife between thy teeth,</u>
   And just against thy heart make thou a hole,
   That all the tears that thy poor eyes let fall
   May run into that sink, and, soaking in,
   Drown the lamenting fool in sea-salt tears.
Marcus. Fie, brother, fie! teach her not thus to lay
   Such violent hands upon her tender life.
Titus. Why, Marcus, no man should be mad but I.
   What violent hands can she lay on her life?
   Ah, wherefore dost thou urge the name of hands;
   To bid Aeneas tell the tale twice o'er
   How Troy was burnt and he made miserable?
   O, handle not the theme, to talk of hands,
   Lest we remember still that we have none.
   Fie, fie, how frantically I square my talk,
   And if we forget we had no hands,
   If Marcus did not name the word of hands!
   Come, let's fall to; and, gentle girl, eat this.
   Here is no drink! Hark, Marcus, what she says;
   I can <u>interpret all her martyr'd signs;</u>
   She says she drinks no other drink but tears,
   Brew'd with her sorrow, mesh'd upon her cheeks:

762

Speechless complainer, I will learn thy thought;
In thy dumb action will I be as perfect
As begging hermits in their holy prayers:
Thou shalt not sigh nor hold thy stumps to heaven,
Nor wink, nor nod, nor kneel, nor make a sign,
But I of these will wrest an alphabet.
And by still practice learn to know thy meaning.
Young Lucius. Good grandsire, leave these bitter
deep laments:
Make my aunt merry with some pleasing tale.
Titus. Peace, tender sapling; thou art made of tears,
And tears will quickly melt thy life away.
Titus Andronicus, 3.2

(Enduring unlimited hardships, Titus is nothing if
not positive-minded. He gives Lavinia some tough
love on how to stop her heart from wildly beating:
'Wound it with sighing, girl; kill it with groans.' Or,
failing that, 'get some little knife between thy teeth.'
And make a hole for the tears to fall into.' Hmm.

Titus is also determined to communicate with
the 'Speechless complainer.' He will 'interpret all her
martyr'd signs' as well as 'begging hermits in their holy
prayers.' From any sign Lavinia makes Titus will 'will
wrest an alphabet' and 'by still practice learn to know
thy meaning.'

Young Lucius says to Titus that he should take it a little easier on Lavinia and 'Make my aunt merry with some pleasing tale. Titus says forget the tears they will, 'quickly melt thy life away.' Titus is insightfully drawn as a well-intentioned but unsympathetic, unforgiving man.)

(NEXT, Will, through Young Lucius, thinks back to his youth and the influence of books he has read, some passed on by grandfather Arden to his mother Mary Shakespeare and then to him.

How do I know this? Because I wrote it that way in a scene from Will's boyhood in the novel 'Discovering Will's Lost Years.' In a later scene from the book, Will, as the new tutor to noble children, goes into the house library for the first time and is overwhelmed by the two-tiered rows of books. He thinks: *Oh, for the time and opportunity to read them all, to grasp them, turn pages, smell them, bathe in—*

The erudite and striking lady of the house enters, sees Will admiring the books, and says, 'I share your proclivity, for books contain and nourish all the world.'

Back to this book: Lavinia chases Young Lucius through Titus' house. He is afraid, because Lavinia is making signs to him, but is reassured by his grandfather.)

Titus. Ah, boy, Cornelia never with more care
Read to her sons than she hath read to thee
Sweet poetry and Tully's Orator.
Young Lucius. For I have heard my grandsire say full oft
Extremity of griefs would make men mad;
And I have read that Hecuba of Troy
Ran mad through sorrow: that made me to fear;
Although, my lord, I know my noble aunt
Loves me as dear as e'er my mother did,
And would not, but in fury, fright my youth:
Which made me down to throw my books, and fly,
Causeless perhaps, but pardon me sweet aunt.
Titus. How now, Lavinia! Marcus, what means this?
Some book there is that she desires to see.
Which is it, girl, of these? Open them, boy.
But thou art deeper read and better skill'd:
Come, and take choice of all my library,
And so beguile thy sorrow, till the heavens
Reveal the damn'd contriver of this deed.
Why lifts she up her arms in sequence thus?
Marcus. I think she means that there was more than one
Confederate in the fact; ay, more there was,

Or else to heaven she heaves them for revenge.
Titus. What book is that she tosseth so?
Young   Lucius.   <u>Grandsire,   'tis   Ovid's</u>
<u>Metamorphosis;</u>
  <u>My mother gave it to me.</u>
Titus Andronicus, 4.1

(Throughout this passage, Will, while previewing a revelation in the play, recollects his youth, summarized neatly in Young Lucius' final two lines 'tis Ovid's Metamorphosis; My mother gave it to me . . .'

For clarity, 'Tully,' or Cicero, was a noted Roman orator around 60 BC.

As noted by Imogen in *Cymbeline,* as 'madded Hecuba.' Hecuba, mentioned above in *Titus,* was a Queen of Troy in Greek mythology. Young Lucius compares her running 'mad with sorrow' to the stricken Lavinia.

Next, we learn why Lavinia chased Young Lucius and the books he was carrying and why she selected the Ovid.)

Titus. Soft! See how busily she turns the leaves!
Help her:
What would she find? Lavinia, shall I read?
This the tragic tale of Philomel,

And treats of Tereus' treason and his rape;
And rape, I fear, was root of thine annoy. . . .
Lavinia, wert thou thus surpris'd, sweet girl,
Ravish'd and wrong'd as Philomela was,
Forc'd in the ruthless, vast, and gloomy woods? . .
.

Give signs, sweet girl, for here are none but friends,
What Roman lord it was durst do the deed:
Or slunk not Saturnine, as <u>Tarquin</u> erst
<u>That left the camp to sin in Lucrece' bed</u>?
Titus Andronicus, 4.1

(The concluding line of the passage refers to The
Rape of Lucrece, Will's poem written around the
same time as Titus Andronicus. In the before-
mentioned work, 'Tarquin' left the Roman camp and
raped the wife of one of his fellow soldiers.

Following Titus' powerful speech, Lavinia takes
a stick between her teeth and writes the names of her
attackers in the dirt: Chiron and Demetrius, the Goth
Queen Tamora's sons.)

(AS a diversionary tactic, Young Lucius delivers
weapons and messages from his grandfather Titus to
the Goth Queen's sons Chiron and Demetrius. They

ask him 'What's the news?' Lucius answers in an aside, 'That you are both decipher'd, that's the news.'

After Lucius leaves, Demetrius unwinds one of the scrolls and reads while his brother and Aaron listen:

Integer vitae, scelerisque purus
Non eget Mauri jaculis, nec arcu.

Translation: 'The man who is of pure life and free from crime needs not the bows and arrows of the Moor.')

Chiron. O, 'tis a verse in Horace; I know it well:
I read it in the grammar long ago.
Aaron. Ay, just, a verse in Horace; right you have it.
Now, what a thing it is to be an ass!
(Aside.) Here's no sound jest! the old man hath found their guilt;
And sends them weapons wrapp'd about with lines,
That wound, beyond their feeling, to the quick.
Titus Andronicus, 4.2

(ONLY the credulous believe that young Goths have been to grammar school. Will, speaking through Chiron, recollects the apt phrase in Horace from his grammar school education, where he studied the classics and read and spoke in Latin.

Aaron comprehends the message from Titus and recognizes that it is 'beyond their feeling,' meaning that Demetrius and Chiron don't know 'the old man hath found their guilt.')

(TRUMPETS are heard. Chiron and Demetrius believe that their mother, the empress Tamora, has had a son by her husband Saturninus. A nurse brings in the baby who is black. The nurse and Tamora's sons want to kill it. 'I'll broach the tadpole on my rapier's point.' They know that the baby will shame their mother and probably result in her death and theirs. Aaron holds and protects his baby at sword-point and goes dramatically poetic. I see James Earl Jones, deep-voiced and majestic as Othello and Lear, in the role.)

Aaron. <u>Sooner this sword shall plough thy bowels up.</u>
Stay, murderous villains! will you kill your brother?
Now, but the burning tapers of the sky,
That shone so brightly when this baby was got,
He dies upon my scimitar's sharp point
That touches this my first-born son and heir!

I tell you, younglings, not <u>Enceladus</u>,
With all his threatening band of <u>Typhon's</u> brood,
Nor great <u>Alcides</u>, nor the god of war,
Shall <u>sieze this prey out of his father's hands</u>.
What, what, ye sanguine, shallow-hearted boys!
<u>Ye white lim'd walls! ye alehouse-painted signs!</u>
<u>Coal-black</u> is better than another hue,
In that it scorns to bear another hue;
<u>For all the water in the ocean</u>
<u>Can never turn a swan's black legs to white</u>,
Although she lave them hourly in the flood.
Tell the empress from me, I am of age
To keep mine own, excuse it how she can.
Titus Andronicus, 4.2

(THE first line of the speech, 'Sooner this sword shall plough thy bowels up,' is spoken after Demetrius threatens to kill Aaron's baby.

In line seven 'the mythological giant 'Enceladus,' and in line eight the monster 'Typhon' are invoked by Aaron to emphasize his will to protect his baby. This is strong company. However, Aaron doesn't think it's enough and claims that even Hercules, born as Alcides, 'nor the god of war,' Ares, can 'sieze this prey out of his father's hands.' I am constantly impressed by how much mythology Will remembered and researched.

Aaron uses creative language to contrast his 'Coal-black' color with the white skin of Demetrius and Chiron: 'Ye white lim'd walls! ye alehouse-painted signs! They may have white-washed walls in Third-Century A.D. Probably no 'Alehouse signs' were in view, but Will saw plenty of them in his times.

A few lines later we have an absorbing phrase:

'For all the water in the ocean
Can never turn a swan's black legs to white,'

The ever-imaginative Will uses a swan, which is immediately thought of as being white, to illustrate that the color of humans, in this case Aaron's baby, is fixed at birth, and can't be washed away. And Will uses a swan's black legs to make the point. Excellent!

This also brings to mind the generalization-defeating statement that there are no black swans. This can only be proved if we are able to inventory all the swans in the world. The black-swan effect is used to label shocks like a stock-market crash, a loose analogy at best.

Back to Aaron who learns from the nurse that in addition to the empress, only 'Cornelia the midwife and myself' have seen the baby. Because he doesn't want witnesses, Aaron promptly stabs the nurse.

Then he instructs Chiron and Demetrius to 'Go
to the empress' and tell her of the scheme, then
purchase with gold a white baby he knows of and take
it to court,

And be received for the emperor's heir,
And substituted in the place of mine
To calm this tempest whirling in the court;
And let the emperor dandle him for his own.

(Lucius, Titus' son, bivouacs with a Goth army on
a plain near Rome. A soldier enters leading Aaron
carrying his baby.)

Lucius. O worthy Goth, this is the incarnate devil
That robb'd Andronicus of his good hand;
This is the pearl that pleas'd your empress' eye;
And here's the base fruit of his burning lust.
Say, wall-ey'd slave, whither wouldst thou convey
This growing image of thy fiend-like face?
Why dost thou not speak? what, deaf?
A halter, soldiers; hang him on this tree,
And by his side his fruit of bastardy.
Aaron. Lucius, save the child,
And bear it from me to the empress.
If thou do this, I'll show thee wondrous things

That highly may advantage thee to hear: . . .
For I must talk of murders, rapes, and massacres,
Acts of black night, abominable deeds,
Complots of mischief, treason, villainies,
Ruthful to hear, yet piteously perform'd:
And this shall all be buried with my death,
Unless thou swear to me my child shall live.
Lucius. Even by my god I swear to thee I will.
Aaron. First know thou, I begot him on the
empress.
Lucius. O most insatiate luxurious woman!
Aaron. Tut, Lucius, this was but a deed of charity
To that which thou shalt hear of me anon.
'Twas her two sons that murder'd Bassianus;
They cut thy sister's tongue and ravish'd her,
And cut her hands and trimm'd her as thou saw'st.
. . .

Indeed, I was their tutor to instruct
That codding spirit had they from their mother,
As sure a card as ever won the set;
That bloody mind, I think, they learn'd of me,
As true a dog as ever fought at head,
Well, let my deeds be witness of my worth.
I train'd thy brethren to that guileful hole
Where the dead corpse of Bassianus lay:
I wrote the letter that thy father found,
And hid the gold within the letter mention'd,

Confederate with the queen and her two sons: . . .
Even now I curse the day, and yet, I think,
Few come within the compass of my curse,
Wherein I did not some notorious ill:
As, kill a man, or else devise his death;
Ravish a maid, or plot the way to do it;
Accuse some innocent, and forswear myself;
Set deadly enmity between two friends;
Make poor men's cattle stray and break their necks;
Set fire on barns and hay-stacks in the night,
And bid the owners quench them with their tears.
Oft have I digg'd up dead men from their graves,
And set them upright at their dear friends' doors,
Even when their sorrows almost were forgot;
And on their skins, as on the bark of trees,
Have with my knife carved in Roman letters,
Let not your sorrow die, though I am dead.
Tut, I have done a thousand dreadful things
As willingly as one would kill a fly;
And nothing grieves me heartily indeed
But that I cannot do ten thousand more.
Titus Andronicus, 5.1

(WHEN Will makes villains, he makes them complete. Aaron is up, or is it down, there with the best. Or, is it worst?

You can see the actor adjusting his sleeve and possibly sniffing, as he delivers the first line in Aaron's fourth speech of the passage on getting Tamora pregnant: 'Tut, Lucius, this was but a deed of charity.'

Eight lines later with the deft, 'As sure a card as ever won the set,' Aaron confirms his tutoring of Tamora's boys, Chiron and Demetrius, who were already-corrupted with her fraudulent spirit. Although he offers with pride, 'That bloody mind, I think, they learn'd of me.'

About halfway through his speech, Aaron reminds of the breadth of his beastly ways with, 'Few come within the compass of my curse.'

The remaining vile litany is highlighted by Aaron bragging on digging up dead men from their graves, propping them 'upright at their dear friends' doors' and carving messages on their skin: 'Let not your sorrow die, though I am dead.'

'Tut,' Aaron's fussy disparagement, or his 'don't worry about it,' is also used in Richard 111, when Gloster says, in effect, 'no problem.' If I can't get the crown this way, "I'll pluck it down.'

Following this loathsome rant, Lucius tells the Goth soldiers to cut Aaron down for he doesn't deserve 'So sweet a death as hanging.'

(Tamora and her sons in disguise knock on Titus' door. He sees through them.)

Tamora. Know thou, sad man, I am not Tamora;
She is thy enemy and I thy friend:
I am Revenge; sent from the infernal kingdom
To ease the gnawing vulture of thy mind
By working wreakful vengeance on the foes.
Come down and welcome me to this world's light;
Confer with me of murder and of death:
There's not a hollow cave or lurking-place,
No vast obscurity or misty vale
Where bloody murder or detested rape
Can couch for fear but I will find them out;
And in their ears tell them my dreadful name,
Revenge, which makes the foul offenders quake.
Titus. Do me some service ere I come to thee.
Lo, by thy side where Rape and Murder stands;
Now give some 'surance that thou art Revenge,
Stab them, or tear them on thy chariot wheels;
And then I'll come and be thy waggoner,
And whirl along with thee about the globe.
Titus Andronicus, 5.2

(TAMORA, posing as Revenge, uses biting language to put Titus' mind at rest in line four of her speech: 'To ease the gnawing vulture of thy mind.'

Five lines later, Tamora reassures Titus that evildoers cannot hide from her. Even a 'vast obscurity' cannot save them.

In line two of his speech, Titus tells Tamora: 'Lo, by thy side where Rape and Murder stands' showing he knows that her two guilty sons accompany her.

Titus invites Tamora to 'tear them on thy chariot wheels.' He will drive the chariot 'And whirl along with thee about the globe.' Note the visual-provoking verb 'whirl' corresponding to wheel.

Also, 'About the globe' harkens back to Tamora's brag that 'No vast obscurity' can hide the 'foes.'

(Titus remarks about Tamora's sons Chiron and Demetrius, posing as Rape and Murder, 'Good lord, how like the empress' sons they are.'

Tamora misses the cues: 'For now he takes me firmly for Revenge.'

Tamora says she will now leave and take 'take my ministers along with me.', Titus says, 'Nay, nay, let Rape and Murder stay with me,' and she agrees to leave her sons with Titus who cuts their throats.)

Titus. And now prepare your throats. Lavinia, come.

Receive the blood: and when that they are dead,
Let me grind their bones to powder small,
And with this hateful liquor temper it;
And in that paste let their vile heads be bak'd.
Come, come, be every one officious
To make this banquet; which I wish may prove
More stern and bloody than the Centaurs' feast.
So, now bring them in, for I will play the cook,
And see them ready 'gainst their mother comes.
Titus Andronicus, 5.2

(Three lines from the end of Titus' grisly speech he hopes to 'Make this banquet' 'More stern and bloody than the Centaurs' feast. In the legends, the Centaurs are invited to a wedding feast, drink alcohol, and borrowing a line from 'Measure for Measure,' 'quite athwart goes all decorum.' Also, a little milder since it refers to how 'the baby beat the nurse,' an appealingly humorous idea.)

(The Emperor Saturninus and the Empress Tamora arrive, along with other dignitaries. Titus presides dressed like a chef, invites them to eat.

Saturninus asks, 'Why art thou thus attired, Andronicus?' Titus answers that he wants all to be well as he entertains them.

Tamora says, 'We are beholden to you,' Titus responds, and the play concludes in a bloodbath.)

Titus. And if your highness knew my heart, you were.

My lord the emperor, resolve me this:
Was it well done of rash Virginius
To slay his daughter with his own right hand,
Because she was enforc'd, stain'd and deflower'd?
Saturninus. It was, Andronicus. . .
Because the girl should not survive her shame,
And by her presence still renew his sorrows.
Titus. A reason, mighty, strong, and effectual;
A pattern, precedent, and lively warrant
For me, most wretched, to perform the like:
Die, die, Lavinia, and thy shame with thee:
And with thy shame thy father's sorrows die!
Tamora. Why hast thou slain thine only daughter thus?
Titus. Not I; 'twas Chiron and Demetrius:
That ravish'd her, and cut away her tongue;
And they, 'twas they that did her all this wrong.
Saturninus. Go, fetch them hither to us presently.
Titus. Why, there they are both, baked in that pie,

Whereof their mother daintily hath fed,
Eating the flesh that she herself hath bred.
'Tis true, 'tis true; witness my knife's sharp point.
Titus Andronicus, 5.3

('Baked in that pie.' Nice twist when Titus gets Tamora to eat pie that contains the baked remains of her sons.

THE 'knife's sharp point' that chopped up Chiron and Demetrius kills Tamora. Saturninus stabs Titus, and Titus' son Lucius stabs Saturninus.

The play ends with Marcus, Titus' brother, asking his nephew, Lucius, to talk:

'Your hearts will throb and weep to hear him speak.'

Lucius speaks lofty words about Rome and Titus. He then turns to Aaron, 'this execrable wretch' and 'the heinous tiger' Tamora.)

Lucius. Set him breast-deep in earth, and famish him;
There let him stand, and rave, and cry for food;
If any one relives or pities him,
For the offence he dies. This is our doom:
Some stay to see him fasten'd in the earth. . . .
As for the heinous tiger, Tamora,
No funeral rite, nor man in mournful weeds,

No mournful bell shall ring her burial;
But throw her forth to beasts and birds of prey:
Her life was beast-like and devoid of pity;
And, being so, shall have like want of pity.
Titus Andronicus, 5.3

PERICLES

(GOWER, serving as Chorus, delivers a long introduction. We truncate this passage, but hint at what's to come, ranging from incest to purity. The relationships of two fathers and two daughters are initially at the crux of the play.)

Gower. The beauty of <u>this sinful dame</u>
Made many princes thither frame
To seek her as a bed-fellow,
In marriage-pleasures play-fellow:
Which to prevent he made a law,
To keep her still, and men in awe,
That whoso ask'd for her his wife,
His riddle told not, lost his life:
So for her many a <u>wight</u> did die,
As <u>yon grim looks</u> to testify.
What now ensues, to the judgment of your eye,
I give, my cause who best can justify.
Pericles, Chorus.

(CHORUS describes the Daughter of Antiochus, King of Antioch.

782

The gist is that 'this sinful dame' is a knockout who is in an incestuous relationship with her father. Potential suitors, or 'wights,' who fancy her, can look but they better not touch or they die, as his 'yon grim looks' attest.

Gower's construction of 'this sinful dame' reads curiously 20th-Century, film-noirish. I see a 1940's movie poster of Barbara Stanwyck in 'Double Indemnity,' or Jane Greer in 'Out of the Past,' the latter released in the UK as 'Build My Gallows High.' Stanwyck and Greer played classic *femme fatales* to perfection.)

(PERICLES, Prince of Tyre, enters Antiochus' palace with wooing on his mind. Antiochus asks him whether he understands 'The danger of the task you undertake.)

Pericles. I have, Antiochus, and, with a soul
Embolden'd with the glory of her praise,
Think death no hazard in the enterprise.
Antiochus. Bring in our daughter, clothed like a
bride,
For the embracements even of Jove himself;
At whose conception, till Lucina reign'd,
Nature this dowry gave, to glad her presence,

The <u>senate-house of planets</u> all did sit,
To <u>knit in her their best perfections</u>.
Pericles. <u>See where she comes, apparell'd like the</u>
<u>spring</u>,
　　Graces her subjects, and her thoughts the king
　　Of every virtue gives renown to men!
　　<u>Her face the book of praises</u>, where is read . . .
　　Ye gods, that made me man, and sway in love,
　　That have inflam'd desire in my breast
　　To taste the fruit of yon celestial tree,
　　Or die in the adventure, be my helps,
　　As I am son and servant to your will,
　　To compass such a boundless happiness!
　　Antiochus. Before thee stands this fair Hesperides,
　　With golden fruit, but dangerous to be touch'd;
　　For death-like dragons here affright thee hard:
　　Her face, like heaven, enticeth thee to view
　　Her countless glory, which desert must gain;
　　And which, without desert, because thine eye
　　Presumes to reach, all thy whole heap must die. . .

　　Here they stand <u>martyr's, slain in Cupid's wars</u>;
　　And <u>with dead cheeks advise thee to desist</u>
　　For going on death's net, whom none resist.
　　Pericles, 1.1

784

(PERICLES is so taken with the idea of wedding the daughter of Antiochus, he thinks 'death no hazard in the enterprise.'

Given the incestuous relationship, it is ironic that Antiochus says, 'Bring in our daughter, clothed like a bride.'

He goes on to say that Jupiter, god of the sky, Lucina, goddess of childbirth, and 'the senate-house of planets' all contributed 'To knit in her their best perfections.'

'Senate-house of planets' is marvelous.

Pericles joins the admiration with, 'See where she comes, apparell'd like the spring,' and the charming, 'Her face the book of praises.'

After more waxing lyrical about his daughter, Antiochus warns Pericles: 'martyr's, slain in Cupid's wars' 'with dead cheeks advise thee to desist.'

I found 'Cupid' bracketed by 'martyrs,' and 'wars' exceptional.)

(PERICLES tells the daughter of his 'unspotted 'fire of love to you.' But he understands the outré circumstances and the danger of getting involved. After Antiochus and his daughter exit, Pericles speaks his thoughts to the audience.)

Pericles. How courtesy would seem to cover sin,
When what is done is like an hypocrite,
The which is good in nothing but in sight!
If it be true that I interpret false,
That were it certain you were not so bad
As with foul incest to abuse your soul;
Where now you're both a father and a son,
By your untimely clasping with your child,
Which pleasure fits an husband, not a father;
And she an eater of her mother's flesh,
By the defiling of her parent's bed;
And both like serpents are, who, though they feed
On sweetest flowers, yet thy poison breed.
Antioch, farewell! for wisdom sees, those men
Blush not in actions blacker than the night
Will shun no course to keep them from the light.
One sin I know another doth provoke;
Murder's as near to lust as flame to smoke:
Poison and treason are the hands of sin,
Ay, and the targets to put off the shame:
Then, lest my life be cropp'd to keep you clear,
By flight, I'll shun the danger which I fear.
Pericles, 1.1

(A speech of insight and feeling: Two gripping lines
made me pause and reread, 'untimely clasping with
your child' and 'she an eater of her mother's flesh.'

786

'Murder's as near . . . and 'Poison and treason . . .' are two aphoristic truisms.

'By flight . . .' indicates that Pericles knows the risks and takes to the sea.

Antioch knows that Pericles knows: 'He must not live to trumpet forth my infamy,' and orders an aide, 'thou must kill him.')

(Thaliard, the lord who Antioch ordered to kill Pericles, goes on his mission but finds that Pericles has gone to sea, where he is shipwrecked and thrown upon the rocky shore. Pericles speaks of his misfortune.

Afterwards, three fishermen talk of the peculiarities of life and then find Pericles.

Pericles. Yet cease your ire, <u>you angry stars of heaven</u>!

Wind, rain, and thunder, remember, earthly man

Is but a substance that must yield to you;

<u>And I, as fits my nature, do obey you</u>:

Alas, the sea hath cast me on the rocks,

Wash'd me from shore to shore, and left me breath

Nothing to think on but ensuing death:

Let it suffice the greatness of your powers

To have bereft a prince of all his fortunes;

And having thrown him from your watery grave,
Here to have death in peace is all he'll crave.

Fisherman 3. Master, I marvel how the fishes live in the sea.

Fisherman 1. Why, as man do a-land, the great ones eat up the little ones: I can compare our rich misers to nothing so fitly as to a whale; 'a plays and tumbles, driving the poor fry before him, and at last devours them all at a mouthful: such whales have I heard on the land, who never leave gaping till they' swallow'd the whole parish, church, steeple, bells, and all.

Pericles. Nay, see the sea hath cast upon your coast,

Fisherman 2. What a drunken knave was the sea to cast thee in our way.

Pericles. A man, whom both the waters and the wind
In that vast tennis-court hath made the ball
For them to play upon, entreats you to pity him;
He asks of you that never used to beg. . . .
What I have been I forgot to know;
But what I am, want teaches me to think on:
A man throng'd up with cold; my veins are chill,
And have more life than may suffice
To give my tongue that heat to ask your help;
Which if you shall refuse, when I am dead,
For that I am a man, pray see me buried.

Fisherman 1. Die, quoth 'a? Now gods forbid! I have a gown here; come, put it on; keep thee warm. Now, afore me, a handsome fellow!

Come, thou shalt go home, and we'll have flesh for holidays, fish for fasting-days, and moreo'er puddings and flapjacks; and thou shalt be welcome.

Pericles, 2.1

(By mentioning the 'angry stars of heaven' and his nature' tells us that Pericles is on the right side, at least according to Elizabethan beliefs.

FISHERMAN ONE has a moral on how fishes live in the sea: 'great ones eat up the little ones,' and how human 'whales' live on land: 'till they swallow'd the whole parish, church, steeple, bells, and all.' Did Will have a lesson on economic inequality over four-hundred years ago that applies today? Or is he simply saying that it's better to be a big fish than a little one.

We have, 'In that vast tennis-court hath made the ball,' a use of tennis as metaphor, this time for the sea. In Henry V, 1.2, the Dauphin of France sends, 'Tennis balls, my liege,' to King Henry as an insult.

Evidence of Will having the common touch, and knowing the innate generosity of ordinary folk, is evident throughout his works. The fisherman doesn't say, 'We'll take you to our home.' Instead he says, 'Come, thou shalt go home.' and then promises, 'flesh for holidays, fish for fasting-days, and moreo'er puddings and flapjacks; and thou shalt be welcome.' How nice, and lovingly-written a sentiment this is, including the surprising 'flapjacks.'

Pericles asks where he is. Fisherman One: 'this is called Pentapolis, and our king the good Simonides . . . and deserves so to be called for his peaceable reign and good government . . . and I'll tell you, he hath a fair daughter, and tomorrow is her birthday; and there are princes and knights come from all parts of the world to joust and tourney for her love.' Dare we guess where Pericles is heading next?

In a net, the fishermen find a coat given to Pericles by his father. Pericles wears it to King Simonides Court, 'Where with it I may appear a gentleman.'

Fisherman Two says, 'I'll bring thee to the court myself.'

(KING SIMONIDES and his daughter, Thaisa, 'Sits there; like beauty's child,' appraise Pericles' five competitors: 'a knight of Sparta,' 'a prince of Macedon,' and so on, all bearing precious and unique gifts for Princess Thaisa.

Pericles is the sixth knight. He offers 'A wither'd branch' with the motto: *In hac spe vivo*, In hope I live.

They like the moral, but wonder at Pericles 'rusty outside,' meaning the coat rescued from the sea. Simonides observes:

> Opinion's but a fool, that makes us scan
> The outward habit by the inward man.

Later, the six knights attend a banquet, at which time Thaisa tells Pericles:

> To whom this wreath of victory I give,
> And crown you king of this day's happiness.

Simonides says of Pericles, 'He is but a country gentleman . . . let it pass.'

Thaisa says, "To me he seems like diamond to glass.'

Pericles speaks of King Simonides, and, when asked by Thaisa, 'Of whence you are, your name and parentage,' tells of himself.

> *Pericles.* Yon king's to me like to my father's picture,
> Which tell me in that glory once he was;
> Had princes sit, like stars, about his throne,
> And he the sun, for them to reverence;
> None that beheld him, but like <u>lesser lights</u>,
> Did vail their crown to his supremacy:

Where now his son's like a glowworm in the night,
The which hath fire in darkness, none in light:
<u>Whereby I see that Time's the king of men,</u>
<u>For he's their parent, and he is their grave,</u>
<u>And gives them what he will, not what they crave</u> .

. .

A gentleman of Tyre, my name Pericles;
My education been in arts and arms;
Who, looking for adventures in the world,
Was by the rough seas reft of ships and men,
And after shipwreck driven upon this shore.
Pericles, 2.2 and 2.3

(NOTE 'lesser lights' in line five.

Four lines later, 'Whereby I see that Time's the king of men' launches the perceptive couplet that follows: 'For he's their parent . . . and suggests that 'time,' like nature, controls destiny.

In his brief resume, Pericles' inelaborate language fits his likable, simple and direct manner.)

(In scene four, the incestuous Antiochus and his daughter sit in a chariot when 'A fire from heaven came' and burned them to death. As Helicanus said, 'sin had his reward.'

We return to the main story in scene four where Simonides tells the knights, that for reasons he does not understand, his daughter Thaisa wishes to wait twelve months before undertaking 'A married life.'

The king discovers a letter written by Thaisa stating that 'she'll wed the stranger knight' 'Or never more to view nor day nor light.' Simonides likes the idea, 'Tis well mistress; your choice agrees with mine.'

Pericles enters and sees the letter. As a tactic to prove his worth, Simonides accuses Pericles of bewitching his daughter. He calls Pericles a traitor and a liar. Pericles says, 'I return the lie,' and, in an aside, the king says, 'I do applaud his courage.'

Act two ends with King Simonides telling Thaisa that either she bends her will to his, or 'I will make you man and wife.'

Thaisa asks Pericles if he loves her: 'Even as my life or blood that fosters it.'

Then Simonides asks, 'What, are you both agreed?' They both say yes, if it pleases him.

Simonides. It pleaseth me so well that I will see you wed;

And then, with what haste you can, get you to bed.
Pericles, 2.5

(Much of the past two acts, not written by Will, are light on great passages and heavy on narrative. However, the continuity is necessary and will be helpful to understanding as we move into the final three acts, written by Will.

Will's imagination ran riot in his later plays like this one, Cymbeline and Coriolanus. They are not long on plot, have fewer soaring speeches, but are rewarding to read and amusing on stage.

Pericles and Thaisa marry and have a child, appropriately called Marina. They learn by letter that with Antiochus dead, Helicanus, a lord of Tyre, may grab the crown. The new family boards a ship that nearly founders in a storm and Thaisa is lost overboard.

Before Pericles learns of his wife's death, Chorus tells us that 'The sea-toss'd Pericles appears to speak.'

Pericles. Thou god of this great vast, rebuke these surges,

Which wash both heaven and hell; and thou that hast

Upon the winds command, <u>bind them in brass,</u>

Having call'd them from the deep! O, still

<u>Thy deafening, dreadful thunders; gently quench</u>

Thy nimble, sulphurous flashes! O, how, Lychorida,

How does my queen? Thou stormest venomously;
Wilt thou split all thyself? <u>The seaman's whistle</u>
<u>Is as a whisper in the ears of death</u>,
Unheard. <u>Lychorida! Lucina</u>, O
Divinest patroness, and midwife gentle
To those that cry by night, convey thy deity
Aboard our <u>dancing</u> boat; make swift the pangs
Of my <u>queen's travail</u>.
Pericles, 3.1

(UNDER Will's pen, Pericles is suddenly a more accomplished poet. Telling the sea god in line three to 'bind them in brass' is a highly-imaginative way of asking that the winds be stopped.

Two lines later, Pericles asks that 'Thy deafening, dreadful thunders; gently quench' the lightning. The use of 'gently' makes the line sing.

We learn, in another dash of poetry, that the storm and crashing sea are so loud that the seaman's whistle is a 'whisper in the ears of death.'

Pericles cries out for help with the 'queen's travail' to Lychorida! his baby's nurse and Lucina, the goddess of childbirth.

Reach back to the second line from the end and enjoy the vivid verb 'dancing.')

(THE NURSE Lychorida enters to offer Pericles his baby: 'Take in your arms this piece of your dead queen.'

Pericles speaks of his 'love of this poor infant, this fresh-new seafarer.'

A sailor tells Pericles of superstition regarding his drowned wife Thaisa, who is still aboard the ship. Pericles then speaks over Thaisa's body and prepares her burial at sea.)

Sailor One. Sir, your queen must overboard: the sea works high, the wind is loud, and will not lie till the ship be cleared of the dead . . .

Pardon us, sir; with us at sea it hath been still observed; and we are strong in custom. Therefore briefly yield her; for she must overboard straight.

Pericles. A terrible childbed hast thou had, my dear;
No light, no fire: the unfriendly elements
Forgot thee utterly; nor have I time
To give thee hallow'd to thy grave, but straight
Must cast thee, scarcely coffin'd, in the ooze;
Where, for a monument upon thy bones,
And aye-remaining lamps, the belching whale
And humming water must o'erwhelm thy corpse,
Lying with simple shells. O Lychorida,
Bid Nestor bring me spices, ink and paper,
My casket and my jewels; and bid Nicander

Bring me the satin coffer: lay the babe
Upon the pillow: hie thee, whiles I say
<u>A priestly farewell to her: suddenly, woman.</u>
Sailor Two. Sir, we have a chest beneath the hatches,
<u>caulked and bitumed ready.</u>
Pericles, 3.1

(Mark in the introductory comments to this passage, Pericles tenderly calling his baby, 'this fresh-new seafarer?'

Line five in Pericles' speech, 'Must cast thee, scarcely coffin'd, in the ooze' is mournful, especially with 'ooze' at its close.

'Nestor' from Greek mythology is one who returns from the sea. Nicander was a Greek poet and doctor and a good candidate to comfort Pericles' baby.

Pericles' final line, 'A priestly farewell to her: suddenly, woman,' is distinctive for the deep feeling in his use of 'priestly' and the last two words: 'suddenly, woman.' I don't know what Will meant by the haunting 'suddenly, woman.' Perhaps someone can help me with a message. Thank you: @rnoyes1

See again the important, underlined clue in Sailor Two's description of the chest in which Thaisa is cast into the sea.)

(Will sets scene two of act three in Ephesus, a coastal city in what is now present-day Turkey.

A servant brings in a chest, 'the sea toss upon our shore,' to Cerimon, a lord of Ephesus, accompanied by two gentlemen. I don't need help in guessing what is in the chest.)

Cerimon. Tis wondrous heavy. Wrench it open straight:
   If the sea's stomach be o'ercharg'd with gold,
   It is a good constant of fortune that
   It belches upon us. . . .
   How close tis <u>caulked and bitum'd</u>!
   Did the sea cast it up? . . .
   O you most potent gods! what's here? a corse! . . .
   Shrouded in cloth of state; balm'd
   With bags of spices full! A passport too!
   <u>Apollo, perfect me in the characters</u>!
   Here I give to understand,
   I e'er this coffin drive a-land,
   I, King Pericles, have lost
   This queen, worth all our mundane cost.
   Who finds her, give her burying;
   She was the daughter of a king:
   Besides this treasure for a fee,
   The gods requite his charity.

798

If thou liv'st, Pericles, thou hast a heart
That even cracks for woe! This chanc'd tonight. . .

Nay, certainly tonight;
For look how fresh she looks! They were too rough
That threw her in the sea. Make a fire within:
Fetch hither all my boxes in my closet.
Death may usurp on nature many hours,
And yet the fire of life kindle again
The o'erpress'd spirits. I heard of an Egyptian
That had nine hours lien dead,
Who was by good appliances recover'd.
Well said, well said; the fire and cloths.
The rough and woeful music that we have,
Cause it to sound, beseech you.
The viol once more: how thou stirr'st, thou
The music there! I pray you, give her air.
Gentlemen,
The queen will live: nature awakes; a warmth
Breathes out of her: she hath not been entranc'd
About five hours: see how she 'gins to blow
Into life's flower again! . . .
She is alive; behold,
Her eyelids, cases to those heavenly jewels
Which Pericles hath lost,
Begin to part their fringes of bright gold;
The diamonds of a much praised water

Do appear, to make the world twice rich
Live,
And make us weep to hear your fate, rare creature,
Rare as you seem to be.
Thaisa. O dear Diana,
Where am I? Where's my lord? What world is this?
Cerimon. Lend me your hands; to the next chamber
bear her.
Get linen: now this matter must be look'd to,
For her relapse is mortal. Come come;
And <u>Aesculapius</u> guide us!
Pericles, 3.2

(IN line five, Cerimon uses the same wording 'caulked and bitum'd' to describe the chest carrying Thaisa as spoken by Sailor Two in the final line of the previous passage. Bitumed probably means made ready, or it may refer to the bottom of the chest. Any ideas?

Just before he reads Pericles' heartfelt note, Cerimon asks interpretive help from the Greek god of many things, including poetry: 'Apollo, perfect me in the characters!'

As known, Will uses music effectively throughout his works. This time to rouse Thaisa from the dead: 'The rough and woeful music that we have' and the exemplary touch, 'The viol once more,' do the job and more.

The lines that touch us as we root for Thaisa to awaken: 'see how she 'gins to blow' 'Into life's flower again!'

In his final line, Cerimon asks for help in restoring Thaisa from 'Aesculapius,' the ancient Greek god of healing.)

(AFTER twelve months of living on Tharsus, Pericles leaves his daughter Marina in the care of the Governor, Cleon, his wife Dionyza, and the baby's nurse, Lychorida.)

Pericles. We cannot but obey
The powers above us. Could I rage and roar
As doth the sea she lies in, yet the end
Must be as 'tis. <u>My gentle babe Marina</u>, whom,
<u>For she was born at sea, I have nam'd so</u>, here
I charge your charity withal, leaving her
The infant of your care; beseeching you
To give her princely training, that she may be
<u>Manner'd as she is born.</u>
Cleon. Fear not, my lord, but think
Your grace, that fed my country with your corn,
For which the people's prayers still fall

Must in your child be thought on. If neglection
Should therein make me vile, the common body,
By you releiv'd would <u>force me to my duty</u>:
But if to that <u>my nature needs a spur</u>
The gods revenge it upon me and mine
To the end of generation! . . .
We'll bring your grace e'en to the edge o' the shore,
Then give you up to the vast Neptune and
The gentlest winds of heaven.
Pericles, 3.3

(PERICLES cannot bear to leave 'My gentle babe Marina', and then he lovingly speaks of her name: 'For she was born at sea, I have nam'd so.'

'Manner'd as she is born' means that Marina was born into royalty and her training will help guarantee that she acts accordingly. Hamlet uses a similar phrase in 1.4 telling Horatio of King Claudius' excessive drinking:

'But to my mind, though I am native here
And to the manner born, it is a custom
More honored in the breach than the observance.'
Meaning that Claudius' habit is more honored by not doing it than doing it.

Cleon makes double-edged, solemn promises not to neglect Marina. First, the people who were fed with Pericles' corn would 'force me to my duty.' Failing that, if 'my nature needs a spur' the gods would punish him. We'll see how that commitment holds up.)

(IN scene four of act three, Cerimon bids farewell to the recovered Thaisa who believes she will 'n'er see my lord again.' She goes to live in 'Diana's temple' in Ephesus attended by Cerimon's niece.)

(We have a complicated plot, spun out over long time periods. Gower, as Chorus, helps the audience to catch up and settle in for the ensuing action.)

Gower. Imagine Pericles arriv'd at Tyre,
Welcom'd and settle to his own desire.
His woeful queen we leave at Ephesus,
Unto Diana there a votaress.
Now to Marina bend your mind,
Whom our fast-growing scene must find
At Tharsus, and by Cleon train'd
In music, letters; who hath gain'd
Of education all the grace,

Which makes her both the heart and place
<u>Of general wonder</u>. But, alack,
That monster envy, oft the wrack
Of earned praise, Marina's life
Seeks to take off by treason's knife.
Pericles, 4. Chorus

(YOU have the nub. Cleon and Dionyza have a daughter, Philoten. Where Marina is gifted and 'Of general wonder,' Philoten lacks most skills. This won't do for Dionyza. She has Marina's nurse, Lychorida, murdered and hires Leonine to kill Marina. They talk privately.

Marina enters sad over the death of Lychorida.

Before exiting, Dionyza speaks soothingly and encourages Marina to walk with Leonine. She resists but finally acquieses.)

Dionyza. Thy oath remember; thou hast sworn to do't.
'Tis but a blow, which never shall be known.
Thou canst not do a thing i' the world so soon
To yield thee so much profit. Let not conscience,
Which is but cold, inflaming love in thy bosom,
Inflame too nicely; nor let pity, which
Even women have cast off, melt thee, but be
<u>A soldier to thy purpose</u>.

Leon. I will do't; but yet she is a goodly creature.

Dionyza. The fitter, then, the gods should have her.
Here she come weeping for her only mistress'
death.

Marina. No, I will rob Tellus of her weed,
To strew thy green with flowers: the yellows, blues,
The purple violets, and marigolds
Shall as a carpet hang upon thy grave
While summer-days do last. Ay me! poor maid,
Born in a tempest, when my mother died,
This world to me is like a lasting storm,
Whirring me from my friends. . . .
When I was born:
Never was waves or winds more violent;
And from the ladder-tackle washes off
A canvas-climber: Ha! says one, wilt out?
And with a dropping industry they skip
From stem to stern: the boatswain whistles, and
The master calls, and trebles their confusion.

Leonine. Come, say your prayers.

Marina. Why will you kill me?

Leonine. To satisfy my lady.

Marina. Why would she have kill'd?
Now, as I can remember, by my troth,
I never did hurt her in all my life:
I never spake bad word, nor did ill turn
To any living creature: believe me, la,

I never kill'd a mouse, nor hurt a fly:
I trod upon a worm against my will,
But I wept for it, How have I offended,
Wherein my death might yield her profit,
Or my life imply her danger?
Pericles, 4.1

(IN Dionyza's insistent final line, she urges Leonine to be, 'A soldier to thy purpose.'

After Leonine says 'I will do't; but yet she is a goodly creature,' we get Dionyza's chilling rationale, 'The fitter, then, the gods should have her.'

'Tellus,' Roman goddess of the earth, is a good choice to strew flowers.

Did you like the verb 'whirring' following the noun storm?

In the second part of Marina's first speech she mentions her experiences on board the ship on the day she was born in a storm: 'A canvas-climber: Ha! says one, wilt out?' Will never tired of writing about the sea, and here we have a young woman speaking of what she saw as a baby. Note the authenticity of the lingo. Will spent time at sea, and some of that in storms.

Midway through her final speech in the passage, Marina talks of never hurting 'any living creature:

believe me, la.' The 'la' is likely an irreverent word or phrase, like 'damn it.'

Leonine tries to kill Marina, they struggle, but are interrupted by pirates who scare Leonine off, abduct Marina, take her to a brothel and barter over who will have her. Marina is determined, 'I still my virgin knot will keep.'

(Cleon believes Marina is dead at Leonine's hand and confronts Dionyza. 'O Dionyza, such a piece of slaughter.' She tells him, 'You'll turn a child again.' Cleon asks what they should do when 'Pericles shall demand his child.' Dionyza and Cleon insult back and forth, and he is no match for her.

Following the bitter exchange, Gower offers continuity at Marina's grave, including reading her epitaph.

Dionyza. That she is dead. Nurses are not the fates,
To foster it, nor ever to preserve.
She died at night; I'll say so. Who can cross it?
Unless you play the pious innocent,
And for an honest attribute cry out,
She died by foul play. . . .
Yet none does know, but you, how she came dead,
Nor none can know, Leonine being gone.

She did distain my child, and stood between
Her and her fortunes: none would look on her,
But cast their gazes on Marina's face;
While ours was blurted at, and held a <u>malkin</u>,
<u>Not worth the time of day</u>. It pierc'd me through.
Cleon. Thou art like the harpy,
Which, to betray, dost, with thine angel's face,
Sieze with thine eagle's talons.
Dionyza. You are like one that superstitiously
Doth <u>swear to the gods that winter kills the flies</u>:
But yet I know you'll do as I advise.
Gower. By you being pardon'd, we commit no crime
<u>To use one language in each several clime,</u>
<u>Where our scenes seem to live</u>. I do beseech you
To learn of me, who stand i' the gaps to teach you
<u>The stages of our story</u>. Pericles
Is now again thwarting the wayward seas,
Attended on by many a lord and knight,
To see his daughter, all his life's delight. . . .
So with his steerage shall your thoughts grow
To fetch his daughter home, who first is gone.
<u>Like motes and shadows see them move awhile;</u>
Your ears unto your eyes I'll reconcile. . . .
(Dumb show.) <u>See how belief may suffer by foul</u>
<u>show!</u>
This borrow'd passion stands for true old woe;
And Pericles, in sorrow all devour'd,

With sighs shot through and biggest tears
o'ershower'd,
Leaves <u>Tarsus,</u> and again embarks. He swears
Never to wash his face nor cut his hairs;
He puts on sackcloth, and to sea. He bears
A tempest which his mortal vessel tears,
And yet he rides it out. Now please you wit
The epitaph is for Marina writ
By wicked Dionayza.
The fairest, sweet'st, and best lies here,
Who wither'd in her spring of year.
She was of Tyrus the king's daughter,
On whom foul death hath made this slaughter;
Marina was she call'd; and at her birth,
Thetis, being proud, swallow'd some part o' the
earth:
Therefore the earth, fearing to be o'erflow'd,
Hath Thetis' birth-child on the heavens bestow'd:
Wherefore she does, and swears she'll never stint,
Make raging battery upon shores of flint.
<u>No vizard doth become black villainy</u>
<u>So well as soft and tender flattery.</u>
Let Pericles believe his daughter's dead,
And bear his courses to be ordered
By <u>Lady Fortune</u>; while our scene must play
His daughter's woe and heavy well-a-day
In her unholy service. Patience, then,

And <u>think you now are all in Mitylen.</u>
Pericles, 4.3

(IN line 12 of Dionyza's vituperative speech to
Cleon, she complains that people think that her
daughter, Philoten, is thought to be a malkin, or
servant wench, compared to Marina. Dionyza goes on
to say that Philoten was deemed 'Not worth the time
of day,' an expression that's fallen into the English
language.

Dionyza then tells Cleon that he is so naïve and
superstitious that he would 'swear to the gods that
winter kills the flies.'

Gower, acting as Chorus, joins the play again to
make certain that the audience, particularly those in
the pit, catch the drift. Gower professes that it's no
crime

'To use one language in each several clime,
Where our scenes seem to live.'

He then asks the audience to let him tell them
'The stages of our story.' Gower is in costume, and,
to make it all work, he adopts, where possible, a light
touch.

He also cautions the audience to accept the
characters shifting around, 'Like motes and shadows,'

until he reconciles their eyes and ears to what is going on in the play. Bits of dust floating among the shadows is subtle imagery.

In the dumb show, when Pericles and his aides enter without speaking to see Marina's grave, Gower says, 'See how belief may suffer by foul show!' Dionyza proves a master of artifice and would be an effective modern politician, or seller of sham.

'Tarsus' is an historic city in Southern Turkey.

In writing Marina's faux epitaph, Dionyza cleverly introduces Thetis, ancient Greek goddess of water: 'Hath Thetis' birth-child on the heavens bestow'd.'

After reading the epitaph, Gower addresses the audience with the relevant:

'No vizard doth become black villainy
So well as soft and tender flattery.'

(At the end of his speech in the previous passage, Gower instructs the audience to 'think you now are all in Mitylene,' the main city on the isle of Lesbos.

And here we are in the brothel with Marina, the pirates, and a bawd, or female whoremaster.

Marina's continuing distress enhances the audience's emotions and builds toward the resolution.

Will also used scenes like this to change the pace and treat the groundlings to some ribald references. Doubtless, some of the groundlings yell out the occasional sexual threat to Marina.

The bawd speaks of Marina as, 'my dish of chastity.'

A man called Boult, whose masters have bought Marina, complains about her lack of sexual cooperation and she answers. His response is surprising. But first the Bawd.)

Bawd. Fie, fie upon her! She is able to freeze the god Priapus, and undo a whole generation. We must either get her ravish'd or be rid of her. What she should do for clients her fitment, and <u>do me the kindness of our profession</u>, she has me her quirks, her reasons, her master-reasons, her prayers, her knees; that she would make a puritan of the devil, if he should cheapen a kiss of her.

Marina. <u>Thou art the damn'd doorkeeper</u>

Boult. What would you have me do? go to the wars, would you? where a man my serve seven years for the loss of a leg, and have not money enough in the end to buy him a wooden one?

Marina. Do anything but this thou doest.

Empty

<u>Old receptacles, or common sewers of filth;</u>

Serve by indenture to the common hangman:
Any of these ways are yet better than this;
For thou professes, a baboon, could he speak,
Would own a name too dear. O that the gods
Would deliver me safely from this place!
Here, here's gold for thee.
If that thy master would gain by me,
Proclaim that I can sing, weave, sew, and dance,
With other virtues I can keep from boast;
And I will undertake all these to teach.
Boult. Come, I'll do for thee what I can; come your
ways.
Pericles, 4.5

(THE Bawd, in line three, of her prose speech
complains that Marina will not, 'do me the kindness
of our profession.' We have here a conflict of values.

Before Bolt's re-readable three-line soldier
speech, the Bawd urges Boult to 'crack the glass of
her virginity,' and he responds to Marina's 'Thou art
the damn'd doorkeeper,' or you could let me out, with
the speech.

Marina encourages Boult in line three of her
speech to empty 'Old receptacles, or common sewers
of filth.' This and other of her persuasive lines get to
him, and he decides to free her to his masters,

assuming they agree. Marina is one more of Will's women of spine.)

(ON CUE, Gower is back to put 'the two-hours traffic' in perspective.)

Gower. Marina thus the brothel scapes, and chances
Into an honest house, our story says.
She sings like one immortal, and she dances
As goddess-like; . . . and with her needle composes
Nature's own shape, of bud, bird, branch, or berry,
That ever her art sisters the natural roses; . . .
And to her father turn our thoughts again,
Where we left him, on the sea. We there him lost;
Whence, driven before the winds, he is arriv'd
Here where his daughter dwells; and on this coast
Suppose him now at anchor. . .
His banners sable, trimm'd with rich expense; . . .
In your supposing once more put your sight
Of heavy Pericles; think this his bark:
Where what is done in action, more, if might,
Shall be discover'd; please you, sit, and hark.
Pericles, 5. Gower as Chorus

(Gower tells us that Marina's needlework is so faultless and pretty 'That ever her art sisters the natural roses.' Again, with 'sister's,' Will supplies the original and unexpected verb.

At this point in the play, the audience really needs Gower to both orient them and help them to continue to suspend disbelief. Get this: Pericles leaves his daughter's gravesite, encounters still another windstorm, and 'driven before the winds, he is arriv'd' on the coast where 'where his daughter dwells.' I can hear a Hollywood mogul saying: 'Wait a minute, hold on. You expect audiences to believe . . . good luck on selling that one. You can't jump the shark again."

Anyway, it's great fun, and Elizabethan audiences lapped it up.

But Gower's not done with his instruction, he tells the audience to 'please you, sit, and hark.' I'll bet one of the groundlings standing in the pit hollers back, 'Sit on what, my arse?' Pandemonium.

(IN deep grief and speaking to no one, Pericles lies on a couch in his barge off Mitylene. One lord speaks of Pericles' suffering over the loss of 'a beloved daughter and a wife.'

Another lord tells of 'a maid in Mitylene' who might be able to help him. Marina is brought aboard and Pericles talks with her.)

Pericles. I am great with woe, and shall deliver weeping.

My dearest wife was like this maid, and such a one
My daughter might have been: my queen's square brows;
Her stature to an inch; as wand-like straight;
As silver-voic'd; her eyes as jewel-like,
And cas'd as richly; in pace another Juno;
Who starves the ears she feeds, and makes them hungry
The more she gives them speech. Where do you live?
Falseness cannot come from thee;
For thou look'st Modest as Justice, and thou seem'st a palace
For the crown'd truth to dwell in: . . .
Tell thy story;
If thine considered prov'd the thousandth part
Of my endurance, thou art a man, and I
Have suffer'd like a girl: yet thou dost look
Like Patience gazing on men's graves, and smiling
Extremity out of act. What were thy friends?
Hast lost thou them? Thy name most kind virgin?
Recount, I do beseech thee, come, sit by me.
Marina. My name is Marina.
Pericles. Thou little know'st how thou dost startle me

To call thyself Marina. . . .
But are you flesh and blood?
<u>Have you a working pulse?</u> and are no fairy?
Pericles, 5.1

(MOVING poetry abounds, as it should with father and long-lost daughter reunited.

'For thou look'st Modest as Justice, and thou seem'st a palace
For the crown'd truth to dwell in.'

'Modest as justice' is a divine metaphor. Also shining is the inventive abstraction: 'crowned truth' dwelling in a palace.

'Like Patience gazing on men's graves,' recalls the bountiful 'She sat like patience on a monument, smiling at grief' from Twelfth Night, 2.4.

In the midst of all the well-placed sentiment, 'Have you a working pulse?' brought a smile.

(After realizing that he has found his daughter, Pericles hears music.

Once he's asleep, Diana, goddess of childbirth, materializes as an apparition and speaks conclusively.

As gods do when they come down in the final scenes
of romantic Elizabethan plays.)

Pericles. The music of the spheres! . . .
Most heavenly music! . . .
It nip me into listening, and thick slumber
Hangs upon my eyes: let me rest.
Diana. My temple stands in Ephesus: hie thee
thither,
And do upon my altar sacrifice.
There, when my maiden priests are met together,
Before the people all,
Reveal how thou at sea didst lose thy wife:
To mourn thy crosses, with thy daughter's call,
And give them repetition to the life.
Or perform my bidding or thou liv'st in woe;
Do it, and happy; <u>by my silver bow</u>!
Awake and tell thy dream.
Pericles, 5.1

(IN the next-to-last line of her speech, Diana tells
Pericles to obey 'by my silver bow' confirming that
she is also goddess of the hunt.

Diana vanishes, Pericles awakes and pledges: 'I
will obey thee.'

(We're gifted with two recognition scenes at the close of Pericles: father and daughter, and now the reuniting of husband and wife, mother and daughter, family rejoined.

As Gower tells the audience at the Temple of Diana:

Now are sands are almost run;
More a little, and then done. . . .
At Ephesus the temple see
Our king, and all his company.

Pericles. I here confess myself the King of Tyre;
Who, frighted from my country, did wed
At <u>Pentapolis</u> the fair Thaisa.
At sea in childbed dies she, but brought forth
A maid-child, call'd Marina; who, O goddess,
Wears yet thy silver livery.
Thaisa. Voice and favour!
You are, you are, O royal Pericles.
Marina. My heart
Leaps to be gone into my mother's bosom.
Gower. In Pericles, his queen and daughter, seen
Although assail'd with fortune fierce and keen,
Virtue preserv'd from fell destruction's blast,
Led on by heaven, and crown'd with joy at last.

ACKNOWLEDGMENTS

I dedicated this book to Boston University Professors Robert Sproat and Harold White. I also thank other B.U. and UCLA faculty who helped me better understand the wonderworking powers of William Shakespeare and other giants of English literature.

Finally, I thank the myriad friends, relatives, classmates, business associates, fellow teachers, workshop leaders and participants, and all others who contributed thoughts, suggestions and criticisms.

ABOUT THE AUTHOR

After long stints with IBM and Westinghouse, Richard J. Noyes was Associate Director of the Center for Advanced Engineering Study at the Massachusetts Institute of Technology. Noyes is now a business consultant for public and private sector organizations. He has published five other books.

Printed in Great
Britain
by Amazon

32259008R00475